ACTA UNIVERSITATIS UPSALIENSIS

Skrifter rörande Uppsala universitet

C. Organisation och historia

38

THE FRONTIERS OF HUMAN KNOWLEDGE

Lectures held
at the Quincentenary Celebrations
of Uppsala University 1977

Editor: Torgny T. Segerstedt

UPPSALA 1978

Distributed by

ALMQVIST & WIKSELL INTERNATIONAL

STOCKHOLM · SWEDEN

HUMANITIES PRESS

ATLANTIC HIGHLANDS · N.J.

ISBN 91-554-0791-9
ISSN 0502-7454

Printed in Sweden by
Borgströms Tryckeri AB, Motala 1978

Technical editing:
Editorial office, Uppsala University

Preface

One of our aims during our quincentenary celebrations was to strengthen the ties between Uppsala University and other centres of research and learning. For that reason, the faculties organized about fifty symposia and conferences with more than 6000 participants. The idea was to get reports from different frontiers of science. We hoped, of course, that the quincentenary-activities would stimulate Uppsala scholars in their research and that contacts would be established with leading international scientists that would be of lasting value. There is no way of evaluating in an objective manner whether we achieved our aim or not. But, intuitively, we feel that we have done so.

Another aim was to inform the general public about our scholarly work and the results and methods of modern research. For this purpose, we kept "open house" that is, we invited the public to visit a number of our departments. This invitation met with an enormous response from the citizens of Uppsala and the experiment was evidently a great success. We have received many requests to repeat these activites. However, they must be very well planned in order to be useful.

We may regard the lectures delivered on the 28th of September 1977 as a kind of synthesis of the two other aims. The faculties had asked their *doctores honoris causa* to give popular lectures on the day before the conferment. The lectures were open to the students and the general public. The majority of the guests of honour gave positive replies, which meant that never before had so many famous scholars lectured in Uppsala and never before had so many scholars, students and other supporters of research listened to so many lectures of high quality.

We felt that the lectures ought to be published. First and foremost, because of their great merit and, secondly, because it may be of considerable interest in the future to be able to determine what were by leading experts regarded as urgent problems in different fields of research in the year 1977.

It is a great pleasure for Uppsala University to have the privilege of publishing this volume. We thank the authors for their generosity and we feel sure that the book will be of lasting values.

Uppsala, May 1978
Torgny T. Segerstedt

Contents

Christian Theology and Inter-religious Dialogue

By John H. Hick
H. G. Wood Professor of Theology
University of Birmingham,
England

I

Dialogue, or discussion, between people of different faiths takes place on various levels and in a variety of contexts. There is, first, discursive theological dialogue, concerned with the truth-claims of the different religions. But this should always broaden out to include ways of life and forms of art and symbolism, and should involve opportunities to observe or even participate in one another's religious life at its focal point of worship and contemplation. Here it may begin to pass into a second form of dialogue, the interior dialogue, practiced and reported by such Christian pioneers as the late Père H. le Saux (Swami Abhishiktananda) and Dom Bede Griffiths in India. And then, third, there is the more immediately practical dialogue concerned with common human problems and exemplified, for example, by the Buddhist-Christian-Hindu-Jewish-Muslim discussions at Colombo in 1974, whose report is entitled *Towards World Community: Resources and Responsibilities for Living Together*.

I shall be concerned here primarily with discursive dialogue, though with the understanding that this may pass naturally into the deeper interior dialogue, and also that a common concern about world community is a very proper part of the agenda of inter-religious dialogue today, and one to which I shall return at the end of this lecture.

Discursive or theological dialogue, then, takes place somewhere on or moving about within a spectrum which ranges between two opposite conceptions of its nature. At one extreme there is purely confessional dialogue in which each partner witnesses to his own faith, convinced that this has absolute truth whilst his partner's has only relative truth. At the other extreme is truth-seeking dialogue in which each is conscious that Transcendent Being is infinitely greater than his own limited vision of it, and in which they accordingly seek to share their visions in the hope that each may be helped towards a fuller awareness of the Divine Reality before which they both stand. Dialogue sometimes takes place nearer to one pole and sometimes nearer to the other, but often varies in character as it proceeds, moving back and forth along the scale.

II

Let us look first at the confessional end of the dialogical spectrum. Here the Christian, in dialogue with people of other faiths, speaks from within his own conviction that God has entered decisively into human history in the person of Jesus Christ, the Second Person of the Holy Trinity incarnate, who has revealed the divine nature and purpose for man in a unique and unsurpassable way in comparison with which all other revelations must necessarily be secondary, in the sense of being incomplete, or imperfect, or preliminary, or in some other way vitally inferior to the Christian revelation.

This confessional attitude to other religions derives in recent theology from the massive dogmatic work of Karl Barth (particularly the relatively early Barth of *Church Dogmatics,* 1/2), and the detailed application of this to the world religions by the great Dutch missionary scholar Hendrik Kraemer in his immensely influential book *The Christian Message in a Non-Christian World,* written for the World Missionary Conference at Tambaram, near Madras, in 1938. So long as this stance was dominant within the World Council of Churches, as it was until the end of the General Secretaryship of Dr. Visser't Hooft in 1966, this great ecumenical vehicle refrained from inter-religious dialogue. Since then, however, dialogue has become the order of the day, and instead of a confessional rejection of dialogue we have now a confessional stance within dialogue. For those who adopt this stance, the Christian revelation is not one among several, but is the only true revelation of God. This has recently been articulated as follows by the distinguished missionary theologian, Bishop Lesslie Newbigin:

A Christian who participates in dialogue with people of other faiths will do so on the basis of his faith. The presuppositions which shape his thinking will be those which he draws from the Gospel. This must be quite explicit. He cannot agree that the position of final authority can be taken by anything other than the Gospel—either by a philosophical system, or by mysticial experience, or by the requirements of national and global unity. Confessing Christ—incarnate, crucified and risen—as the true light and the true life, he cannot accept any other's alleged authority as having right of way over this. He cannot regard the revelation given in Jesus as one of a type, or as requiring to be interpreted by means of categories based on other ways of understanding the totality of experience. Jesus is—for the believer—the source from whom his understanding of the totality of experience is drawn and therefore the criterion by which other ways of understanding are judged. ("The Basis, Purpose and Manner of Inter-Faith Dialogue, *Scottish Journal of Theology,* Vol. 30. No. 3 (1977), p. 255.)

From this point of view the Christian, however personally open and charitable towards people of other faiths, is necessarily bearing witness, or confessing his faith, and he is bound to hope that his hearers will respond to the Word of God which reaches them through his words, and commit themselves to Christ as the way, the truth and the life. Thus Bishop Newbigin says that the Christian's purpose in entering into dialogue with people of other faiths 'can only be obedient witness to Jesus Christ. Any other pupose, any goal which subordinates the honour of Jesus Christ to some purpose derived from another source, is impossible for the Christian. To accept such another purpose would involve a denial of the total lordship of Jesus Christ. A Christian cannot try to evade the accusation that, for him, dialogue is part of his obedient witness to Jesus Christ' (p. 265). Here we see the confessional position adopted as an explicit stance within dialogue.

Needless to say, there is an equivalent confessional stance for the adherents of any other of the religions and ideologies. It is important to keep this fact in mind, because whilst from within a particular confessional circle of faith one has the impression of standing at the centre of the world of meaning, with all other faiths dispersed around its periphery, from the point of view of global history it is evident that there are many different circles of faith, with the inhabitants of each living under the same impression of their own unique centrality. Let us, then, briefly take note of this plurality of centres, by referring to Islam, as another semitic faith; to advaitic Hinduism, as representing a very different kind of religion; and to Marxism, as a powerful secular rival to the traditional religions.

The confessing Muslim, in inter-religious dialogue, will speak from within his own faith that Islam represents the latest and fullest revelation, taking up and completing the earlier revelations through Moses and the prophets down to and including Jesus. He will see much good in other religions, particularly in Judaism and Christianity as kindred religions of the Book; but it will be his firm conviction that Islam is the final revelation; and he will inevitably hope that in confessing his faith he may be the instrument of Allah in leading others to commit themselves to the living relationship to God which is Islam.

Again, the Hindu who adheres to the truth revealed in the Vedas and Upanishads as interpreted in the advaitic tradition will speak with people of other faiths from within his conviction that the Absolute Reality is beyond all human categories, and that the worship of a personal God occurs on a lower and preliminary level of the religious life. He will see all religions as paths towards the final good of union with the Ultimate, but will see these paths as eventually converging upon the direct way revealed in Advaita Vedanta. Unlike the Christian and the Muslim, however, he will not feel obliged to try to press his own spiritual knowledge upon others, for he believes that they will accept it for themselves when they are ready for it, if not in this life then in some future life.

Then there is the Marxist in dialogue with religious believers. Whether Marxism is to be accounted a religion is a matter of definition. Personally I prefer a definition of 'religion' which involves an essential reference to the Transcendent and which consequently does not include Marxism. But nevertheless Marxism borders on the religions in that it is a systematic interpretation of human existence which issues in a distinctive way of life; and as such it constitutes one of the most powerful options among the world's living religions and ideologies. And when a Marxist engages in dialogue with people of other faiths than his own he does so from within his conviction that Marxism teaches the truth about man and his history, including the truth that man's religions are projections of human hope, whose historic function has been to enable the exploited masses to bear their servitude patiently rather than rise up against their oppressors. And it must be his hope that through his proclamation of Marxist truth his hearers will be converted and enlisted among the forces of progress.

When these four come together in confessional dialogue, each must in the end be bearing witness to his own faith. But it may be that each is also of an open-minded and enquiring disposition, desirous of learning as well as of bearing witness. They will then come to know about one anothers' convictions, and will be able to compare the different features of their respective belief systems. But still, insofar as they hold to the absolute truth of their own traditions, each will be basically concerned to try to bring the others to share his own faith.

For example, the Christian may enunciate what has traditionally been regarded as the central truth of his faith, namely that Jesus Christ was God the Son incarnate. The Muslim will respond that Jesus was indeed the greatest of the line of prophets before Mohammad himself; and he will acknowledge that Jesus was born of a virgin mother, as the scriptures say. But he will insist that it would be blasphemy to hold that he was actually and literally God, in the sense of being one of the three Persons of a Divine Trinity. The Hindu will say that Jesus was indeed a divine incarnation, one of the series of *avatars* which continues down perhaps to Sri Ramakrishna and Mahatma Gandhi in the nineteenth and twentieth centuries. And the Marxist will say that since God is an illusion, it must be an illusion to think that Jesus was in any sense God incarnate. He was rather a great moral revolutionary whom the church has captured and used for its own counter-revolutionary purposes.

And so long as they all stand firmly within their own respective circles of faith, the dialogue will consist basically in the display and comparison of these incompatible beliefs.

However, inter-religious dialogue undertaken just like that, as two (or more) people bearing mutual witness to their own faiths, each in the firm conviction that his is the final truth and in hope of converting the other, can only result either in conversion or in a hardening of differences—occasionally the former but more often the latter. In order for dialogue to be mutually fruitful, lesser changes than total conversion must be possible and must be hoped for on both (or all) sides. In principle this is readily acknowledged by many contemporary Christian advocates of the confessional stance. Thus Bishop Newbigin says that 'We are eager to receive from our partners what God has given them, to hear what God has shown them. In our meeting with men of other faiths we are learning to share in our common patrimony as human beings made by the one God in his own image' (p. 266). He also grants, and indeed affirms, that not only the non-Christian but also the Christian himself should be changed in the course of the dialogue. Indeed he says, 'Much of his own "Christianity" may have to be left behind in this meeting. Much of the intellectual construction, the piety, the practice in which our discipleship of Christ has been expressed may have to be called in question' (p. 268).

Here we approach the living heart of our problem, as it affects the Christian. For the question is, how serious and how radical can this possibility of change be in the Christian partner? Suppose that, in the experience of dialogue, *more* of 'the intellectual construction ... in which his discipleship of Christ has been expressed' is called in question than he anticipated? Are there then to be reserved areas of belief which must remain exempt from the possibility of change? May it indeed turn out that he was only playing at openness to change in his own understanding, but that in reality he stood throughout firmly upon a dogmatic conception of what his Christianity must be—a conception which simply corresponded to the traditional structure of Christian orthodoxy?

Let us pursue these questions a little further. In allowing for significant change in the Christian as a fruit of his dialogue with non-Christians it is customary to draw a very important distinction (suggested by that of Karl Barth) between, on the one hand, the historical phenomenon called Christianity, which is one of the religions of the world, and on the other hand personal discipleship and devotion to Jesus Christ. We have here an entirely proper and helpful distinction between Jesus—the actual Jesus who lived in Palestine in the first third of the first century, the reports and rumours of whose life and teaching have inspired millions ever since to try to live as his disciples—and the historical development of Christianity, the latter being recognised to be a human, and often all-too-human, affair. And the contemporary confessionalist often suggests that we should engage in dialogue, not primarily as adherents of historical Christianity but simply as disciples of Jesus.

This is, I think, a very fruitful approach. But where it will lead must depend to an important extent upon investigations concerning the historical Jesus, to whom it appeals, and of the ways in which the Christian interpretation of him has been formed over the centuries. The all-important question concerns the extent to which the man Jesus is to be understood in terms of the developed theology of the church. For the confessionalist it is usually an unquestioned assumption that belief in the doctrines of the Incarnation and the Trinity are essentially involved in personal discipleship to Jesus. But it is precisely this assumption that has been directly questioned in many recent discussions of Christian origins and of the development of Christian thought, and that is today at the centre of a considerable debate. To cite just one major evidence of this, in the 1976 Report of the Church of England's Doctrine Commission, the chairman, in his own essay, wrote that in using traditional Christian language about Jesus as God's only Son he is 'using language in a very indirect, even poetic, way to express the central role of Jesus in giving form and life to our faith in God' (*Christian Believing*, p. 129); and, concerning the doctrine of the Trinity, that 'I cannot with integrity say that I believe God to be one in three persons' (p. 126). If the Commission's chairman, who is also Regius Professor of Divinity at Oxford, can take this view—a view, it should be added, with which some of his colleagues agreed but with which others strongly disagreed,—we are clearly in a period of theological reflection in which these doctrines which were once accepted largely without question have now become matters of open debate. And the publication earlier this year of the book *The Myth of God Incarnate* by seven British theologians has opened this debate to a larger public. We can all see at least the possibility that the doctrines of Incarnation and Trinity may turn out to be part of the 'intellectual construction' which has to be left behind when the disciple of Jesus discards the cultural packaging in which western Christianity has wrapped the gospel.

III

To indicate how this has come about I would remind you that fifty years ago it was widely assumed in Christian circles that Jesus lived his life in the awareness of being God the Son incarnate. It was assumed that he knew himself to be divine; that he walked the earth with conscious divine authority, knowledge and power; and that he taught his own unique divine status in such sayings as 'I and My Father are one', 'No man cometh unto the Father but by me', 'He that hath seen me hath seen the Father'. But that position has become very difficult to sustain in the light of continuing biblical study. It is now widely accepted that the great christological sayings of the Fourth Gospel express the theology of the church—or at least of an important part of the church—towards the end of the first century; that it is uncertain whether the historical Jesus accepted the designation of messiah or christ; that the meaning of the phrase which he undoubtedly did use of himself, namely 'son of man', is still unclear; and that it cannot be established historically that Jesus thought of himself as more than that as which he seems to have been presented in the earliest christian preaching, namely: 'Jesus of Nazareth, a man attested to you by God with mighty works and wonders and signs which God did through him in your midst' (Acts, 2:22). It is accordingly widely acknowledged that if Jesus was indeed God the Son incarnate, he did not know this during his earthly life. Indeed, because of the implausibility of maintaining the divine self-consciousness of the historical Jesus many are today attracted by the new theory that it was in his resurrection that Jesus either became, or became conscious of being, Son of God or God the Son.

Such speculations have moved a long way from the original proposition that Jesus of Nazareth presented himself as God incarnate, Son of God or God the Son living a human life. A further move which many today feel constrained to take acknowledges that the idea of divine incarnation is a poetic or symbolic or mythological way of speaking of God's powerful presence to a faithful human being and through him to others. Whether such a development of Christian understanding is right or wrong is not a matter to be quickly or easily settled, and the current renewed phase of intense christological discussion may well have to continue for a long time. My own view is that the Christian mind will almost inevitably come to see the doctrine of the Incarnation, and the doctrine of the Trinity which grew out of it, in a new way, no longer as precise metaphysical truths but as imaginative constructions giving expression, in the religious and philosophical language of the ancient world, to the Christian's devotion to Jesus as the one who has made the heavenly Father real to him. Or at any rate, I would suggest that this is the kind of development which the more intellectual part of the Christian mind (appropriately, in the human brain, the left hemisphere!) is likely to undergo, whilst its more emotional other half perhaps continues to use the traditional language of Christian mythology without raising troublesome questions about its meaning. In that case the Christian position in interfaith dialogue will change in character. It will no longer be necessary to insist, however gently, upon the uniqueness and superiority of Christianity; and it may be possible to recognise the separate validity of the other great world religions, and both to learn from them and enable them to learn from the Christian tradition.

This development is continuous with some three centuries of internal change in response to the challenges of modern science and philosophy. Christianity is the first of the ancient world faiths to have attained—however unevenly and falteringly—to a new selfunderstanding in the light of the scientific revolution; and its gift to the other great religious traditions can now be its own experience of modernisation, communicated both in inter-faith dialogue and in other ways. This is the role of 'critical catalyst' of which Hans Küng has recently written (*On Being a Christian,* pp. 100 f.). The Christian responsibility and opportunity are both alike great. For it is for the most part Christian agencies—such as the World Council of Churches' Programme on Dialogue with People of Living Faiths and Ideologies—that are today most actively promoting inter-religious dialogue; so that the ethos of the Christian ecumenical movement tends at the same time to set the tone for the wider world ecumenical dialogue.

If it is to fulfil its special role during this new period of religious history, Christianity must, I believe, move emphatically from the confessional to the truth-seeking stance in dialogue. And indeed to a great extent this has already happened, as is shown by the Guidlines for Inter-Religious Dialogue formulated in 1972 by Dr. Stanley Samartha of the World Council of Churches. In this document it is first affirmed that 'The basis of inter-religious dialogue is the commitment of all partners to their respective faiths and their openness to the insights of the others. The integrity of particular religions must be recognised'. This statement acknowledges the degree of validity within the confessional stance, but places it within the context of religious pluralism. It is then said that the objective of dialogue is not a superficial consensus or a dilution of convictions, but 'It must lead to the enrichment of all in the discovery of new dimensions of Truth'. Finally, after a series of valuable recommendations about the need to go beyond purely intellectual discussion and even to participate in one another's worship, and also to be prepared to take concrete action together for world peace, the document concludes with a statement of the truth-seeking ideal for dialogue: 'Inter-religious dialogue should also stress the need to study fundamental questions in the religious dimension of life. Religions are man's responses to the mystery of existence and quests for meaning in the midst of confusion. World religious organisations should support the long-range study of the deeper questions which today ought to be taken up not just separately by individuals of each religion, but also together in the larger interests of mankind.' ("The Progress and Promise of Inter-Religious Dialogues",

Journal of Ecumenical Studies, 1972, pp. 473 f.). This seems to me to be the right method and approach.

The main impact, in response to which Christianity has undergone the transformations of the last three centuries, is of course that of modern science; and we must ask how the other world religions are likely to respond to the same impact, coming to them from the west in a more powerful form as the impact of an already formed scientific outlook. Will they be able to survive the spread among their populations of the scientific attitude?

We can only speak of probabilities; but the probability seems to me to be that they will survive to about the same extent that Christianity has survived in the west. For the fact that science first developed within Christendom does not establish Christianity in an exclusive or proprietary relationship with the scientific enterprise. Ever since A. N. Whitehead suggested the idea, in his *Science and the Modern World* (1926), it has frequently been said that distinctively Christian theology is responsible for the rise of modern science by providing the idea of an objective order of nature waiting to be explored by man. Since the universe is God's creation, it is said, it must have a rational structure; and science is the attempt to uncover this structure. And it does indeed seem reasonable to suppose that the Christian assumption that nature forms an intelligible system must have constituted one of the conditions for the rise of science. But that this condition was not by itself sufficient is shown by the fact that for the first fifteen centuries of its history Christianity showed little sign of giving birth to the scientific enterprise. Science, then, can hardly have arisen spontaneously out of the inner logic of the Christian faith. Further the Christian tradition has for much of its history nourished a dogmatic mentality opposed to the freely searching spirit of scientific enquiry; so that for several centuries scientific growth was generally impeded and opposed by the leaders of Christian civilisation. Those who today hail modern science as the glorious child of the Christian faith may well be great grandchildren of those who denounced Charles Darwin as an agent of the devil. Indeed the general record of the churches in relation to the rise and progress of modern science, from the time of Galileo to at least the end of the nineteenth century, has been so largely negative that what has happened since then can only be described as a mass conversion.

The origins of the scientific revolution of the 16th and 17th centuries lie in the many-sided awakening of the European mind from its dogmatic slumbers in the period which is comprehensively called the Renaissance. This was a renaissance of the ancient Graeco-Roman civilisation, whose literature was spread throughout Europe by the new technique of printing. Science was thus a product of an interaction of cultures. For the rationalistic and enquiring spirit of Greek philosophy seems to have been the main new fertilising agent which stimulated the rise of modern science in Christian Europe, bringing its medieval phase to an end. And once the scientific enterprise was launched it has generated its own increasing momentum, rapidly establishing its independence from the Christian world-view, and indeed continually challenging the Christian faith and forcing it to undergo major transformations in order to remain credible in the light of growing empirical knowledge.

Thus we may say that Christianity provided, unconsciously, an intellectual soil in which the Greek spirit of unimpeded rational enquiry could blossom into the modern scientific outlook; and that this has now in turn largely transformed the intellectual content of Christianity into a faith which does not contradict the findings of the sciences.

It is impossible to know whether, if the course of world history had been different, and something corresponding to the European Renaissance had occurred within one of the civilisations dominated by another world religion, it would have produced the scientific outlook and its practical out-working. For the question which arises concerning the other great world religions is not whether they too can give birth to modern science—for it could only be born once, and this has already happened—but whether they can come to terms with the already formed scientific outlook. So far as technology is concerned, there seems no doubt that this has been successfully exported to many non-Christian cultures, including Hindu India, Buddhist and Shintoist Japan, Maoist China, and some of the Muslim countries of the Middle East. But the deeper question which has yet to be answered is whether the belief systems of these other faiths can assimilate the modern scientific outlook and its results.

The eastern religions of Hinduism and Buddhism may, I would think, be expected to come to terms with the methods and discoveries of the natural sciences without too much difficulty, and indeed perhaps with rather less trauma than Christianity has experienced. It is true that great parts of India and of the Buddhist lands further east are only now emerging from feudal social conditions resting on a basis of mass ignorance and superstition. But it does not follow from this that Hindu and Buddhist theology must be intrinsically resistant to the development of the modern experimental investigation of the world. That the natural world is *maya* does not mean that it is an illusion in the ordinary sense of that word, but that it is time-bound, is in incessant process, and is dependent upon a more ultimate divine reality—this being essentially what Christian theology says when it describes the natural universe as a contingent order. Again, the cyclical conception of the universal process is not, as is sometimes said, antiscientific. On the contrary, the notion of a pulsating universe, beginninglessly and endlessly expanding and contracting, is one of the models under discussion in contemporary scientific cosmology. It could turn out that the balance of cosmological evidence and argument will point to the 'big bang' being unique, or to its being one of a series, perhaps an infinite series, of moments of compression between contractions and expansions. But science as such does not depend upon a 'linear' as opposed to a 'cyclical' conception of the process of the universe; the issue will be settled, if it is ever settled, by empirical evidence.

There is however another aspect of the scientific outlook and method which is directly relevant to the world religions and which must seem particularly challenging and threatening to Islam. This is the historical and critical study of ancient literature, including sacred scriptures. Christianity has gone through agonies of internal conflict during the last hundred years in breaking away from its former virtually universal assumption concerning the books of the Bible that, to quote a pronouncement of the first Vatican Council, 'having been written by inspiration of the Holy Ghost, they have God for their author'. Christian scholars now accept that the Bible was written by a variety of human beings over a period of about a thousand years, and that in telling the story of Israel's encounters with God over many generations the biblical writings at the same time express the pre-scientific assumptions of their authors. Instead of consisting of infallible divine oracles, the biblical writings are the culture-related utterances of men and women of faith as they experienced the divine presence in a variety of historical situations. But to come to this view of the scriptures has been a still unfinished agony for Christendom.

How will Islam respond to the historico-critical study of the Qur'an? In one way the problem is less acute than for Christians, in that the Qur'an has a unitary authorship and was writtten during a single lifetime; so that the kind of source criticism by which, for example, the Pentateuch and the synoptic Gospels have been analysed has little scope in relation to the Qur'an. But on the other hand the Qur'an is regarded with even greater veneration by orthodox Muslims than the Bible has ever been by Christians. For it is seen as the Word of God incarnate in human language, as Jesus is seen in orthodox Christian theology as the divine Word incarnate in human flesh. It will therefore not be easy for Muslims to reconcile the divine authority of the Qur'an, written in seventh century Arabia, with the modern scientific picture of the universe. It seems likely that in the process there will be a split between Quar'anic fundamentalists and liberals paralleling, but perhaps deeper and more bitter than, that between Christian fundamentalists and liberals. We must hope that the experience of interfaith dialogue will be helful to Islam during this difficult period of its history.

IV

Finally, let us turn from the impact of science and technology to the moral and social criticisms and suggestions which the world's faiths may have to offer one another as the interactions between them develope. We can at this point resume the Christian-Muslim-Hindu-Marxist dialogue which we began earlier. This is of course only a segment of the larger and more complex network of world dialogue; and even within this limited segment I am only going to pick out a single question from among the many that will be directed to each of the partners to the dialogue. But this will perhaps serve to illustrate the kind of mutual questioning that is to be expected.

One of the questions put to Hindu India in the dialogue of faiths will concern the caste system—officially rejected in India since 1949 but still in practice persisting in many ways—according to which each individual is born into a particular caste and sub-caste which determines his or her occupation, social circle, choice of marriage partner, and spiritual status; and leaving outside the system, with no social or spiritual status at all, the outcastes or untouchables, whom Mahatma Gandhi renamed Harijans, children of God. Is not this a fundamentally unjust system, denying the basic concept of the equality of all mankind? The answer can, surely, only be that this is so. The caste system stands under the same condemnation as feudal social hierarchies, the class structure in many modern western societies, and the assumption of white superiority and black and brown inferiority which is still so evident among most white Christian populations. But we must remember that in condemning distinctions of caste, class and colour we are speaking from the point of view of a modern liberal concept of human equality which has only recently come to widespread consciousness. If we ask where this immensely important concept has come from, the answer would seem to be that the abstract idea is present in all the major religious traditions, but that its activation as a political force in the world, first in Europe and the U.S.A. and then increasingly throughout the world, has resulted from the general undermining of hierarchial authority as a modern has superseded a medieval mentality. India has not yet completed this transition from the medieval to the modern world, and is still in its struggle to throw off the ancient caste system. It must be added that conservative Hinduism continues to be the last stronghold of caste, and that the influence of Christianity, Marxism and Islam upon Hinduism must be towards the final purging of the blight of caste from the life of India.

One of the questions put to Islam in the multilateral dialogue of faiths will concern the status of women in Muslim societies. The issue here is partly polygamy and partly the traditional subordination of women within patriarchical societies. The respective merits of monogamy and polygamy deserve to be debated in the light of the growing knowledge of human nature offered by psychology and sociology. But polygamy must also be seen in relation to the different stages of social history. Why is it that polygamy was practiced in the societies reflected both in the Qur'an and in the earlier strata of the Old Testament, but has subsequently died out in Jewish society and is today dying out in Arab societies? It may well be that the liberation of women, which naturally excludes polygamy, is part of a general process of liberation as humanity 'comes of age' in the modern world. But the challenge faces Islam to come to terms with this new outlook, including its effect in liberating women.

One of the major questions put to the Marxists and Maoists in their dialogue with the religions will concern individual human freedom. The religions will have increasingly to recognise a considerable element of truth in the Marxist analysis of the economic dynamics of human society, and a common aim with Marxism in the ideal of a classless society in which men no longer exploit one another. Indeed the moral basis for the criticism both of the Hindu caste system and of polygamy and the traditional subordination of women is most clearly articulated in Marxism. For Marxism embodies in its pure form the mentality produced by the scientific revolution. Marxism is modernity without religion, in contrast to much of contemporary Christianity, which is modernity in a religious form. But the Marxist societies have to face the question whether, in their opposition to capitalist-Christian civilisation, they have not themselves become hierarchical and authoritarian, thus negating the concept of human liberation on which they are based. For there are clearly as many features of Marxist as of Christian, Muslim and Hindu societies which contradict the modern ideal of human equality and freedom.

What questions will the other partners in the ecumenical dialogue put to Christianity? We have seen that the most distinctive feature of the societies of Europe, North America and Australasia has been that they belong to the modern world. They look across the great gulf of the scientific and technological revolutions to their own medieval past and to the lingering medieval present of many other parts of the world. For Christendom was the civilisation within which the transformation of medieval into modern man first took place and through whose influence it is therefore taking place elsewhere. This is Christianity's unique historical role. If we relate the contingencies of history to an overarching divine purpose of creating children of God out of human animals, we can say that it has been Christianity's special vocation to give birth to the modern mentality. But this calling also has its perils and temptations. In being the first science-based culture, Christendom is also the first culture to experience the domination, possibly leading to the destruction, of human life by its own technology. For technology has created the self-consuming consumer society, with its selfish assumption of a continually rising standard of living. This assumption—together with the population explosion made possible by medical technology—is rapidly exhausting the earth's basic mineral and energy resources and creating the prospect of ecological disaster, perhaps in the early decades of the next century. Western civilisation may thus be in process of strangling itself by its own unbridled lust for ever greater wealth and luxury; or may indeed destroy itself abruptly in a massive thermo-nuclear exchange in which the deeply ingrained western habit of violence puts the marvels of modern technology to suicidal use. Christianity has so far offered no effective resistance to this trend, but is on the contrary deeply implicated in the self-destructive lifestyle and violent tradition of modern western man. The question is now whether Christian civilisation, having become the first bearer of the modern scientific spirit, can avoid being so dominated and corrupted by it that it leads the whole world to destruction.

I am not going to end with any ringing statement of confidence that mankind will succeed in overcoming its immense problems—with the Islamic, Hindu and Buddhist worlds making their transition from a medieval to a modern mentality without succumbing to the dangers so evident in the west; with the Marxist and Maoist civilisations developing their own forms of personal freedom and creativity; and with the Christian west learning non-violence from the profoundly peaceful tradition of Buddhism, and learning a certain detachment from material possessions from traditional Hindu wisdom. I do not profess to know whether any of these things will happen. But what can be said with assurance is that each of the great streams of faith within which human life is lived can learn from the others; and that any hope for the future lies largely in the world ecumenical dialogue which is taking place in so many ways and at so many levels.

Some Trends in Contemporary Indian Christian Theology

By M. M. Thomas

Director of the Christian Institute for the Study of
Religion and Society,
Bangalore, India

I

Robin Boyd's book: *An Introduction to Indian Christian Theology*[1] gives ample evidence of the fact of a distinct tradition in India of understanding Christ and Christianity in terms of Indian culture, and also of its legitimacy in the history of the Indian Church. In 1938 at the time of the meeting of the International Missionary Council at Tambaram, South India, an Indian group of Christian laymen and theologians published the Symposium, *Rethinking Christianity in India;*[2] but it was at that time rejected as syncretistic. Since then much water has flown under the bridge of missionary and ecumenical theology. Today there is world-wide recognition in dominant theological circles, that the gospel of Jesus Christ transcends all cultures, ideologies and religions. But more importantly, there is also the conviction among wide circles that the universality of the gospel should find its expression in its ability to penetrate all cultures, ideologies and religions and transform them into its media. This in part is the result of Biblical theology and in part the result of the ecumenical fellowship of Churches encountering and living in dialogue with various cultures and historical experiences throughout the world. Therefore in the ecumenical theological education programme today, there is a good deal of talk and action, not only about the liberation of Christian theology from its Hellenistic, Latin or European continental captivity, but also about every Church building its theology in its own context of culture and historical experience. Universality and contextuality always go together. Thus, though many have hesitations the ecumenical community of theologians have welcomed the emergence of a theology of liberation in Latin America, a theology of Black Power rooted in the historical experience of the struggle of the blacks for racial justice, a

---

[1] R. H. S. Boyd, *An Introduction to Indian Christian Theology.* CLS, Madras 1969.
[2] Madras 1938.

theology of dialogue with ancient but living religious faiths in Asia, a theology of renewal of Technological Humanism in Western Europe and America and of Marxism in Eastern Europe. Like the traditional Western and Eastern theologies they express the truth of the gospel and like them are liable to fall into heresies. It is in this ecumenical setting that the tradition of Indian Christian theology has received spiritual support and theological legitimacy as an integral part of the history of the Church of Christ sojourning in India.

All theologies are rooted in dialogue between the gospel and the world and take seriously the communication of the gospel to the self-understanding of the people it encounters. That is why the fear of dialogue, whether internally of the Christian convert with his own ideological background or his religious past or externally with people of different ideological or religious persuasion destroys theological creativity. In fact, fear of syncretism after Tambaram 1938 has been theologically destructive for the Indian Churches, because it made the Churches close in on themselves and live in imported shells of Western confessions rather than open themselves to their own milieu with a view to confessing Christ in categories of the self-understanding of people in their own situation. In the ecumenical fellowship even today, theologians who are afraid of syncretism are also afraid of dialogue. It seems to me that it would help theological advance in all parts of the world if we defuse the fear by defining syncretism in a neutral way as is done in the academic discipline of the History of Religion as the phenomenon of mutual interpenetration inevitable in any meeting between cultures and religions, and then by distinguishing between right and wrong kinds of syncretism.[3] Thus we can speak of the Church standing for Dialogue leading to a Christ-centred Syncretism. This would liberate the Churches from fear of dialogue which is almost the essence of any living theology which is the handmaid of the evangelistic and social mission of the Church. I realise that theologians who have long defined syncretism so as to condemn it cannot easily accept this semantics. But I hope that once they begin to accept dialogue as essential to theologising, they will see the point here made.

In any case it is my thesis that Indian Christian theology has come into being as a result of dialogue with the living cultures, ideologies and religions of India; that the crucial problems of its future are related to the task of developing the syncretism it represents along the path of true Christ-centredness; and that this cannot be done without risking deviations and heresies.

The Indianness of Indian Christian Theology has developed along three lines. Firstly in dialogue with the popular religion of the tribals and village

[3] See *Breaking Barriers*. Ed. David M. Paton, BPCK, London 1975, p. 236, where in his Moderator's Report to the Nairobi Assembly this idea was presented by the author.

people. Secondly in dialogue with the modern secular ideologies within the movements struggling for national freedom and nationbuilding. In this talk I shall specially concentrate on the third, namely the development of Indian Christian theology in dialogue with philosophical Hinduism that is Hindu *darsanas*. I was asked to "concentrate particularly on the differences in emphasis and orientation of those on the one hand who try to interpret the Christian message with reference to *advaita* speculation, and those on the other who relate to the Vaishnavite tradition and explore the idea of *avatara* as a valid concept of interpreting the ministry of Christ".[4] This is too vast a subject and I am not metaphysically trained enough to feel any competence in doing an adequate job. So I thought it would be more appropriate for me to indicate the major trends as I see them, and raise some questions from the standpoint of Theology as a struggle for a Christ-centred syncretism.

II

Before we look at some of the Indian theologians who pursue *advaita* and *avatar* traditions of Hinduism, it is necessary to point out that these traditions are in various stages of reinterpretation in India on their own respective fundamentals, and have many variations within each system as thus reinterpreted. So that they cannot be viewed now as closed systems incapable of absorbing new insights and transforming themselves in new directions within certain limits. The dynamism within the *darsanas* are maintained not only in their restatements by the modern Hindu philosophers to make Hinduism more relevant to modern India, but also by the national leaders of political action who seek in them the spiritual anchorage and dynamic for their struggle for a new society and state. Both Western culture and Christianity and the pressures of modernity in India have made the traditions more open to inner transformations. This is an important point to grasp.

No doubt *advaita* as a total system is a monism which sees Nirguna Brahman the Absolute as the undifferentiated one without a second. The world of multiplicity has no ultimate reality though it may appear as real to *avidya* (ignorance) as the rope may appear a snake to the ignorant. In the transcendent world of Reality (Paramarthika realm), the atman (self) of man is identical with the Brahman, the universal self, though the *jiva* (empirical self) moves in the relativities of the empirical world of plurality (the Vyavaharika realm) and may even live as though they are real till the knowledge (jnana) of atman-Brahman identity dawns. Of course it is disputed whether Sankara the main exponent of advaita can be interpreted in these terms of

---

[4] Letter from Prof. Hallencreutz.

monism. But it cannot be disputed that such an interpretation of advaita is part of the tradition. And this extreme monistic interpretation of advaitic philosophy is maintained because of the continuity of those who have the advaitic experience of atman-Brahman identity, the long line of rishis of old up to Ramakrishna and Ramana Maharshi in the modern period. In such a metaphysical monism clearly the world of society, history or persons or even personal God (*Iswara*) can have no ultimate spiritual significance or purpose. But other forms of advaita and other interpretations of Sankara are current; and they emphasise the subtle distinction between monism and nondualism, between the categories of one and not-two. The former denies two, the latter affirms that while there are two, they are essentially not two. Advaita means non-duality. It does not deny diversity but emphasises unity in diversity. This is the opening in which Radhakrishnan affirms the dynamism and reality of the personal God, the world of multiplicity, moral distinctions and regeneration and sees the advaitic spiritual vision not as the destruction but as the fulfilment of human values and historical purposes. The *Jivanmukta* who has realised unitive vision does not cease to be in the world but is incorporated into *Iswara* the creative principle of the world to lift all mankind to the same vision that *Brahmaloka* may be realised. Aurobindo Ghosh's Integral Yoga rejects monistic interpretation of advaita, which he attributes to Sankara, and sees Brahman as involved in the creative evolutionary process of the world. It passes from matter through mind and ego-conscious persons to supermind and to the goal of a spiritual community of *jnanis,* with each stage of the creative process supported by Brahman and transcended by the next stage. Swami Vivekananda sees the movement from duality through modified non-duality to non-duality as an ascending ladder of reality. And *Jivanmukta* who has come to the last stage stays on in the world to serve the world; he thus develops advaitic vision as the spiritual basis for service to the world.

From another side, leaders of political and social action who are antireligous and are committed to secular democratic and socialist ideologies and struggles look to advaitic philosophy and its unitive spiritual vision as a necessary corrective to the spirit of division and conflict in which they themselves are engaged and as providing a boundary where conflict ceases and unity in diversity is affirmed. Jawharlal Nehru saw the crusading spirit pervading the modern political and social ideologies like Capitalism, Communism and Fascism as having its roots in the "crusading religions" Judaism, Christianity and Islam; he sees the antidote to this spirit in the advaitic spirituality which can tolerate many gods including an unknown god because of its spiritual indifference to *nama* and *rupa* (names and forms). He found this spirituality as a possible basis for his foreign policy doctrine of "peaceful coexistence" of different ideologies and social systems without crusading for mutual destruction.[5] Jai Prakash Narain has said, that "the root of morality lies in the endeavour of man to realise the unity of existence or to put it differently to realise the self. For one who has experienced this unity the practice of morality becomes as natural and effortless as the drawing of breath."[6] Asoka Mehta thinks that Indian Socialism would have within it "the search for the unitive way of life through a path that is suffused with pantheistic awareness or a search for unity in diversity."[7] Even the more militant Socialist Ram Manchar Lohia underlines "the emotive basis and the search for oneness of all life and things" as the greatest contribution of India to social and political ethics. He adds that the Western spirit of "a too onesided acceptance of appearance" and the Indian spirit of "an equally onesided acceptance of the reality behind things" can receive mutual correction. If Western spirituality has led to militancy of "strife", Indian spirituality has led to the peace of "stagnation". He himself has no doubt that he would "prefer to die of strife rather than stagnation" but both have dangers inherent in them. He sees the possibility of a third alternative which synthesises the two and therefore keeps the militant strife for justice within the framework of an advaitic spiritual vision, which has within it the experience of "the joy of being one with the universe (and) of being equal with everything in it". As he puts it "the method of dialectic materialism informed by spirituality may unravel the moment of history. The method of spirituality informed by dialectical materialism may raise the edifice of being."[8]

In a way the *avatar* (descent of God) tradition of Vaishnavism with its many divine *avatars* especially Rama and Krishna and the warmth of *bhakti* (devotion) for them expressed in song and prayer was an earlier protest against the cold abstract impersonality of Sankara's advaita tradition. Its philosophical theistic basis was provided by Ramanuja's *Visishtadvaita* (qualified nondualism) and the *avatar* doctrine of the *Bhagavadgita*. Its highest religious expression was *bhakti* mysticism, communion with the *avatar*. Here also there have been reinterpretations in the modern period by leaders of the Indian renaissance in philosophy, religion and politics. Among them Govinda Ranade of Maharashtra, an economist and liberal nationalist and a member of the Prarthanasamaj was foremost. His doctrine of Indian theism with its belief in Providence at work in Indian history and in the necessity of the moral regeneration of Indian society was based on the distinction and relation between *achit* (nature), *chit* (man) and *Brahman*

[5] M. M. Thomas, *Secular Ideologies of India and the Secular Meaning of Christ*. CISRS/CLS 1976, p. 64.
[6] Ibid. p. 66.
[7] Ibid. p. 67.
[8] Ibid. pp. 69–70.

(God) combining Ramanuja's Visishtadvaita, Protestant Christianity and western idea of Progress. Tagore's *Gitanjali* was very much in the Bhakti tradition. Mahatma Gandhi, not only had his roots in Vaishnavism, his scripture was the *Bhagavadgita* with its avatar doctrine. In fact many of its philosophical advocates affirm the bhakti tradition as the one spiritual tradition in which men and women had transcended caste to experience social equality, and therefore as more adequate for providing a spiritual basis for Indian democracy.

I have given this survey to show that the *advaita* and *avatar* traditions of Hinduism are both allied to each other as *darsanas* and that they are both in process of reinterpretation and transformation in dynamic terms in the context of modern India. Early Christian converts like Nehemiah Goreh were engaged in refutation of Hindu systems of thought because they appeared as closed systems. But later converts from Hinduism, especially some of the Brahmin converts found it important to penetrate the spiritual and philosophical traditions of Hinduism with Christ; and this was possible because these traditions were themselves in flux and open to change. Already according to them history was putting pressure on them for change and they had to ensure that change went in the direction of Christ and not in the direction of new Western idols. In part they were only reckoning with their own past. In part it was also necessary to communicate the Christian gospel in the thought-forms of cultured Hindus. In fact, when the Church of South India was inaugurated in 1947 its Constitution had a statement which said that the expression of the universal truth of the gospel in the thought-forms and life-patterns of India would be a basic theological task of the Church in India.

III

Indian Christian theological trends which utilise the *advaitic* and *avatar* traditions may be distinguished within the setting of this common theological mission. This may be done with respect to two specific areas of Indian Christian theology—one which attempts to understand the spiritual experience of fellowship with God through Jesus Christ in terms of the interiority of the experience of advaitic or Bhakti mysticism; the other which seeks to interpret the person of Jesus Christ as Redeemer of the world in the metaphysical categories of *advaitic* or *avatar* tradition.

One of the crucial challenges to Indian Christian theology comes from the fact of the spiritual depth and interiority of the mystic experience of self-realisation in the advaitic experience. This experience of God transcends all religious names and forms (nama-rupa) and is claimed to be unmediated. In its highest reaches it is the realisation of the atman-Brahman identity leading to the awareness of identity of the self with the whole universe. This is a cosmic spirituality of liberation from the distinction between one and many in the world to the transcendent one, the real behind all the appearances. Many Christians are deeply attracted by this unitive vision, and more so now with the divisions and conflicts in the world becoming more intense than ever. Brahmabandava Upadhya and following him the French Sannyasins Jules Monchanin and more recently Swami Abhishektananda and a group of Christian Asramites and theologians with him have been seeking to define the Christian advaitic vision in terms of the Trinity. They see a parallelism between the trinity of Brahman as Sat-Chit-Ananda (Being-Consciousness-Bliss) and the Christian trinity of Father-Lagos-Spirit. They follow the tradition of Christian mysticism represented by Eckehart, St. John of the Cross and the Eastern Orthodox doctrine of theosis which define Christian personalism as beyond the limitations of human persons and beyond the impersonality and the unipersonality of the Divine. Swami Abhishiktananda in his book *Hindu-Christian Meeting Point in the Cave of the Heart* says: "We may proclaim for ever to Hindus that many truly encounters God as Creature, Son and Sinner. India will never take this message seriously until it is freed from the dualistic presuppositions which too often colour our conceptualisation and expression of it .... Only when his ego is fully purified and removed in the Spirit will the Christian be capable of preaching with authority the Personal nature of God and the reality of human personality."[9] Mark Sunder Rao in his pamphlet *Ananyatva: Realisation of Christian Non-duality*[10] distinguishes between monism and nonduality and shows that the Greek doctrine of *perechoresis* (co-inherence) underlying the doctrines of Trinity and Incarnation provide a framework for incorporating the advaita experience into Christian personalism. In his opinion, mystica, theosis, and perechoresis used by the Greek fathers point to a divine human union not unlike that of the advaita union; only unlike the advaita it is not ontological but pneumatological, that is the union in the Holy Spirit and not identity of nature. He also makes a difference between Christ's oneness with God which is hypostatic (in substance) and the disciple's union with God which is mystic mediated through Christ. Rejecting I-It and I-Thou, Rao asks for a relation of I-in-Thou and Thou-in-me that is of mutual interpenetration in the Spirit. Of course the Christian advaitins would consider the personalism of the Bhakti tradition as personalism of a low order. But Bishop Appasamy[11] and others who follow the Bhakti tradition think that Christian personalism with its affirmation of

---

[9] *Hindu-Christian Meeting Point* by Swami Abhishiktananda CLS/CISRS 1969, p. 127.
[10] Mark Sunder Rao, *Ananyatva: Realisation of Christian Nonduality.* CISRS 1964.
[11] A. J. Appasamy, *Christianity as Bhakti marga.* CLS. Madras 1928. *My theological Quest.* CISRS 1964.

creatureliness, sinfulness and sonship is never safe in the advaitic context; and therefore the Mahavakyam of Christian mysticism for them is "Abide in Me and I in You" denoting mutual indwelling and not "I and Father are one" which is often interpreted by advaitins as monistic identity. Therefore they stand for Bhakti-mysticism as the pattern of Christian realisation of God through Christ. The difference between Appasamy's doctrine of mutual indwelling in the Spirit and Mark Sunder Rao's doctrine of *ananytva* through co-inherence in the Spirit is very slight and subtle but it may be important.

In this dialogue between Christian mysticism and Hindu mysticism and the theology of Christian non-duality which has developed out of it, one sees a preoccupation with the spiritual interiority to the exclusion of all bodily and social exteriority and a concentration on the Eternal Christ to the exclusion of the historical Jesus. This may be an antidote to the cults of objectivity and historicism which have bedevilled a good deal of Christian theology. But the question remains whether such interiorisation can do justice to the truth and meaning of Jesus Christ. In fact Swami Abhishiktananda himself has raised the question sharply. He asks whether Christianity as a historical religion "dated in time—the birth of Jesus under Caesar Augustus, his teaching under Tiberius, his execution under the procurator Pontius Pilate" can be "interiorised" without losing its "temporal nature".[12] His own answer is, that "stated in these terms the problem is insoluble"; he opts for a solution at the level, not of theology but *anubhava* (spiritual experience). But Christian theology cannot be so satisfied. Perhaps I should add, that the place of interiority of self-understanding and self-realisation in any Christian definition of the human person and human history is a very crucial question in many theologies both traditional and modern. Not only the theologies of Western Christian mysticism and Eastern theosis, but also the pietist revivalism in Protestantism and Sectarianism and even the more sophisticated theology of Bultmann have raised the same question.

Let us now look more closely at some of the attempts at using *advaita* and *avatar* traditions by Indian theologians to understand Christ in relation to Creation and Renewal of Creation, providing a theological basis for the moral regeneration of persons and historical action to transform nature and society.

It is Keshub Chunder Sen's understanding of Jesus Christ as the Incarnation of *Chit* (consciousness) in Sat-Chit-Ananda Brahman into Divine Humanity which claims our foremost attention. He knows that in his attempt to restate advaita to give room for Christ he is transforming the system of Hindu metaphysics itself. Speaking of Pantheism, he defines it as "the

---

12 Swami Abhishiktananda. Op.cit. p. 30.

identification of all things with God'' and goes on immediately to contrast Hindu Pantheism with Christ's pantheism. He says, ''Hindu pantheism in its worst form is proud, being based upon the belief that man is God; it is quietism and trance. Christ's pantheism is the active self-surrender of the will. It is the union of the obedient, humble and loving Son with the Father. In Christ, you see true pantheism.'' Sén wants to retain the Hindu framework, but restates it. This is also his approach to Brahman in relation to Creation, Incarnation and Cosmic Redemption. The *Chit* of Sat-Chit-Ananda is the agent of God's creative and redeeming activity. He equates *Chit* with *logos* and *sophia*. He says: ''What was creation but the wisdom of God going out of its secret chambers and taking a visible shape . . . . That voice once uttered has ever since rolled backwards and forwards . . . has gone on increasingly through the ages ever since it began . . . . a continuous evolution of creative force, a ceaseless emanation of power and wisdom from the Divine Mind.'' Just as he used the idea of pantheism by reinterpreting it, here he uses the idea of emanation by reinterpreting it as creation. Jesus Christ for Keshub Sen is the ultimate in the cosmic creative process. Elsewhere he pictures the total scheme of Divine Salvation thus: ''The apex is the very God Jehova, the Supreme Brahman of the Vedas. Alone in his own eternal glory He dwells. From him comes down the Son, in a direct line, an emanation from Divinity. Thus God descends and touches one end of the base of humanity; then running all along the base permeates the world and then by the power of the Holy Ghost, drags up the degenerated humanity to Himself. Divinity coming down to humanity is the Son, Divinity carrying up Humanity to heaven is the Holy Ghost.'' Regarding the incarnation of God in Christ, Sen says that as Jesus had renounced his ego in self-surrender, it was filled by God through His *kenosis,* thereby incarnating Himself as Divine Humanity.[13] Manilal Parekh, himself coming to Christ through the path trod by Sen has criticised Sen's scheme of Divine Salvation as giving no place for the radicality of the Sin of man and of the Cross of Christ.[14] I may remark here that this is the defect of all theologies including Tiellard de Chardin's which have the axis Creation-Incarnation-Consummation as contrasted with theologies with the axis Sin-Cross-Eschatology. These latter theologies however runs the danger that Christ never gets fully involved in Creation; He remains as a tangent. These two theological types always need mutual correction.

Advaita defined as monism does not and cannot have a doctrine of creation which gives spiritual reality to the world of relations, except as the

---

[13] Quotation from Sen's speeches quoted in M. M. Thomas, *The Acknowledged Christ of the Indian Renaissance.* pp. 61–67.

[14] Ibid. p. 68.

illusion of *avidya* induced by *maya*. Brahmananda Upadhyaya[15] reinterpreted *maya*, not as illusion but as the power to produce and sustain the world of relations as "contingent" as contrasted with "necessary" being. Such reinterpretation is now very much in vogue, thanks to Radhakrishnan and other Neo-Sankarites; but it was not so when Upadhyaya propounded it. But Upadhyaya dared not equate Christ with *Iswara* or *avatar* because they have no reality in ultimate Brahman. He grants in the world of maya many avatars (descents of God) for re-establishing the moral order disturbed by evil. Especially he considered Krishna as such an avatar. But Christ is for him the Incarnation, one and once for all embodiment of the *chit* in Sat-Chit-Anand trinity of Brahman, following Keshub Chunder Sen. Only he elaborates it further. Later of course Raymond Panikkar does equate Christ with *Iswara* the personal God and agent of Creation in the advaitic darsana.[16] This was possible without denigrating Christ to a lower order of reality as Radhakrishnan and others have begun to interpret *Iswara* as Brahman from the cosmic point of view (the ultimate in relation to the world) and more or less as of the same order of reality as Nirguna Brahman (God as He is in Himself).

Chenchiah of the 'Rethinking Christianity' group follows the Upanishadic tradition which, he says, is not advaitic in the Sankara sense. According to him, the Upanishads see plurality as real but affirms their separation from God and each other as unreal. Brahman emptying himself to find himself through the creative process is more real than Brahman the Absolute. Chenchiah theologises within the metaphysical framework of Sri Aurobindo whose Integral Vedanta has brought reality to the creative evolution through natural and historical process in relation to Brahman. Though Aurobindo rejects Sankara, Aurobindo also can be spoken of as coming within the tradition of Neo-advaita; and as Chenchiah uses his framework for developing his Christology, we may consider him also as broadly standing within the Christian advaitic tradition in Indian theology. Advaita here means the vision of unity and not of the Absolute. Chenchiah wants a God who becomes man and stays on with man as permanent man and does not leave the world as Hindu *avatars* do after they have discharged their temporary mission on earth. In fact Chenchiah's criticisms of the philosophy of Sankara and Radhakrishnan and of the theology of Karl Barth and Hendrik Kraemer are along the same lines—that they are too much preoccupied with an Absolute God who can never involve Himself in the creative and historical processes. The Christ of Barth and Kraemer is "the advent of an incognite God who touches the world as the tangent touches the circle, (that is), touching without touching and does not enter into it, taking his

[15] R. H. S. Boyd, Op.cit. pp. 69–82.
[16] R. Panikker, *The Unknown Christ of Hinduism.* London 1964.

place in creation, but only tears the texture of history and creates a void". He goes on: "There is a humorous side to this Barthian-Advaitic Kraemer-Radhakrishnan dual. Both believe in the Absolute. Both discard relativism, the one as sin and the other as *maya*." Chenchiah calls himself a Relativist believing in a God who is involved fully in the finitude of creative evolution, with metaphysics absorbed into the physical, spirit into matter, to bring the creative process to its divine goal. In this setting Jesus is the *adipurusha* of the New Creation, the new jump which takes creation to a new dimension, not unlike the jumps which took place when matter evolved into life, or animal into man. His Christ may be considered as similar to St. Paul's Second Adam; only he is more earthly than heavenly bringing the realisation of the New Humanity within the historical process. And the Holy Spirit as *Sakti* present in history reproduces Christ in men and women and incorporates them in the New Humanity.[17]

One should also mention Stanely Samartha who follows the framework of Radhakrishnan's Neo-advaita for his theologising. He sees a polarity, rather a paradox between historicity and ontology, between fact and being, in any true Christology; and as he finds the same polarity expressed in Neo-advaita, he thinks that Indian Christology might very well be worked out within its framework. More so because it is the dominant *darsana* of India. Robin Boyd in giving the title *Christadvaita* to his new book on "a theology for India", seems also to indicate the greater relevance of advaita Vedanta for Indian Christian theology.

It was the clearly understandable and easily practisable personal devotion of the *bhakti* and *avatar* tradition which brought many Indian theologians to seek to interpret Christianity in its terms. Avatar tradition is theistic from the start, gives spiritual reality to the world and the human soul in their distinctness from God; it takes warm loving devotion or bakti as the key to human appropriation of the Divine and it takes human sin and Divine Grace seriously. In fact Otto had considered the bhakti religion as the religion of Grace in India and as nearer to Christianity than other Indian traditions.

Thus Bishop Appasamy has developed his Indian Christian theology interpreting Christianity as *Bhaktimarga*, as contrasted with the *jnanamarga* of advaita. Philosophically he works within the framework of Ramanuja's *Visishtadvaita* and speaks of God as Creator of the world which is His body and therefore rejecting identity and separation. God is also the *antaryamin* (indweller) immanent in the world. And following the Prologue of the Gospel of St. John, Appasamy affirms that the *antaryamin* has taken flesh in Jesus, so that "He is fully embodied in Jesus". Here Appasamy develops a Christian doctrine of *avatara*, emphasising over against the Hindu doctrine,

---

[17] See M. M. Thomas, op.cit. pp. 167–170.

the once-for-allness of God's avatara in Jesus and his real bodily humanity in history. Above all, God's purpose in Jesus's *avatara* is not re-establishment of harmony disturbed by evil by slaying the wicked but furthering the Divine purpose of Salvation of the world. The suffering love of God manifested in Jesus not only liberates mankind from sin understood as alienation from God but also shifts from man to God the burden of *karma* understood as the cosmic law of moral retribution.[18] Chakkarai Chettiar gives the title *Jesus the Avatar* to his book on Christianity. To him, Jesus is the *satpurusha* in whom *maya* is cast off and transcended so that the full divine glory and light shine in the world, and shared with his bhaktas. And he interprets the Cross as the point at which no ego can exist, "but is burnt up in the *homa* or sacrificial fire that burns in the deepest heart of God and necessarily of humanity, which is Jesus in history". He adds that the incarnation and the cross continue "from stage to stage, from the historical to the spiritual, from time to eternity". The Holy Spirit is the permanent presence with us of Jesus the avatar himself. In union with him the *bhakta* receives, not metaphysical advaita, but an advaita which is *sambhava* an event in history which transforms him and makes him the centre of cosmic transformation.[19] S. K. Rudra follows the Indian line of the impossibility of the "conditioned being" of man to "know with certainty in and through his own conditioned existence the essential character of unconditioned God" the Brahman Nirguna; but goes on to speak of Jesus as the one in whom God has revealed himself as Brahman Saguna. The life, death and resurrection of Christ expresses "the eternal unchanging reality" of God in ways in which "the philosopher as well as the peasant" can understand. Participation in the life of Christ through abiding in Him as Love is the destiny of man. It results in social progress and human community. He says: "When at last humanity has found its centre in Christ the Son, a fully organised human society embracing all the world in one common brotherhood will be both possible and practicable .... Without a centre, humanity can never become one. We can conceive of no other ultimate centre but Christ the Incarnate God."[20]

IV

This brief and unsystematic survey of two streams of Indian Christian theology makes clear that we are dealing with the struggle of Indian Christians to understand and communicate the truth and meaning of Jesus Christ in the traditional language of Hindu metaphysics and spirituality. They are

[18] R.H.S. Boyd, op.cit. pp. 118–135.
[19] Ibid, pp. 167–174.
[20] M. M. Thomas, op.cit. pp. 272–274.

syncretistic in the sense of intermixing of fragments from different cultural and religious traditions. They need to be evaluated to see whether they have developed an inner coherence to the syncretistic thought and far more important, whether the coherence is centred in the Jesus Christ of God. Evaluation of Christ-centredness depends however on the meaning of Personalism and Historicity which the Old and New Testaments of the Bible, more especially the picture of Jesus Christ in the Gospels represents. Both Christian advaita and Christian Bhakti traditions are pursuing the true personalism as they severally understand it. The advaitin is afraid of reducing God to a person among persons and affirms Him as the ground of being. Even Karl Barth has spoken of the possibility of idolatry in certain conceptions of God as personal, but what is the right meaning of speaking of God as personal? Bhakti theology affirms the Personal Being of God as the ground of human personal beings, and are afraid to follow *advaita* which might lead to denial of the creatureliness and sinfulness of man. There is a further question whether either of the metaphysical framework of Hinduism or even Neo-Hinduism can sustain the affirmation of a Divine Purpose for the world and an *eschaton* for human history, without which the idea of personal being either of God or man cannot be Christ-centred. Paul Devanandan says that Neo-Hinduism has to go much further in the restatement of Vedanta to evolve such a metaphysical framework. He feels that "the actionlessness of the mystic advaitism of the finite self and the Infinite self still upheld as the desirable end of all religious pilgrimage" which is common to all Hindu religious metaphysics is the ultimate stone of stumbling. Against this, Fr. Samuel Rayan of Vidyajoti of Delhi[21] has recently come out with a defence of the relation between Faith and History depicted in the Bhagavadgita and pleading for a re-examination of the concepts of History current in Western theologies. He thinks that the Gita concept of History is more adequate than the objectively linear concepts of secular history and salvation history which informed the liberal and dialectical theologies of the West which now lie in ruins or the many other concepts of history which have more recently been canvassed by Bultmann, Pannenberg and Von Balthasar.

Rayan points out that the moment which faces Arjuna in the battlefield of *Kurushetra* raises the crisis of history for the human person and the world and that the Gita is a theological treatise which relates Faith to History in a radical manner. The fact that commentaries on the Gita have been written by all philosophers and national leaders of modern India from Tilak to Radhakrishnan, Gandhi and Bhave is evidence of its relevance to the historical decisions Indians are called to make in our time, and that it contains "a solid basis for the use that has been made of it in modern times and down the

---

[21] S. Royan: Indian Theology and the Problem of History, in *Society and Religion* (ed. R. W. Taylor). CISRS 1976, pp. 167–193.

centuries". His own exploration of this "solid basis" is indeed very illuminating. He shows how in *Kurushetra*, man has come into an hour of historical crisis. But crisis is also the time of *kairos* where "the Lord creates himself on earth and when he is acknowledged Charioter of man in the midst of history-making struggle". The Sankhya position that no earthly action really matters, the call of caste duty and the attraction of personal gain are all powerless to move Arjuna. They have to ultimacy, and are irrelevant before God. And the real problem is that of "work as at once necessary for life and dangerous for salvation", and of existence without the hope of reaching the goal of life. The solution is offered in *Nishkamakarma,* "work without selfish desire" and *Lokasamgraha* "the gathering and holding together and wholeness of the world". Thus selfless action for human community is given as the point at which history becomes salvation history. But this action is provided further spiritual depth by "linking it up with the Person of the Lord and with personal loyalty to Him" who is present within the stream of history, as the Self established in the heart of all, the *antaryamin*. This presence as creative activity may be impersonal, but in redemptive activity it is deeply personal. Krishna says "Those who commune with Me in love's dwelling abide in Me and I in them" thus transforming *chronos* into *Kairos*. To quote: "Time is saved from its cyclic quest and brought home to the Lord. It is a live moment when man stands addressed by God as his *bhakta* and friend." Thus "History is time open to God and on the move, maturing towards its own wholeness which is already present in the presence of the Lord within its heart"; and the central message of the Gita according to Rayan is that "the recurring consequences of Karma can be overcome, and mechanical time can be led to meaningful personal goal and thus redeemed by relating in faith to the Lord who loves us. The possibility of a definite End to *Samsara,* the Great Fear, is affirmed".

Christ-centredness is a challenge, not only to the syncretism of Indian Christian Theology but to all theologies in all parts of the world which are all syncretisms. Moving towards Christ-centred syncretism is the ecumenical theological task.

The Model Health Service— A Search for Utopia

By Odin W. Anderson

Professor of Sociology
Center for Health Administration Studies
University of Chicago, USA

I. Rationale

The efforts by nations to develop a model health service have been a search for Utopia—adequate number of hospital beds, doctors, nurses, adequate distribution, equal access, and above all, reasonable cost. Note the words adequate, equal, and reasonable. None are definable according to scientifically established criteria. All are results of temporary equilibria in perceptions of demand, resources available and allocated, and professional prerogatives of doctors. More mundanely this balance depends on the endurance of the public and the degree of dedication of the profession compounded by the pressures on the welfare state to spend beyond the capacity to produce a surplus for humane purposes.

The foregoing observations led me to international comparisons, because one system cannot be its own reference point. There is need to compare ranges of differences in utilization, personnel, facilities, and expenditures between industrialized countries. Are there repetitions in patterns; are there relationships between various factors that are predictable; are there problems which are solvable by direct intervention; and are there generic problems which do not respond to intervention, but must be regarded as in the nature of things regardless of time, place, and circumstances?

In the United States I discovered a wide range of patterns of use and expenditures from state to state. In other industrialized countries I found great variations between countries in the use of hospitals, e.g., from 85 admissions per 1000 population to 200. The variations in use of physicians' services were not as great, but significant. These kinds of crude data indicated the need for some systematic comparisons. I selected three industrialized countries which exhibited a range of characteristics from loosely structured to highly structured systems, plurality of sources of funding, public or private ownership of facilities, and a host of other factors. They were the United States, Sweden, and Great Britain (limited to England and Wales).

II. Comparative Developments—The United States, Sweden, and England

The countries and economies known as the liberal democracies which replaced the mercantilist and highly regulatory concept of the state during the 19th century conceived of the state as limited to the maintenance of law and order, ultimate sanctioning of private property, taxing power, and some concept of minimal subsistence for the poor who could not function in the labor market. The means of production and distribution were in private ownership in a market economy of price competition. The private sector—public sector dichotomy shaped the evolution of the health services. Each country had to decide on the extent to which health services were primarily a private sector concern or a public sector concern. In all three countries the autonomous practicing physician charging fees emerged and was licensed by the state. In the United States and England the voluntary hospitals capitalized by the new wealthy upper middle class became the backbone of the hospital system to which private physicians applied for privileges to admit patients. In Sweden the hospitals, with exceedingly few exceptions, were from the start owned and funded by the local governments. The facilities were later taken over by the county governments when they were created in 1862. The Swedish political and social system never entertained the concept of private or voluntary hospitals because no upper middle and wealthy middle class on the order of the United States and England emerged. Sweden did not have the economic base for it. Significantly, Sweden under Queen Christina divorced the hospitals from the poor laws, making the public hospitals agencies for the entire community. In England the voluntary hospitals were built for the worthy poor, i.e., low-income workers, with a small percentage of beds reserved for the small wealthy class and their private doctors, plus some private hospitals. Further, municipal hospitals in the major cities were built for the paupers, the really destitute, not connected with the labor market, or in contemporary parlance the unworthy poor.

In the United States the voluntary hospitals became—and still are—the backbone of the general hospital system to serve the emerging and large middle and upper income groups as early as the latter 19th century. The hospitals were capitalized in the main by private philanthropists as acts of charity, but for the community in general rather than the working poor or paupers. The latter groups were—and are—regarded as a residual of the system which hospitals by their charters were obligated to serve, but they accounted for roughly only one-third of the hospitals' income obtained from taxation and private charity. From the start the voluntary hospitals received their major operating income from private patients. As a spillover for the voluntary hospitals many cities built general hospitals for the poor, but they remained residuals of the main system. The physicians, like those in England until the National Health Services Act of 1946, were largely free-standing private entrepreneurs whether with hospital connections or not. In Sweden, however, the hospital connected physicians were salaried from the early days and were in a class separate from private practitioners on the outside. It seems that economies of the United States and England could support a profession largely on a fee-for-service basis from a relatively large clientele, unlike a less affluent country such as Sweden.

As for the supply of health service personnel, the United States and England until 1946, both private and publicly supported medical, nursing, dental, and pharmacy schools trained personnel. In Sweden the State assumed major responsibility from the beginning.

So far, I have dealt mainly with personal health services—a one to one relationship between a patient and a physician—as contrasted to public health services dealing with mass control of disease through environmental sanitation and immunization. The liberal democratic market economy began to recognize in the middle and latter 19th century that individual initiative was not equal to controlling diseases that were communicable through water, milk, and food. Collective action was necessary. Thus publicly supported health departments expanded rapidly as a proper function of the state but separate from and parallel to the personal health services emanating in large part from the private sector and being regarded largely as a private responsibility even for the poor. The division between the public health and personal health sectors continued conceptually and administratively in the United States and England, and until recently in the latter. In Sweden, however, there was a pragmatic amalgam of public health officers—practitioners from the latter 18th century up to the present for sparsely populated areas of the country.

Inevitably, personal health services became more costly as medical technology expanded in scope and number—radiology possibly being the first conspicuous example at the turn of the century. Surgery became safe because of antisepsis, and relatively painless because of anesthesia. Naturally the demand for services began to increase as well, a pressure which has not yet abated. Increasing unit price and increased demand resulted in a higher total expenditure from all sources. The philanthropists and the government helped to increase the supply; the next problem was to enable the general self-sustaining public to buy the services.

Naturally enough each country evolved its own method of entrance into health insurance, private or public. It was noted that Sweden had a free hospital service for generations, particularly after 1862. She did not enter into government insurance for physicians' services outside the hospital until 1955 after 20 years of sporadic public discussion. England took its first health insurance step for workers under certain incomes and then for general practitioners' services in 1911. The United States entertained the possibility of government health insurance in 16 states between 1916 and 1918, but nothing came of it. There was insufficient political support even from organized labor. The United States later broke through by means of private health insurance in the 1930's, expanding during World War II, and growing even more rapidly thereafter. This blunted general political interest in government health insurance until the last few years. National health insurance was enacted for an age group in 1965—those 65 years of age and over. Returning to England, nothing officially happened to national health insurance until World War II forced a reconsideration of the entire personal health services apparatus culminating in the comprehensive National Health Service based on two fundamental principles: Comprehensive as to services and free at time of service. The United States and Sweden were more incremental in their approaches and their systems still hardly approach the comprehensiveness of the National Health Service.

III. Trends Since 1950

The limited but extremely suggestive data that stimulated comparative research between the United States, Sweden, and England are revealed in the table below. They are from around 1960.

Comparison of the United States, Sweden, and England on generally quoted utilization indices

Type of Use	United States	Sweden	England
General hospital admission rates per 1000 population	130	130	85
Mean length of stay	8	12	12
Percent of population seeing a physician at least once during a year	65	65	65
Number of physician visits per capita	5	3	5

These data are difficult to explain in that in the United States only about two-thirds of general hospital care was paid for by insurance while in

Sweden and England it was virtually free at time of service. Although there was little insurance coverage for out-of-pocket physicians' services in the United States, while physicians' services were mostly paid by insurance in Sweden and were entirely free at time of service in England, the proportions of the population seeing physicians at least once a year were approximately the same in all three countries. Furthermore, on average there appeared to be just as many physicians' visits per person in the United States as in England, and more than in Sweden. Clearly use of health services revealed mystifying variations from country to country. The reasons for these great variations have not been elucidated yet. The best we have now is conventional wisdom inferred from at best descriptive data.

To show the dynamics of health services systems, it is necessary to show changes over time within and between systems. The national data from each country are quite adequate for this purpose. Very little is known about what happens inside the system—more specifically, the physicians' consulting room. This is the "black box" in health services research. We are learning more about what happens before and after a patient has been in the "black box", but how physicians make decisions is a largely unexplored area.

In order to compare changes over time between the three countries, I made the assumption that 1950 would be an appropriate benchmark for comparisons within and between systems. By 1950 the health services in industrialized countries had absorbed the medical and chemotherapeutic technology which accelerated during and after World War II.

The most popular indicator of change is the amount of money spent on the respective systems. By any standard the increase in each country has been phenomenal and by magnitudes not imaginable in the early 50's. Between 1950 and 1974 the per capita expenditures in the United States on all health services increased by fully 500 percent, or five-fold. In Sweden the increase was fully 2500 percent, or 25 fold, and in England the increase, as in the United States, was around 500 percent, again five-fold. In the three countries expenditures for health services as a percent of gross national product rose from under five percent in all three in the 50's to over eight percent in the United States, almost ten percent in Sweden, and over six percent in England (the U.K.). Expenditure for health services has exceeded the growth in the gross national products in all countries and is one of the leaders in expenditures for consumption goods. Correcting for inflation in the three countries between the early 50's and the early 70's does not essentially change the comparisons.

As a crude indicator of possible control over expenditures it is useful to show the major sources of funding among the three countries.

Sources of Funding in %

	U.S. (1974)	Sweden (1973)	England (1973)
Private			
Patient direct	35	15	15
Insurance	26	—	—
Other	1	—	—
	62	15.0	15.0
Public			
Central government	24	17	80
Local government	13	64	5
	38	85	85

These distributions of sources of funding reflect the potential ability of each system to direct its resources from a central point if the public policy so dictates. The diversity of sources of funding in the United States reveals a multi-nucleated decision-making system not even apparent in these figures. The insurance sector itself is extremely diversified among 500 or so private insurance agencies. The major trend is the increasing role of the Federal government, and one destined to continue.

Sweden reveals the division of fiscal and administrative responsibility between the state and the counties, one which has remained quite constant during the last 25 years. And England reveals the highly centralized nature of the funding of its system. Buried in all three systems are the relative contributions from employers and employees adding to the diversity, being highest in the United States and lowest in England.

In all three countries it is felt that the health system is overemphasizing hospital care at the expense of primary or out-of-hospital care. Early 1970 data reveal that both the United States and England devote 39 percent of all health service expenditures to the hospital (exclusive of physicians' salaries) and Sweden devotes 48 percent. All three countries devote approximately the same proportion of expenditures to physicians' services. The Swedish proportion has been increasing as the number of physicians has expanded. Sweden's system has been hospital intensive since the latter 19th century after the counties were given exclusive responsibility for ownership and operation, and possibly even before.

As reflected in the expenditure data, each country has been in a 25-year period of variable expansion in personnel, facilities, and use. The differences have been mainly in pace. In 1950 the United States started with the highest physician supply, followed by England and Sweden. Sweden's supply of physicians was unusually low, 40 % of that of the U.S. and 70 %

of that of England. Since then Sweden has more than doubled its supply of physicians, beginning to approximate that of the United States and exceeding that of England. In all three countries the number of nurses has increased phenomenally. In 1950 the number of nurses per 100,000 population was 249 in the U.S., 182 in Sweden, and 131 in England. By 1974 the number had increased to 404, 612, and 238 respectively. As for dentists, the U.S. ratio has remained quite constant at under 60 per 100,000 population, Sweden increased its ratio from 49 to 88 and England remained quite constant, under 25.

To avoid unnecessary details and tedium I will give a quick review of hospital beds and hospital staffing ratios and use. General hospital beds per 1000 population has increased significantly in the United States from 3.3 beds per 100 in 1950 to 4.5 in 1975. England has dropped slightly from five to around four beds. Sweden has also dropped slightly from 5.7 beds to 5.5. It is difficult to break out general hospital beds from all types of hospital beds, but clearly Sweden has always had a high bed-population ratio compared to other industrialized countries and until recently a significantly lower physician-population ratio.

Admissions to general hospitals have increased in all countries from 110 per 1000 in 1950 to 157 in the U.S.; from 113 to 156 in Sweden; and from 64 to 104 in England. Paralleling these increases there has been a shortening of the average length of stay from slightly over 8 to slightly under 8 in the U.S.; from 16 to 10 in Sweden; and from 15 (1960) to 10 in England. The number of general hospital days per capita continues to vary widely. In 1974, for example, the United States used 1.2 days per person. Sweden 1.5, and England 1. The differences in the use of mental hospitals are truly staggering, around one-half day per capita in the United States, 2 days in Sweden, and one day in England.

Finally, an intriguing system difference is the number of personnel per patient day in general hospitals exclusive of physicians. In 1950 the United States recorded 1.78, Sweden 1.31 and England 1.51. By the early 70's the U.S. had climbed to over 3, Sweden almost 2 and England over 3.5.

The foregoing indicators of performance of health service systems should logically be regarded as inputs, i.e., the elements necessary to affect health outcomes, recovery, stabilization, or death. In many instances they are also regarded as outcomes, particularly if the intent is to increase access and equalize access to services, the egalitarian objective. More use of services may, therefore, according to this objective, be regarded as output measures. The desired measure of output, however, is the impact on the standard health indicators: mortality rates by age, sex, and cause and the average length of life and morbidity. Morbidity is much more difficult to measure than mortality. Both are difficult to relate directly to personal health services. Nevertheless, a popular international sport is to compare the mortality rates between countries as possibly reflecting the impact on them of their personal health services.

Let us start with average length of life. In recent years the average length of life in the United States is estimated at 72 years; Sweden 75, and England, also around 73. Universally, women live longer than men by as much as five years. The rank order of average length of life is Sweden, England, and the U.S.A. Very popular indicator is infant mortality, number of infants who die under one year per 1000 live births. Here England and the United States are virtually similar in 1974, 16–17. Sweden is a spectacular under 10. In all three countries the rates continued downward. Sweden's infant mortality rate has always been very low—at the turn of the century 99. The United States recorded its first national figure in 1915, 15 years later, and the figure was 100 when Sweden's was around 76! In the United Kingdom the rate was even higher than in the U.S. It is of interest that the range of variations by income classes or residence is as wide in England as in the United States, as high as 40 in some areas. Sweden's range is exceedingly narrow. From the 1950 levels to 1974 the United States infant mortality rate has declined 43 percent, Sweden 54 percent, and England 49 percent.

The maternal mortality rate is exceedingly low in all three countries. In the early 70's the rate had dropped to 1, 5 or less per 1000 live births in the United States and 1.1 in England. In Sweden the rate has become so low that it is almost zero and not worth reporting since 1965.

IV. Meaning of the Indicators

The foregoing review of the differences in expenditures, facilities, personnel, use, and health indicators reveals no clear relationships. Research in health services has not yet been able to isolate the variables that account for the variations. Indeed, it appears as if there are fundamental social and biological forces which operate regardless of expenditures, number of facilities and personnel, and health indices. All the indicators are in the same directions in all systems, up or down, as the case may be, but there appears to be no relationship between the expenditures and their impact on the standard health indicators. England spends much less on health services than does the United States, but her health indicators are approximately the same. Sweden spends as much and possibly more than the United States and appreciably more than England, but her health indicators have been low for several generations before the advent of a modern health service. In fact, Sweden decided to double its number of physicians at the same time that she had the lowest health indicators in the world! It seems reasonable to assume that after a country has reached a level of industrialization and affluence personal health services have very little influence on the standard health indicators. The removal of personal health services would probably not drastically change the indicators for the worse—but this is speculation, and very difficult to prove one way or another.

What has been cruelly learned is that there is no neat and measurable reservoir of morbidity which can be cleaned up with comprehensive medical care because other and more subtle morbidities by definition surface. Theoretically, need for medical care cannot possibly be inexhaustible, but so far, no country has yet tried to find out what may be the saturation point.

What I then propose are indicators of performance appropriate to the egalitarian political context in which the major programs in the welfare state are being formulated. The driving ideology behind national health insurance has been the equalization of access, hence a performance indicator can be the extent to which people are obtaining access to services in equal amounts regardless of family income and residence. Even so it is only recently that all systems have become seriously concerned with equalizing *distribution* of facilities and personnel, making them more easily accessible by distance as well as by no price at time of service. Indeed, implicit in the egalitarian philosophy is that a measure of the proper fit of need/demand and services is that all people should die of the same rank order of causes, regardless of family income and residence.

V. Strains and Tendencies Common to All Systems

Until the last decade or so there was little political concern with the direct management of the health services. All countries were in an expansive mood, reflecting the expansiveness of their economies. Each year, the health services were allocated more money regardless of type of organization, ownership, and sources of funding. Even though the general public appears to be happy to have a free or near-free service when they seek care, the politicians and public administrators are universally alarmed at the amount of money going to the health services in competition with other priorities and obligations assumed by governments. How, then, can the system be managed to relate expenditures to results? Are there measures of net outcomes so that intelligent public policy can be formulated in relation to choices of alternatives? Are there management principles which can be borrowed from industry which can be applied to health services management? So far, the answer is in essence "no", although this does not, of course, preclude the possibility of developing management methodology applied to the management of the health services. But this is for the future. It would seem that the evidence for this observation was made clear in the foregoing. I can add still more by stressing that in reviewing not only the expenditure patterns of the three countries under discussion in this paper, but also a number of other industrialized countries, including the U.S.S.R., there appears to be no relationship between how health services delivery is organized, who owns the facilities, how the health personnel are paid and how the total system is financed and the total national expenditures devoted to health services. This is a sobering and distressing observation. I then conclude that in any system the amount spent for health services is mainly a political decision because there are no performance indicators of any substance which can be used to guide policy other than equal access and cost sharing. Whether the health services are financed largely by private sources as in the U.S., or by almost completely public funds as in England and the U.S.S.R., the fundamental problem of resource allocation is inherent. So far, countries have responded to popular demand and the public has liked it. Now, public authorities are beginning to question this demand—how much of it is necessary, how much unnecessary. The answer everywhere is planning and rationalization of the systems.

Planning and rationalization to fit need, services, and expenditures have been considered seriously for the first time in liberal democratic economies only recently, although the U.S.S.R. has engaged in them for several decades. Even so, to date, planning has to be quite arbitrary because health services cannot be managed like an automobile factory, life insurance company, or even a grammar school. The health services are by their very nature open-ended because of people's perceptions of illness and physicians' discretionary authority inherent in professional work settings. How does one encompass and manage this system so that public authorities know what the public treasury or private financing is getting for its money? In the main we do not know. It is of interest, however, that countries are still spending 5 to 10 percent of their gross national products without having measuring rods of accomplishment. Still, people are happy because they are assured of care at low or no cost—shared by all when they are sick, a most vulnerable condition for anyone.

Because of the openness of the health services and because of the lack of performance measuring rods, all countries are responding similarly to rising expenditures. Planning and rationalization introduce some structure into health services organization: some boundaries such as regionalization, limiting supply of beds and physicians accepting rationing by inducing queueing, by more salaried positions for physicians, and thereby better control over physicians' incomes, fewer entry points for patients, and constrictions to opportunities for a viable private health services sector. A private sector might result in a two-class system, assuming a one-class system is ever possible in a governmental system.

Although it does take imagination, not to mention boldness to formulate plans on a national scale, the distinct trend towards more and more structure is a natural concommitant of planning in that the openness of the system hardly allows any other recourse. Planning then requires more political skill than technical skill given the current state of the art.

VI. Observations and Prognosis

In all countries the primary concern will be a profoundly political one; how to balance the need/demands of the public, the priorities the countries will give to health services in competition with other national concerns and the form the organization of health services will take. In essence, as is true of all health and welfare programs, the tolerance of the public for politically minimal endeavors will be tested. The length of the queue is one such crude but politically real indicator. Another test of tolerance is the willingness of the medical profession to function in what appear to be increasingly constricted circumstances as to traditional and powerful professional prerogatives inherent in professional work.

Nevertheless, I predict that the allocations to health services will continue to increase both relatively and absolutely for the next generation. The desire for health services to cure immediately when possible, to care over the long term when cure is impossible.

What may reverse this trend is a change in the attitudes of the public towards sickness, pain, and dying and a turning way from professional service. Such imputation of rationality, however, does not seem realistic.

The pressures on the system will continue and the response will be as much rationalization through scientifically established criteria as possible. I am not sanguine, however, that criteria of sufficient depth and scope can be developed so as to encompass any more than a limited range of diagnoses that lend themselves to such specifications. A health service which can be managed with as much prior specifications of results as an automobile factory would not be a health service. It would be impersonal. The ideal patient would be a breathing brick.

There will be increasing attempts to monitor the decision-making of physicians as exemplified in the United States by the legally mandated Professional Standards Review Organizations (P.S.R.O.). Its efficacy is yet to be tested. The objectives are far ahead of the methodology to implement them.

Should governments really contain costs through rationalization, priority will then likely be given to high technology and correspondingly expensive procedures rather than to skillful management of long-term illness. A truly comprehensive health service will be regarded as too expensive for a national economy.

What countries may be driven to is the targeting of problems for special attention. The setting of, and the carrying out of priorities within the entire spectrum of health services is still at a crude stage. The tendency is toward comprehensiveness. For example, there are pockets of infant mortality in the United States and the United Kingdom which have rates twice that of the national average. There are diseases that lend themselves to quite specific cure or prevention such as venereal disease which continues to be rampant.

It is of interest that both the United Kingdom and Sweden have established Royal Commissions, to study their health services and make recommendations. The United States had a series of analogous commissions in the latter sixties. Regardless of overlapping sources of funding, and reorganizational structure these commissions were concerned with the same problems—rising costs, inequitable distribution of services, inadequate management, and so on. Looking ahead to the mid-eighties, the proportion of the G.N.P. the United States, Sweden, and England devote to health services will be higher, but in the same rank order—Sweden, 15 %, the U.S., 12 %, and England, 7 %. In essence, the United States will continue to have a more loosely structured system than either Sweden or England, but will be moving toward them in rationalizing the system; England in her Reorganization Plan of 1974 will be edging toward equalization between regions so slowly that no one will feel threatened. Sweden will continue to have a County-State division of responsibilities and keep on chipping away at fee-for-service prerogatives for private practitioners. The respective problem solving styles will continue to be process (open negotiation and bargaining between interest groups) in the United States, structural reorganization in England (and covert negotiating among interest groups), and consensus through facts in Sweden. High technology will be adopted at a variance pace; the U.S. the fastest, followed closely by Sweden, and a distant last by England. In fact, England might well send patients needing heroic procedures to the U.S. and Sweden. It would be cheaper than building up her own services. The proper management of chronic illness will continue to be intractable. The reservoir of need will be vast and larger than today. The capacity of the society and the health services to cope adequately with this problem will continue to be limited, not only because of low priority in resource allocation, but fundamentally because the kind of care required by patients with long-term and intractable illnesses is beyond price. They need the kind of care that can normally be expected only of wives, husbands, and relatives.

In sum, the health services will continue to be a growth industry and in public demand. It will continue to be labor intensive. High technology developments will continue. All of this will be expensive. There is no cheap way out. Health services cannot be efficient; they will continue to be provided with a great deal of faith. Health services will continue to receive a high priority because they are wanted—regardless of so-called outcome measures. Therefore, health services will be given high priority despite the anguish of politicians and administrators because they share the same desire for services when they are sick, in pain, and dying.

Comparative research in national health services systems has helped greatly to understand the nature of the entity called health services and generic similarities. It will take this kind of research to tell us how to manage the system as a whole, in part, or perhaps even leave it alone. Perhaps no enterprise has emerged in modern society in which we spend so much, and about which we know so little. The search for Utopia will continue—adequate resources, equitable distribution of supply, equal access, at reasonable cost.

BIBLIOGRAPHY

This is a highly selected bibliography supporting the data in this paper and the background literature for cross-national studies. The latest data for expenditures, facilities, personnel, and vital statistics are from the standard official sources worked up by Larry Corder and exist in unpublished form.

Brian Abel-Smith. *Paying for Health Services*. Public Health Papers No. 17. Geneva, World Health Organization, 1963.

Christa Altenstetter. "Planning for Health Facilities in the U.S. and in West Germany." *Milbank Memorial Fund Quarterly: Health and Society*, 51:41–71, Winter, 1973.

American Scandinavian Foundation, *Scandinavian Review*, "Health: A Major Issue," 1975.

Ronald Andersen, Björn Smedby, and Odin W. Anderson. *Medical Care Use in Sweden and the United States*, Research Series No. 26, Chicago, Center for Health Administration Studies, University of Chicago, 1969.

Ronald Andersen, "A Framework for Cross-National Comparisons of Health Services Systems." in: Manfred Pflanz and Elizabeth Schach, eds. *Cross-National Sociomedical Research: Concepts, Methods, Practice*. Stuttgart, Georg Thieme, 1976, p. 25–46.

Odin W. Anderson and George Rosen. *An Examination of the Concept of Preventive Medicine*. Health Information Foundation. Research Series No. 12, New York, The Foundation, 1960.

Odin W. Anderson. *Health Services in the U.S.S.R.* Selected Papers, No. 42, Chicago, Graduate School of Business, 1973.

Odin W. Anderson. "All Health Care Systems Struggle Against Rising Costs." *Hospitals,* 50:97–102, Oct. 1, 1976.

Odin W. Anderson. *Health Care: Can There Be Equity: The United States, Sweden, and England.* New York, Wiley-Inter Science, 1972. All historical references prior to 1970 and trend data from 1950 to latter 1960's.

Spyros Andreopoulos, ed. *National Health Insurance: Can We Learn from Canada?* New York, Wiley, 1975.

John H. Babson. *Health Care Delivery Systems: A Multinational Survey.* Bath, England, Pitman Medical, 1972.

Ragnar Berfenstam and Inger William-Olsson. *Early Child Care in Sweden.* London, Gordon and Breach, 1973.

David A. Ehrlich, ed. *The Health Care Explosion: Which Way Now?* Berne, Switzerland, Hans Huber, 1975.

Ray H. Elling. "Health Planning in International Perspective," *Medical Care,* 9:214–234, May-June, 1971.

Karl Evang, David S. Murray, and Walter J. Lear. *Medical Care and Family Security: Norway, England and the U.S.A.,* New York, Prentice-Hall, 1963.

Mark G. Field, "The Concept of Health Systems at the Macrosociological Level," *Social Science and Medicine,* 7:763–785, 1973.

John Fry. *Medicine in Three Societies: A Comparison of Medical Care in the U.S.S.R., U.S.A., and U.K.,* New York, Elsevier, 1970.

Robert M. Gibson and Marjorie Smith Mueller, "National Health Expenditures, Fiscal Year, 1976." *U.S. Social Security Bulletin,* 40:3–22, April, 1977.

William A. Glaser. *Social Settings and Medical Organization: A Cross-National Study of the Hospital.* New York, Atherton Press, 1970.

William A. Glaser. *Paying the Doctor—Systems of Remuneration and Their Effects.* Baltimore, Johns Hopkins Press, 1970.

James Hogarth. *The Payment of the Physician—Some European Comparisons.* New York, Macmillan, 1963.

Morris Janowitz. *Social Control of the Welfare State.* New York, Elsevier, 1976.

Egon Jonsson and Duncan Neuhauser. "Hospital Staffing Ratios in the United States and Sweden," *Inquiry* (Supplement) 12:128, June, 1975.

M. Kaser. *Health Care in the Soviet Union and Eastern Europe.* London, Croom Helm, 1976.

Robert Kohn and Kerr White, eds. *Health Care: An International Survey.* London, Oxford University Press, 1976.

Paul Lembcke. "Hospital Efficiency—A Lesson from Sweden." *Hospitals* 33:34, April 1, 1959.

Theodore J. Litman and Leonard L. Robins. "A Comparative Analysis of Health Care Systems: A Socio-Political Approach." *Social Science and Medicine,* 5:573–581, December, 1971.

Alan Maynard. *Health Care in the European Community.* London, Croom Helm, 1975.

A. Mizrahi and A. Mizrahi. *L'enquete de 1970 sur les Consommations Medicales.* Paris, Centre de Recherches et de Documentation sur la Consommation, 1970.

Milton I. Roemer. *Health Care Systems in World Perspective.* Ann Arbor, Michigan, Health Administration Press, 1976.

Romuald K. Schicke. *Die Stellung des Arztes in Systems der Gesellschaftlichen Sicherung in der Bundesrepublik Deutschland, in England und in der U.S.A. und ihre Bedeutung für die Versorgung mit Gesundheitsgutern.* Dissertation, University of Hamburg, Hamburg, 1969.

Dorothy Swaine Thomas. *Social and Economic Aspects of Swedish Population Movement, 1750–1933*. New York, Macmillan, 1941.

Tapani Purola, Esko Kalimo, and Kauko Nyman. *Health Services Use and Health Status under National Sickness Insurance*. Helsinki, Research Institute for Social Security, 1974.

Richard M. Titmuss. *Birth, Poverty, and Wealth: A Study of Infant Mortality*. London, Hamish Hamilton Medical Book, 1943.

Harold L. Wilensky. *The Welfare State and Equality; Structural and Ideological Roots of Public Expenditures*. Berkely, Calif., University of California Press, 1975.

Nancy L. Worthington. "National Health Expenditures, 1929–74." *U.S. Social Security Bulletin*, 38:3–20, February, 1975.

Experiences in the Development of a Clean Air Operating Room

By Sir John Charnley

Professor of orthopaedic surgery
Centre for Hip Surgery
Wrightington Hospital, Wigan, England

Ultra-Clean Air in the Operating Room Environment

Though the author is a known proponent of clean air operating rooms he has so far avoided public utterances suggesting that total hip replacement cannot be justified unless performed in an ultra-clean environment. This reticence during the first half of the last decade was prompted by scientific doubt. The case for clean air had not been proved and even in 1978 it is still strongly contested in many quarters.

More recently reticence was based on the argument that thousands of elderly patients with painful hip conditions could be deprived of the boon of this operation if a campaign had been launched to declare clean air systems obligatory. If an unfortunate few have become infected through the lack of a clean-air installation they have suffered therefore for the benefit of many.

But the situation is changing. Whereas it can be argued that risks can be taken if they are not scientifically proved, and especially in the case of elderly patients with gross disability, this policy surely is rapidly becoming no longer tenable in the case of young patients. Many surgeons are currently accepting for operation patients under 30 years of age. The level of suffering commonly deemed to justify the operation is now much lower than it was even 5 years ago.

If governments impose strict criteria for clean rooms when pharmaceuticals are being packaged, surely the same level of cleanliness is aesthetically reasonable for operations on human beings. Admittedly a sealed ampoule does not contain the anti-bacterial mechanisms of the living body, on which those who denigrate clean air are totally dependent, but when ampoules are being filled they are not open to the air for the one or two hours of a surgical operation.

The Argument Against Ultra-Clean Operating Rooms

Bacteriologists and general surgeons maintain against the ultra-clean operating room environment that the potential for infection in an ordinary operating room is insignificant compared with the patient infecting himself with his own bacterial flora and with cross-infection from other patients in the hospital.

The only preventive measures available from this policy relate to identifying specific strains of pathogenic bacteria and the 'carriers' in the ward and the operating room.

Accepting that 'carriers' (at least for well-known organisms such as Staph. Aureus which can be typed) do exist, this line of thought seems to fail to consider the physical route by which organisms from a carrier reservoir do actually reach a sterile wound. One presumes that those who hold this point of view fall back on a vague idea of some type of bacteraemic transit.

An important argument against ultra-clean air is the undisputed fact that for total hip replacement infection rates vary so widely in different hospitals (from less than 1 % to about 10 %) yet in modern operating rooms there cannot possibly be an order of magnitude difference in the environmental contamination. The conclusion therefore is that different infection rates must be explained by different skills of the surgical teams.

In a conventional modern operating room with 20–40 air changes per hour it is recognised that the wound is being contaminated from the air throughout the period of the operation and the factor of surgical skill which decides infection concerns the classical matters of the leaving of dead spaces, the production of haematomata, and excessive damage to tissue. All of these factors are potentiated many times over by the presence of a large foreign body such as the implant. In total hip replacement there is in addition the special sensitivity to infection caused by acrylic cement.

A criticism of claims made at Wrightington for ultra-clean operating room conditions reducing infection after total hip replacement is that the fall in infection rate in the early days of this experience (Charnley and Eftekhar 1969 (1)) merely reflected a change from what originally were primitive operating room conditions (exhaust fan in the ceiling, etc.) to conditions representing those of an up-to-date conventional theatre. This criticism is considered in the next section.

An argument against ultra-clean air in the operating room, advanced by Shaw, Doig and Douglas (1973) (2), is the undisputed fact that different operation sites have different tendencies to develop post-operative infection. They give the example of lumbar sympathectomy carrying a 0.8 % infection rate whereas incisions to expose arteries in the groin during the same operation carry an infection rate of 26 %. But this could be explained by local factors, such as blood supply, affecting the dosage of organisms necessary to establish an infection. In orthopaedic surgery infection is notorious following operations to suture the Tendon Achilles and this is certainly explained by the poor blood supply in that region.

The Special Case of Acrylic Cement

The whole subject of an ultra-clean operating room environment has evolved from experience in implanting considerable volumes of acrylic cement. The making of a permanent implant of any foreign body, especially if large, always carries with it a risk of being rejected by infection; but acrylic cement has demonstrated special features in this respect which, compared with a simple metallic implant, are quite characteristic. These features are:

1. For the infection to manifest itself for the first time several weeks, or even months, after uncomplicated primary healing of the wound.

2. A tendency to fail to grow organisms from biopsy material, or to grow Staphylococcus aureus in only about 30 % of cases with the majority of organisms being of a type considered in the past to be non-pathogenic for surgical wounds.

3. For symptoms to be associated with radiological signs of osteitis and often with the spontaneous appearance of a sinus.

An important characteristic of an infected cemented implant when compared with infected Thompson and Austin-Moore femoral prostheses inserted without cement is the radiological appearance of osteitis. These latter, even when proved to be infected (as when changing to a total hip replacement) rarely show osteitis in the X-ray and rarely produce a sinus. This might be explained by the fact that the smooth surface of the metallic implant lies in a track lined with strong, collagenous fibrous tissue and even if organisms are present they are restrained from invading the cancellous bone by the fibrous membrane. An acrylic cement surface on the other hand does not evoke a fibrocyte response as does metal, but a macrophage response. If the implant is sterile and the cement is mechanically firmly fixed in relation to the skeleton, the macrophage response remains dormant, but if infection is present even by organisms of very low pathogenicity it seems as though the macrophage layer is unable to restrain the extension of the inflammatory process to the bone surrounding the track of the prosthesis stem.

There is no doubt that our experience with acrylic cement has opened up a new field of bacteriology. When the author first encountered these complications when using Teflon (PTFE) (1958–62), and for years after, pathological material was repeatedly reported sterile and such organisms as were recovered were attributed to contamination. Nowadays, though infections occur ten times less commonly it is becoming increasingly rare for a laboratory to fail to grow an organism when alerted to the special circumstances.

The Ultra-Clean Environment and total Hip Replacement

The criticism that the reduction of the infection rate at Wrightington from its original high level of about 7 % before 1962 was merely the result of changing from primitive operating room with air having a known high bacterial count, to conditions equal to a modern operating room of conventional design does not explain the facts. Even ten years after the author's original experience Patterson (3) in Vancouver, and Wilson (4) in New York, both in 1972, reported respectively 7.4 % infection in 403 operations and 11 % in 100 operations yet both were working in modern operating rooms. As in the author's case, major orthopaedic operations with prolonged exposure of large areas of tissue were not followed by post-operative infection when acrylic cement was not implanted. This surely must incriminate acrylic cement, though admittedly not proving that the organisms were acquired by the air-borne route.

Surgical Skills

It is a well-recognised fact at Wrightington that new surgical residents (five every six months) do not have a higher infection rate than the permanent, consultant staff despite the fact that the majority of the residents have not before had much personal experience of major surgery.

Over 4000 primary interventions for osteoarthrosis were performed in the 5 years 1970 to 1974 inclusive and the residents had an infection rate (assessed more than 18 months from the operation) of 0.5 % and the permanent consultant staff 0.4 %. Statistically this is identical. The residents performed more than twice the number of operations performed by the consultants though the consultants performed more difficult operations.

If this very low rate of infection for residents, we believe as a result of using the ultra-clean environment, were not a fact Wrightington would have had to close down many years ago.

Fig. 1 compares two slit sampler plates (7 inches, 17.5 cm in diameter) making one rotation in one hour; the clean plate is from the interior of the operating room enclosure during an operation (with the team all wearing 'body exhaust' clothing); the contaminated plate from the anaesthetic room opening into the operating room and flushed with clean air escaping from the enclosure (because this particular enclosure is not a recirculation system but

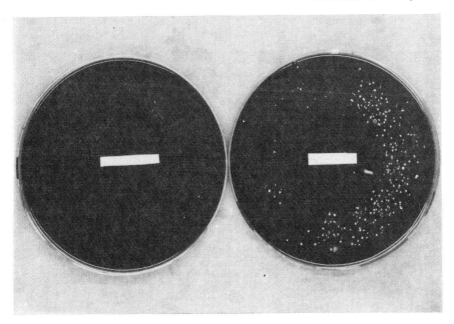

Fig. 1.

uses filtered fresh air at 4 000 ft³/min; 112 m³/min). The contaminated plate corresponds to 5 colony producing particles/ft³ (180/m³). This amount of contamination is generally accepted as indicating a high standard of air cleanliness in a conventional operating room and very few conventional theatres reach this level when a major operation is in progress.

Superficial Wound Infection

Superficial wound infection is rare with very experienced operators but 'imperfect superficial wound healing' (to quote from our proforma for recording this parameter) occurs at a rate of between 3 % and 5 % in the work of the whole unit. The phrase 'imperfect wound healing' is used to describe the *appearance* of the wound while in hospital and it comprises sterile complications (i.e. haematomata and skin necrosis) as well as true infections because the two conditions can be differentiated only retrospectively. One cause of superficial infection is too tight tying of sutures causing strangulation of tissue which then gives free rein to the multiplication of organisms present in the sweat glands and hair follicles.

On the other hand tight tying of sutures is always used when we suture the deep fascia but the inevitable necrosis round these tight sutures in the deep fascia is not followed by infection because the deep fascia, unlike skin, does not contain bacteria.

If there were a significant number of bacteria in the wounds at the end of operations at Wrightington, the residents would almost certainly have a higher infection rate than the consultants, if one is to judge from the rate of superficial wound infection.

Definition of Infection

Superficial infection often is difficult to diagnose, except retrospectively because sterile haematomata and skin necrosis can obscure the early diagnosis. Deep infection also, even when acquired early, is often difficult to diagnose until six weeks to six months after the operation on a retrospective review of the behaviour of the patient and the radiological picture.

Infection Rate at Wrightington

The total infection rate at Wrightington in relation to the development of the clean air environment is shown in Table I.

TABLE I

		Air Changes per hr.	Air Contamination CPP/hr.	Total Infection Rate %	Total No. Operations
First Enclosure	June 62 May 66	130	0.34–1.8	3.0	1 023
Second Enclosure	June 66 Oct 67	300	0.13	1.5	865
Second Enclosure +Aprons	Nov 67 Dec 69	300	0.10	1.0	1 681
Third Enclosure +Body Exhaust	Jan 70 Jan 76	300	0.10	0.7	6 467

It is to be noted that air contamination of 0.10 'colony producing particles' per hour on a 3 1/2″ diameter (8.75 cm) blood-agar Petri dish is equivalent in our experience to 0.01–0.02 colonies/cubic ft of air by slit-sampler (i.e. 1 or 2 colonies per 100 ft³, 35–70/m³). It will be noted in Table I that the air contamination remained at the same low level, even though the infection rate fell; this we take to indicate that impervious clothing eliminated about 0.80 % of infection which must have occurred previously by direct contamination from the surgeon's body independent of the air-borne route.

Infection Rate and Diagnosis

Breaking down infection rates into disease categories is shown in Table II.

TABLE II

	No. of Cases	% Infection	
Primary Osteoarthrosis	4 938	0.5	(0.47)
Rheumatoid Arthritis	566	2.0	(1.9)
Secondary Operations	965	1.5	(1.35)
	6 467		

The fact that the infection rate for rheumatoid arthritis is 4 times higher than for primary osteoarthrosis is compatible with a blood-borne source. This is consistent with the systemic nature of this disease and the recognised tendency for spontaneous pyoarthrosis to occur even in the absence of operations on the joints (Kellgren et al. 1958 (5); Mitchell et al. 1976 (6)).

Prophylactic Antibiotics

It is important to emphasise that in this fifteen years study of post-operative wound infection after total hip replacement prophylactic antibiotics have not been used. This was a deliberate policy in an attempt to assess the contribution of blood-borne infection to the total infection rate. When antibiotics are not used a fall in infection rate must be the result of reducing contamination from the environment and especially from the environment of the theatre; because the ward environment has been constant throughout. These results show that if blood-borne infection occurs at all the incidence must be very low, at least in primary operations for osteoarthrosis, because in this condition the total infection rate was only 0.5 % over 4 936 operations in six years. This rate of infection is lower than is reported from units where heavy antibiotic prophylaxis has been a routine for many years.

Bacteraemic Infection

Experience inclines the author to the view that the vast majority of so-called 'late infections' after total hip replacement have in fact been acquired at the time of the operation and only in the case of rheumatoid arthritis is there good evidence for the possibility of bacteraemic infection.

In most cases of late manifesting deep infection factors in the early post-operative period compatible with an early infection can often be found; such as pyrexia lasting perhaps two weeks, or a superficial infection, or the clinical result at three to six months being disappointing when there was no reason in the patient's personality why it should be poor.

The idea that symptomless bacteraemic infection is rare is supported by the success of the policy of performing primary operations in the presence of sepsis elsewhere in the body. Our experience gives us confidence to perform arthroplasty on the second hip after failure of the first by infection.

When claiming a blood-borne infection it is important that the nature of the organism should be compatible with the blood-borne route. To claim for instance that a late infection of a total hip by a coagulase negative staphylococcus was blood-borne following a dental extraction, is not as likely as would be by a Strep. viridans or a Staph. aureus.

In the early days of our experience we not infrequently attributed late infections by C. Coli and B. Proteus to a urinary tract origin; but over the last five years infections by these organisms have become much less frequent and records of the early post-operative state of the superficial wound have often made it unnecessary to invoke a blood-borne explanation. The frequency of urinary infection in our elderly female patients is almost certainly as high as ever it was and though we attempt to sterilise the urine by a week or two on antibiotics prior to surgery this can hardly be expected to avoid a risk if indeed it were a very real one.

Septicaemic Infection

Late infection by septicaemia on the other hand is a very real thing, though the incidence of this in our experience at Wrightington would seem to be not higher than about 1 in 1 000 or even perhaps 1 in 2 000.

When septicaemic infections occur the clinical picture is that of the arthroplasty which has been completely, and even notably, successful for 6 to 18 months but is then interrupted by an episode involving prostration, with the high temperatures and the systemic reactions typical of a septicaemia.

Ward Procedure and Post-Operative Infection

It is important to emphasise that the progressive fall in infection rate extending over a period of ten years at Wrightington has been achieved without any change in ward ritual. At Wrightington the vast majority of patients are nursed in wards of 20 to 35 beds. There has never been any attempt to isolate new patients from the pre-existing ward population prior to operation. There also has never been any attempt to isolate patients who have developed post-operative infections from the rest of the patients in the ward. Because of the success of this policy over many years patients are even admitted to such a ward, often from other hospitals, with old infections and even with a sinus.

Skin preparation is started in the ward 24 hours before operation and consists of washes with hibitane soap and in male patients shaving of the operation site with an electric razor (never with a sharp razor). On the morning of operation the patient is transferred from the ward to the operating room with the hip for operation wrapped in sterile drapes (including the foot) after the last skin preparation.

In the anaesthetic room and when the patient is under anaesthesis, one of the first tasks is to isolate the patient's perineum by sterile adhesive drapes. The skin is degreased with commercial ether and painted with 2 % iodine in 7 % spirit (sensitivity having been tested 48 hours previously by painting the skin with iodine on admission and covering with a plastic spray).

On admission to the clean air operating enclosure the skin is again painted with 2 % iodine in spirit, this time by the operating surgeon prior to draping the wound, and this is repeated a third time after removing drapes and immediately prior to suturing.

Philosophy of Operating Room Asepsis

In the Wrightington theatre routine the author's attitude to asepsis is that "half-clean equals dirty". There exists no stage between total sterility, as inside the clean air enclosure, and the level of cleanliness (or dirtiness) of a ward.

The concept of asepsis in the operating room at Wrightington has much in common with procedures in the bacteriological laboratory where absolute sterility is produced by flaming a platinum loop and a culture is transferred aseptically even though the operator does not wear a cap, mask or gloves, or even wash his hands.

The interior of the clean air enclosure is to be regarded as a 'diverticulum' of the interior of the autoclave. The instruments pass from the interior of the autoclave to the interior of the operating enclosure inside sealed bags crossing dirty air (even more safely than does a platinum loop) and carried by unsterile circulating personnel.

Bacteriology of Infection

Bacteriological statistics for the whole series will be published in due course, but for the present purpose the statistics from January 1974 to January 1976 (van Niekerk (7)) from 2 136 operations performed in those recent two years are offered.

Superficial Infection

In patients with superficial infection (Table III) Staph. Aureus was cultured in 31 out of 73 patients (42.5 %); coagulase negative staphylococcus in 6 out of 73 (8 %). In 19 out of 73 (26 %) cultures no organisms were grown. Mixed cultures were obtained in 11 out of 73 (15 %).

TABLE III. Bacteriology of Superficial Infection (1974 and 1975)

	Number of Patients No.	%
Staph. Aureus	31	42.5
No growth	19	26
Coag. Neg. Staph.	6	8
Strep. Faecalis	2	2.7
Proteus	2	2.7
Haemolytic Strep.	1	1.4
Coliform	1	1.4
Mixed Infections Staph. Aureus ⎱ Staph. Faecalis ⎰	3	4
Coag. Neg. Staph.⎱ Coliform ⎰	2	2.7
Staph. Aureus ⎱ Coliform ⎰	1	1.4
Staph. Aureus ⎱ Coag. Neg. Staph. ⎰	1	1.4
Staph. Aureus ⎱ Strep. Haemolyticus ⎰	1	1.4
TOTAL	73	

Deep Infection

Coagulase negative staphylococci were cultured in 6 out of the 18 infections in this series and Staph. Aureus (Staph. Pyogenes) in 4. The full picture of the organisms responsible for deep infections is shown in Table IV.

TABLE IV. Bacteriology of Deep Infection (1974 and 1975)

	Number of Patients No.	%
Coagulase Negative Staph.	6	33
Staph. Aureus	2	11
Staph. Pyogenes	2	11
Not valid (late Sinus)	2	11
Sterile	2	11
Haemolytic Strep.	1	5.5
Pseudomonas	1	5.5
Propionibacterium	1	5.5
Citrobacter frendii ⎱ A. calcoaceticus ⎰	1	5.5
TOTAL	18	

Acute Post-Operative Infection

While there is no doubt about the tendency of acrylic cement to produce chronic deep infection, it is quite certain that acrylic cement does not tend to precipitate early acute infection.

Since 1969 we have not had one instance of high pyrexia within a week or two after the operation, terminating with the evacuation of a large volume (500 mls) of pus, obviously connecting with the deep implant. This type of infection is almost certainly acquired in the operating room. Prior to 1969 we had three such instances.

The possibility that very serious early infections such as these could follow from the presence of a carrier of staphylococci in the operating room (perhaps a visitor) is not contested even by those opposed to the theory of the ultra-clean operating room environment.

The total abolition of this dangerous type of fulminating staphylococcal post-operative infection is in itself a considerable matter. This dramatic feature is not evident in the mere statistics of a reduction of post-operative infection from original levels of 7 % or 3 %, to the present 0.5 %.

Final Comment

The main argument against ultra-clean operating conditions in total hip replacement comes from orthopaedic surgeons, but only those who do not perform large numbers of these operations. When postgraduates leave Wrightington to use their new skills in total hip replacement in their own hospitals the author has observed, on three or four occasions, that often they will perform 200 or 300 of these operations over two or three years without a single infection; but not long after this we find they are taking steps to install clean-air units!

The problem will never be truly evaluated until total joint replacement is concentrated in special centres where complications cannot, even subconsciously, be "swept under the carpet" as a result of surgeons having other types of interesting operations to perform which enable them to forget complications which affect only part of their weekly work and (in the hard discipline of private practice) only part of their livelihood. In a centre such as Wrightington specialising in hip replacement if there were to be a post-operative infection rate of 2 % this would produce 24 new infections every year (for an annual operation throughout of 1 200 operations). At the beginning these infected patients would probably report to outpatients every three months, making 96 septic attendances per year. But there might be the same number attending at longer intervals from the previous years. Add to this infections incurred in other hospitals and referred to the specialised unit and it becomes clear that it would be impossible for sensitive and conscientious surgeons to pursue a career in such an atmosphere.

The nation-wide result of an infection as low as 1 % in the U.K. would be 200 new cripples a year if 20,000 total hip replacements are being performed annually.

From an administrative point of view it does not seem to be realised that when the cost of an ultra-clean installation is amortised over 10 years the capital sum is not very high and, which is most important, annual running costs also are not necessarily high.

The last ¹/₂% of the infection rate

In attempts to trace the origin of the 0.5 % of deep infection in primary operations for osteoarthrosis which so far has defied clean environment precautions in the operating room, the author still believes that the most likely source of the infecting organisms resides in the bodies of the four human beings who, for an hour or more, are in close proximity to the open wound. All different organisms which have been grown from deep infections of total implants have at some time or another in our investigations been found on human skin.

Because transfer of bacteria from the operating team to the open wound through the medium of the air is out of the question in the clean-air environment one must continue to look for some as yet unrecognised pathway for direct transfer responsible for the 'last ¹/₂ %'. A possibility which interests the author might be the sweat which sometimes saturates the cuffs of the surgeon's gown at the point where this enters the cuff of the rubber glove.

The role of sweat in wound infection has never been positively decided though it has been the source of countless tests over the years. The general opinion is that it is not very significant.

In his own case the author has observed a variable amount of saturation with sweat of the cuff of the gown proximal to the glove. Under the rubber cuff of the glove where evaporation is prevented saturation can be heavy. The amount of saturation would appear to depend on the surgeon's general physical condition at any particular time, as well as on the amount of muscular energy expended during a difficult operation. *Even if sweat is harmless this must be considered a failure of asepsis because the sweat has not been sterilised.*

When surgeons wear two pairs of gloves it is not unusual to change the outer pair if any suspicion of contamination is thought to have been incurred. In changing the outer gloves it is impossible to be certain that one or more digits of the new pair of gloves have not been contaminated by contact with the damp textile of the gown.

The essential point is that this mechanism makes possible direct contamination of the *exterior* of the digits of the gloves and therefore *direct contamination of the implant or the cement*. This type of contamination is unique, because it is 100 % certain to enter the depths of the wound.

To investigate this matter the author and his colleagues encircled their bare wrists with short lengths of sterile stockinette (2'' diameter and 2'' long) immediately before applying the first pair of gloves. In the first series of tests at the end of the operation two specimens were cut off the cuffs (while still in the clean enclosure) and dropped into separate bottles of Robertsons meat broth. Out of 55 cultures 26 produced a growth; 21 grew coagulase negative Staph. (38 %), 3 grew Staph. Aureus (5.5 %) and 2 grew an aerobic spore-bearing bacillus (3.6 %).

Because this method of culture is too sensitive to be very significant, another series of 39 tests was carried out in which the whole of the test cuff was put into a dry, sterile container and sent to the laboratory for the making of viable counts by shaking in a known volume of fluid. The lowest limit of sensitivity of the test was about 40 organisms per cuff. Out of 39 tests 5 (13 %) indicated about 300 coagulase negative staph. per cuff; 3 (7.7 %) about 900 coagulase negative staph. per cuff; and 1 (2.5 %) about 300 aerobic spore-bearing bacilli.

In one test the author refrained from applying the bactericidal cream, and the two cuffs were estimated as holding 12,300 and 66,600 organisms of coagulase negative staph; for obvious reasons this test was not repeated.*

In view of the ease with which this breach of asepsis can be closed the author now routinely takes precautions.

The method which has been found simple and satisfactory (Charnley 1977) is as follows:

Cylindrical cuffs are made of two layers of towelling material, measuring 6'' (15 cm) in length and of a circumference just large enough to permit the surgeon to insert the widest part of his hand (heads of the metacarpals). The author puts these on as the first act after the hand scrub. The first pair of gloves is then pulled on taking care that the rubber cuffs overlap the distal ends of the absorbent cuffs. The gown is then put on, followed by the second pair of gloves. The pulling on of the second pair of gloves is delayed till the draping has been completed and operation is about to start.

The mechanism of this arrangement is that movements of the surgeon's wrists exert a pumping action on the rather voluminous porous mass and thus ventilate away the humid air before it can condense as moisture. This results in the exterior of the textile cuff of the gown, and even that part inside the rubber cuffs of the outer pair of gloves, remaining perfectly dry.

---

* I am indebted to Miss Carol MacKenzie, Senior Laboratory Technician, Wrightington Hospital, for advising on and carrying out these tests.

REFERENCES

1. Charnley, J. and Eftekhar, N.—Post-operative Infection in Total Prosthetic Replacement Arthroplasty of the Hip Joint. British Journal of Surgery. Vol. 56 No. 9 September 1969
2. Shaw, D., Doig, C. M. and Douglas, D.—Is Airborne Infection in Operating Theatres an Important Cause of Wound Infection in General Surgery? Lancet 1973 Vol. 1 pp. 17–26
3. Patterson, F. P. and Selby-Brown, C.—Preliminary Results of the McKee-Farrar Total Hip Replacement. Journal of Bone & Joint Surgery 1972 54A
4. Wilson, P. D., Amstutz, H. C., Czermecki, A., Salvati, E. A. and Mendes, D. G. Total Hip Replacement with Fixation by Acrylic Cement. Journal of Bone & Joint Surgery 1972 54A
5. Kellgren, J. H., Ball, J., Fairbrother R. W. and Barnes K. L.—Suppurative Arthritis Complicating Rheumatoid Arthritis. British Medical Journal Vol. 1 1958
6. Mitchell, W. S., Brooks P. M., Stevenson R. D. and Buchanan W. W.—Septic Arthritis in Patients with Rheumatoid Disease: a Still Under-diagnosed Complication. Journal of Rheumatology Vol. 3 Part 2 June 1976
7. Van Niekerk, G. A. and Charnley, J.—Post-operative Infection After Charnley Low Friction Arthroplasty of the Hip. Wrightington Hospital Internal Publication No. 68

Drug regulation by government: the nature of regulatory choices

By J. Richard Crout

Director
Bureau of Drugs, Food and Drug Administration
Rockville, Maryland, USA

> The central moral problem of government has always been to strike a just and effective balance between freedom and authority ....,
>
> Dr. Henry Kissinger[1]

In late July 1937 Mr. Harold C. Watkins, chief chemist of the Massengill Company of Bristol, Tennessee, undertook the problem of finding a palatable solvent for modern medicine's first wonder drug, sulfanilamide—the purpose being to produce a convenient liquid preparation of this medicine. He settled on a diethylene glycol/water mixture flavored with raspberry extract, personally checked its taste and fragrance, and sent the formula to the manufacturing section of the company on August 28. Seven days later the firm began shipping the first of 240 gallons of the new product. "Elixir Sulfanilamide".

On October 11, 1937, scarcely one month later, the American Medical Association received two telegrams from physicians in Tulsa, Oklahoma reporting six deaths in patients who took the product. By October 15 distribution had ceased, and the Food and Drug Administration was beginning a massive search for every bottle sold. Before this tragic episode was over, 107 people died of ethylene glycol poisoning. Dr. S. E. Massengill, President of the company, was later to reveal that the product had not been tested at all in animals prior to marketing. In spite of this, he issued the following press release in the midst of the epidemic of poisonings:

My chemists and I deeply regret the fatal results, but there was no error in the manufacture of the product. We have been supplying legitimate profes-

---

[1] Kissinger, H. W., Morality and power: the role of human rights in foreign policy, Washington Post, p. C3, September 25, 1977.

sional demand and not once could have foreseen the unlooked for results. I do not feel that there was any responsibility on our part. The chemical sulfanilamide had been approved for use and had been used in large quantities in other forms, and now its many bad effects are developing.[2]

The unfortunate chief chemist, apparently a more sensitive person, committed suicide in despair to bring the overall toll to 108.[3]

The "Elixir Sulfanilamide" episode of exactly 40 years ago triggered the beginning of our current system of new drug regulation in the United States. Within a few months the Congress passed the Food, Drug and Cosmetic Act of 1938 establishing, among other things, the principle of preclearance of new drugs by the FDA before they could enter the market place. The administrative mechanism developed to accomplish this was the New Drug Application (NDA), a document to be submitted by the manufacturer containing evidence that the drug is safe for its intended use. To provide a procedure for appeal of regulatory decisions and to protect the constitutional principle of due process, the new law provided that an adverse decision by the FDA can be appealed to the courts. Such decision may then be remanded to the Agency if its original handling of the matter was procedurally incorrect. The courts do not overrule FDA on matters of scientific judgment, however, provided proper procedures are followed.

This law served with few modifications for 24 years, until in 1962 history repeated itself. But this time the drug disaster occurred in Europe with thalidomide. Although thalidomide was never marketed in the United States, it was rather widely distributed to thousands of patients, ostensibly for investigational use. In truth, however, most of this distribution occurred through Richardson-Merrill's detailing force and had no research purpose whatsoever. The intent was simply to interest a large number of physicians in a new drug about to be approved by the FDA, a technique known in marketing circles as "seeding the market".

Congressional hearings conducted by Senator Kefauver over the preceding two years had already brought to light many slipshod practices in the field of drug evaluation, including widespread distribution of investigational drugs to practitioners for promotional purposes, absent or inadequate records on patients in investigational studies, and lack of informed consent. The physicians and clinical investigators who testified at the hearings also made clear that the prevailing practice of the day was to conduct uncontrolled studies on new drugs and therefore that the effectiveness of many drugs already in the market place was in doubt.

[2] Wallace, H. A., Elixir sulfanilamide, a report of the Secretary of Agriculture, Senate Document No. 124, 75th Congress, 2nd session, November 26, 1937.
[3] Young, J. H., The "elixir sulfanilamide disaster," Emory University Quarterly, Vol. 14, pp. 230–37, 1958.

In response to these problems, which were well known to the drug industry and clinical investigators but not to the public, the Congress included several important policy innovations in the 1962 amendments. Among these were the requirements that subjects participating in drug research give their informed consent, that all clinical testing of investigational drugs be conducted under applications approved by the FDA (the IND requirements), that new drugs be proven effective as well as safe for their intended use prior to marketing, and that the standard of scientific evidence acceptable for demonstrating effectiveness shall be "adequate and well controlled investigations, including clinical investigations, conducted by experts qualified by scientific training and experience to evaluate the effectiveness of the drug involved". As I will discuss in a moment, this rigorous requirement for clinical trials of high scientific excellence has, in my judgment, had a far greater impact on drug development and evaluation in the United States than the effectiveness requirement per se.

Today the winds of change are blowing again. Congressional hearings on drug regulation have been held by major legislative health committees on many occasions over the past several years, and important new bills have been introduced to both houses of Congress. Again modern drug disasters have been recognized and widely publicized. This time, however, they are not isolated dramatic episodes of obvious, serious toxicity. Instead they highlight the more difficult problem of serious, but uncommon, adverse events confounding an otherwise valuable or desired therapy. Examples include such problems as endometrial carcinoma and estrogens, thromboembolism from oral contraceptives, and (for those of us impressed with the UGDP study) cardiovascular deaths and oral antidiabetic therapy. The new bearer of bad news is not the classical toxicologist or forensic pathologist, or at least not he alone, but the epidemiologist.

An important difference this time around, however, is that broad public discussion is occurring over the genuine dilemmas posed by governmental regulation. We are learning that health regulatory agencies are not simply technical institutions whose mission is to review and approve applications. Regulatory agencies are increasingly becoming the focal point for societal debate on such major issues as the degree of risk which is acceptable for chemicals in the environment, the extent to which regulation constrains the innovative process, and the role of the state vs. the individual in making benefit/risk decisions about drugs and food additives. The shaping of public policy on these important and sensitive issues is one of the most fascinating aspects of working in a health regulatory agency today.

*

There was a time, not very long ago, when I thought the quality of public discussion on our drug regulatory system in the United States was extraordinarily low. In those days it was typical for most critics of the FDA to cast all criticism into one of two models, depending upon their point of view. The first of these might be called the "political" model and is highly popular among physicians, clinical investigators, and the drug industry. According to this construct, the regulation of drugs is conducted by slow, unimaginative bureaucrats who are intent on disapproving drugs so as to avoid criticism by congressional committees for approving anything with risks. By combining such qualities as lack of perspective, overconcern with safety, and inefficiency, they manage to bog down all of drug regulation into a mire of technicalities. Admirers of this model tend to see regulatory decisions as contests between science and politics, and they plead for an FDA which is "more scientific" and "more reasonable".

The other model might be called the "sellout" model and is particularly popular among consumer activists, certain congressional committees, and the press. According to this formulation, the agency is also slow and bureaucratic—a point on which all critics seem to agree—but largely because it lacks commitment in enforcing the law. Because of personal allegiance to the medical profession and the drug industry, the regulator is seen as quick to approve new drugs without adequate evidence of safety or effectiveness but as slow and inept in withdrawing drugs from the market. The net effect is an industry-dominated agency which fails to enforce the law. Adherents to this model tend to regard regulatory decisions as contests of will between those serving the public interest and those representing special interests, and they plead for an FDA which is "less industry-oriented" and "more aggressive".

Each of these models has the virtue of being readily understandable and inherently plausible. It appeals to the biases of nearly everyone to view regulatory controversies as basically one-on-one contests between the virtuous and the untrustworthy. Both models have the additional appeal of permitting their followers to debate the motives and character of their opponents rather than the issues at hand—and obvious advantage for those who feel no obligation to cope with the complex of scientific, legal, and policy considerations that enter into a regulatory decision.

Perhaps it is wishful thinking, but I believe there has been an improvement in the past year in public understanding of the true nature of regulatory decisions. Also, the quality of public debate in the United States appears to have risen from F to C-minus, and I have hopes that we may some day achieve a B. I attribute part of this improvement to a waning of our post-Watergate atmosphere of hostility toward government. We seem to be regaining our capacity for reasoned discourse on complex matters. The larger part of this improvement in our understanding of the nature of drug regulatory decisions, however, I would attribute—and this may surprise you—to saccharin and laetrile.

*

The FDA decision to take formal action to ban saccharin as a food additive was announced last spring. This decision has provoked more mail to the Congress and the White House than any other contemporary issue. Such matters as energy policy, nuclear control, and environmental protection have generated trivial consumer interest by comparison. Once the first wave of public shock was over, the proposed saccharin ban began to raise deep and thoughtful questions that go to the heart of health regulatory policy and to the basic human right of personal freedom. What has happened to our health priorities, that a major human carcinogen like cigarettes should go untouched while a low-risk carcinogen like saccharin is to be banned? What kinds of benefit-risk decisions are properly made by government, and what kinds are reasonably made by the consumer himself? What standards are appropriate when one is attempting to weigh the value of quality-of-life benefits like soft drinks against uncommon but life-threatening risks like cancer?

Laetrile has raised an equally profound, but different, set of questions. The issue in this case is whether a highly promoted but untested cancer remedy should be kept off the market because it cannot meet the effectiveness requirements of the drug law. Its advocates argue that laetrile is really a vitamin, that its beneficial effects cannot be appraised by the usual methods of science, that its use is being suppressed by the medical establishment and the FDA as part of a conspiracy against unorthodox treatments, and that banning is an unconstitutional infringement on the right of dying patients to "freedom of choice" in the therapy they take. Opponents counter that laetrile is simply one in a long sequence of cancer frauds that have been thrust upon the public, that its claims of effectiveness are fictitious, that misleading promotion of the drug is leading unsuspecting patients away from genuinely effective treatments for cancer, and that the hard-core promotors of laetrile are basically money-seekers who exploit the sick and vulnerable for personal gain.

The saccharin and laetrile controversies are important because the public is beginning to understand through the debates now in progress the true nature of the choices involved in regulatory decisions by government. It is obvious that the conflict in these cases is not between such simplistic alternatives as science vs. politics, the public vs. industry, or good vs. evil. Instead the true conflict is between competing *good* values, *all* of which we as a rational democratic nation support and value. The true confrontation in these cases is between such lofty and valued societal objectives as protecting the health of the individual, protecting the public against exploitation and protecting personal freedom.

This brings me to the fundamental thesis of this lecture: Debate over health regulatory issues should be seen as a proper and necessary form of competition among those representing the *good* values in our society. Thus each participant is a stakeholder, to a greater or lesser degree, in *both* sides of the argument. In the business of regulation, there are few clear-cut choices between vice and virtue. There are only hard compromises among competing desirable goals. The moral imperative of the regulator is thus to implement the law with vision and perspective. He must find balanced solutions to regulatory problems which preserve the principle of the greatest good for the greatest number.

The role of the regulatory agency is thus to serve as a focal point for resolution of conflict among some of our most precious societal values. The health regulatory agency occupies a particularly sensitive position in the public mind because it deals with life-and-death issues on occasion, and important quality-of-life issues always. It is essential that those of us in science and medicine come to understand the basic role of regulatory agencies so that we can interact with them effectively and appropriately. Too often scientific experts see drug regulatory agencies, for example, as instruments for imposing their own value judgments on all of society. We must not forget that regulatory decisions must meet *several* standards in order to serve their larger social purpose: they must be based on sound scientific facts, they must be legal, they must be in tune with contemporary standards regarding benefits and risks, and they must be arrived at through accepted processes of government which have the confidence of the people.

*

I began this talk by describing the dramatic episode of obvious drug toxicity that led to enactment of the Food, Drug and Cosmetic Act almost forty years ago. I then tried to emphasize that regulatory issues have now evolved to the point where easy choices of that type no longer exist. Today's regulatory decisions involve complex choices between competing good values, and all are, by comparison with former days, close calls.

As an example of the complexity behind an apparently simple policy choice, may I cite the current debate over whether the effectiveness requirement adopted in 1962 should be continued. Mounting pressure for repeal of this requirement is coming from a loosely-knit alliance of persons who in other respects have little in common. They include (a), on the one hand, some conservative economists and academic physicians who argue that the effectiveness requirement is inhibiting innovation and that the usual competitive forces of the free marketplace are sufficient to keep ineffective drugs from entering medicine to any great extent, and (b), on the other, the laetrile promoters who argue that patients have a right to freedom of choice. Both suggest that in all other areas of our society fraud is controlled by requirements for honest labeling and full disclosure, not by banning. Why the say, should not the same philosophy apply to drugs?

There is of course no compelling reason why drugs could not be regulated in this way. On the other hand, we should not fool ourselves that such a change in the law will really have any meaningful effect on new drug development. A requirement that drugs be accurately and honestly labelled is tantamount to an effectiveness requirement, given the desire of physicians and patients for therapies that are something more than placebos. Legitimate drug manufacturers thus have little to gain from repeal of the effectiveness requirement—a fact they seem to have recognized, since they are by and large not among those supporting such a change in the law. Promotors of unorthodox remedies such as laetrile, however, have much to gain from this proposed change in the law. They are quite willing to market products without explicit labelling claims and to let sales be encouraged by the indirect word-of-mouth promotion of believers. In my judgment, then, the scholarly community concerned about the effect of regulation on innovation has, in attacking the effectiveness requirement, fastened on to an inappropriate solution to its concerns and has unwittingly blessed a movement that is interested only in the easy marketing of unproven remedies.

It is time we realized that the effectiveness requirement is not the feature of the law with greatest impact on innovation. There are, in my opinion, at least two aspects of the law of much greater importance in this regard: (a) the requirement for adequate and well controlled trials and (b) the requirement that clinical research on drugs be regulated under the IND process. The great importance of the adequate-and-well-controlled standard to FDA decision-making is not well understood outside of drug regulatory circles. This is the provision of the law which forces decisions on effectiveness to be based strictly on the results of scientifically valid studies and not on expert opinion. This requirement has literally revolutionized the field of drug evalation in the past fifteen years, and correspondingly the quality of evidence presented to the FDA today is far more extensive and detailed than could have been imagined two decades ago. The fruits of this effort are everywhere around us, in the form of a more rational set of drugs on the market, improved drug labelling, and a vastly improved knowledge base for the practice of scientific therapeutics. But it is no secret that these gains have been purchased at the cost of increased time and money for new drug development.

The investigational drug review (IND) process has also had a profound effect on new drug development, both in the United States and overseas. There is no doubt that federal regulation has stimulated many improvements in the research process and has helped assure that drug studies are conducted accordingly to high scientific and ethical standard. But again these gains have not been cost-free. The drug industry (and now the medical device industry) is the only industry in our society to have both the entry of its products into the marketplace and its research on those products subject to preclearance by government. It is inevitable that such an arrangement will produce its share of bureaucratic problems and slightly bruised researchers. The central question is not whether these problems can be avoided but whether the benefits of this system to the public are worth these costs.

We must not mislead ourselves that there is some easy solution to the problem of regulation and its dampening effect on innovation. To those who seek more rapid review and approval of new drugs in this country, I must ask: what do you think we as a society should give up to accomplish this objective? Should we drop our current system of Institutional Review Board reviews of research protocols? Should we at FDA stop scrutinizing these protocols so carefully? Should we permit the earlier evaluation of drugs in humans on the basis of less rigorous testing in animals? Are we willing to see drugs marketed in this country after their evaluation in only a few hundred patients—a common practice abroad—or should we continue to require extensive premarketing testing during Phase III of clinical investigation? If we are overburdened with paperwork—and who isn't?—what particular records can we abandon without undermining public confidence in the integrity of our data collection and review systems?

If drug development is to move faster in this country, the public must come to accept the idea that less control over research, is in the long run, safer than the alternative, because freedom is essential to discovery and insight. This is a sophisticated concept, not easily explained to the public, and certainly not about to be readily accepted by those already suspicious of science and technology, and of physicians. The challenge to those concerned about the innovative process is to defend that point of view in public on its merits, not to promote some simplistic, extraneous "solution" such as repeal of the effectiveness requirement. The challenge to those also concerned about ponderous government decision-making is to articulate in the positive sense what new standards and procedures would better serve the public interest. Pretending that these complex problems can be solved by a simple legislative change in the effectiveness requirement however, is to mislead both the Congress and the public.

In contrast to those concerned about the effect of regulation on innovation, the laetrile supporters really do want, I suspect, simple repeal of the effectiveness requirement. There is in all parts of the world mounting interest in what might be called non-scientific or unorthodox medicine. Examples include the health food movement, Chairman Mao's emphasis on traditional as well as Western medicine in China, and the popularity of such techniques as yoga and transcendental meditation. The drug laws were never intended to regulate these activities but inadvertent confrontation occurs when substances used as part of such unorthodox therapies come up against the effectiveness requirement in the law. The solution to this problem, however, is not to tear down the effectiveness requirement but rather to define a separate category in the law for such substances. If society wants such products as high dose vitamins, herbal remedies, homeopathic drugs, and laetrile, they should be accomodated for what they are—unproven remedies, folk medicines, or frauds depending on your point of view.

For myself, I can get along without such a category of products in our society, but I also recognize that that may be is a minority point of view. And all of us have trouble defending a public policy which treads heavily on personal freedom when the health risks are low in comparison with such dangerous substances as cigarettes and alcohol. It may not be wise, however, to continue the pretense that substances such as laetrile must either be accepted as therapeutic drugs or be suppressed. The drug regulatory law deals with science, and to risk its essential features in the political arena over relatively innocuous products is to court a serious long-term setback to the rational control of powerful chemicals in our society.

We may well be better off to tolerate a few follies in the marketplace. But again the choice is between competing good values—do we want scientific rationality or personal freedom? And if we want the latter, are we willing to pay the price of a few frauds here and there?

*

In closing may I return to my central theme. Modern choices in regulatory policy are seldom simple. Neither is the choice among competing options in any specific regulatory decision. Today's regulator must weigh a complex of factors—each inherently valuable in its own right—in an attempt to find optimal solutions to important health problems. Though our health regulatory agencies began historically with a more limited mission of law enforcement, and this remains an essential aspect of their work today, they have also taken on a judicial role in society. With its power to issue regulations, to enforce laws, and to resolve conflicting views, today's health regulatory agency is a microcosm of government itself.

*

On this occasion of the 500th Anniversary of the founding of Uppsala University, may I compliment both the University and the Swedish government for placing your own drug regulatory agency on this historic campus. What better setting for the intellectual struggle that attends difficult regulatory choices than this institution, with its renowned tradition in the sciences and humanities? My colleagues at the Food and Drug Administration and I envy this remarkable association, which to my knowledge is unique in the world, between a leading governmental drug control authority and a distinguished university. To both institutions we pay our sincerest respects for your past service to humanity and anticipate with great interest your continuing contributions to the scientific and medical progress of mankind.

To your faculty of Medicine, I offer my most heartfelt thanks for including me as one of your own by the award of an honorary Doctor of Medicine. This is an extraordinarily great honor which I shall remember and cherish always, and I accept it also as an expression of your respect for my institution, the Food and Drug Administration. For this honor my colleagues and I are deeply grateful.

Medical Education—A Personal View

By John R. Ellis

Dean
London Hospital Medical College,
London, England

To be here today in Uppsala fills me with great joy and pride. It is more than forty years since I came here first as a young undergraduate from Cambridge. I remember very clearly my first sight of the city, glistening under snow, as I came along the Uppland plain from Riseberga near Knivsta.

I am told that as I walked around the University and town I appeared a little arrogant as though I missed the courts of Cambridge, the lawns and the pinnacles of King's College Chapel—but in truth I fell in love with Uppsala then and it has remained special to me since. My arrogance, of course, was no more than the defence reaction of a boy startled by something quite unexpected. I was aware that there were other countries and other peoples—people who spoke other languages than English who were called foreigners, and others who spoke rather bad English and were called Americans. I had genuine sympathy for their misfortune, as I saw it, in through no fault of their own not living within sight of the British flag. Then, suddenly and unexpectedly in this outer world was Uppsala.

My happiness today is increased by being here with three friends who have done so much for medical education. It is a strange subject. Few, to my mind, are more important. None can bring one into more conflict with so many people—yet few aspects of Medicine in the past 20–30 years have created such a band of brothers out of doctors from many lands and many disciplines. All the battles, set-backs and vicissitudes that a lifetime in medical education have inevitably brought, have been offset for me by the chance it has given me to make so many good friends in so many countries.

Since first I came to Uppsala I have returned many times. My first close study of the medical school was made in the early fifties when I was sent by the Royal College of Physicians of London to study medical education in Scandinavia and was able to meet everyone from students to the Chancellor of the Universities of the Realm.

Uppsala was then well settled in its ways—those ways which had been established by the great reorganisation of medical education that had taken place everywhere in the last half of last century, when medical schools were formed or reformed to produce that innovation of the late nineteenth century, the generalist doctor. But here in Uppsala in the fifties those established ways were under challenge, and the process of again reforming medical education, to adapt it to the Medicine of our time, had already begun. Since then I have watched that process, in Uppsala and in Sweden, with admiration and envy. So much has been achieved. Maybe the adaptation of medical education to modern Medicine is not yet complete but more, I think, has been achieved here than in any comparable country.

Elsewhere, including the United Kingdom, there has been perhaps less success but nonetheless I think that everywhere, even in those countries where it may seem no progress at all has been made, the first phase of the process of adapting medical education to modern Medicine is over—for the first need was to delineate the problem and clarify what had to be done.

I think it is now clear that to adapt medical education to our new, increasingly powerful, increasingly dangerous, increasingly demanded and continually changing Medicine it is necessary

to educate our doctors as well as to train them
to give them command over Science—

> enable them to think critically like scientists while still being able to act like doctors

to enable them to be holistic in their approach to

> the individual (while being conscious that they also have responsibilities to the community as a whole) and aware of the social and behavioural factors affecting the health of both individuals and society

We know that

> our doctors must be equipped to face a changing future and prepared to work as members of teams in a greater Medicine containing many other health professions;
> that they must retain professional attitudes, accept that they are members of a service-orientated organisation and be prepared to submit themselves to a corporate discipline which exists for the good of others (the public in contact) and not for the good of themselves;
> and that they might profitably help Medicine to become a commonweal organisation capable of guiding society as a whole.

That is not a comprehensive list but most people are likely to agree with it.

What is equally important is that there is now clarification of what has to be done to achieve such aims.

We have a new and growing understanding of educational processes, of teaching and learning—and of the new armament of educational technology.

We know how to make better teachers and that we must make good teachers only out of good doctors. We know that bad doctors who are good teachers can do incalculable harm. We know that those teachers who teach Medicine must continue to practise Medicine.

We have the greatly improved power of evaluation (of students, teachers and courses) which can result in us exchanging those examinations which in the past have exerted a bad influence on education and training, for a most valuable educational tool.

We know that in learning clinical method and in acquiring empirical knowledge, coercive teaching is helpful, but that it is essential to use quite different educational processes to inculcate curiosity, critical thinking and the ability to learn for oneself—and that it is, therefore, essential to offer problem-solving in the clinical setting, together with special educational opportunities for study in depth at some stage. So we know that the course must include both active and passive teaching. It is not a matter of one or the other but of the right blend and the right timing.

We know that in consequence the course must contain flexibility, options and electives. We know that it must also be both sequential and integrated–a series of stages of growth and development with, in each stage, as much integration as is possible to maximise relevance and acceptability, to overcome the complications of specialisation and to save time for educational opportunities.

We know, too, that flexibility demands knowledge of the individual student if it is to be effectively used, and that care of the student as an individual in *and out of* medical school is necessary also, both because good clinical method depends on individual care, and because his attitudes will be developed largely by his personal experience (in and out of school) and because students are more diverse than ever before.

We know that flexibility, individualised learning, integration and a course which is designed to develop an individual, cannot be achieved so long as medical schools are governed by departments. We know that, in consequence, the governance of the medical school must be changed to include representation of inter-departmental and extra-departmental activities—and to include representation of junior teachers and students.

We know that the school requires not only a new atmosphere but also a new structure, with learning space and new kinds of teaching space—and that school and university must collaborate in new ways with medical care in all its aspects.

We know we have to pay even greater attention to clinical training than in the past, lest we produce scientists (physical, chemical, biological or behavioural) instead of doctors. We know we have to be careful not to sacrifice the quality of clinical training by using it as a carrot to overcome the inherent problems of a long course (in which there is much to be learned which does not immediately appear relevant to a vague long-term goal) and that clinical competence can be satisfactorily acquired only by participation in medical care.

We know that all these things can be done *only* when we change the format of medical education from a medical school course and internship to a two stage process—basic medical education and post-basic (postgraduate) training.

That list of what we know about what has to be done in medical education is not comprehensive—but few of those who work in the subject will argue the principles. All will agree that if we do those things we will not be doing too badly, and even if we discover more that has to be done it is unlikely to affect the main direction of reform. True there are gaps in our knowledge, some problems as yet unsolved—like what to do with Deans, but they are not of primary importance.

I would claim that much has been done already in many places to implement these reforms. Of course there are countries where medical schools continue on the old traditional lines—there are teachers, of fame and power, who remain wholly oblivious of educational processes, see education solely as teaching, and teaching solely as talking, and have infinite faith in the certainty that they know precisely how their subject should be taught. Thus equipped by divine guidance they appear immutable, especially where the divine right of professors is enshrined in the law of the land.

Nothing, however, is completely immutable, given a little time. Even in lands where there is great respect for tradition, changes may occur. I have seen them happen even in London. It is not so long since an esteemed senior colleague of mine, still alive but no longer preaching, used formally to complain to me in my capacity of Sub-Dean "You are teaching the students to be rude, again today I was asked questions". I received a formal report that two students had "confessed to reading the Lancet" and was told that "that kind of thing has got to be stopped". I remember the Academic Board of a medical school considering a proposal that the library should be shut in the daytime because students had been seen reading in it. When one re-members such things one realises how much change has occurred.

Many think progress has been much too slow, but we should remember that when medical education last had to be reorganised, in the middle of last century, so as to replace the previous specialised training of Physicians, Surgeons and Apothecaries, with a training for general practitioners, that too took time—and it was a simpler process.

My own school was founded in 1785 "to be a complete medical school within a hospital on the model of the faculty of medicine of a university". It was a long time before it was able to provide a training of the typical nineteenth century kind for general practice, which eventually it did extremely well. It was still geared to that task twenty-five years ago when it had five professors in post. Today it has thirty and a commensurate or even greater increase in more junior academic staff. Recent progress has been quite fast and when one looks at postgraduate medical education it is encouraging to see that in England and Wales between 1960 and 1970 some 300 postgraduate medical centres were established in district hospitals. Attitudes have changed also. In the nineteen fifties we recognised in Britain, as we have always recognised, research in Medicine as something which might profitably be pursued by a few doctors in the hope of making important discoveries. We did not recognise the virtue of that other exercise which here in Sweden has been described as "making science" and thought of as a necessary activity on the part of most doctors as a way of keeping mentally fit. Now it is no longer unusual for British doctors to engage in such pursuits.

In most countries the leaven has been working in the loaf. Ideas have changed and they have not been changed from outside Medicine, by educationalists altering our ideas. Change has come from within, and to some extent it has been engendered by the new attitudes of students, of the young who have chosen to take up Medicine and entered the medical schools bringing their new attitudes with them.

Yet everywhere, even where most change has been achieved, there is frustration and anxiety at the difficulties which stand in the way of completing the task of adapting medical education to modern Medicine, and which prevent the implementation of those changes which we now know have to be made. In this A.M.E.E. meeting, of which these lectures are the concluding part, a part of the programme is entitled "Barriers to progress".

The Barriers are real and formidable, of many kinds and no doubt differ in different places. They fall, however, or so it seems to me, into two main categories: internal barriers (within medical education and within medical schools) and external barriers, barriers that are external to medical education. It is the latter which seem to me to be the more serious and to be the ones we should be tackling.

It is right and natural, in my view, in this first Phase of adapting medical education to the new Medicine to concentrate on defining the problem and delineating the answers and this had to be done within medical education and with much help from the science of education itself. We have concentrated our energies within medical education, our much needed national and international meetings have been between those most concerned with educational processes. But that first phase is ending and it is urgently necessary now to engage more strongly, more consistently in communication with those not engaged in medical education; the medical profession, the other health professions, those responsible for the organisation of medical care, the public and governments.

The greatest barriers to advance, and greatest dangers for the future, I believe, are not in medical schools, not in postgraduate medical authorities, but outside them both. In many countries the importance, the new nature and the needs of medical education are simply not understood. There is next to no awareness of either the changes that have been made or the changes that have to be made—nor is there any awareness of the nature of contemporary Medicine and of the ways in which it differs fundamentally from that of the 1930's.

It is not perhaps the task of those in medical education to bring about an understanding of what contemporary Medicine is all about, but it is our task to make known what medical education needs—and what it can do—what kind of doctors can be made and what kind cannot, and that task has not been completed. The need for more education is accepted maybe—but not its implications in money, space and manpower. There is much acclamation when we talk about the need for more behavioural science. The concept of students working with General Practitioners or in preventive medicine or in rural areas is accorded the warmest of receptions and felt, like motherhood, to be wholly good, but there is little awareness that like motherhood it is possible to have far too much.

There is at the same time a popular view that students are too close to "science" and should be protected from what are perceived as its dangers by being removed from it, and at best taught how to apply a selected few of its advantages. The basic fact is not realised that the only way to prevent doctors from becoming cold scientific technicians, is to give them by education the power to control science, and at the same time to make them first class clinicians.

Sadly and strangely we have, it seems to me, totally failed in many countries to get across the message that the generalist, and not the specialist, is the most difficult doctor to prepare—requiring the greatest care and the longest time. There is little realisation that the generalist doctor emerged only in the second half of the nineteenth century, as much a phenomenon of the Victorian era, as the aspidistra, the anti macassar and the Albert Memorial. It says much, of course, for the excellence of the general doctors produced in the first quarter of this century and of the training which evolved to produce them, that there is so great a longing to maintain their like today and so great a fear of abandoning the traditional way in which they were produced.

Even so there are people who see no need for generalist doctors in the future—who would see only specialists in hospital, and other specialists outside combining to offer preventive medicine, primary care and the management of psycho-social disorders. But the need still exists and will always remain for some physicians, not necessarily many, who are generalists and are able to care

for patients who present with undifferentiated clinical problems and who, whether acutely ill or not, must be cared for during the often long period before their problems are elucidated;

for patients requiring the help of many specialists;

for patients suffering from the most common disorders which occur in the major specialised fields.

The need for such generalists is far greater in developed than in developing countries, where disease is more acute and organic and its presentation more florid—but soon those countries will have an increasing need for generalists of the kind now needed in the most developed parts of the world.

General Physicians of this kind require a more careful preparation than any specialist and require for their work facilities, support and purpose built premises. They differ wholly from the kind of generalist who will emerge from a basic course in medical school—the kind so beloved by those who in their innocence would wish to see them turned out in thousands by mass production from conveyor belts in medical schools in developing countries—each country producing a model fitted closely to its believed immediate needs—by using the old traditional form of programming in medical school.

That system does not work. Always the graduates, especially the brightest and most conscientious, are well aware of their gaps and inadequacies at the end of the course, and move heaven and earth (or at least move far across the earth) to get for themselves some form of postgraduate training, often in a specialty. One of the greatest tragedies of our times is to see countries such as India making more and more medical schools in the hope of gaining more doctors, only to see their graduates migrating elsewhere to obtain the postgraduate unobtainable at home. Many never return, but the country anyway is denied the young doctors in postgraduate training who not only provide medical care, but also fill an important place in the teaching team. Without them the quality of undergraduate education and training falls, and the need for postgraduate training increases still further. The vicious circle is completed. Turning the taps full on will not fill the bath if the plug is out.

General physicians have never been produced by a basic course of programming in medical school, and never will be. In the past a useful General Practitioner could be produced by such a process, and remain useful for many years, because the practice of Medicine changed little compared with our time. But now no generalists, other than those of superficial and time-limited competence, will ever again be made out of a medical school course even of six or more years' duration—though good specialists could be. Generalists in Medicine, as opposed to generalists in other health professions with limited licenses, require a two or even three stage preparation, and if possible specialists should have the same. Yet still so many countries are resistant to this vital reorganisation of medical education on which its sucessful adaptation to modern Medicine primarily depends.

In no other way can it be possible:

to concentrate in medical school upon that education (that sharpening of the mind) which alone can equip a doctor satisfactorily to deal with a constantly changing future,

to ensure the acquisition of that clinical competence which can only be acquired by participation in medical care under supervision;

to cut and contain the cost of medical education;

to conserve manpower;

to maintain junior teachers in adequate numbers, and to preserve the immense value of academic freedom.

If there is a two-stage preparation for Medicine—a university course designed primarily to educate and a postgraduate course designed primarily to train—then the postgraduate training can be tailored to meet the current needs of medical care, branch by branch, specialty by specialty. Medical education does not have to change en bloc with every change in Medicine; and in the university course academic freedom can continue, to the benefit of all. If there is no more than a medical school course it must of necessity be vocationally orientated, be a training rather than an education, and its content must be dictated by the current needs of medical care as perceived by those who are responsible for, or would like to be responsible for, deciding what care shall be given.

Many countries have had a two-stage preparation for Medicine for many years and have required that all doctors pass through both stages. Elsewhere the second stage has been available for some, and taken by some, but it has not been available or not required for all of those generalists who need it most. Many countries still cling to the old traditional format of a one stage medical school preparation, and sadly many are encouraged to do so by international authorities who are concerned to see more doctors but are innocent of full understanding of the complexity of medical education. This situation must be changed.

Those who work in medical education must, I believe (while continuing to develop better education and learning, better teaching methods, better organisation of courses, while continuing in brief to deal with the internal barriers to progress) begin to communicate, coherently, consistently and cohesively, with the professions in Medicine, with the public and with governments, to ensure an understanding of what has to be done, and why, and of why it is so important to do it now. It is not a matter of lobbying, of pressure groups, of selling new ideas. It is a matter of making known the facts, a matter of information.

We have now besides a huge number of medical schools, an organisation in almost every country capable of linking its schools together, and of providing data about them and their needs, constraints and possibilities. We also have our international organisations in medical education. We are well situated to explain the facts, and the facts are powerful. If we do not give time and effort to this aspect of medical education then from ignorance and unawareness the barriers to progress will remain, and indeed are very likely to increase. We will find ourselves in every medical school ever increasingly aware of what we should be doing and less and less well able to do it.

All of us in all our countries face, to different degrees, the same difficulties and albeit manifested in different ways. In the most democratic countries there are extreme difficulties as, very rightly and correctly, the public in one way or another, comes to play an increasingly large part in decision making in regard to health care and to education and training for it. This is right and proper, but that does not make the public well informed. Everywhere the costs of health care and education necessitate more government intervention, but that does not make governments well-informed. Decisions on Medicine and medical education should not be made by people who can say of Medicine only what some say of music, "I do not play myself and I have never studied it, but I know what I like and what I like is what everyone else is going to hear."

We in Medical education have studied it and practised it, and we know now a lot about it. We know what it needs—but no one else does. We have to ensure that they do—and we must ensure that everyone understands that one of the ingredients essential to good medical education is the University, and its academic freedom. That does not mean freedom for professors and departments to do what they wish. It means freedom to develop, to experiment and above all to search always for something better. It means, too, freedom for the University student to develop his full potential, and not to be proselitised, recruited or drafted into this or that type or branch of Medicine.

In many countries academic freedom does not exist. In those where it does exist it is imperilled. It must be maintained and strengthened—and this necessitates that medical education consists of a basic University Course which is followed by postgraduate training—and during that training, through it and not through the University Course, medical education is related branch by branch to the current health needs of the people.

The quality of present health care depends primarily on postgraduate training. The quality of health care in the future depends on the quality of university education in Medicine. Man alone among the animals has the power to see where he stands in the path of evolution and affect the future. He can, we can, to some extent invent the future and pull ourselves into it. Because Medicine, health care, can do so much to ensure that the environment of the future is a good one, the responsibilities of medical education in medical school are heavy, the onus on the University is great, and its potential for good is enormous.

We must somehow get the message across that it is not enough for our medical schools to be centres of excellence—we need the right, the freedom and the chance to pursue excellence—and that is different.

I often in the past hoped to see the day when I could say my School medical education in my country, medical education everywhere is fine. I know now that if ever I come to think that such is the case then that day I will have lost sight of what education is all about. It is not quality, but the pursuit of quality that matters.

We do not, therefore, in my personal view, have to fear the barriers that obstruct progress, nor fear that they cannot be overcome. They will be, so long as we set ourselves to overcome them and strive—and in education it is the striving that matters most. More even than succeeding.

Recent Developments
In Political History:
The Case of the United States

By Allan G. Bogue

Frederick Jackson Turner Professor of History,
University of Wisconsin,
Madison, USA

I

Fortunately, perhaps, we cannot know the meaning that historians of the year 2077 will find in the historical activities and publications of our present era. Will the period between the end of the Second World War and the celebration of the Bicentennial of the Independence of the United States be viewed as one of business as usual or a golden age of scholarship, or an era in which an old order was fatally undermined as a new dispensation appeared? Although the clock and calendar may in the end confound us, it is useful to begin this discussion of the current state of political history by briefly noting those developments in the history profession which serve particularly to distinguish this era from the earlier twentieth century.

The years between 1945 and 1977 were ones in which the number of historians in academic life grew tremendously as enrollments increased and this growth involved not only the multiplication of historians in old specialties but the active development of fields of history which in the 1930s or early 1940s were viewed as minor subareas of older intellectual provinces or thought to be so exotic that it was out of the question to find either specialists who could teach them or students interested in enrolling in their courses. The 1940s were characterized by a considerable increase in the number of history departments in the United States offering Latin American or Russian history although the number of history professors who could speak or read Russian with proficiency grew more slowly. During the 1950s and the 1960s we saw the wide-spread development of courses in the histories of the so-called Third World Countries. To the history student in the United States and Canada these curricular developments offer a much more varied bill of fare. The history teachers involved work in company with those whose interests, skills, and knowledge of historical developments are much more varied in sum than used to be the case. These circumstances should certainly enhance the perspective of all concerned. And while these changes have taken place in history similar developments have occurred in the related disciplines whose members study the current manifestations of the events, social processes, and individual decision making that historians try to describe and analyze through time.

In general also, historians since World War II have achieved a greater diversity of interest within their national specialties in the discipline. Many still are interested in elites and important institutions, but ideas, social, economic and political processes, and men, women, and children, individual and in group, below the elite level, have attracted the attention of many within the historical profession. "History from the bottom up", "people's history", and "working class history" are all expressions that mean something both to those who come to praise and those who prefer to deplore. Such perspectives are, however, facts of the historian's life. And in consequence of these interests historians have become more interested in using the records of local governments, institutions, and individual citizens as well as quantitative data that depict historical activity in the aggregate.

There have also been great changes in the availability of historical research materials. Great microfilm and microfiche projects and xerography have made it possible for historians to obtain relatively easy access to a range of materials that our predecessors of the 1920s would think a veritable King Solomon's mines. When one considers technical innovation of course the computer leaps to mind. The application of this device to historical research is unqualifiedly a contribution of the last 25 years. Although the computer and the type of research that it symbolizes has roused the latent Luddite in Jacques Barzun and others, computers have thus far changed the lives of historians in general much less than some uneasy members of our profession believe.[1]

Although some members of the first generation of those administering computer services argued that learning to use the computer would inevitably change the character of research because of the orderly thought processes that it inculcated in those who wrote programs for it, such men misread the degree to which mastery of computer languages would be essential to using the computer successfully. Rather such machines are allowing some historians to effectively use types of historical records that were so massive or required such painstakingly tedious or detailed quantitative analysis that scholars in the past either ignored them or exploited them so selectively or subjectively that their conclusions had little general relevance. Thanks to those willing to use the computer, census manuscripts,

---

[1] Jacques Barzun, *Clio and the Doctors: Psycho-History, Quanto-History* (Chicago: University of Chicago Press, 1974).

election returns, legislative roll calls, and a great range of other governmental data and records are contributing to historical analysis as never before.[2] Since the same computerized data might be useful to numbers of scholars, and the task of converting some important records to machine-readable form was beyond the resources of individuals, collaborative and foundation funded data processing projects have been developed during this era. Machine-readable data has demanded special archiving skills and techniques and brought the machine-readable data archive into being. And as governments began to computerize their record keeping and data anlysis, government archivists have been challenged to develop data evaluation techniques and machine-readable data archives in order to preserve basic governmental information which in the past would have been preserved in some sort of a paper record.[3]

The effective use of quantitative data demanded statistical skills beyond the abilities of all but the very occasional political historian of the 1950s. As established historians have labored to acquire such expertise and urged their graduate students to incorporate training in statistics and data processing in their programs a communication problem has developed within the profession. Are the quantitative historians responsible for making themselves understood among their conventionally-trained colleagues or should the latter be responsible for understanding the discourse of the odd fellow down the corridor. Put in these terms the onus might well seem to fall on the quantifiers—certainly the general public will not retrain itself—but there is an additional dimension to the problem. Those same skills that place a barrier between historian colleagues are found quite generally among social scientists, and the historian who cannot understand the quantitative historian cannot fully comprehend much that is said or published in various disciplines that have furnished the historians with organizing themes and interpretive insights in the past. There has been much anguish that Grade School Johnnie cannot read or write during this era, but the formal requirements that John History Major must meet also produce B.A.s who cannot read a great deal of what is published in the disciplines that historians used to describe as "related".

The behavioral revolution that occurred in disciplines such as political

---

[2] The useful life of introductions to data processing is short and historians badly need a new one. See, however, Edward Shorter, *The Historian and the Computer: A Practical Guide* (Englewood Cliffs, N. J.: Prentice Hall, 1971), and Jerome M. Clubb, Erik W. Austin, and Michael W. Traugott, *Computers in History and Political Science* (White Plains, N. Y.: IBM Corporation, 1972).

[3] Allan G. Bogue, "The Historian and Social Science Data Archives in the United States," in *Social Science Data Archives: Applications and Potential, American Behavioral Scientist* 19, ed. Richard I. Hofferbert and Jerome M. Clubb, (1976): pp. 419–42 and other contributions to this publication.

science and sociology in the 1930s, 1940s, and 1950s was not only quantitative in character; it was also notably ahistorical or even antihistorical. Although some social scientists clung to analytical methods that were basically historical in nature and some of the leading behavioralists understood or emphasized the importance of historical variables, the overwhelming emphasis on statistical analysis and survey research—the latter approach seemingly denied to historians—forced the interested historians to learn new skills to understand the research of scholars who showed little appreciation of history and which historians suspected might well be of little use to them.[4] The situation of the earlier twentieth century in which some presidents of the American Political Science Association also served in the same capacity in the American Historical Association seemed gone forever. But even while the behavioral tide was at its flood, counter trends were appearing and now increasing numbers of social scientists are rediscovering history.

Where stands political history in this era of apparent change? Table I is a crude attempt to show the relative importance of political history in the offerings of a number of major journals in Canada, England, and the United States.

TABLE 1. *Political history: in major professional journals: 1948–50 and 1973–75*

		Pages of Political History	Total Article Pages	Percent Political History	Percent Quantitative Political History
Canadian Historical Review:	1948–50	399	806	49.5	5.8
Canadian Historical Review:	1973–75	415	733	56.6	00.0
English Historical Review:	1948–50	579	780	74.2	00.0
English Historical Review:	1973–75	684	1146	59.7	10.6
American Historical Review:	1948–50	300	713	42.1	3.3
American Historical Review:	1973–75	231	1272	18.2	5.0
Journal of American History:[a]	1948–50	454	1100	41.3	00.0
Journal of American History:	1973–75	683	1233	55.4	15.3
Journal of Economic History:	1948–50	179	375	47.7	18.4
Journal of Economic History:	1973–75	430	2202	19.5	16.9

[a] Known as *The Mississippi Valley Historical Review* until 1964.

[4] Some idea of the interaction between historians and political scientists in the Twentieth Century United States is given by Richard Jensen in "History and the Political Scientist," and "American Election Analysis: A Case History of Methodological Innovation and Diffusion," Chapters 1 and 9 in Seymour Martin Lipset, *Politics and the Social Sciences* (New York: Oxford University Press, 1969), pp. 1–28 and 226–43. See also the extensive editorial introductions in Joel Silbey, Allan G. Bogue, and William Flanigan, *The History of American Electoral Behavior* (Princeton: Princeton University Press, 1978).

The message of the table, as in the case of many other tables, is not completely clear, but some trends are apparent. In absolute terms, four of the five journals increased the number of pages devoted to political history across the last twenty-five years. But relatively speaking, only two of the journals increased the number of pages assigned to this type of history—the *Canadian Historical Review* by a minor amount and the *Journal of American History* somewhat more substantially. The publications in political economy that represented almost forty-eight percent of the pagination of the *Journal of Economic History* during the late 1940s diminished relatively in amount but as that journal's editors found the resources to expand its available pages greatly across the twenty-five-year period its contributors still produced a substantial amount of material dealing with the political system. In various respects the record of the *American Historical Review* has been the most striking. During the late 1940s the proportion of political history appearing in its pages was similar to that found in the other periodicals but during three years of the mid 1970s its editors allocated only 18 percent of a considerably larger pagination to contributions in political history. Does this change represent a decline in the interest in political history within the profession or an effort on the part of the editors to serve a tremendously varied constituency? The record of the other journals seems to suggest the latter explanation.

The "new political history" is a familiar phrase and we may inquire as to the impact of that particular *genre* of political history on the publication programs of our major journals. Actually definitions of the "new political history" vary, but there is some consensus: in varying degree such political history involves the use of quantitative methods, and concepts or theory from the social science disciplines concerned with political behavior as well as some effort to approach the analytical rigor of the social sciences.[5] Although one can cite contributions in which there are no quantitative presentations or, conversely, no use of theoretical constructs, a tabulation of articles in political history in which the authors use graphs, charts, or tables does provide a measure of the presence of quantitative history within political history generally. When we apply this standard to the five

[5] Allan G. Bogue, "United States: The 'New' Political History," in *The New History: Trends in Historical Research and Writing since World War II,* ed. Walter Laqueur and George L. Mosse (New York: Harper Row, 1967), pp. 185–207; David S. Landes and Charles Tilly, eds., *History as Social Science* (Englewood Cliffs, N.J.: Prentice Hall, 1971), pp. 71–73, presents a definition of "social-scientific history," distinguishing three basic characteristics of the *genre:* "aggregation, the marriage of theory and empiricism, and systematic comparison." This book represents the collective wisdom of the members of the History Panel of The Behavioral and Social Sciences Survey and is an excellent introduction to the basic professional issues involved; as an account of the development of social science history and the relative importance of its various varieties it is less satisfactory.

journals, the most striking exhibits are those of the *Canadian Historical Review,* which was somewhat *avant garde* during the late 1940s but which apparently backslid during the mid 1970s, and the *Journal of American History,* which was chastely narrative in form during the late 1940s but allocated some fifteen percent of an expanded pagination to such material in the years 1973–75.

Analysis of established journals of course does not tell the whole story. When established publication outlets are inadequate to serve the volume of material offered or are slow to recognize new styles and different concerns, new journals appear. And this has certainly happened within the new histories in the United States—at least three journals whose editors are interested in publishing the new political history have developed within the last ten years and, on occasion, several other new special interest publications publish material that bears upon political history.[6]

The results of a number of major book competitions in the United States from 1946 through 1975 largely confirm the evidence of the periodical literature. The two major prize committees of the American Historical Association allocate the Beveridge and the Dunning awards. Since 1946 the judges in these competitions awarded prizes to books in political history in twenty-five and thirty-three percent of the contests. But in competition for the Bancroft Prize, administered by Columbia University, and in the Pulitzer history competition the proportion of winners in political history has stood at forty-one and fifty percent, although a more rigorous effort to distinguish between political history and other subdisciplines, particularly intellectual history and diplomatic history, might lower these percentages somewhat. Also, specialists in political history have not shared in the prize distributions of the early 1970s to the same degree as in earlier years. Of the 177 awards in the four competitions only four were given to authors whose work might be described as illustrating the new political history.[7] Studies of Joseph McCarthy's sources of political support and the political community of Washington D. C. in the Early National Era by Michael Paul Rogin and James Sterling Young illustrate both theoretical and quantitative dimensions, as might be expected from authors who are political scientists; Sheldon Hackney's study of Alabama's Populists and Progressives was

[6] *The Historical Methods Newsletter* is now in its tenth year of publication, the *Journal of Interdisciplinary History* has reached volume seven, and *Social Science History* has published its first numbers as the official journal of the Social Science History Association. Among the other journals publishing occasional articles that might well be categorized as new political history are the *Journal of Social History* and the *Journal of Urban History.*

[7] Olga S. Weber, *Literary and Library Prizes* (New York: R. R. Bowker Company, 1970), lists the Beveridge, Dunning, and Bancroft Prizes through 1970, pp. 26–27 and 38–40. Subsequent winners are listed in the *Annual Reports* of the American Historical Association and in the *Reports of the Trustees* of Columbia University. The Pulitzer History Awards are listed in *The World Almanac and Book of Facts* (New York: New York World Telegram, 1976), p. 547.

in part quantitative, and Eric McKitrick infused his study of Andrew Johnson with various insights derived from social science theory.[8] Significantly the book that has had the greatest influence in popularizing quantitative political analysis among historians, Lee Benson's *Concept of Jacksonian Democracy,* does not appear in any of the lists, although the copies in graduate school libraries usually show signs of considerably heavier use than do various volumes awarded prizes in the American Historical Association prize competitions.[9]

Finally, of those historians responding to a questionnaire circulated by the Quantitative Data Committee of the American Historical Association in 1973, forty-five percent of those involved in research in quantitative history reported that either they or their graduate students were working on topics that clearly were political in nature or had political dimensions.[10] Within the group twenty-eight percent of the full professors reported political history as an area of interest whereas fifty-six percent of a considerably larger group of assistant professors described research topics in political history. Although this perhaps suggests a swing toward quantitative political history among the younger members of the profession, we must remember that, excepting only economic historians, political historians were the first members of the craft to experiment with quantitative techniques during the present era. Currently young historians seem to be turning to topics in social history, including demography, to a much greater extent than formerly and very possibly in greater numbers than those working in political history.

Obviously political history does not dominate the profession today as when the young Frederick Jackson Turner found Freeman's dictum "History is Past Politics and Politics Present History" emblazoned above a bulletin board in the famous history seminar room at John Hopkins, but it is still very important.[11] On the other hand, although quantitative political history, or social science history emphasizing politics, has created a considerable stir within the profession, its advocates have not carried their subdiscipline by storm, and quantitative political historians are as yet a very minor

[8] Sheldon Hackney, *Populism and Progressivism in Alabama* (Princeton: Princeton University Press, 1969); Eric L. McKitrick, *Andrew Johnson and Reconstruction* (Chicago: University of Chicago Press, 1960), Michael Paul Rogin, *The Intellectuals and McCarthy: The Radical Specter* (Cambridge, Mass.: M.I.T. Press, 1967); James Sterling Young, *The Washington Community, 1800–1828* (New York: Columbia University Press, 1966).

[9] Lee Benson, *The Concept of Jacksonian Democracy: New York as a Test Case* (Princeton: Princeton University Press, 1961).

[10] Allan G. Bogue. "The Quantitative Data Questionnaire," A.H.A. *Newsletter* 11 (1973): 27–30. The proportions given here are based on a retabulation of the original questionnaire returns.

[11] Ray Allen Billington, *Frederick Jackson Turner: Historian, Scholar, Teacher* (New York: Oxford University Press), p. 62.

element within the profession as a whole. But they are significant because they are the agents of change among political historians. With few exceptions they are the scholars who most fully understand the vocabulary and methods of political scientists and political sociologists, and as such are a major conduit through which the ideas of those disciplines are spread among historians generally. Painfully, and with a good deal of lost motion, they are changing the contours of political history rather substantially. They have problems and in a sense they themselves constitute a problem, although a beneficial one, for political historians in general. For these reasons I shall devote much of the remainder of this paper to a discussion of the contours and implications of the new political history. This is not to suggest that the political biographer who disdains psychiatry, the student of political ideas, the scholar who prefers to describe the development or change in political institutions in narrative or to use other of the well established techniques of the political historians, is unimportant—far from it. But the newer developments are important to those who practice the conventional skills whether they wish it so or not. Old worlds can seldom be recaptured; change must be faced constructively if historians are to meet their obligations both to students and the general public.

What are the unique concerns of political historians? Obviously they are the political aspects of the human experience. But within this broad mandate, the scholar may focus on the actors, ideas and symbols, processes, institutions, and the social and economic context of politics as well as combinations of these subjects. In such study any historical method is appropriate that contributes to the production of reliable and interesting results. But the new political historians do differ somewhat in approach from earlier generations both in their methods and in their conceptual approach, as I have already suggested. As late as 1955 or even 1960 it was most unusual to find a correlation coefficient in the work of American political historians; now such statistics are not only commonplace in the work of quantitatively-oriented scholars but dozens understand that this measure is only one, and often the least illuminating, of various measures generated in the process of regression analysis. We know too that the ecological fallacy is less to be feared than once thought and that regression analysis may allow conjuring tricks hitherto believed impossible, such as the estimation of specific numbers of party voters within ethnic groups or, somewhat more dangerous, the numbers of voters who crossed party lines in successive elections. Quantitative historians have explored the use of numerous summary measures useful in the analysis of legislative behavior and moved far toward a more sophisticated understanding of those most appropriate for various purposes. Although some authorities have strongly cautioned historians against the use of factor analysis, there are undoubtedly particular historical problems in which one of the various techniques of that kind of procedure are highly effective. And although they have not been used heavily by historians as yet, techniques such as multiple classification analysis, discriminant analysis, probit analysis, and multidimensional scaling will undoubtedly serve historians well in the right circumstances. Some historians are now wrestling with the unique problems involved in the use of time series data in political history, and current advances in demography will yield payoffs in political history as well since political behavior is related in some degree to age, cohort membership, and family status.[12]

The quantitative methods used by some historians have intimidated potential readers, and some zealots have become so enthralled with technique that innovation has become an end in itself, irrespective of whether the new methods provide substantially better answers than the old. This is technological faddism and self-defeating in the end. Even some of the founding fathers of quantitative history have moments of doubt about the transformation that they have helped produce. Although quantitative data should not be ignored, they suggest, neither should it displace conventional analysis; such material should be presented without making undue demands on the mathematical knowledge of the reader. Writing in the *Journal of Interdisciplinary History* a few years ago, Samuel P. Hays deplored what he considered to be excess emphasis on technique in the work of the new political historians.[13]

II

Although Hays and others apparently believe that the emphasis on applying new statistical methods in political history has been overdone, they have also urged political historians to push ahead in the use and development of theory. In reviewing the theoretical or broadly conceptual component in

[12] There have been two courageous efforts made to provide introductory statistical texts for historians: Charles M. Dollar and Richard J. Jensen, *Historian's Guide to Statistics: Quantitative Analysis and Historical Research* (New York: Holt, Rinehart and Winston, 1971); and Roderick Floud, *An Introduction to Quantitative Methods for Historians* (Princeton: Princeton University Press, 1973). When supplemented with standard statistics texts such Hubert M. Blalock's, *Social Statistics* (New York: McGraw-Hill in various editions) these books are extremely useful but the serious quantitative historian will wish to use the wide range of more specialized books and articles dealing with particular varieties of analysis.

[13] Samuel P. Hays, "Historical Social Research: Concept, Method and Technique," *Journal of Interdisciplinary History* 4 (1974): pp. 475–82. In this review essay, Hays uses the word "technique" to refer to what I have described as quantitative or statistical methods and the word "methods" to refer to what some would call research design. He concludes by urging the new historian to "move from . . . initial enthusiasm with technique to a concern for methods and theory (82)."

political history, I shall confine myself to illustrative literature dealing with the political experience in the United States between the 1780s and the outbreak of World War I. Most political historians, writing in the years 1900–1939, used theory—that is they chose their topics, gathered their data or evidence, and composed their narrative in terms of some basic scheme of interpretation and generalization that explained why political actors behaved as they did. But in much such writing the theory is implicit. Certainly, however, two somewhat related theories were stated by their best known advocates with some precision and are worth particular attention. Frederick Jackson Turner wrote, "from the point of view of the rise and growth of sectionalism and nationalism, it is much more important to note the existence of great social and economic areas, independent of state lines, which have acted as units in political history, and which have changed their political attitudes as they changed their economic organization and divided into new groups," than to emphasize the "state as a political factor".[14] Here is a statement of political interplay based largely on regional differentiation. But Charles Beard selected a different model when he turned to Madison's statement in *The Federalist*, "A landed interest, with many lesser interests, grow up of necessity in civilized nations and divide them into different classes, actuated by different sentiments and views. The regulation of these various and interfering interests forms the principal task of modern legislation, and involves the spirits of party and faction in the necessary and ordinary operations of government."[15] However, at a higher level of generalization, Gene Wise portrays the work of both Turner and Beard, reformist and presentist in tone and resolutely committed to the importance of economic influences, as part of a broader Progressive paradigm that prevailed into the 1940s.[16]

In Chapter 1 of *An Economic Interpretation of the Constitution*, Beard presented not only a statement of his basic theory but a precise description of the research design which he proposed to use in testing it: a collective biography in which the economic attributes of the members of the Constitutional Convention of 1787 were to be independent variables.[17] Strictly speaking Beard was a political scientist but like many others of his era enjoyed dual citizenship in both that discipline and in history. Unlike Beard,

[14] Frederick Jackson Turner, Editor's Note to *The Geographical Distribution of the Vote of the Thirteen States on the Federal Constitution*, by Orrin G. Libby (Madison: University of Wisconsin, 1894), p. 3.

[15] The Federalist: *A Commentary on the Constitution of the United States* ... (New York: Modern Library, Random House), p. 56.

[16] Gene Wise, *American Historical Explanations: A Strategy for Grounded Inquiry* (Homewood, Ill.: Dorsey Press, 1973).

[17] Charles A. Beard, *An Economic Interpretation of the Constitution of the United States* (New York: Macmillan Company 1913, reprinted with new introduction in 1935), pp. 1–18.

many, perhaps most, of the historians of the 1920s and 1930s believed that it was inappropriate or unnecessary to engage in formal explications of their frame of reference, theory, or explanation sketch. The reader must dig deeply into their work to reconstruct the author's general understanding of why events occurred and men and women behaved as they did. And many historians who tried to present the long sweep of American political history fell back on the presidential administration as the basic building block in their narrative—the so-called presidential synthesis.

During the last thirty years political historians have not completely discarded the old models of the 1930s and the 1940s.[18] Although a good deal of energy was expended during the years 1945–1960 in refuting Beard's explanation of the drafting of the federal constitution and the Civil War, neo-Beardian interpretations still appear, sectionalism still is regarded as playing an important part in American political behavior, and that unique section the frontier, quite appropriately, is still being examined.[19] Historians by the hundreds study the politics of the American South, convinced that there are unique dimensions in the political behavior of this region which will repay intensive examination. Indeed one model of the years between the great wars is with some improvement, a very important contender among our current explanatory theories of political behavior.

In the introduction to his doctoral dissertation, *The Democratic Machine, 1850–1854* in 1923, Roy F. Nichols defined a political man who was essentially similar to economic man, or as David Potter summarized it, politicians were "distinguished by the fact that they deal in power and not in commodities—they acquire or lose status as their quantum of power increases or diminishes".[20] Some forty-four years later, as his career was drawing to a close, Nichols wrote in the last of a series of increasingly broad analyses of the American party system, "art has been constantly brought into play to supply ever more intricate devices to meet the needs of a self-governing community becoming increasingly complex". Among the "most elaborate of these inventions," was the "American political party machine ... a device which enabled the community to carry on the periodic contests for power which are one of the chief features of the practice of self-govern-

---

[18] Thomas C. Cochran, "The 'Presidential Synthesis' in American History," *American Historical Review* 53 (1948): pp. 748–59 was a free swinging attack upon conventional political history and one of the premonitory rumblings of the new political history.

[19] See Barton J. Bernstein, ed., *Towards a New Past: Dissenting Essays in American History* (New York: Random House, Pantheon Books, 1968), pp. 5–13, and the essay in this volume by Staughton Lynd, "Beyond Beard," pp. 46–64. Also note the melding of Turner and Beard in William Appleman Williams, *The Roots of the Modern American Empire: A Study of the Growth and Shaping of Social Consciousness in a Market Place Society* (New York: Random House, Vintage Books, 1969) and other books by this author.

[20] Don E. Fehrenbacher, *History and American Society: Essays of David M. Potter* (New York: Oxford University Press, 1973), p. 206.

ment".[21] Professor Potter credits Nichols with doing much to restore respectability to American political history during his lifetime of assiduous research upon the Democratic politics of the antebellum period and upon the history of political parties in the United States. Nichols, he noted, explicitly specified a theoretical model of mid-nineteenth century American politics in his Pulitzer Prize winning *Disruption of the American Democracy* (1948) that made the disruption of parties during the 1850s more understandable than did purely narrative accounts. That statement of theory of course leaves a good deal to be desired, but Nichols listed various postulates and variables and consciously tried to meld narrative and analytical approaches to his subject.

Within the context of the Nichols' model one understands the decision making of political actors in terms of their search for votes and the political appointments and other perquisites of power.[22] Ideology is played down; rather, jobs and legislative outputs reward the faithful and attract converts. Such a model is particularly attractive to the analyst in cases where formal statements of competing parties did not exist, when the objectives of two or more parties were similar or where the commitment to the party seems to have largely reflected personal commitment to political personalities. Currently dispute prevails about the degree to which one can argue that the developing Whig and Democratic parties of the 1830s subscribed to unique ideologies or were composed merely of place seekers and the champions and detractors of Old Hickory but Nichols, it should be remembered, developed his model of the American political party machine while studying the 1850s, an era marked by intense ideological conflict and he was deeply aware of what he termed "cultural federalism", the tendency of specific regional or cultural entities to develop group attitudes.[23]

---

[21] Roy F. Nichols, *The Invention of the American Political Parties: A Study of Political Improvisation* (New York; Macmillan, 1967), pp. xi-xii. Nichols's other major works in this context were *The Democratic Machine, 1850–1854* (New York: Columbia University Press, 1923); *Franklin Pierce* (Philadelphia: University of Pensylvania Press, 1931); *The Disruption of American Democracy* (New York: Macmillan, 1948); *Blueprints for Leviathan: American Style* (New York: Atheneum, 1963). See also Nichols's autobiography, *A Historian's Progress* (New York: Alfred A. Knopf, 1968), a fascinating account of his intellectual and institutional progress.

[22] Nichols had numerous students who followed his analytical lead. One of the most eminent has been Richard P. McCormick whose book, *The Second American Party System: Party Formation in the Jacksonian Era* (Chapel Hill: University of North Carolina Press, 1966) has had great influence.

[23] See Herbert Ershkowitz and William G. Shade, "Consensus or Conflict? Political Behavior in the State Legislatures during the Jacksonian Era." *Journal of American History* 58 (1971): pp. 591–621, and for a conflicting view, Peter Levine, "State Legislative Partie in the Jacksonian Era: New Jersey, 1829–1844," *Journal of American History* 62 (1975): pp. 591–608. Ronald P. Formisano tries to put the various approaches into perspective as they appear in the literature relating to the Jackson Era in "Toward a Reorientation of Jacksonian Politics: A Review of the Literature, 1959–1975," *Journal of American History* 63 (1976): pp. 42–65.

Some historians have pointed out that the political party as broker of power and place creates backlash and that efflorescences of anti-party sentiment occurred in the antebellum years, particularly during the processes of party realignment.[24] Certainly disenchantment with machine politics has on occasion created political alienation and the contemporary explanations are not unique to any age in the United States: politics should deal with ethical and social issues that *really matter;* mere power brokerage leads to corruption; it does not matter which party wins or controls government, since major parties are alike in their subservience to regional or national elites that specify what the outputs of the political system are to be. In the writing of a few historians, notably Gabriel Kolko, this latter argument attains the status of a full fledged model, but his is a minority position.[25]

Although there has been striking development of the machine theme in the work of Richard McCormick and others dealing with the reemergence of parties during the Jacksonian period, Nichols believed that the Civil War occurred because the political party machine broke down.[26] And other causal interpretations of the great conflict may be set within his framework—such as David Donald's suggestion that there was an excess of democracy or even James G. Randall's earlier and related description of a war produced by a "blundering generation" of political leaders.[27] Such inductive generalizations are of course highly underdeveloped as theories go. Nor can we be sure that authors, such as Randall or Donald, would themselves admit that their interpretations fit the pattern developed here or that they would necessarily agree with any given effort to link the political policy "outputs" of the 1850s to a particular theory of human behavior.

The contributions of intellectual historians to our understanding of American political history contrast sharply with the theory of the political machine. The growth of interest in intellectual history has been one of the most striking developments of the last thirty years and it was to be expected that the political system should intrigue some intellectual historians. Perhaps the greatest luminary to follow the pioneer generation of intellectual historians,

[24] Ronald P. Formisano, "Political Character, Antipartyism and the Second Party System," *American Quarterly* 21 (1969): pp. 683–709.

[25] Gabriel Kolko, *The Triumph of Conservatism: The Roots of American Foreign Policy* (Boston: Beacon Press, 1969), pp. 3–26. Significantly when Kenneth Prewitt and Alan Stone devoted a chapter to "Elites and American History," in *The Ruling Elites: Elite Theory, Power, and American Democracy* (New York: Harper and Row, 1973), pp. 31–52, they depended most heavily on Kolko of the relatively small number of historians cited. Radical historians generally have been more successful as critics of the various political interpretations advanced than in developing articulated models. See Michael A. Lebowitz, "The Jacksonians: Paradox Lost," in Bernstein, *Towards a New Past*, pp. 65–89.

[26] Richard P. McCormick, *The Second American Party System.*

[27] James G. Randall, "A Blundering Generation," *Mississippi Valley Historical Review* 27 1940): pp. 3–28. David Donald, *Lincoln Reconsidered* (New York: Random House, Vintage Books, 1961), pp. 209–35.

Richard Hofstadter, maintained a lively interest in political history and wrote a number of studies that brilliantly combined the history of ideas with political analysis and provided a number of conceptual frameworks of varying breadth and subtlety.[28] Among these was one of the earliest statements of the consensus theory of American politics, emphasizing the broad areas of agreement on political fundamentals shared by spokesmen of the contending parties throughout the history of the United States. In other publications he posited a theory of political change and action related to the concept of "status politics" and status anxiety as contrasted with interest or class politics. Hofstadter's analysis of the ideas of the Populists and Progressives rested, according to his memorialists, upon recognition of the fact that political ideas and acts fulfill both manifest and latent functions for the actors involved. Thus he emphasized the antisemitism of the Populists, their belief in conspiracies and crank monetary nostrums rather than their more constructive programs. Indeed the Populist style gone sour, he would later argue, might be justly called paranoid and found classic expression in the political style and rhetoric of Joe McCarthy and the legions of the Radical Right. When this writer asked various informed American political historians to identify the five works in American political history that they considered to have most influenced teaching and research since World War II, almost all of the respondents cited one or other of Hofstadter's books. Sophisticated, subtle, and witty Hofstadter inspired a host of imitators but few, if any, have succeeded in emulating his subtlety, wit, or ability to excite readers.[29]

Various important works by other authors concentrating in a rather different style on the ideological aspect of politics have appeared since 1960 of which two at least are particularly interesting to the historian of nineteenth century politics: Eric Foner's *Free Soil, Free Labor, Free Men: The Ideology of the Republican Party before the Civil War* and James M. Banner's *To*

---

[28] Richard Hofstadter, *The American Political Tradition and the Men Who Made It* (New York: Alfred A. Knopf, 1948; the Vintage Edition of 1973 includes an interesting forward by Christopher Lasch); *The Age of Reform: From Bryan to F.D.R.* (New York: Alfred A. Knopf, 1955); *The Idea of a Party System: The Rise of Legitimate Opposition in the United States, 1780–1840* (Berkeley: University of California Press, 1969); *The Paranoid Style in American Politics and Other Essays* (New York: Random House, Vintage Books, 1967) includes papers published in the years, 1954–1964. See also "Pseudo-Conservatism Revisited: A Postscript (1962)," in *The Radical Right*, ed. Daniel Bell (New York: Doubleday, Anchor Books, 1964), pp. 97–103.

[29] Commentary upon Hofstadter's approach and contributions is provided in: Lasch *supra;* Arthur M. Schlesinger, Jr., "Richard Hofstadter," in Marcus Cunliffe and Robin Winks, *Pastmasters: Some Essays on American Historians* (New York: Harper and Row, 1969), pp. 278–315; Stanley Elkins and Eric McKitrick, eds. and contribs., *The Hofstadter Aegis: A Memorial* (New York, Alfred A. Knopf, 1974), pp. 300–67. Elkins and McKitrick discuss Hofstadter's indebtedness to Robert K. Merton for the idea of latent and manifest functions, pp. 317–19.

the Hartford Convention: The Federalists and the Origins of Party Politics in Massachusetts, 1789–1815.[30] Ideology, wrote Foner is "the system of beliefs, values, fears, prejudices, reflexes, and commitments—in sum social consciousness—of a social group, be it a class, a party, or a section". As he showed, the ideas of members of the same political party often differ to some degree—presumably it is the common denominator that is the important thing. But Foner also wrote, "the two decades before the Civil War witnessed the development of conflicting sectional ideologies, each viewing its own society as fundamentally well-ordered, and the other as both a negation of its most cherished values and a threat to its existence.... The existing political system could not contain these two irreconcilable ideologies .... And in the end the South seceded .... rather than accept the victory of a political party whose ideology threatened everything southerners most valued". Or again, "the fundamental achievement of the Republican party before the Civil War" was "the creation and articulation of an ideology which blended personal and sectional interest with morality so perfectly that it became the most potent political force in the nation".[31] Ideology in this view is obviously political dynamite.

The interpretive structure that has been particularly associated with the rise of the new political history in the United States is the so called ethno-cultural model of electoral behavior. Although one can point to forerunners of the new political history in terms of interest, subject matter, or method, and identify a group of historians who, during the 1950s and early 1960s contributed to the *genre,* either through their writings or their direction of graduate students, Lee Benson was the historian who contributed most strikingly to these developments. His long article, "Research Problems in American Political Historiography", was the first important contribution by a historian to the electoral aspects of the new political history, calling for the systematic analysis of popular voting data in terms of time, space, and rate of change and identifying also certain key explanatory variables, sectionalism, urban-rural differences, class and ethnicity.[32] In 1961 he published the one study indispensable to an understanding of subsequent developments in quantitative political history, *The Concept of Jacksonian Democracy: New York as a Test Case.*

Illuminated by Benson's broad reading and personal contacts among social scientists interested in the political process, particularly Paul Lazars-

---

[30] Eric Foner, *Free Soil, Free Labor, Free Men: The Ideology of the Republican Party before the Civil War* (New York: Oxford University Press, 1970); James M. Banner, *To The Harford Convention: The Federalists and the Origins of Party Politics in Massachusetts, 1789–1815* (New York: Knopf, 1970).

[31] Foner, *Free Soil,* pp. 4, 9, 309.

[32] See Mirra Komarovsky, *Common Frontiers of the Social Sciences* (Glencoe, Ill.: The Free Press, 1957), pp. 113–83.

feld, *The Concept of Jacksonian Democracy,* was a rather self-conscious attempt to popularize a behavioral approach and rigorously analytical methods among historians as well as to reinterpret Jacksonian Democracy on the basis of substantive evidence. The book is not, however, merely an effort to present a documented case in support of the proposition that ethno-cultural religious groupings were the major determinant of party choice and voting behavior during the Jacksonian Era in the State of New York. Although Benson argued that members of the same ethno-cultural-religious groups tended to make their political decisions in reference to their fellows and suggested that groups which he described as "puritan" tended to make common cause against those subscribing to more latitudinarian or "nonpuritan" religious doctrine or practice, he did not suggest this was universally the case in the political experience of the United States. Rather he argued that, "In an extremely heterogeneous society whose members tend to have high personal levels of aspiration, with a federal government system and agreement on political fundamentals, it seems logical to predict that a wide variety of factors will significantly determine voting behavior and that political parties will function essentially as decentralized aggregates of state and locally based organizations."[33] Disclaiming the ability to propose a complete model of American voting behavior at the time, he suggested a tentative classification of voting determinants that included the (1) pursuit of political goals by individuals or groups; (2) individual or group fulfillment of political roles; and (3) negative or positive orientation to reference individuals or groups.

Since the publication of the *Concept of Jacksonian Democracy* other scholars have filled a bookshelf with historical analyses of electoral behavior that patently built upon the foundations laid by Benson and upon the efforts of Samuel P. Hays to integrate the various analytical trends of the time under the rubric, "the social analysis of political life", as well as revealing the tendency of these latter authors to shop among the offerings of social scientists interested in the political process.[34] Of midwestern politics

---

[33] Benson, *Concept of Jacksonian Democracy,* p. 276.

[34] Samuel P. Hays, "New Possibilities for American Political History: The Social Analysis of Political Life," paper delivered at the Annual Meeting of the American Historical Association, December 29, 1964 (Ann Arbor, Mich.: Inter-University Consortium for Political Research, 1964) and "The Social Analysis of American Political History, 1880–1920," *Political Science Quarterly* 80 (1965): pp. 373–94. Hays' first effort toward such a formulation was "History as Human Behavior," *Iowa Journal of History* 58 (1960): pp. 193–206. Because this article antedated the publication of *The Concept of Jacksonian Democracy* there has been some tendency to present Hays as the major influence in stressing the importance of the ethno-cultural factor in American political life. This disregards the fact that Benson had emphasized the importance of ethno-cultural divisions in the political reorganization of the 1850s in a widely circulated paper, "An Operational Approach to Historiography," delivered at the American Historical Association meeting in December, 1954 and that a preliminary version of

one such author wrote, "Partisan affiliations were not rooted in economic class distinctions. They were political expressions of shared values derived from the voter's membership in and commitment to, ethnic and religious groups."[35] And another maintained, "religion was the fundamental source of political conflict in the Midwest."[36] In such hands the puritan-nonpuritan dichotomy became one of pietists and ritualists, or pietist or evangelical and liturgical.[37]

The new political historians have by no means restricted themselves to a consideration of electoral behavior.[38] Although their most striking achievements lie in that field, they have worked industriously in legislative behavior

The Concept of Jacksonian Democracy was widely circulated in 1958 under the title, "Public Opinion and the American Civil War: An Essay in the Logic and Practise of Historical Inquiry" (Stanford: Center for the Advanced Study of the Behavioral Sciences, 1958). It is in this study that Benson used the specific phrase "ethno-cultural" in describing this category of variables.

[35] Paul Kleppner, *The Cross of Culture: A Social Analysis of Midwestern Politics, 1850–1900* (New York: Free Press, 1970), p. 35.

[36] Richard J. Jensen, *The Winning of the Midwest: Social and Political Conflict, 1888–1896* (Chicago: University of Chicago Press, 1971), p. 58. Space does not permit a listing of all the articles and books that make substantive contributions to this approach but see also: Ronald P. Formisano, *The Birth of Mass Political Parties: Michigan, 1827–1861* (Princeton: Princeton University Press, 1971); Fred C. Luebke, *Immigrants and Politics: The Germans of Nebraska, 1880–1900* (Lincoln: The University of Nebraska, 1969). Despite the rather strong statements quoted above, most of the authors involved recognize that noncultural variables may play some role in shaping political outcomes. Particularly valuable in this respect are, Samuel T. McSeveney, *The Politics of Depression: Political Behavior in the Northeast 1839–1896* (New York: Oxford University Press, 1972), and James E. Wright, *The Politics of Populism in Colorado, 1860–1912* (New Haven: Yale University Press, 1974).

[37] The most perceptive critiques are provided by: James E. Wright, "The Ethnocultural Model of Voting: A Behavioral and Historical Critique," in *Emerging Theoretical Models in Social and Political History*, ed. Allan G. Bogue (Beverly Hills, Cal.: Sage Publications, 1973), pp. 35–56; and Richard L. McCormick, "Ethno-Cultural Interpretations of Nineteenth-Century American Voting Behavior," *Political Science Quarterly* 89 (1974): pp. 351–77. Despite its penetrating analysis of the literature this article goes awry in presenting the relative contributions of Hays and Benson to the "model." The chronology of their contributions is given in note 34. This writer circulated Benson's 1954 paper among members of my seminar and discussed his ideas with my colleague, Professor Hays, during academic year 1954–55. Thereafter ethno-cultural patterns were a subject of keen interest in both his seminar and mine. All four of the studies by Iowa graduates cited on page 355 of McCormick's article as contributing to the development of the model, were done in my seminar or by my advisees. But a much more important distortion of fact occurs on that same page when he quotes Hays (1960) concerning the impact of cultural factors on elections and then continued, "In 1961, Lee Benson generalized Hay's hypothesis ...," although Benson had made the basic points in widely circulated papers considerably antecedant to Hays' article of 1960. For a discussion of methodological problems involved, see J. Morgan Kousser, "The 'New Political History;' A Methodological Critique," *Reviews in American History* 4 (1976): pp. 1–14. Kousser's book, *The Shaping of Southern Politics: Suffrage Restriction and the Establishment of the One-Party South, 1880–1890* (New Haven, Conn.: Yale University Press, 1974) represented a new bench mark in methodological expertise.

[38] For an analysis of developments and prospects in various fields of the new political history see the editorial essays in Lee Benson, et. al., *American Political Behavior: Historical Essays and Readings* (New York: Harper and Row, 1973). See also Robert P. Swierenga, *Quantification in American History: Theory and Research* (New York: Atheneum, 1970).

and in the analysis of political elites. And in this latter respect there has been interesting convergence with the work of Richard Hofstadter. In advancing the proposition in the *Age of Reform* that the declining status of political actors accounted for political unrest during the late nineteenth century and the reform activities of progressive leaders, Hofstadter cited biographies of Progressive leaders or legislators reflecting the rather general interest in prosopography among both the new political and, subsequently, the new social historians as well.[39] Although seldom specifying it precisely, the historians who followed the collective biography approach to the Progressive period and other eras were using a model in which the behavior of their subjects provided dependent variables, and economic and social change were independent variables. They assumed that when economic or social change threatened the status of individuals, the latter would take ameliorative political action. In "operationalizing" this model such scholars in effect used biographical data series as proxies for the impact of social and economic change.

If historians have contributed in a major way to the increased emphasis upon ethno-cultural factors in the study of electoral behavior, social scientists have performed much of the labor in the development of an electoral realignment model that, many believe, provides a distinct improvement on the presidential synthesis. Social scientists have long noted alternations in the control of the national and state governments by the competing political parties but the refinements of the current model are rooted particularly in the work of V. O. Key, Jr., with additional contributions by members of the Center for Political Studies at the University of Michigan. Many others, including a growing number of historians, have further elaborated or tested the model in various time periods of the history of the United States.[40]

[39] Jerome M. Clubb and Howard W. Allen. "Collective Biography and the Progressive Movement: The 'Status Revolution' Revisited", *Social Science History* 1 (1977): pp. 518–34 is a trenchant critique.

[40] A massive bibliography has now accumulated: See particularly, James L. Sundquist, *Dynamics of the Party System: Alignment and Realignment of Political Parties in the United States* (Washington, D. C.: The Brookings Institution, 1973); Walter Dean Burnham, *Critical Elections and the Mainsprings of American Politics* (New York: W. W. Norton, 1970); Walter Dean Burnham, Jerome M. Clubb, and William M. Flanigan. "Partisan Realignment: A Systemic Perspective," and Lee Benson, Joel M. Silbey, and Phyllis F. Field, "Toward a Theory of Stability and Change in American Voting Patterns, New York State, 1792–1970," in *The History of American Electoral Behavior*, ed. Joel M. Silbey, Allan G. Bogue, and William M. Flanigan (Princeton, N. J.: Princeton University Press 1978): pp. 45–105. A useful collection that includes contributions of both historians and political scientists in Joel M. Silbey and Samuel T. McSeveney, *Voters, Parties and Elections* (Lexington, Mass.: Xerox, 1972). Although the seminal writings on which the stability-realignment model rests are V. O. Key, Jr., "A Theory of Critical Elections," *Journal of Politics* 17 (1955): pp. 3–18, and Angus Campbell, "A Classification of the Presidential Elections," in *The American Voter*, ed. Campbell, Philip E. Converse, Warren E. Miller, and Donald F. Stokes (New York: Wiley and

Realignment theorists divide the political history of the United States into a succession of political systems that, beginning at least with the Jacksonian Era, are separated from the succeeding system by one or more realigning elections. These occurred, allegedly, in the 1850s, the 1890s, and the 1930s with some spillover in the first instance into the 1860s and premonitory shifts in the electorate during the 1920s. A recent writer defines a political realignment as a "durable change in patterns of political behavior"[41] and, more specifically, scholars using this conceptual scheme describe changes of the following kinds: A state of relative stability in the political system is disrupted by a crisis. Elements of the voting population in the United States change allegiance either permanently or for an extended period during the resultant realignment era. Such change is effected by patterns—sometimes very complex—of voter shifts that may involve the development of third parties and their subsequent maintenance or absorption. Voters move disproportionately into a party or parties that were out of power at the beginning of the realignment and both the legislative and the executive branches fall to the party profiting from the realignment. A reform agenda, developed during the realignment period, although perhaps with more extensive antecedants, becomes the major concern of the law makers immediately subsequent to realignment. As the system moves beyond realignment, the initial objectives or ideological commitments of the alignment period are gained or lost and political brokerage functions play an increasingly important role in the concerns of party leaders and members. Despite minor intra-party movement, both short run and long run in nature, the system is in general stable until another major crisis occurs. Within this general context, elections may be described as realigning (V. O. Key's adjective was "critical"), deviating, maintaining or, in the case in which a party retained control of the government while the composition of its support changed substantially, converting.

Realignment theory does not necessarily exclude the operation of other processes. A reform ideology is involved in realignment, and those who have developed the emphasis upon ethno-cultural reference group behavior may explain electoral realignment as being effected by the differential impact of the realignment issue or issues on particular cultural groups in the population. Those primarily interested in the behavior of elites may view realignment as illustrating the failure of governing elites to adjust successfully to new issues—Randall's blundering generation for instance—or as the mechanism by which a new elite generation varying from the old in its social

---

Sons, 1960), pp. 531–38 one derives some perspective as to the hardiness of the idea of electoral periodicity by referring to W. B. Munro, "The Law of the Pendulum," in *The Invisible Government* (New York, 1928), pp. 58–84.

[41] Sundquist, *Dynamics of the Party Systems*, p. 5.

and economic bases, its agenda, or role conception asserts control within the political system. Those who think basically of the political system as a machine in which votes buy power and power buys place can also accommodate the realignment concept as one which suggests that party dominance is not equally at issue in every election but that at particular times party performance will determine the control of power and the nature of system outputs not just for two or four years but for a generation to come.

Just as economists distinguish between micro and macro economics, we can move beyond the level of generalization illustrated by realignment analysis and identify a macropolitical history in which the historian or social scientist studies political processes that facilitate comparisons across national or state boundaries. Here, of course, the major catch word has been "modernization". Social scientists of the current generation have produced a vast literature exploring the concept from many different perspectives, general or specific, theoretical or substantive, and case study or elaborate cross-national comparison. Specifying a basic dichotomy between modern and traditional, scholars have suggested that the transition from traditional to modern generates processes involving: urbanization, industrialization, secularization, individuation, rationalization, participation, literacy, communications, bureaucracy, and integration. Of these concepts, some, as for instance "participation", are particularly political in nature; in other cases the impact of the modernizing processes on politics are indirect in effect. Some scholars are willing to accept the term political development as descriptive of the political side of modernization—others would define their terms somewhat differently.[42]

Quibbles over vocabulary aside, scholars in various social science disciplines have identified a considerable number of political processes that seemingly occurred in the western nations during the last several centuries, and related them in conceptual schemes of varying complexity. To the list above, one may add the terms identification, legitimation, distribution and penetration, which, along with participation, one group of scholars main-

---

[42] The literature is overwhelming; for instance, John Brode, *The Process of Modernization: An Annotated Bibliography on the Sociocultural Aspects of Development* (Cambridge, Mass.: Harvard University Press, 1969) lists 12,304 entries. Daniel Lerner, *The Passing of Traditional Society: Modernizing the Middle East* (Glencoe, Ill.: Free Press, 1958) is a classic study, as is Samuel P. Huntington, *Political Order in Changing Societies* (New Haven, Conn.: Yale University Press, 1968). Of particular interest to the political historian should be the series, "Studies in Political Development," sponsored by the Committee on Comparative Politics of the Social Science Reseach Committee, some of which are cited below. Both some account of the history of the developmental approach and candid assessment of the problems involved in it are given in S. N. Eisenstadt, "Studies of Modernization and Sociological Theory," *History and Theory* 13 (1974): pp. 225–52, and by Gabriel A. Almond, "Approaches to Developmental Causation," in Gabriel A. Almond, Scott C. Flanagan and Robert J. Mundt, *Crisis, Choice and Change: Historical Studies of Political Development* (Boston: Little, Brown, 1973), pp. 1–42.

tains, were the problems of political development.[43] These they suggest may be examined within a conceptual scheme that posits variations in equality, capacity, and differentiation as other variables. When we place such a typology within the perspective of time, viewed either as the point when crisis begins or in terms of phases or stages embracing or delimiting crises, and in terms of location, as in the contrast of center versus periphery, and take the initial institutional structures into consideration, there is obviously a good deal of challenge here for those who wish to use substantive data in testing developmental models.

The first historian to confront the modernization process in a major way was Cyrus E. Black who posited four successive "critical problems" which modernizing countries faced: (1) the challenge of modernity; (2) the consolidation of modern leadership; (3) economic and social transformations; and (4) the integration of society. Black devoted much of *The Dynamics of Modernization* to categorizing nations in terms of the time at which they confronted the critical problems and noted the speed with which they moved through the various phases. His scheme allowed him to summarize the histories of more than 160 national states or dependencies under seven basic patterns of modernization.[44]

In a recent publication Charles Tilly has summarized the field of political development by distinguishing sequence or stage theories, developmental models in which relationships between variables are analyzed but which do not specify "particular paths or priorities", less embracing functional theories, and historical theories in which the authors relate the experience of individual states to "transformations affecting the world as a whole", a category which also, in his view, includes Marxian or other interpretations of "dependency and underdevelopment".[45]

One historian with impressive credentials in quantitative history has recently stigmatized modernization theory as a "fad".[46] But unquestionably the modernization and developmental literature is influencing historians and will continue to do so. Indeed some historians have used modernization concepts without greatly emphasizing the fact. Van Beck Hall, Jackson Turner Main, and Samuel P. Hays have all recently distinguished in their work between political actors who thought in terms of local interests and

[43] Leonard Binder, James S. Coleman, et al., *Crises and Sequences in Political Development* (Princeton, N. J.: Princeton University Press, 1971), particularly pp. 283–316.
[44] C. E. Black, *The Dynamics of Modernization: A Study in Comparative History* (New York: Harper and Row, 1966). The critical problems are outlined pp. 67–68.
[45] Charles Tilly, ed., *The Formation of National States in Europe* (Princeton, N. J.: Princeton University Press, 1975), pp. 601–38. The quoted phrases appear on pp. 611, 624, and 628.
[46] Formisano, "Toward a Reorientation of Jacksonian Politics." p. 65. "'Modernization'" he writes, "bids fair to become the kind of catchword whose incantation magically resolves the problem by failing to confront it."

those who brought a cosmopolitan point of view to their decision making processes.[47] And, although he adds his own refinements, Professor Wiebe's segmented society is obviously a highly differentiated one.[48] Explicit acceptance of the modernization model is also to be found and is illustrated by the recent book of Richard D. Brown, who apparently views the Republican Party as the political vehicle of modernizers in the United States.[49]

III

The explanatory models of historians are, we know, linked not only to the time, place, and events under study but also reflect the time and place at which historians are writing and their personal interests and backgrounds. And the time, place, and interests of the individuals who read the work of the historian will affect their evaluation of it. The assumptions underlying the hackneyed phrase, "an idea whose time has come", has applied all too well in historical writing. Even so we can still suggest some basic principles that are useful in evaluating the models that scholars have used in interpreting the politics of the past.

There are a number of characteristics that any interpretive scheme should have, whether in history or not, if it is to be useful. The theory, model, or interpretive framework should (1) be grounded in an established body of social or political theory or some satisfactory substitute; (2) be concerned with matters of importance rather than trivialities; (3) have definite explanatory power: (4) be clear, precise, and parsimonious; (5) be consistent with other accepted and reliable knowledge; (6) allow empirical validation; and (7) appear to fit the evidence of the case in hand. In considering the politics of the past from the standpoint of social scientific history specifically there are a number of other useful evaluative criteria: (8) the model should be comparative in nature—that is the variables examined should be applicable in other cases than that under examination; (9) the model should explain change; (10) it should be appropriate to the level of political activity at which it is applied; and (11) the greater the number of levels of political activity or different processes which it usefully illuminates the more convincing the

[47] Samuel P. Hays, "Political Parties and the Community-Society Continuum," in *The American Party Systems: Stages of Political Development,* ed. William N. Chambers and Walter Dean Burnham (New York: Oxford University Press, 1967): pp. 152–81; Van Beck Hall, *Politics Without Parties: Massachusetts, 1780–1791* (Pittsburgh: University of Pittsburgh Press, 1972); Jackson Turner Main, *Political Parties Before the Constitution* (Williamsburg, Va.: Institute of Early American History and Culture, 1973). For "local" read "traditional"; for "cosmopolitan" substitute "modern".

[48] Robert H. Wiebe, *The Segmented Society: An Introduction to the Meaning of America* (New York: Oxford University Press, 1975).

[49] Richard D. Brown, *Modernization: The Transformation of American Life, 1600–1865* (New York: Hill and Wang, 1976).

model.[50] Beyond such principles, of course, are matters of validation—the specific research design, the nature and use of evidence and its presentation. The argument or test should be logically convincing, the evidence adequate in quantity and quality and the presentation clear. An effort to use such criteria exhaustively in evaluating the interpretations or models sketched in this paper is clearly beyond our scope, but we may note a few of the more obvious applications.

When we consider the work of Professor Nichols, we are, in the view of many, dealing with an approach that is essentially "good old-fashioned, common-sense" political history. Nichols uses the analogy of the political party as machine or, in one book, the government as leviathan, but the protagonists, he never allows us to forget, are people. His politicians sought power and they used that power to benefit themselves, the constituencies that they represented, and the parties of which they were members. Like all men, Nichols' politicians shared, in greater or lesser degree, the attitudes characteristic of their regions and cultures, but they were essentially rational decision makers trying to maximize the benefits of their participation in politics. Nichols did not advance his analysis of political power much past the point of arguing that it motivated his politicians and that some obviously had more than did others. The research of this generation has shown that power is a very slippery and difficult concept and Nichols specified and subjected his model to empirical validation in only the most perfunctory way. His political history was basically the history of political elites—the machinations of the party leaders appear in painstaking detail but there was much less attention paid to the mass electorate. And in the hands of less gifted scholars than Nichols his approach has often become a mere pedestrian accounting of the political details of the past.

As argued, Professor Hofstadter's theory of consensus was clearly system wide in its application and most useful therefore in the comparative study of the development of a number of nations. To look at state or local politics within that perspective adds little to the illumination that analysis at the national level gave us. The formulation does not explain change in the American political system effectively and in effect it merely defined one of the basic ground rules of American politics, a contribution that should in no way be denigrated. We now realize also that Hofstadter defined conflict

---

[50] I am indebted to my colleague, Paul K. Conkin, for showing me a passage that he wrote in an unpublished commentary concerning the characteristics desirable in assumptions, facts, and theories taken from other disciplines: "It is clear and precise in statement; it is consistent with other accepted and reliable knowledge; it is of a type that allows empirical validation; it has already been investigated and endorsed by competent inquirers: and, finally, and closely related to the above, it commands the respect of all, or almost all, recognized experts in its field." See also Samuel P. Huntington, "Paradigms of American Politics: Beyond the One, the Two, and the Many." *Political Science Quarterly* 89 (March 1974), 1–26, pp. 12–14.

narrowly, that his evidence was selective and that the credibility of the formulation was achieved by ignoring a substantial portion of the inhabitants of the United States, qualifications he came to share.

From the standpoint of understanding the internal politics of the United States, the status-anxiety model was much more interesting. It explained change, it accounted for behavior at both the elite and the mass level, although Hofstadter's primary concern was with the elites, and the model also accomodated variations in behavior at the various levels of the political system, as well as regionally. Hofstadter's presentation was, of course, more suggestive than substantive and his use of evidence was essentially illustrative rather than rigorously analytical. When other scholars tried to subject the status anxiety model to empirical validation in a rigorous quantitative fashion they failed. These analysts used crude and even fallacious methods and perhaps the prize merely eluded them. Certainly historians should be able to design quantitative research designs that provide results congruent with social-psychological explanations and the effort should be continued.

Interest in using the concept of ideology in political history is running at full tide. But if we accept Foner's definition, it is clearly difficult to apply the concept of ideology to specific problems in any but the most general way. In the hands of some historians, ideology becomes a reified Frankenstein and politicians mere puppets at his command. The American party system, wrote Kelley, "gives expression" to American ideologies.[51] Well and good, but when does an ideology raise up a party? When, where, and why do ideologies change and why on occasion do they refuse to change? What proportion of the members of a political party shared what amounts of the various attitudes that melded into ideology? To what degree are gradations in such matters allowable? What are the proper techniques that historians should follow in reconstructing the ideology of a group? Were the statements of any given one of Foner's Republican informants given equal weight with those of any other? Unquestionably the students of ideology primarily use elite statements and infer mass behavior from them. Although the model is attractive in various respects, the links between ideology and the brute details of general electoral politics and even of legislative roll call votes are as yet highly tenuous; empirical validation has been vague, loose and marked by a good deal of selective quotation. Some, indeed, may view ideology as an obfuscating intervening variable which impedes our view of the American politician's response to the social, cultural, and economic

[51] Rober Kelley, "Ideology and Political Culture from Jefferson to Nixon," *American Historical Review* 82 (1977), p. 558. See Lee Benson, *Toward the Scientific Study of History: Selected Essays* (Philadelphia: Lippincott, 1972), pp. 287–303 for an extended critique of Foner's position.

realities of the time, a concept which in its present state of development has a good deal in common with phlogiston.

In assessing the ethno-cultural model, one finds much to commend in the efforts of Benson and others to use theory in explicit fashion and in their attempts to develop research designs that incorporate quantitative as well as literary evidence, thereby improving the processes of empirical validation. The theoretical foundations rest explicitly in reference group theory, but it is also true that researchers using this formulation have shown little interest in developing the full implications of that body of theory in context. Some researchers have emphasized the ethno-cultural variables, that Benson identified as being most important within his model in the special case of New York, so as to suggest that other variables were of little general significance, but it is also true that research dealing with other times and places has provided useful correctives in this respect. None of the ethno-culturalists have adequately emphasized the highly inferential character of the linkages that they posit between belief systems, ethno-cultural-religious group membership, and aggregate voting patterns. And due to the initial inexperience of historians in the use of empirical methods the quantitative foundations of the ethno-cultural research have been considerably less firm than desirable. Most of these scholars view electoral behavior within the framework provided by periodic political realignments but the empirical illustration of ethno-cultural electoral shifts at such times have not been completely convincing. Although the model does have important implications for the study of legislative behavior and policy outputs, these have not been explored in any detail as yet. Thus, although scholars applying the ethno-cultural model have worked an important transformation of the historical landscape they have no reson as yet to believe that their task is complete.

The stability-realignment model has attracted some researchers with relatively sophisticated empirical skills and the results have been impressive, although a variety of technical problems similar to those found in ethno-cultural research can be identified in this work in general.[52] But much of the research has been essentially taxonomic in nature and devoted to precise description of the mechanics of the realignment process. The formulation is concerned with political change, but in the hands of most researchers change is initiated by an exogenous shock. Cannot we go further than simply maintaining that changing societal ethics, the redistribution of power within society as a result of industrialization, or the impact of major econo-

---

[52] Allan G. Lichtman, "Critical Election Theory and the Reality of American Presidential Politics, 1916–40," *American Historical Review* 81 (1976), pp. 317–48, cites much of the relevant recent literature and advances most of the stock criticisms of the realignment model with perhaps some overstatement of its shortcomings.

mic depressions, generate political issues of such concern, or which are handled so badly by the leadership cadres of the existing party system, that the realignment process is initiated? Why do some exogenous shocks produce realignment while others do not? Some have pointed out that elements of realignment may proceed over very long periods of time, affect different regions at different times, affect some electoral groups and leave the allegiance of others untouched. Why has this been so? The reference group theory incorporated in the electoral survey analysis research at both Columbia and subsequently at the University of Michigan may be appropriately applied in this model and there is some suggestion now that a generational succession model may be useful in explaining this cyclical model of American politics.[53] Finally we should note that, as in the case of ethno-cultural research, realignment analysis has focussed primarily on elections; the precise ways in which legislative behavior and policy outputs are associated with electoral realignment remain a relatively undeveloped aspect of realignment analysis theory at this time.

The modernization literature in general has inspired a massive, and in the eyes of some, a devastating critique. Historians should neither embrace the concept uncritically nor allow the strictures of disillusioned social scientists to drive them from the field. But caution certainly will be appropriate. Given the fact that modernization theory in large part is an abstract set of propositions derived from the history of the western democracies, there is real danger that historians will engage in self-fulfilling prophecy in their use of modernization or developmental analysis. Some have criticized scholars using this calculus for their failure to recognize the importance of external relations upon the internal development of individual countries. And closer examination of the linkages between the various processes has sometimes shown that posited time sequences do not hold. Nor are institutional processes always a mirror of changes in the attitude of the individual actors involved in them. The modernization literature has more than its share of ambiguities, and much of the analysis thus far is based on very soft indicators in comparison-say-to the electoral realignment literature in the United States. The historical quantitative data series needed to "operationalize" developmental models have seldom been used nor in some areas are they even constructed as yet. When they are available the historian will face problems in the use of time series analysis that may be truly formidable.

IV

In a session, organized by the Quantitative Data Committee of the American Historical Association at that organization's Annual Meeting in 1964,

[53] Huntington, "Paradigms of American Politics."

Samuel P. Hays concluded that "Political history ... can well restore itself as the major integrative context of history. But it ... must greatly broaden its perspectives to encompass the full range of value conflicts throughout society, it must develop concepts concerning structure and process and focus more directly on patterns of human relationships; and it must be willing to use the vast store of available quantitative data."[54] Although not all of the early quantifiers would have agreed that this was an adequate agenda for the future, and the statement illustrated the developing ideas of a considerable number of American historians rather than of Hays alone, this charge forecast the future in various respects and serves as an appropriate backdrop for some discussion of the situation, prospects, and needs of political history some twelve years later.

Looking backwards from the vantage point of 1977, we can agree that the new political historians have made very substantial alterations in the historical landscape of the United States since the first examples of the *genre* appeared during the late 1950s and early 1960s. Our understanding of nineteenth-century politics is I think very different from what it was at that time. And even those who remain committed to older forms of analysis frequently now attempt more rigorous analysis than was true a generation ago, a by-product undoubtedly of the quantitative and theoretical concerns of the new historians. But the lot of the innovator is hard—the additional training obtained by an established historian is done at the expense of a larger output of conventional history, the Barzuns and less polished critics rise in denunciation to protest that social science history is a contradiction in terms and that, whatever it may be, it is not history. Journal and press editors have been discomfited by a kind of history that they fear will alienate their subscribers on the one hand or will not sell on the other. And even the fair-minded editor finds it very difficult to find competent referees to evaluate manuscripts; "cookbook" self-trained, historians have blind spots and are uncertain in their judgments. Social scientists understand quantitative methods more thoroughly but their views of what is an interesting or worthwhile subject for investigation may differ sharply from those of historians. A cannibal gene seems present in many of the innovators and they pelt each other with unmerciful vigor concerning issues which are merely matters of fine tuning while delighted conventional critics pick up the stones and brickbats for use in their own reviews or lectures though they may have little true understanding of the argument. And most frustrating of all perhaps is the indictment of the self-promoting reviewer who examines the efforts of some quantitative historian to provide an authoritative answer to questions that have intrigued generations of historians and solemnly affirms, "this author is asking the wrong question".

[54] Hays, "New Possibilities," p. 56.

The stock arguments against the new political history need not be reviewed at length. Of course some of the so called new history is poorly written—but who can argue that the political history of the 1930s and 1940s invariably moved the sensitive to tears or the strong to mighty deeds. Sometimes the new political history substitutes involuted discussions for narrative, but does not the point well proven or the logical solution of a difficult problem carry its own compelling interest? Of course some historians use special purpose vocabulary—the "dismal patois" of the social scientist as Schlesinger calls it—and this deserves to be stigmatized as jargon when misused but appropriate special vocabulary also allows researchers to raise the threshold at which they can begin useful research.[55]

There are, of course important historical problems that do not now and perhaps never will yield to quantitative methods or to which theory brings little illumination. But to suggest that the venturesome should never enter such terrain runs counter to the principles of free inquiry that has been the glory of academic research in the past. In much criticism of the new histories also, perhaps excepting cliometric history, there runs the assumption, explicit or implicit, that there is an immutable intellectual product that is called history. But once we move past the proposition that historians study the people and events of the past, one discovers many kinds of history, differing in subject matter, in sources, methods, theoretical constructs, and objectives. The new political or social science historian differs manifestly in objectives and methods from the writer of narrative political biography; there is no valid intellectual reason to deny a hunting license to either.

It is also true that some critics apply a double standard when evaluating the work of quantitative historians. Historians are taught that they should use all the available evidence. And certainly the researcher should use as much relevant evidence of as many different kinds as is necessary to produce explanations that cannot be overturned by the mere marshalling of additional evidence. In practice this is often impossible and exhaustive analysis of one particular type of evidence bearing on a problem may constitute a contribution in its own right, provided that the findings are indeed qualified by the reservation that they are but a partial explanation of events. Indeed much conventional political history can only be defended on these grounds. Historians who have scrupulously searched the surviving manuscript collections of prominent politicians and read exhaustively in newspapers and political party literature have often ignored or paid little attention to the story that legislative roll calls and electoral returns have to tell. Unfortunately some such historians have seen nothing incongruous in

[55] Schlesinger, "Hofstadter," p. 295.

criticizing the quantitative historian who has rigorously analyzed such data exhaustively because the quantifier has not worked literary sources. One such reviewer declared primly in the *American Historical Review:* "A computer program is not a substitute for research in the primary sources."[56] To which social science historians, knowing full well that computer programs merely allow the effective analysis of certain types of often neglected primary sources, could have agreed no less than the muddled scholar who penned it.

Those critics who denigrate method or technique while urging the development of theory are both wrong and right. The current theoretical models in use are incomplete, inadequately specified, and of less explanatory power than one would wish. We should by all means think hard and long about the constructs we use, the ways that we use them, and the possibility of developing something better. We should also remember that middle-range theory is better than none at all, but certainly we have by and large failed to construct and exploit models that will allow us to see political change in its broadest perspectives. Those interested in ideology have too often ended by suggesting that ideology is the dominant element in producing political change; the student of the political machine has found the explanation of political crisis in the shortcomings of the system or the elites who direct it. We must do better. But uncritical borrowing of models from related disciplines is a high risk business also.

In their suspicion of methodological innovation current critics are assuredly in error. The development of theory should proceed hand in hand with the development of greater skill in using appropriate methods of electoral, legislative, and content analysis, collective biography, time series, and sampling techniques—to name only the most obvious areas of interest. Appropriate methodology is not always the most sophisticated or complex. There are numerous examples of quantitative history in which inappropriate methods were used or the right methods were used in inappropriate ways. And the assurance, "if I keep it simple, I cannot go wrong", is unfortunately also untrue. At the other extreme is the attitude that a new or complex technique is automatically better than one that has been in use for some time.

Although today we have statistical and data processing texts written with historians particularly in mind in great contrast to the situation ten years ago, we in general still make a hard road for both historians who wish to retrain themselves and for graduate and undergraduate students in history. How many undergraduate curricula in history require undergraduates to take even one course in statistics? Few indeed. By failing to provide such an

[56] Linda Grant DePauw, *American Historical Review* 80 (1975): pp. 719–20.

option or requirement we not only foreclose our own majors from full comprehension and use of the new histories, we deny them the cross fertilizing effects of the social sciences.

Changes are coming at the graduate level as the employment notices that cross my desk show very clearly in their frequent description of vacancies where Ph.D.s capable of teaching quantitative methodology courses are desired. But most such courses will be at the graduate level, and we are still depending on the summer "quickie" courses offered by the Inter-University Consortium for Political and Social Research and at the Newberry Library to do what our own graduate curricula should have done long since. The alternative to action on this front is to encourage the social sciences to develop their own history and historians. To some degree this is already taking place.

Although we also think of the new histories as essentially utilizing method and theory from related disciplines, there rests in the mind of many the commitment to modify the borrowed theory or methods to better fit the data and time dimension of history or even ultimately to generate methods and theory that are uniquely appropriate to the historical context. Or perhaps more realistically that the historian will take the methodology from the statistician or mathematician without an intermediate stage in which the political scientist, the sociologist, or the geographer demonstrates its usefulness.

One of the by-products of the new histories has been the development and use of machine-readable quantitative data. The story of the process by which the Quantitative Data Committee of the American Historical Association and the Inter-University Consortium for Political Research assembled the machine-readable data series of popular voting returns and congressional roll calls that served as the foundation for the Historical Data Archive of the Inter-University Consortium for Political and Social Research is well known.[57] That archive continues to grow and the political and social data there have greatly facilitated the development of the so-called ethno-cultural model and research on political realignments. But the days when granting agencies placed large sums in the hands of archival agencies for use in collecting, processing, and archiving quantitative data have long since passed in the United States. Now the machine-readable data archives are growing by soliciting and accepting donations of data from scholars who have completed or made substantial progress on research for which they have prepared their own data series. Thus the accumulation of data sets needed to develop and test theoretical models is proceeding less rapidly

[57] Bogue, "Historian and Social Science Data Archives", pp. 424–27.

than one might wish. We need electoral, legislative, ecological, and elite data series covering at least the national period of most major nations, freely available in machine-readable form, plus at least well-selected samples of major data types at all levels of political activity in all of the varying areal units in which political activity is found. Fulfilling these needs would represent a staggering addition to the present holdings of machine-readable data archives but it is difficult to imagine that we can have a truly definitive political history until that work is well advanced. Nor is it clear as yet how much decentralization of these library holdings will be appropriate. Conventional college and university libraries have been slow to recognize their obligations to gather machine-readable data. In the meantime, national- and lower-level government archives are just now starting to face the awesome task of dealing with the preservation of data files that governmental agencies have placed in machine-readable form—a process which in many cases means that paper records of the type preserved a generation ago have not been retained. Historians have a tremendous stake in this enterprise also.

V

I would not argue that any one of the scholarly edifices that I have been describing should be boarded up and a sign placed upon the front lawn reading, "No longer safe for occupancy". I am inclined to believe, however, that the greatest returns in the immediate future will accrue to those historians who embrace a "new pluralist" model, that is built on the assumption that a wide range of determinants may be at work in the politics of the United States at any time, that their salience will change through time and from region to region, and that they involve socio-cultural, economic, and institutional-structural variables. The approach will be such as to illuminate the study of both limited and extended time periods. It will not merely explain electoral behavior, but legislative behavior and policy agenda and outputs and their various interrelationships and integrate ideology and political symbolism with the other elements of the political system. The major evidence should be the platforms and other statements of political groups, biographical data, popular voting returns, legislative roll calls, and specific policy outputs as these appear in legislation, supplemented but not dominated by those old standbys, the newspapers and manuscript collections. In the long run developmental models and data series may have a great impact on American political history. Whether this be a realistic assessment of our needs and capabilities or mere fantasy, time of course will tell but certainly the last twenty-five years have shown historians that they have both the capacity and the tools to produce a political history that is truly new and closer to the actualities of the past than ever before.

Perspectives actuelles
sur les origines du monachisme

Par Antoine Guillaumont

Professeur au Collège de France
Paris, France

Un fait nouveau apparaît dans l'histoire du christianisme au cours de la 2e moitié du IIIe siècle : on voit des chrétiens, de plus en plus nombreux, quittant la communauté des fidèles, s'en aller dans les déserts et y mener une vie exclusivement consacrée à l'ascèse. On pense communément que le monachisme est né en Egypte, avec saint Antoine qui se retira au désert en 270, ou, peut-être, quelque 20 ans plus tôt avec saint Paul ermite, s'il faut en croire la biographie, pour le moins romancée, écrite par saint Jérôme : de là il se serait répandu dans le monde chrétien, où on le voit partout établi dès la fin du IVe siècle : en Palestine, en Syrie, en Mésopotamie, en Asie Mineure, en Grèce, en Italie, en Gaule, etc. C'est là un fait d'une immense portée dans l'histoire du christianisme, car l'idéal monastique a très profondément marqué la spiritualité, voire la morale, chrétiennes traditionnelles, aussi bien en Orient qu'en Occident. Qu'on s'en loue ou qu'on le déplore, comme on le fait souvent aujourd'hui, en dehors même des églises issues de la Réforme, c'est un fait qui s'impose à l'historien et dont les origines font problème.

D'où provient ce mouvement? Quelles en furent les causes? Des explications de nature diverse et demeurées classiques ont été avancées par la science historique, depuis la fin du XIXe siècle. Je ne puis que les énumérer brièvement, en signalant les éléments nouveaux que les études et découvertes plus récentes ont apportés à telle ou telle d'entre elles.

On a fait appel à des influences extra-chrétiennes, qui seraient venues, à un moment donné, infléchir, dans son développement, la spiritualité évangélique:

– influences venues de l'Inde, spécialement du bouddhisme, où le monachisme s'est développé bien avant qu'il n'apparaisse dans le christianisme. Il y a certes bien des analogies entre le genre de vie des moines chrétiens et celui des moines bouddhistes. Mais la difficulté est dans l'établissement de rapports historiques. L'écart est grand, sous le rapport du temps et de l'espace.

Les inscriptions d'Asoka qui ont été découvertes, ces dernières années, en Afghanistan, le long de la route de l'Inde à Palmyre et à la Méditerranée et qui témoignent des activités missionnaires bouddhistes en direction de l'Occident, si elles réduisent quelque peu cet écart, sont encore bien loin de le combler !

– influence du judaïsme, qui, à l'époque hellénistique, offre quelques exemples célèbres de vie au désert : Jean Baptiste, Bannous, l'ascète auprès de qui Flavius Josèphe passa trois ans, dans la solitude, les Thérapeutes de Philon, établis dans les faubourgs d'Alexandrie, et surtout les Esséniens des bords de la mer Morte; à cette dernière hypothèse, les découvertes de Qumrân sont venues apporter un regain de faveur. Le groupement que nous fait connaître le « Rouleau de la Règle » présente certains caractères d'une communauté monastique; le genre de vie qui y est décrit évoque d'ailleurs, plutôt que l'anachorétisme de saint Antoine et de ses émules, l'organisation des communautés cénobitiques fondées, en Haute Egypte, par saint Pacôme. Mais comment établir une filiation entre une secte juive de Palestine, disparue peu après le milieu du Ier siècle, et un mouvement qui se manifeste en Egypte à la fin du IIIe? On réduit quelque peu cette difficulté en cherchant à établir un lien entre la secte de Qumrân et le monachisme chrétien, non pas d'Egypte, mais de Mésopotamie et en supposant, selon une thèse qui connaît actuellement une certaine faveur, que des sectaires de Qumrân, gagnés au christianisme, ont quitté, après 70, la Palestine et sont allés vivre en Mésopotamie. Mais nous sommes là, de toute évidence, en pleine hypothèse.

– influence de l'hellénisme lui-même, au sein duquel s'est développé, vers les alentours de notre ère, un certain idéal de solitude et de retraite, qui a pu, du reste, imprégner les milieux juifs dont je viens de parler. Il est certain que la philosophie grecque, et tout spécialement le stoïcisme, a profondément influencé la littérature monastique chrétienne et a fourni au monachisme, quand celui-ci s'est constitué une doctrine, maintes notions fondamentales. Mais peut-on admettre une telle influence sur les initiateurs eux-mêmes, un saint Antoine, un paysan de la vallée du Nil, dont son biographe, saint Athanase, nous assure qu'il était illettré? De fait, à ses origines, le monachisme chrétien, du moins en Egypte, apparaît comme un phénomène essentiellement rural.

– une autre influence pourrait être invoquée, avec plus de vraisemblance : celle du manichéisme, dont la connaissance a beaucoup progressé depuis les découvertes de documents manichéens en Asie Centrale et, vers 1930, au Fayoum, en Egypte. Nous savons que, né en Mésopotamie vers le milieu du IIIe siècle, le manichéisme a connu une très rapide expansion et s'est diffusé notamment en Egypte, dès la seconde moitié de ce siècle, c'est-à-dire au moment même où y apparaissait le monachisme chrétien. Ne tiendrait-on pas là l'explication recherchée? L'« élu » manichéen est bien une sorte de moine, dont le genre de vie se rapproche plutôt de celui des moines itinérants syriens que de celui des anachorètes égyptiens. En réalité, les contacts sont à situer non en Egypte, mais en Mésopotamie et c'est, à mon avis, le manichéisme qui a subi l'influence du christianisme mésopotamien, de ses tendances ascétiques et de sa structure communautaire, sur lesquelles j'aurai à revenir.

Enfin on a fait appel à d'autres causes, de caractère religieux ou politique, sur lesquelles je puis passer rapidement. Le monachisme aurait été la réaction de « purs », de « spirituels », héritiers des martyrs, contre la sécularisation de l'Eglise constantinienne; mais on oublie que le monachisme est apparu nettement avant la paix de l'Eglise, en 312. On a invoqué aussi l'influence des persécutions elles-mêmes, qui ont poussé nombre de chrétiens à se réfugier au désert, ce qu'illustrent aussi bien les actes des martyrs de Perse sous Sapor que ceux d'Egypte sous l'empereur Dèce; je pense qu'il y a du vrai dans cette explication (j'y reviendrai), mais cela n'a pu être qu'une cause occasionnelle : si ces chrétiens, poussés au désert par la persécution, y sont restés une fois la persécution finie, c'est parce qu'ils avaient découvert là un mode de vie qui répondait à des exigences, à un idéal, qu'ils portaient déjà en eux.

En réalité, les nombreux travaux consacrés au monachisme primitif depuis la dernière guerre, surtout, ont beaucoup modifié les façons de voir traditionnelles que je viens de rappeler. Deux perspectives nouvelles se dégagent.

D'abord, le monachisme, dans l'Eglise, n'est pas un phénomène uniquement égyptien à l'origine. Il est vrai que l'Egypte devint de bonne heure le pays de prédilection du monachisme; les premières grandes oeuvres de la littérature monastique, *Apophtegmes des Pères, Histoire lausiaque* de Pallade, l'*Histoire des moines d'Egypte,* traduites dans toutes les langues de la chrétienté, portèrent au loin la renommée des moines d'Egypte, au point que ceux-ci revêtirent bientôt, aux yeux de tous, une valeur exemplaire; en tout pays, les institutions monastiques cherchèrent, pour rehausser le prestige de leurs origines, à se rattacher au monachisme égyptien, de même que, peu auparavant, beaucoup de chrétientés locales s'étaient pourvues, à tort ou à raison, de prestigieuses origines apostoliques. Mais bien des indices portent à croire, maintenant, que le monachisme est apparu en plusieurs points de la chrétienté de façon indépendante et presque simultanée. A coup sûr, le monachisme mésopotamien, à ses origines, est autochtone et il ne subit, massivement, les influences égyptiennes qu'après le Ve siècle : et c'est bien plus tard – pas avant le IXe siècle – que se constitua la légende de mar Awgin dans le but de pourvoir le monachisme mésopotamien de lettres de noblesses, en le rattachant à celui d'Egypte. En Palestine également on a la preuve de l'existence, dès le début, d'établissements monastiques indépendants de saint Hilarion, que saint Jérôme présente comme un disciple de saint Antoine. Dans ces conditions, il n'est plus possible de se représenter le monachisme chrétien comme né d'une étincelle qui, apportée d'ailleurs et tombée quelque part en Egypte, aurait rapidement embrasé la chrétienté entière.

D'autre part, nous connaissons mieux maintenant la préhistoire du monachisme. Celui-ci, tel qu'il se manifeste dans l'Eglise à la fin du IIIᵉ siècle, n'est pas une phénomène radicalement nouveau; l'essentiel des éléments constitutifs de sa doctrine existait dans l'Eglise depuis le premier siècle. En d'autres termes, il y eut, avant le monachisme proprement dit, un pré-monachisme. C'est dans les forts courants ascétiques, mieux connus maintenant, qui marquèrent profondément le christianisme des trois premiers siècles, que se trouve la source principale de ce que nous appelons, au sens propre, le monachisme chrétien.

Pour donner à mon exposé la base la plus concrète possible, je vais envisager l'histoire primitive du mot *monachos* lui-même, qui, par le latin *monachus,* a donné notre mot français « moine ». On associe communément le mot *monachos* à un autre mot grec, *monos,* qui veut dire « seul » : le moine, comprend-t-on, est celui qui vit seul, dans la solitude du désert. Mais tel n'est pas la premier sens du mot *monachos.* On a, en effet, quelques attestations de l'emploi de ce mot avant l'apparition du monachisme proprement dit, c'est-à-dire avant qu'il y ait des « solitaires » dans les déserts. Le mot, étranger au grec classique, a d'abord désigné, dans l'Eglise ancienne, un ascète qui – et c'est là le trait essentiel – garde la continence, ne se marie pas, celui qui reste « célibataire » pour raison d'ascétisme religieux. Significatif à cet égard est l'emploi que fait de ce mot Symmaque, un des traducteurs grecs de la Bible, au IIᵉ siècle, en *Genèse* 2,8, pour désigner la condition d'Adam avant la création d'Eve : il était alors *monachos* (hébreu lᵉ*badô*), c'est-à-dire sans femme, célibataire. Le *monachos* est donc bien, primitivement, celui qui vit seul, qui est « solitaire » si l'on veut, mais non pas parce qu'il vit dans la solitude du désert, loin des hommes, mais simplement parce qu'il n'a pas de femme. Le célibat est donc lié à l'essence primitive du monachisme : le moine est d'abord l'ascète célibataire.

Le célibat religieux, de l'un et de l'autre sexe, était une pratique fort répandue dans l'Eglise des premiers siècles; les témoignages en sont nombreux, spécialement dans le christianisme de Mésopotamie. Certains savants – comme Burkitt, Vööbus – ont même pensé que, dans cette église, le baptême n'était, primitivement du moins, conféré qu'à ceux qui renonçaient au mariage. Le fait apparaît clairement dans les *Actes de Thomas,* ouvrage composé à Edesse vers le milieu du IIIᵉ siècle et qui prétend raconter l'évangélisation de l'Inde par l'apôtre Thomas; la question se pose, il est vrai – et on peut en débattre –, de savoir si cet ouvrage provient de la grande Eglise, ou d'une secte hétérodoxe. On y voit Thomas imposer la rupture du lien conjugal à ceux qui, gagnés par sa prédication, demandent le baptême. L'*Evangile de Thomas*, recueil de paroles de Jésus constitué au IIe siècle et trouvé en Egypte, il y a quelque 30 ans, en version copte – mais je le crois d'origine syriaque – fait du célibat la condition du salut. On lit au logion 75: « Jésus a dit : Il y en a beaucoup qui se tiennent près de la porte, mais ce sont les *monachoi* qui entreront dans la chambre nuptiale » ; la version copte a simplement transcrit le mot grec qui, ici, désigne – le contexte est clair – l'ascète célibataire : pour entrer dans la chambre nuptiale de l'époux céleste, il faut renoncer, ici bas, au mariage.

Si les emplois du grec *monachos* en ce sens, que l'on peut appeler pré-monastique, sont assez rares, en revanche très nombreux sont ceux du mot syriaque *îhîdâyâ*, qui est l'exact équivalent du grec *monachos* : c'est le mot usuel, en syriaque, c'est-à-dire dans la langue de la Syrie et de la Mésopotamie chrétiennes, pour désigner le « moine ». Mais avant de se fixer dans ce dernier sens, le mot, tout comme le grec *monachos,* mais d'une façon beaucoup mieux attestée, a d'abord désigné l'ascète célibataire. Le genre de vie des *îhîdâyê* (pluriel de *îhîdâyâ*) est bien connu par deux ouvrages syriaques du IVe siècle, les *Démonstrations* d'Aphraate, le « Sage persan », et le *Livre des degrés,* d'un auteur inconnu. Les solitaires que sont les *îhîdâyê* vivent au sein de la communauté des fidèles : ils se distinguent des autres fidèles par le fait qu'ils ont abandonné toute possession terrestre pour mener une vie errante, consacrée à la prière et à la prédication, et aussi par le fait qu'ils ont renoncé au mariage pour garder la « virginité » (*b^etûlûtâ*), ou, s'ils étaient mariés, à l'usage du mariage, pour observer ce qui était appelé la « sainteté » (*qaddishûtâ*) : c'est en ce sens seulement qu'ils sont des « solitaires », par le fait qu'ils vivent « seuls », sans femme.

Quel est le motif de ce renoncement au mariage? C'est là une question délicate et complexe. Plusieurs motifs ont pu intervenir, en particulier la conception biblique et juive des rapports existant entre sacralité et sexualité. Aphraate explique qui les *îhîdâyê* doivent garder la continence parce que celle-ci est requise de celui qui est au service de Dieu : il invoque une tradition juive, attestée par ailleurs, selon laquelle Moïse aurait renoncé à toute vie conjugale à partir du jour où il se sentit appelé par Dieu et se mit au service de celui-ci. De plusieurs passages de la Loi il ressort que le prêtre, les jours où il était de service au Temple, devait s'abstenir de tous rapports avec sa femme : il y avait donc incompatibilité entre service liturgique et activité sexuelle, celle-ci étant considérée comme cause d'impureté. Cette raison explique, je pense, le célibat des Esséniens, et aussi celui des Thérapeutes, ces ascètes juifs qui, selon Philon, vivaient dans la banlieue d'Alexandrie. Elle a pu jouer un rôle aussi dans les origines du célibat monastique, le moine étant, en quelque sorte, comme l'Essénien ou le Thérapeute, en permanence au service de Dieu et devant, par conséquent, se trouver en état permanent de pureté.

Mais il y a, au célibat monastique, une autre raison, plus profonde, qui s'inspire, elle aussi, d'idées bibliques et juives. Par là nous allons entrer plus profondément dans l'analyse du sens du mot *monachos* et de son équivalent syriaque *îhîdâyâ*. La racine sémitique sur laquelle est formé ce dernier, hébreu *iâhad*, veut dire, non seulement « être seul », mais aussi « être un ». Et c'est bien là, je crois, le sens fondamental du mot *monachos* : celui qui est un, unique, unifié. On lit dans le psaume 86, 11 :

> « Enseigne-moi, Iahvé, ta voie
> et je marcherai dans ta vérité :
> unifie mon coeur, pour qu'il craigne ton nom ».

« Unifie « , hébreu *iahêd,* que le traducteur Aquila a rendu par *monachoûn,* première attestation de ce verbe correspondant au substantif *monachos.* « Unifie mon coeur », cela veut dire « fais que je n'aie pas un coeur partagé », « deux coeurs », ou, selon une expression biblique fréquente, « un coeur et un coeur ». Cette expression couvre une notion biblique importante, qui est celle de l'intégrité du coeur : il faut aller à Dieu, l'aimer, est-il dit, « de tout son coeur » , d'un coeur entier *kōl lêb.* Le service de Dieu interdit tout partage. Dans la religion juive, le partage ainsi proscrit est l'attitude de celui qui voudrait tout à la fois servir le Dieu unique et rester au service des idoles. Cette notion, transposée, est restée fondamentale dans l'éthique judéo-chrétienne sous le nom grec de *haplotês,* « simplicité », vertu qui s'oppose à la duplicité, *dipsuchia,* le fait d'avoir l'âme, le coeur, partagés. Je pense que l'idéal primitif du *monachos* a des attaches profondes avec cette vertu judéo-chrétienne de « simplicité » : le moine est celui qui se met au service de Dieu tout entier, sans partage. Il y a dans l'oeuvre exégétique d'Eusèbe de Césarée, au IIIe siècle, un passage qui est un *locus classicus* pour l'histoire du mot *monachos* et qui illustre fort bien l'idée que je veux mettre en relief. Commentant le verset 7 du Psaume 68 : « Elohim fait habiter les solitaires *(iᵉhîdîm),* dans une maison », Eusèbe fait remarquer que le mot hébreu *iahîd* (parent du syriaque *îhîdâyâ*) est traduit chez Symmaque par *monachos,* tandis que la version des Septante a choisi le mot *monotropos*; ces deux termes grecs sont donc équivalents; or, ajoute-t-il, *monotropos* se dit de celui qui, au lieu de se comporter tantôt d'une manière, tantôt d'une autre, a une activité uniforme, toute orientée vers une seule fin. Ainsi doivent donc être les *monachoi,* et ce sens fondamental du mot est resté longtemps sensible chez les auteurs anciens qui ont voulu définir l'idéal monastique. C'est la définition du moine que l'on trouve encore, au début du VIe siècle, chez le pseudo-Denys l'Aréopagite : « Les moines sont ainsi appelés – *monachoi* – parce que leur vie, loin d'être divisée, demeure parfaitement une, parce qu'ils s'unifient eux-mêmes par un saint recueillement qui exclut tout divertissement, de façon à tendre vers l'unité d'une conduite conforme à Dieu et vers la perfection par l'amour divin ». Je m'empresse de dire qu'il faut faire chez Denys, et très largement, la part de l'influence du néo-platonisme, où la notion d'unification joue un grand rôle. Mais qu'il y ait, dans ces lignes, un écho de la conception primitive du *monachos* est prouvé par le fait que l'on retrouve une définition analogue du moine chez des auteurs du même temps, spécialement en Syrie (le pays d'origine, vraisemblablement, du corpus dionysien), par exemple chez Philoxène de Mabboug, chez qui l'influence du néo-platonisme n'intervient pas : « Le moine, dit-il, doit réaliser son nom de manière effective et être moine *(îhîdâyâ* unifié) en son extérieur et en son intérieur. Et il ne doit y avoir en lui rien d'autre que lui seul et Celui qui habite en lui, je veux dire le Christ, lequel ne consent à s'établir en lui que s'il est seul » ; et pour illustrer cette idée, Philoxène cite le Psaume 68,7, dont nous venons de voir le commentaire d'Eusèbe : « Dieu fait habiter les solitaires dans une maison ».

Si l'on part de ce sens fondamental du mot *monachos,* synonyme de *monotropos,* désignant celui dont toute l'activité est unifiée, orientée vers une seule fin, alors tout ce qui définit la condition monastique devient clair, et d'abord le renoncement au mariage. Un texte célèbre de saint Paul prend tout son sens, remis dans les perspectives qui viennent d'être évoquées. L'Apôtre écrit aux Corinthiens (*I Cor.* 7,32 s.) : « Je voudrais que vous soyez sans soucis; or celui qui n'est pas marié se soucie des choses du Seigneur et de la manière dont il plaira au Seigneur; mais celui qui est marié se soucie des choses du monde et de la manière dont il plaira à sa femme et *il est partagé (mémeristai) ».* L'Apôtre explique ensuite qu'il en est de même pour la femme et il ajoute : « Je vous dis cela dans votre propre intérêt, et non pour vous tendre un piège, mais pour que vous soyez empressés et assidus auprès du Seigneur, sans tiraillement », *aperispastôs*; ce dernier terme réapparaît souvent dans les textes qui définissent l'idéal monastique : le moine ne doit pas être partagé, « tiraillé », et c'est pour cela qu'il renonce au mariage, celui-ci étant représenté comme cause de division et de partage.

Sur ce point aussi les influences issues de l'hellénisme sont venues s'ajouter. Le sage épicurien, lui aussi, évite de se marier pour échapper aux difficultés que le mariage crée pour celui qui veut s'adonner à la sagesse. La diatribe cynico-stoïcienne a largement exploité le thème des inconvénients du mariage, et ce lieu commun a été trop souvent repris par les auteurs chrétiens (un saint Jérôme, et Grégoire de Nysse) pour défendre, avec des arguments d'une qualité douteuse, l'idéal chrétien de la virginité. Mais ces développements rhétoriques, dont on a abusé, ne doivent pas faire méconnaître l'idée qu'ils recouvrent, et que je crois fondamentale dans l'éthique chrétienne des premiers siècles et dans l'idéal primitif du *monachos*, du moine.

Si nous envisageons maintenant, rapidement, les démarches essentielles qui caractérisent l'état monastique, tel qu'il s'est développé à partir de la fin du IIIe siècle, nous allons voir que toutes s'expliquent fort bien à partir de cette idée fondamentale : le moine est celui qui ne veut pas être partagé, et qui veut avoir une vie unifiée.

La première de ces démarches est le renoncement, en grec *apotagê* ou *apotaxis*. Il ne s'agit pas seulement du renoncement au mal et à Satan, comme l'était, pour tout fidèle, le renoncement baptismal; mais il s'agit de renoncer même à des choses qui, en elles-mêmes, ne sont pas mauvaises : la famille, non seulement celle que le moine fonderait s'il se mariait, mais aussi (nous le reverrons) celle où il est né, sa parenté charnelle; puis les biens et richesses de ce monde. Tout cet ensemble se résume dans le mot « monde », *kosmos* : le renoncement monastique est un renoncement au monde. Mais ce mot, comme on le sait, est ambigu; ici, il désigne, non pas ce qui est essentiellement mauvais, mais ce qui est mauvais relativement, dans la mesure où ce peut être un obstacle pour qui veut devenir parfait. Pourquoi faut-il renoncer à ces choses, si elles ne sont pas essentiellement mauvaises? Parce que les biens de ce monde sont source de soucis et de division. Cela est net dans le récit de la conversion de saint Antoine : saint Athanase nous dit que la première chose qu'il fit après sa conversion à l'ascétisme fut de vendre les terres héritées de ses parents et d'en distribuer le prix aux pauvres : cela, certes, pour obéir au précepte évangélique qu'il avait entendu lire à l'église : « Si tu veux être parfait, va, vends tout ce que tu as et donnes-en le prix aux pauvres, puis viens et suis-moi » (*Matt.*19,21); mais aussi, précise le texte, pour que ces biens ne soient pas pour lui une source de soucis et d'embarras.

Le but que le moine recherche, en effet, en renonçant aux biens de ce monde, c'est de devenir « sans soucis », en grec *amérimnos*; ce qu'il recherche, c'est la bienheureuse *amérimnia,* l'absence de soucis, qui le rendra entièrement disponible pour le service de Dieu. C'est aussi, nous l'avons vu, cette absence de soucis qu'avait en vue l'Apôtre Paul quand il recommandait le célibat : « Je voudrais que vous soyez sans soucis ... ». Le renoncement aux biens de ce monde procède donc du même motif que le renoncement au mariage. Saint Basile, un des grands théoriciens du monachisme à la fin du IVe siècle, définissant le renoncement, écrivait dans ses *Grandes Règles* : « Il faut renoncer à tous les attachements passionnés du monde, qui peuvent faire obstacle sur le chemin qui mène vers le but fixé par la religion ... En effet, l'esprit qui est partagé entre différents soucis ne peut pas réussir dans ce qu'il s'est proposé ». Et il cite *Matthieu* 6,24 : « Nul ne peut servir deux maîtres …». D'une façon plus naïve, l'abba Isaïe, un moine du Vᵉ siècle, écrivait, de son côté : « Du même qu'il n'est pas possible à quelqu'un de regarder le ciel d'un oeil et de regarder la terre de l'autre oeil, de même il n'est pas possible à notre esprit de s'occuper à la fois des choses de Dieu et des choses du monde ». Le renoncement est donc fondé sur le postulat qu'il y a incompatibilité entre le monde et Dieu, entre l'attachement à cette vie et le service de Dieu.

Ce renoncement ne doit pas être seulement une attitude intérieure, un détachement purement spirituel. Il doit se réaliser effectivement, se concrétiser par la séparation, l'éloignement, ou, pour prendre le mot propre, l'anachorèse, *anachôrêsis*. C'est précisément avec l'anachorèse, la retraite loin du monde, que commence ce que nous appelons, au sens courant du mot, le monachisme. Mais, ce qu'il faut bien voir, à mon avis, c'est que le motif qui a poussé à l'anachorèse est celui-là même qui a inspiré, avant l'apparition du monachisme proprement dit, le célibat religieux et le renoncement à toute forme de possession. Des causes occasionnelles ont pu intervenir pour provoquer l'anachorèse, notamment les persécutions, qui ont contraint nombre de chrétiens à se réfugier au désert, nous dirions maintenant à prendre le maquis, et à découvrir ainsi la vie au désert; mais si l'anachorèse ainsi découverte a été maintenue, réitérée en dehors de toute contrainte, c'est parce qu'elle répondait au motif profond qui avait inspiré l'ascétisme pré-monastique et qui n'est autre que la volonté qu'a l'ascète de se soustraire à l'emprise du monde pour être tout à Dieu.

L'anachorèse n'est d'ailleurs pas une démarche faite une fois pour toutes, car le moine a toujours à lutter, même au désert, pour sauvegarder sa solitude. Un bel exemple d'anachorèse est donné par l'abba Arsène, dont on disait qu'il avait été précepteur des fils de l'empereur Théodose et qui se retira au désert de Scété, l'un des plus célèbres habitats monastiques d'Egypte. Etant encore au palais, Arsène priait en demandant à Dieu de lui dire comment il serait sauvé; il lui fut répondu : « Arsène, fuis les hommes et tu seras sauvé ». Et, au désert même, Arsène, faisant la même prière, entendit cette réponse : « Arsène, fuis, tais-toi et garde la solitude (*hésychia* : nous reverrons ce mot) : ce sont là les racines de l'impeccabilité ». De fait, à Scété, Arsène changea plusieurs fois de cellule, pour s'éloigner toujours davantage des cellules des autres moines. A un jeune moine qui lui demandait : « Pourquoi nous fuis-tu? » Arsène répondit : « Dieu sait que je vous aime, mais je ne puis être en même temps avec Dieu et avec les hommes », et il ajoutait : « Les milliers et les myriades d'en haut – c'est-à-dire les anges – n'ont qu'une seule volonté, mais les hommes ont des volontés multiples; je ne puis, dans ces conditions, abandonner Dieu pour suivre les hommes ». Ces derniers mots évoquent un thème important que je ne puis qu'effleurer : celui de l'imitation de la vie angélique, celle-ci étant représentée comme une vie unifiée, libérée des soucis multiples, donc de parfaite insouciance, *amérimnia*, toute entière tendue vers une seule fin, le service de Dieu.

Cette anachorèse, cette retraite, par laquelle le moine met une distance entre le monde et lui, peut être d'ampleur variable : Antoine, au début, se retire simplement à l'écart de son village, puis il s'établit de l'autre côté du Nil, puis il gagne l'autre extrémité du désert arabique, aux confins de la mer Rouge. Quand le moine, en s'éloignant ainsi, va dans un pays étranger, l'anachorèse prend le nom de *xénitéia,* mot difficile à traduire en français : exil, dépaysement, expatriation. C'est ce que fit l'abba Arsène, dont je parlais il y a un instant, lorsque, quittant Constantinople, il gagna l'Egypte. La *xénitéia* est la condition d'étranger (le mot est formé sur *xénos*, étranger), condition que le moine embrasse quand il quitte son pays natal pour aller vivre dans un pays où nul ne le connaîtra, par conséquent où il devra vivre dans le dénuement et dans le mépris. Elle est un complément naturel du renoncement : c'est l'arrachement de l'homme à son milieu naturel, à sa famille, à sa parenté, à sa patrie. Le principe en est formulé par saint Jérôme dans une lettre fameuse adressée à son ami Héliodore ; il cherche à montrer à son ami qu'il lui sera impossible de mener la vie ascétique dans son propre pays : le Christ lui-même a dû quitter les siens, car « nul n'est prophète en son pays »; « de là il ressort, conclut-il, que le moine ne peut devenir parfait dans son pays ». A cet égard, le prototype du moine est le patriarche Abraham, à qui Dieu dit : « Quitte ton pays, ta famille, la maison de ton père et va vers le pays que je te montrerai » (*Genèse* 12,1). Dans le pays où il est venu, le moine ne doit pas cesser de vivre en étranger, sinon il risque de s'y créer une nouvelle patrie, une nouvelle famille. Et si cela se produit, il n'a plus qu'à s'expatrier une nouvelle fois. Cette démarche peut être réitérée plusieurs fois et alors le moine devient un pèlerin, un perpétuel voyageur : ainsi est né le monachisme errant, qui s'est beaucoup développé en Syrie et, jusque dans les temps modernes, en Russie. Ce mode de vie n'était pas apprécié partout : en Egypte notamment on n'aimait guère les moines vagabonds, et il s'est développé, dans les milieux monastiques de ce pays, une conception plus spirituelle de la *xénitéia* : celle-ci, le moine pouvait, pensait-on, la pratiquer en restant dans sa cellule, à condition de ne jamais s'y sentir « chez soi », de ne pas laisser se développer en lui ce sentiment de familiarité qui nous lie habituellement aux êtres et aux choses qui nous entourent. Cela implique une certaine discrétion du regard. On citait le cas d'un moine qui avait vécu plusieurs années dans une cellule sans s'apercevoir qu'il y avait un lit!

L'anachorèse, ou fuite du monde, pouvait donc pousser le moine à s'expatrier. Elle pouvait aussi lui suggérer de s'enfermer dans une cellule, en coupant toute relation avec l'extérieur : en d'autres termes, le conduire à la réclusion. L'un des plus célèbres reclus fut, en Egypte, Jean de Lycopolis, qui vivait enfermé dans une grotte des environs d'Assiout. La vie de l'abba Isaïe, dont j'ai déjà parlé, fait bien comprendre le motif qui pousse à la réclusion. Isaïe jeune, se retire au désert : c'est l'anachorèse; au bout de quelques années, pour fuir le renom que lui vaut son ascèse, il quitte l'Egypte pour gagner, en Palestine, la région de Gaza; de nouveau, la célébrité l'importune et alors, au lieu de s'expatrier une nouvelle fois, il se fait reclure dans sa cellule et ne communique plus avec l'extérieur que par l'intermédiaire d'un disciple. Il se trouve ainsi à l'origine de toute une lignée de reclus qui se succèdèrent, pendant au moins deux siècles, dans la région de Gaza.

La fuite du monde peut enfin conduire à une forme d'anachorèse plus étrange encore : le stylitisme. Le moine, pour fuir la foule, se fait construire une colonne. Ainsi fit, dans la région d'Antioche, saint Syméon le Stylite : après avoir, sans succès, d'abord changé de lieu, puis s'être fait enfermer dans un enclos, il finit par s'installer sur une colonne, où il vécut pendant 30 ans : haute d'abord de 5 mètres, elle fut portée à 15, puis à 20 mètres! Pour comprendre ce singulier mode de vie, qui, à vrai dire, n'eut guère d'adeptes en dehors de la Syrie et des abords de Constantinople, il faut le situer dans les perspectives que je viens d'évoquer : c'est la fuite du monde, mais, cette fois-ci, selon la verticale!

En définitive, que cherche le moine quand il se retire au désert, comme l'abba Arsène, quand il s'expatrie ou se fait reclus, comme Isaïe, ou quand il se hisse sur une colonne, comme Syméon? Il cherche ce qu'on appelait, en grec, l'*hésychia,* mot difficile à traduire, car il désigne tout à la fois le silence, la tranquillité, la solitude, le recueillement. En Orient surtout, le moine est resté, par excellence, un « hésychaste », quelqu'un pour qui toutes les démarches précédentes, renoncement, anachorèse, expatriation ou réclusion, n'ont qu'un seul but, lui procurer l'*hésychia*, la liberté, la disponibilité nécessaires à qui veut vivre en ne pensant qu'à Dieu, en entretenant constamment en lui, comme on disait, le « souvenir de Dieu ». Selon l'enseignement des moines égyptiens, la *xénitéia,* ou expatriation, n'était légitime qu'en vue de cette seule fin : « Si tu ne peux pas vivre facilement dans l'*hésychia* dans le pays où tu es, alors résous-toi à la *xénitéia* », dit Evagre. Aussi bien, pour être vraiment un hésychaste, le moine doit, selon l'expression consacrée, « rester assis dans sa cellule ». La garde de la cellule est, pour le moine, un précepte fondamental sur lequel les textes insistent inlassablement. L'abba Moïse, un moine de Scété, disait à quelqu'un qui lui demandait un conseil : « Va, assieds-toi dans ta cellule, et ta cellule t'enseignera tout! » Même conseil donné par l'abba Arsène, non sans quelque humour; un moine vient le trouver en lui disant : « Mes pensées me troublent en me disant : tu ne peux pas jeûner ni travailler; va donc visiter les malades, car c'est en cela que consiste la charité ». Arsène, voyant en cela, comme dit le texte, « les semences du démon », lui répond : « Va, mange, bois, dors, ne travaille pas, mais ne quitte pas ta cellule! ». Conseil qui est à prendre, évidemment, *cum grano salis!*

« Mes pensées me troublent », disait le moine à Arsène. En effet, l'*hésychia,* si elle assure au moine la tranquillité extérieure et la solitude, ne lui confère pas, *ipso facto,* la paix intérieure et l'unification de l'âme. Séparé du monde par l'anachorèse, il n'a plus à lutter, comme on disait, avec les « objets », mais il connaît une autre guerre, plus difficile, assurait-on, celle qu'il a à soutenir contre ses pensées; ces pensées, faites du souvenir et des représentations des objets, étaient l'arme subtile dont les démons, disait-on, se servaient contre les solitaires. La psychologie du solitaire a été remarquablement analysée par Evagre, un moine originaire du Pont et qui vécut, à la fin du IVe siècle, aux Kellia, désert voisin de Scété; à une large culture et à un esprit hautement spéculatif, Evagre joignait une grande finesse dans l'analyse psychologique. Je ne puis résister au plaisir de vous citer, pour finir, l'analyse qu'il a faite de la pensée dite d'« acédie » dans son livre intitulé le *Traité pratique.* L'acédie – nous sommes obligés, en français, de garder le mot grec, *akédia,* car il est intraduisible, s'agissant d'une tentation qui est propre au solitaire : c'est, tout à la fois, l'ennui, le découragement, la paresse, le doute que le moine éprouve à l'égard de lui-même, des autres, à l'égard de son état de vie et de la fin qu'il s'est proposée : « Le démon de l'acédie, qui est appelé aussi démon de midi (expression prise au Psaume 91,6 : c'est le fameux *daemonium meridianum*) est le plus pesant de tous les démons; il attaque le moine vers la 4e heure et il assiège son âme jusque vers la 8e heure. D'abord il fait que le soleil lui paraît lent à se mouvoir, ou même qu'il est immobile, et que le jour semble avoir 50 heures. Ensuite, il le force à regarder continuellement vers la fenêtre, à bondir hors de sa cellule, à observer le soleil pour voir s'il est loin de la 9e heure (c'est l'heure du repas!), et à tourner les yeux de-ci de-là pour voir si quelque frère vient! En outre, il lui inspire de l'aversion pour le lieu où il est, pour son état de vie lui-même, pour le travail manuel et, de plus, suggère l'idée que la charité a disparu parmi les frères et qu'il n'y a personne pour le consoler. Et si, dans ces jours-là, il se trouve que quelqu'un ait fait de la peine au moine, le démon se sert de cela pour augmenter son aversion. Il l'amène à désirer d'autres lieux, où il pourra trouver facilement ce dont il a besoin et exercer un métier moins pénible et plus rémunérateur. Il ajoute que plaire au Seigneur n'est pas affaire de lieu : partout, en effet, est-il dit, la divinité peut être adorée. Il joint à cela le souvenir de sa famille et de son existence d'autrefois; il lui représente combien longue est la durée de la vie et il met devant ses yeux les fatigues de l'ascèse. Il dresse, comme on dit, toutes ses batteries, pour que le moine abandonne sa cellule et fuie le stade! ». Comme on le voit, l'acédie est la tentation par excellence du solitaire, celle qui s'en prend à l'*hésychia,* au précepte fondamental de la garde de la cellule, et finalement à la condition monastique elle-même. Elle n'est cependant qu'une des huit pensées principales contre lesquelles a à combattre le moine qui veut parvenir à l'impassibilité, l'*apathéia,* ce qui est, sinon la suppression, du moins la victoire sur les passions; et c'est cette impassabilité qui, selon Evagre, ouvre les portes de la contemplation, ou, comme il dit lui-même, de la gnose. Mais je n'ai nullement l'intention de vous y entraîner à sa suite !

Je crains d'avoir été trop abstrait, et je le regrette d'autant plus que la littérature monastique, surtout celle qui concerne les moines d'Egypte, est pleine de pittoresque et d'anecdotes hautes en couleurs. Mais mon intention n'était pas de vous présenter un tableau de la vie des communautés d'Egypte ou d'ailleurs. J'ai cherché à me mettre, délibérément, plus sur le plan de la phénoménologie que sur celui de l'histoire. J'ai voulu surtout étudier le monachisme comme phénomène religieux, et montrer par conséquent qu'il est pourvu d'une structure propre, qui commande à la fois à sa formation et à son développement : en d'autres termes, montrer comment, en partant d'une donnée qui, pour moi, est fondamentale, l'idée d'unification, s'expliquent toutes les conduites, toutes les démarches essentielles de la vie monastique, célibat, renoncement, anachorèse, expatriation, etc., comment elles se déduisent en quelque sorte les unes des autres, suivant la cohérence interne du phénomène. De ce point de vue, ce qui importe, c'est moins la détermination des influences qui ont pu s'exercer que l'étude de la genèse et du développement d'un phénomène qui, se nourissant dans le contexte religieux qui est historiquement le sien, se développe selon une logique interne et ses propres virtualités. Phénomène qui, en lui-même, n'est pas spécifiquement chrétien : c'est une forme religieuse qui peut avoir, idéologiquement, des contenus divers. Moines bouddhistes et moines chrétiens ont ceci de commun qu'ils sont, les uns et les autres, moines, mais il reste que les uns sont bouddhistes, les autres chrétiens. Mon dessein n'a pas été de montrer jusqu'à quel point les moines d'Egypte, de Mésopotamie ou d'ailleurs ont été chrétiens, mais plutôt comment ils ont été moines, c'est-à-dire tributaires d'une forme de vie qui, fondée sur le désir de l'unification, obéit, je crois, à une des exigences fondamentales de la conscience religieuse.

Some Aspects of Hittite Prayers

Hans G. Güterbock

Professor of Hittitology
University of Chicago, USA

To be here and to have this opportunity of talking to you is not only a great pleasure but has a very special meaning for me. While expressing my thanks to the colleagues who arranged this visit, foremost among them Professor Nils Simonsson and Folke Josephson, I also want to mention my lasting gratitude to the University for having invited me as a guest lecturer in 1948 when I was forced, as it were, to emigrate a second time. It was the late Axel Persson who arranged that invitation and also personally helped us no end in getting used to the new environment. It was a great experience to teach here and to meet the colleagues, and it is a special pleasure for me to see quite a few of them still around now. It was from here that I was called to the University of Chicago, and now this invitation—not to speak of the great honor your University is bestowing on me—comes shortly after my retirement from teaching, symbolically closing the circle.

Twenty-eight years is a long time, and it would be sad if Hittitology had not progressed during that period. The field has gained a great number of workers in many countries, and they all have made their contributions. These include a large amount of tablets excavated and made available in cuneiform copies, a significant number of new editions (or "Bearbeitungen") of Hittite texts, and many penetrating studies of various aspects of Hittite language and civilization.

Permit me to continue for a moment with my personal reminiscenses. In 1952, only three years after I left Uppsala, Prof. Bittel resumed the excavations at Boğazköy and invited me to join his expedition again. Thus I had the privilege of being present when one of the most important finds was made. I was in the house one day when a messenger brought a piece of a tablet from the excavation with a note from Prof. Naumann saying that this had been found in an old level, and could I tell what it said. It was what is now known as the Zukraši text,[1] i.e., part of an account of Hattušili I (about 1620 or so)

---

[1] Hittite texts are quoted here by reference to numbers in E. Laroche, *Catalogue des textes hittites* (Paris, Klincksieck, 1971), abbreviated CTH. Other abbreviations are: ANÉT = J. B. Pritchard, ed., *Ancient Near Eastern Texts Relating to the Old Testament* (Princeton Univ. Press, [1]1950, [3]1969); JAOS = *Journal of the American Oriental Society;* JNES = *Journal of Near Eastern Studies;* KBo = *Keilschifttexte aus Boghazköi;* KUB = *Keilschrifturkunden aus Boghazköi;* StBoT = *Studien zu den Boğazköy-Texten* (Wiesbaden, Harrassowitz).—The text here mentioned is CTH 15, A.

of his war against the city of Haššuwa and the troops of Aleppo which were under the command of a certain Zukraši. This is the tablet that not only comes from a dated level but is inscribed with an historical text in the Old Hittite language and in a peculiar kind of cuneiform handwriting. This handwriting is now known under the name of "typical old ductus" or simply "Old Script", and both Prof. Otten and I have used it for the dating of texts. But if my memory does not deceive me it was I who, at Boğazköy in 1952, first said "We have seen this type of writing before; let's see whether it can be used as a criterium for dating other tablets."

As you know the problem of determining the date of a text has occupied many scholars since then, and there has been much discussion and even controversy. But slowly some points become clearer. The recognition of a specific Old Script has made possible the inclusion of many more texts in the corpus of Old Hittite than those few historical inscriptions which previously had been the sole basis for the recognition of an Old Hittite stage of the language. Since the additional texts include rituals, the Laws, epic tales, and other genres they offer a larger and more varied vocabulary as well as repertory of grammatical features.

A warning is, however, in place here: not all tablets in Old Script are necessarily 'originals' in the sense of being the actual first manuscript or archetype of a text. A mistake like *la-a* for *kar* in the old copy A of the Laws[2] can only be a copying mistake and thus shows that this manuscript is indeed a copy, not the archetype. (The case of a one-time document like a sealed land deed is, of course, different.) But whether 'originals' or not, the increase of manuscripts in the old script is most welcome. As announced by Prof. Otten in the Jahrbuch of the Academy of Mainz for 1975,[3] Prof. Erich Neu is preparing an edition of all the ritual texts written in Old Script. Orally Prof. Neu told me that he had not seen a single fragment in Old Script that is not also in the Old Hittite language, an observation which is welcome as confirmation of our first hypothesis.

Whereas this oldest phase is now clear—or will be, when Neu's publication will come out—, the later phases are harder to define. One can safely say that the New Hittite language first appears under Muršili II (second half of the 14th century). The Huqqana treaty[4] of his father, Šuppiluliuma I, is so close to the language of the preceding period that I would call it Middle Hittite. The lingusitic term Middle Hittite has nothing to do with the old term, introduced by Forrer, of a "Middle Kingdom", but rather refers to the language of the time of the first rulers of the New Kingdom, i.e., the

---

[2] KBo 6.2 i 8 as against KBo 6.3 i 15 (J. Friedrich, *Die hethitischen Gesetze* (Leiden, 1959), p 16, n. 23).
[3] *Jahrbuch 1975 der Akademie der Wissenschaften und der Literatur*, p. 130 f.
[4] CTH 42.

predecessors of Šuppiluliuma. I see no reason why one should not, on the basis of the Huqqana treaty, extend the duration of the Middle Hittite language period to include the reign of Šuppiluliuma himself.

What distinguishes Middle Hititte from New Hittite is the number of features that it shares with Old Hittite. And this is just where the difficulty lies. Given the fact that texts were copied and recopied and partly modernized in the process, but given the other fact that late manuscripts sometimes preserve Old Hittite forms faithfully, how can we tell whether Old Hittite forms in a given text indicate that it was composed in Old Hittite times and that the actual manuscript, though late, happened to preserve these forms, or whether such forms were still part of the living language in Middle Hittite times? In the latter case the text might be a Middle Hittite composition.

Now it so happens that among royal prayers there are some that lend themselves to a diachronic analysis. These same prayers also contain many Babylonian motifs; so the problem of when they were written might be of interest for the literary history of the Near East in general. Before going into this it will be best to look at the prayers themselves. About Hittite prayers there is the important paper by E. Laroche, "La prière hittite",[5] and Ph. Houwink ten Cate published an excellent analysis of Hittite Royal Prayers.[6] It goes without saying that I have much profited from both. Still, another look may be useful.

The Old Hittite ritual for the purification of the royal couple (edited by H. Otten and V. Souček)[7] contains a few short prayers pronounced by the officiating priest on behalf of the king and queen. While this text is preserved in manuscripts in Old Script the prayers contained in it are hardly more than spells pronounced in conjunction with the ritual itself, like "Mercy, o gods! Behold, I have removed the impurities of the king, the queen and the people of Hatti" or "Just as the Sungod and the Stormgod are everlasting, so let the king, the queen and the children be everlasting!"

A text known as "Prayer to the Sungoddess of the Earth"[8] contains a number of old forms but also some newer ones. It has been classified as Old Hittite by some, as Middle Hittite by others. A recent collation showed the script to be Middle Hittite. Here as in the Old Hittite ritual just mentioned the prayer is pronounced by the officiant on behalf of the king. At the broken top of the tablet one still reads: "He/she pours a libation to the Sungoddess of the Earth and the gods, and speaks as follows: 'Behold, the

---

[5] In: École Pratique des Hautes Études, (Vᵉ Section) Sciences Religieuses: *Annuaire* 72 (1964–1965) pp. 3–29.
[6] In: *Numen* 16 (1969) 81–98.
[7] *Ein althethitisches Ritual für das Königspaar*, StBoT 8 (1969), esp. col. ii 9–12 and ii 54—iii 2 (pp. 22–31).
[8] CTH 371.

king entreats you *(mukiškizzi)*.'" Indeed this prayer belongs to the class which Laroche calls *mugauwar*, "entreaty".

The Sungoddess of the Earth is known as a Netherworld deity, but here she is only asked not to listen to calumny:

If his father denounces him, do not listen to him!
If his mother denounces him, do not listen to her!
(and so on: If his brother, sister, in-law, companion
denounce him) do not listen!
   Incline your good eyes, lift your thousand eyelashes and look friendly upon the king; incline your ear and listen to the good word!

This is followed by a general request for blessing and the promise of offerings. There follow identical sections addressed to the satellites of the goddess:

Mercy, o vizier of the Sungoddess of the Earth! May good will be yours! Eat and drink! Speak well to the Sungoddess about the king, and pronounce the name of the king before the Sungoddess in a friendly way! If his father, mother, brother, sister, in-law or companion denounce him, do not let him do so!

The list of these subservient deities who are asked to intercede is interesting. The first is *taknaš* ᴰUTU-*aš* ᴰLAMA-*ŠU* "the Protective deity of the Sungoddess of the Earth". The vizier is second, then come "her servants who put her to sleep and strengthen her". There follow two named deities, Darawa and Paraya, the chief of the LÚ.MEŠ.SAG (eunuchs), the chief of the barbers, and finally, Hilašši, the deified courtyard. The goddess has quite an entourage! Also as an early example of a prayer for intercession this text is of interest.

A hymn to the Stormgod is written in a language that I would call Old Hittite; the manuscript is later (CTH 313).

It is a difficult text; no part lends itself easily to translation. Even so, one finds many Babylonian elements in it, such as: "He gave you the Enlilship", references to Anu and Enlil, to the ocean of Ea, to "Sippar, the eternal city of the Sungod", "Babylon, the city whom Anu gave its name, ... beloved of Marduk." A broken paragraph near the end of the tablet contains the words "scribe of Babylonian", but even without it it is clear that this text is fashioned after Akkadian models, although no Adad hymn has been found of which this could be a direct translation. Whatever model or models existed in Babylonia, they must have been available when the Hittite text was written; if it really is Old Hittite, this would mean late Old Babylonian times.

When first looking for criteria by which to date texts we quite naturally used texts connected with historical figures as starting point. Thus, for the Chicago Computer Program of the 1960s we considered two prayers as Middle Hittite: the prayer of king Arnuwanda I and queen Ašmunikal,[9] whose time certainly falls before the reign of Šuppiluliuma I, and the prayer of Kantuzzili,[10] assuming that this person was identical with a royal prince who is mentioned in connection with events that probably fall a short time before the accession of Šuppiluliuma. Houwink ten Cate, in this monograph on The Records of the Early Hittite Empire, which was based on the computer printout, listed these two texts as Middle Hittite,[11] and so did Josephson in his study of The Function of the Sentence Particles,[12] in which he also used the printout. But already in 1971 Carruba observed that (in his words) "the language of the Kantuzzili prayer hardly differs from that of the genuine Old Hittite texts in Old Script,"[13] and in a recent Harvard dissertation its author, Craig Melchert, lists the Kantuzzili prayer together with its parallels as Old Hittite, though, respectively, in New Hittite and Middle Hittite manuscripts. In the case of the Kantuzzili prayer it is a priori quite possible, either, that an older prayer was adapted to the use of the prince of the Early New Kingdom, or that the author was a namesake of an earlier age. In the case of the prayer of Arnuwanda and Ašmunikal, however, its contents are so directly linked to events of their reign that we are on safe ground if we call it Middle Hittite.

Let us briefly look at the prayer of Arnuwanda and Ašmunikal.[14]

The main subject is a lament about the ravages inflicted by the Gašga people upon the Hittite cult centers of the north. In order to underline the magnitude of this calamnity, the text begins with the assertion that nowhere else but in Hatti the gods used to receive this kind of careful worship. The text is exceptional in some respects: it follows no known pattern; it is almost pedantic in listing the areas plundered by the enemy: eighteen names beginning with Nerik, and in listing the objects taken and the personnel enslaved.

The text then turns to the present. Because the Gašgas have taken Nerik, the offering materials for the Stormgod of Nerik are now being sent to Hakmiš. The Gašgas are made to swear not to interfere with these trans-

---

[9] CTH 375.
[10] CTH 373.
[11] Philo H. J. Houwink ten Cate, *The Records of the Early Hittite Empire (C. 1450–1380 B.C.)*, Uitgaven van het Nederlands Hist.-Arch. Instituut te Istanbul 26 (1970), p. 5.
[12] Folke Josephson, *The Function of the Sentence Particles in Old and Middle Hittite* (Uppsala,1972), p. 46 f.
[13] O. Carruba, "Über historiographische und philologische Methode in der Hethitologie," *Orientalia* 40 (1971) 208–223; p. 222: ".... die Sprache dieses Textes [sc., the Kantuzzili prayer's] sich kaum von der der echten altheth. Texte mit altheth. Duktus unterscheidet ...."
[14] CTH 375.

ports, but they immediately break these oaths, so that the offerings do not reach the god. Here the tablet is broken. In some copies of the text there follow lists of Gašga towns with their rulers. The connection between these lists and the main text is lost. The lists could name such towns whose rules now pledged their support for the future, and this could be stated as part of the prayer just like the list of towns and objects afflicted, which we mentioned, and thus the list might serve the purpose of securing the sanction of the gods for the new oaths. However that may be, the greater part of the text, that is, almost the entire tablet of the main manuscript, can still safely be called a prayer.[15]

Turning now to the Kantuzzili prayer and its parallels, we find essentially three texts. One in which the praying person calls himself Kantuzzili; a second text in which he calls himself king, using only the title without a specific name; and in a third, it is "the Son of Mankind" who pronounces the prayer. These texts have been analyzed and compared with one another previously, but it will be useful to look at them again.

The best preserved text is that of the long composition which begins with a hymn to the Sungod followed by a personal prayer. This is the version in which the worshipper is called Son of Mankind. It is the most 'modernized' of the three versions. It is mainly represented by one fairly complete tablet which is full of erasures and corrections. I have asked myself whether this might have been a draft for the modernized version, but this remains a hypothesis. Most copies of this text are from the late Empire, but some of the fragments which have been taken as its duplicates contain variants which, as far as one can judge from so few examples, represent the older forms and probably belong to the older version, which calls the praying person "king".[16] This version contains more archaic features.[17] It also begins with the hymn to the Sungod and continues with a personal prayer, but the latter is shorter than in the Son-of-Man version. We shall see details later.

Finally, the Kantuzzili version[18] seems to have preserved even more of the old features. It exists in only one copy, a single-column tablet the beginning of which is lost. From the length of the missing part and from the

---

[15] The colophon of the newly published text KUB 48.107, which begins with such a list of towns with their rulers, reads: DUB.2KAM *PANI* DINGIR. MEŠ-*kan* GIM-*an anda memiš-kanzi ŠA* ᴰUTU ᵁᴿᵁ*Arinna QATI* "Second tablet (about) how they speak ... in the presence of the gods, pertaining to the Sungoddess of Arinna. (Text is) complete." The preverb *anda* with *memai-* in other contexts means "on that occasion, at that time, there-with". Does the colophon refer to what the Gašga rulers speak when the prayer is pronounced, or to what the Hittites pronounce in the presence of those rulers, viz., the prayer?

[16] This amounts to putting the fragments listed in CTH as 372 C and E rather under no. 374.

[17] CTH 374.

[18] CTH 373.

fact that the first preserved lines belong to the transition from the hymn to the personal prayer I concluded that it, too, must have started with the Sun hymn; whether it was exactly the same we cannot tell.

The structure of these compositions is similar to that of Babylonian prayers and of those of other cultures as well: a hymn of praise is followed by a transitional part leading to the prayer itself, which again may consist of several parts. In it the individual laments his ill fate and asks the gods for help and for blessing. Since the prayers here under discussion contain a number of individual Babylonian motifs we may safely assume that the overall plan also followed a Babylonian model.

The hymn of praise, addressed to the Sungod Ištanu, is best preserved in the Son-of-Man version. I shall shorten it here, picking out some of the most characteristic parts.[19]

> O Istanu, my lord,
> just lord of judgment,
> king of heaven and earth!
> You are ruling the lands,
> you are giving strength.
> You are a just god,
> you are having mercy.
> . . . . .
> O Ištanu, fully grown son of Ningal!
> Your beard is of lapis lazuli.
>
> . . . .
> O Ištanu, great king!
> Your father Enlil has put the four corners of the land
>   into your hand.
> You are the lord of judgment,
> and in the place of judgment there is no tiring of yours.
> Also among the Former Gods you, Ištanu, are mighty.
> You set the offerings for the gods,
> and you set the shares of the Former Gods.
> The door of the sky they open for you, Ištanu,
> and you pass through the gates of the sky.
>
> . . . .
> You are father and mother of the oppressed and the bereaved.
>
> . . . .
> The cause of the dog and the pig you decide,
> also the cause of the animals who do not speak with their
>   mouth, that, too, you decide,
> and the verdict of the bad and the evil person you give!
>
> . . . .
> The Four (draft animals) whom you, Ištanu, have harnessed,
> behold, the son of mankind has heaped up barley for them.

[19] CTH 372. For a full translation of the hymn see JAOS 78 (1958) 239–241.

So let your Four eat!
And while your Four eat the barley,
Live, o Ištanu!
Behold, the son of mankind, your servant, speaks a word to you
and listens to your word.
O Ištanu, mighty king!
You stride through the four eternal corners
(while) on your right the Fears are walking,
and on your left the Terrors are walking.
(a few lines later others are accompanying the god:)
Bunene, your vizier of the ri[ght], is walking on your right,
and Mīšaru, your vizier [of the left], is walking on your left,
and (thus) you, Ištanu, pass through the sky.

The next few lines are too fragmentary for translation. Before we go on let us pause.

What we just read are excerpts from a composition which can rightly be called a hymn to the Sungod. In his classification of prayers Laroche pointed out that the Hittites used the verb *walliya-* "to praise" when addressing a deity in this way. The verb is attested introducing hymns of praise, but—as far as we know—there is no noun "praise" or "hymn of praise" used for such compositions. Besides, all the texts preserved that can be classified as hymns have a foreign background; mostly Babylonian, but in one case, Hurrian. In the one just read, the Babylonian motifs are so obvious that I do not have to point them out. However, the composition as a whole is not found in Akkadian; it also contains details which are alien to Babylonian thought, such as the judgment over dogs, pigs, and mute animals, or the image of man feeding the animals of the Sungod's quadriga. It so happens that a small fragment of a bilingual, that is, Sumerian and Akkadian, hymn to Šamaš was found in Boğazköy and published years ago.[20] On the obverse, UTU/Šamaš himself is praised as *rē'i tenišēti* "shepherd of mankind", *dayyān nīši dašâti* "judge of the numerous people", etc., while the reverse lists his *sukullū* "viziers": [*kit*] *tum* "law" on the right, *mīšaru* "order of justice" on the left, Bunene, etc. This is not a verbatim model, obviously, but a welcome documentation of the scribes' familiarity with this kind of Babylonian literature.

Returning now to our Hittite prayers, the remaining words in the fragmentary next section of the Son-of-Mankind version show that it duplicates the first lines preserved in the Kantuzzili prayer. In both versions there follows the transition from the hymn to the personal prayer.

From here on I shall use the Kantuzzili text as basis.

[20] KUB. 4.11 (CTH 793), where obv. and rev. should be interchanged.

[Whichever(?)] god became excee[dingly(?)] angry,
that god has turned his eyes to another side
and does not permit Kantuzzili to act.
If that god is in the sky,
or if he is on the earth,
you, o Sungod, shall go to him.
Go, speak to that god
and transmit to him the words of Kantuzzili.

This, then, was the purpose of the hymn to the Sungod! There follows a first
prayer of Kantuzzili to his personal god:

O my god,
ever since my mother gave birth to me
you, my god, have been bringing me up.
My name and my reputation are you, my god;
you, my god, have put me among good people.
In a strength-giving place you, my god, have entrusted
    action to me.
My god, you have called Kantuzzili the servant of your
    body and your soul.
The guidance of my god which I have not known since
    childhood, I experience [now(?)].
. . . .
Never did I swear by my god
and never did I break an oath.
What, (being) sacred to my god, was not right for me
    to eat,
that I never ate,
and I did not (thereby) make my body unclean.
I never separated an ox from the pen,
I never separated a sheep from the fold.
When I found bread, I never ate it by myself,
when I found water, I never drank it by myself.

In the last section just read, Professor Lambert recognized a parallel to one
of the incantations called dingir.šà.dibba "incantation for appeasing an
angry god", which he reconstructed from Late Assyrian and Late Babylonian tablets. So the author of this Hittite text used Babylonian models not
only for the hymn but also for the personal prayer (in this case, of course,
older versions of Lambert's text).[21]

I cannot readily translate the whole text of Kantuzzili. Let me briefly
mention that he complains of his illness and asks the god to reveal to him the

---

[21] See W. G. Lambert, "Dingir.šà.dib.ba Incantations", JNES 33 (1974) 267–322, with an
appendix: "Hittite Parallels", by H. G. Güterbock, pp. 323–327; see esp. pp. 278 f. (lines
80–84) and 288 f.

cause of his anger. Thus, the purpose of the prayer is indeed that of the Babylonian incantations. Kantuzzili then turns to the Sungod again:

> O Ištanu, you are the shepherd of all,
> and your message is sweet to everyone.
> The god who was angry at me and rejected me,
> let him consider me again and make me well!
> . . . .

A few lines later a new section reads:

> O Ištanu, my lord!
> Behold, I, Kantuzzili, am [beseeching] my god,
> (so) let my god hear me!
> What have I, Kantuzzili, ever done to my god?
> And in what have I sinned?
> My god, you made me
> you created me.
> But now, what have I, Kantuzzili, done to you?
> The merchant, a man, holds the scales in plain sunlight
>   but falsifies the scales;
> (but I), what have I done to my god?
> Now my house, because of sickness, has become
>   a house of anxiety,
> and from anxiety my soul is dripping away!

This section again is a parallel to part of the Akkadian incantation.[22] The continuation mainly stresses the misery which the sickness has caused. The end of the prayer is lost in the Kantuzzili version; the Son of Mankind version concludes with the following verses:

> Just as I was born from the womb of my mother,
> o my god, put that same soul back into me!
> Let your soul, my god, become for me the soul of
>   my mother, father, and family!

Just as the hymnic part makes free use of individual Babylonian motifs, so also the personal prayer. As a whole the text is not a translation. The text of the Kantuzzili prayer contains some passages that are still not understood. But even a cursory reading of Goetze's translations[23] conveys the impression of a vivid, in parts even touching, document of personal piety.

The hymnic part of this composition had its own history, to which we shall now turn.

The scribes of king Muršili II, the son of Šuppiluliuma, composed a very intricate prayer to the Sungoddess of Arinna, the chief goddess of the

---

[22] Ibidem, esp. lines 71–77 on p. 278 f., and p. 288 f.
[23] ANET, p. 400 f.

kingdom. This prayer was edited and analyzed by Professor Gurney many years ago.[24] The first part of the prayer was called by him "Invocation". It begins like this (according to a parallel published later):[25]

> O Sungoddess of Arinna!
> King Muršili, your servant, sent me (saying)
> "Go and speak to my lady, the Sungoddess of Arinna!
> I shall entreat the Sungoddess of Arinna, the goddess
>   of my person."

The goddess is then asked to return from wherever she may be and to listen to the prayer. In a section reminiscent of the prayer of Arnuwanda and Ašmunikal, but not identical with it, she is reminded of the fact that she receives proper worship only in Hatti.

The next section is a hymn. Its first six verses run as follows:

> You, Sungoddess of Arinna, are a honored deity!
> Your name is honored among names,
> your godhead is honored among godheads.
> Among the gods You are honored,
> great are you, Sungoddess of Arinna!
> And no other god is more honored or greater than you!

The next line reads:

> You are the lord of just judgment.

Obviously this is a quote from the Sun hymn translated above, though with an interesting change in the syntax: the adjective "just" is here in the genetive, to go with "judgment", not in the nominative, with "lord", as there. Also the next 23 lines are taken from the Sun hymn. The scribe did not even change the word "lord" into "lady" (EN into NIN or GAŠAN), but he did omit a few of the epithets of the male god, like the address "grown-up son of Ningal", the reference to his lapislazuli beard and to the fact that his father Enlil gave him the four corners of the universe. Also, the space available in the break is too short for restoring the entire Ištanu hymn. Obviously other traits of the male Sungod must have also been omitted in the missing part.

A newly found fragment restores the transition from the hymn to the prayer:[26]

---

[24] O. R. Gurney, "Hittite Prayers of Mursili II", *Annals of Archaeology and Anthropology* 27 (Liverpool, 1940), esp. his text C = KUB 24.3 (CTH 376, A)

[25] KUB 36.80 (CTH 376, E).

[26] Field number 544/u (found in 1962), recognized by H. Otten, unpublished, but listed in CTH under 376, A.

> The person at whom the gods are a[ngry]
> and whom they reject,
> you, Sungoddess of Arinna, [take care of him].
> Now bestow blessing upon Muršili, the king,
> and [take] king Muršili, your servant, by the hand.
> Lend your ear to the [words] which king Muršili speaks to you
> and listen to them!

The specific prayer which these words introduce is a Plague Prayer. A brief explanation of the term may be in place.

One epidemic which afflicted the Hittite lands has been known for a long time. It was brought into the country by the Egyptian captives which Šuppiluliuma had taken in the war he fought against Egypt in order to revenge the murder of his son. The most beautiful of Muršili's prayers were written in order to end this scourge.

But the plague prayer that concerns us at this point is quite different. As I said it is part of a long composition. The same plague prayer also exists independently, as a tablet of its own in several copies, and that version has all the characteristics of the Middle Hittite language.[27] In the composite text of Muršili its wording was 'modernized'. The older version contains no royal name. As stated above, Middle Hittite was used no later than the reign of Šuppiluliuma; with Muršili standard New Hittite came into use. Besides, the epidemic is not the only subject of this prayer. We read:

> From one side the plague oppressed it (sc. the country),
> from the other side the enemies oppressed it.
> The independent countries which are around it,
> the land of the Hurrians, Kizzuwatna, and Arzawa,
> they all were hostile.
>   . . . .
> And these regions of the land of Hatti:
> The land of the Gašga—they are swineherds and linen weavers—
> the lands of Arawanna, Kalašma, Lukka, and Pidašša,
> they freed themselves . . . .
> and abolished the tributes and attacked Hatti.
>   . . . .

As Houwink ten Cate pointed out[28] this fits the situation at the time before Šuppiluliuma, so that the historical allusions of the text point to the same period as its language. Obviously, then, an epidemic occurred already at that time.

When Muršili came to the throne, he found the pestilence introduced from

---

[27] See Houwink ten Cate, op.cit. (above, n. 11), pp. 5 and 8–21, where the text is referred to as "283 C".
[28] Ibid. p. 68 f.

Egypt continuing since his father Šuppiluliuma's days and a political situation not unlike the one alluded to in the older prayer, although not all the countries are the same. His scribe took the old prayer, modernized the language, and only omitted Kizzuwatna, which at that time was no longer an independent country, but did not change the names of the local enemies.

After the invocation, the hymn to the Sungoddess, the prayer about the pestilence and the enemy attacks there follows, in this composition, first a section in which the goddess is asked to inflict the illness on the enemies, and a final prayer for blessing.

Muršili's writers went still further. His Daily Prayer to Telibinu has a similar composition: invocation, hymn of praise, and prayer for blessing. Large portions are exact parallels to the composite prayer to the Sungoddess of Arinna, but this composition does not include a section concerned with the epidemic, and the hymn is different. According to the size of the lacuna it must have been much shorter, and there is no reason for restoring any of the solar traits here. When these prayers first became known, it seemed that all parts were equally addressed to both Telibinu and the Sungoddess. But already Gurney in his edition of these prayers had noted the difference in length and kept the Telibinu and the Sungoddess versions apart, and now we know that the old assumption was wrong. Unfortunately, because this section was mechanically reproduced from the first edition, even the latest printing of Pritchard's Ancient Near Eastern Texts still retains the old error.[29]

Among other prayers of Muršili let me mention only one that begins with an invocation of the Sungoddess of Arinna duplicating that found in the composite prayer just discussed.[30] Unfortunately most of the tablet is lost, but in the preserved part of the fourth column the king is concerned about the relation of his wife, Gaššuliyawiya, to the dowager queen. This is another example of the free use of existing prayer sections.

The Plague Prayers of Muršili are well known and free of such borrowings. In the context of this lecture I shall therefore leave them out even though the best of them is a beautiful piece of religious writing. I shall also omit the prayers of Muršili's successors, Muwatalli and the couple Hattušili and Puduhepa, although their prayers are important in their own right. But they are available and have been discussed in literature. Of interest in our investigation of the use of older material in later compositions I only have to mention the fact that Muwatalli included a very short hymn to the Sungod in the large composite prayer.[31] Here the god is addressed as shepherd of

---

[29] ANET, p. 396 f., "Hymn" on p. 397.
[30] KUB 36.81 (CTH 376, F); cf. Güterbock, JAOS 78 (1958) 244.
[31] KUB 6.45 (CTH 381) iii 13–17 with dupl.; cf. E. Tenner, "Zwei hethitische Sonnenlieder", *Kleinasiatische Forschungen* 1 (1930) 387–392, esp. p. 390.

mankind and said to rise from the sea and to judge man, dog, swine and the beasts of the fields. The sources are evident, but these few lines are all that is left of them.

We may now return to our problem of determining the date of the various texts.

If we start from Muršili's big composite prayer to the Sungoddess of Arinna, we already found that the part which deals with the plague is taken from a text which exists by itself and reflects the political situation of an earlier time. The wording is almost the same, but there are enough archaic spellings in the model text to justify its determination as Middle Hittite by Houwink ten Cate.

A comparison of the hymnic part of Muršili's prayer with the Sun hymn reveals greater differences. For one, in the many nominal sentences with the second person pronoun as subject (of the type "You are the judge" etc.) Muršili's text consistently uses the enclitic particle -*za*, the Sun hymn never: neither in the Son-of-Man nor in the King version. H. A. Hoffner observed that the consistent use of the particle in such sentences is an innovation of the New Hittite language.[32] Muršili's version also adds connective particles where the older hymn has asyndesis. DINGIR-*LIM*-*iš* (*šiuniš*) replacing DINGIR-*uš* (*šiuš*) is a case in point, and so is the dative of the personal pronoun, -*ta*, replacing the possessive pronoun, *tiš*, "thine". In a few places where the King version differs from the Son-of-Mankind version, Muršili goes with the former, i.e., as far as we have seen, with the older. Occasionally this results in the preservation of an older form. Thus, e.g., he writes the middle form *šarriškitta* instead of the active *šarreškiši* of the Son-of-Mankind text.

As for the manuscripts of the three versions of these prayers, inspection of the originals in the summer of 1977 showed that the Son-of-Mankind version exists in New Hittite manuscripts only; Kantuzzili's prayer is in Middle Hittite script, and so is also the King version. Also those fragments which I wanted to shirt shift from the Son-of-Mankind to the King version (above p. 130 n. 16) are in Middle Hittite script.

On the whole one gains the impression that the differences between Muršili's composition and its Vorlagen are greater in the hymn than in the plague section. In the latter they mostly concern spelling; in the former, on the other hand, they concern syntax, morphology, and vocabulary. Since most of these pecularities are also found in Old Hittite, the view of those scholars who attribute the original hymn to the Old Hittite period gains in probability.

In the prayer of Kantuzzili the hymn, as we saw, is not preserved. Of its remaining parts the obverse, containing the transitional section and the first

---

[32] H. A. Hoffner, "On the Use of Hittite -*za* in Nominal Sentences", JNES 28 (1969) 225–230.

personal prayer, is paralleled only by the Son-of-Man text. The variants, as expected, show the Kantuzzili text to be older. For a large part of the reverse with the second personal prayer, all three versions exist. There are considerable discrepancies. Some of them are quite enigmatic, partly because of loss of text in one or the other version, but partly also because of our ignorance. Occasionally one is tempted to suspect that some scribe misunderstood what he copied. It is not easy to decide whether the King version or the Kantuzzili prayer represents the older wording, since both contain a mixture of older and younger features. Occasionally the Son-of-Man version preserves an older form than the other two, and in one place all three have *mān* in a context where I can only understand it as conditional, not temporal, a use of this conjunction which is definitely young—Middle Hittite at the earliest. Obviously none of the existing manuscripts is even close to the archetype, and therefore we may take this use of *mān* as an innovation common to all three texts rather than as indication of Middle Hittite origin.

To sum up, I am inclined to go along with those scholars who consider all three versions as ultimately going back to Old Hittite originals although the actual manuscripts are later. And if this is true it means that the Babylonian prototypes must have existed at least as early as the late part of the Old Babylonian period.

Nogle hovedtræk af det danske sprogs udvikling i middelalderen

Av Kristian Hald

Professor i nordiske sprog
Københavns universitet, Danmark

Som bekendt er dansk det af de nordiske sprog, der i middelalderen undergår de største forandringer både med hensyn til lydforhold, bøjning og ordforråd. I det følgende må jeg begrænse mig til sprogets lydlige ændringer i middelalderen og inden for dette område til nogen af de vigtigste ændringer, nemlig dem, der har bidraget mest til at fjerne middelalderlig dansk fra de andre nordiske middelaldersprog. Som de vigtigste ændringer betragter jeg udvikligen af de tryksvage vokaler og udviklingen, den såkaldte svækkelse, af de oprindelige spiranter og klusiler.

De forandringer, jeg taler om, begynder tidligt i middelalderen, og de sparsomme kilder gør det vanskeligt at følge udvikligen i detailler, både geografisk og kronologisk. Bortset fra håndskriftet B 74 af Skånske lov, der dateres til c. 1250, begynder håndskrifter på gammeldansk først at optræde omkring år 1300 på et tidspunkt, da udviklingen på nogle af de punkter, jeg har nævnt, allerede var vidt fremskredet eller afsluttet – i alt fald i nogle af de danske dialekter.

Til supplering af det sparsomme håndskriftmateriale har vi de tidligt-middelalderlige runeindskrifter, men de er desværre få og de fleste af dem yderst kortfattede. Mere givende er det store materiale af sted- og personnavne i latinske kilder, Necrologier, diplomer osv. (diplomer på folkesproget tilhører jo i Danmark en senere periode). Ved hjælp af dette sprogstof kan man belyse vigtige sider af sprogets udvikling i tiden mellem den egentlige runestensperiode og de ældste gammeldanske håndskrifters tid. Dette materiale er også benyttet i betydeligt omfang, fx i Brøndum-Nielsens store Gammeldansk Grammatik, men man kan ikke sige, at det endnu er fuldt udnyttet. Og man har nok heller ikke helt udnyttet de moderne dialekters muligheder for belysning af ældre perioders sprogforhold.

Det er en almindelig opfattelse, at af de danske hoveddialekter står skånsk på det ældste, mest oprindelige trin, mens jysk har fjernet sig længst fra oldsproget, og sjællandsk og de andre danske ømål indtager en mellemstilling. Dette gælder, hvad enten man betragter sproget i de gamle tekster eller ser på forholdene i de moderne dialekter. Taget i meget grove træk er denne opfattelse også rigtig, men det er dog ikke sådan, at fx alle jyske dialekter på alle punkter står på et yngre trin end de skånske.

Ser vi på udviklingen af de gamle infortisvokaler, er det tydeligt, at skånsk på dette punkt stort set står på et ældre trin end ømål og jysk. I de fleste skånske dialekter er infortisvokalen -a bevaret, mens vokalerne -i og -u er svækket; -a er også retableret i de tilfælde, hvor vokalen i middelalderen var svækket som følge af fænomener som vokalharmoni og vokalbalance.

Vokalharmoni kan i Skåne konstateres i det ældste danske, latinsprogede diplom, Knud den Helliges gavebrev till Lunds domkirke 1085. Brevet er tabt, men dets oprindelige tekst kan med næsten fuld sikkerhed rekonstrueres på grundlag af de bevarede afskrifter, dels i Necrologium Lundense, ifl. Weibull fra 1123, dels i Lundebogen 1494. Vi kan i gavebrevet se, at infortisvokalen -i er svækket til -e efter vokalharmoniske regler. Dativformer af stednavne på -høgh ender på -e: scialshoge, flatoige, hildeshoge. Derimod er dativendelsen bevaret som -i ved efterled med a og y i rodstavelsen: byurstingarythi, upaccri (formerne efter necrologiet).

Sandsynligvis indeholder afskriften i necrologiet også et indirekte vidnesbyrd om vokalharmoni ved infortisvokalen -u, hvor vokalharmoni ellers først kan konstateres betydelig senere i skånske kilder. Lundebogen skriver a thurgislo, hvor necrologiet har a thurgislu. Brøndum-Nielsen mener i Gammeldansk Grammatik § 446 anm. 1, at endelsen i thurgislu "maa forklares som analogisk bestemt efter den ret omfattende Gruppe af Kvindenavne af Typen Gunnuru". Dette synes dog lidet sandsynligt. Forklaringen er sandsynligvis den, at Lundebogen her, som i andre tilfælde, har bevaret originalens form, som da er at opfatte som en regulær latinsk ablativ. Skriveren af necrologiet har ikke været opmærksom på, at thurgislo er en latinsk bøjningsform, men ændrer ud fra sin vokalharmoniske fornemmelse o til u efter vokalen i rodstavelsen. På svækkelse af infortisvokalen -a er der ingen eksempler i gavebrevet.[1]

I de ældre sjællandske tekster er hovedreglen den, at de oprindelige infortisvokaler er faldet sammen i en midttungevokal, der normalt skrives æ, men der er dog i disse tekster eksempler på, at den oprindelige infortisvokal er bevaret, ganske særlig oprindeligt -a, hvad der stemmer godt med forholdene i skånsk. Endnu i en tekst som Roskildebispens jordebog fra c. 1370 kan man finde adskillige eksempler paa infortisvokalen -a.[2] I moderne sjællandsk er vokalen blevet en [ə]-lyd, der dog fakultativt kan vær e apokoperet.

Videst fremskredet er udviklingen i jysk, idet man her i meget stor

---

[1] Om rekonstruktionen af gavebrevet og dets sprogform se Acta Philologica bd. 21 p. 105 ff.
[2] Kousgård Sørensen i Ti Afhandlinger (= Navnestudier udg. af Stednavneudvalget nr. 2). p. 234 ff.

udstrækning har fået apokope; sporadisk viser apokopen sig i oprindelige tostavelsesformer allere de i de ældste jyske lovhåndskrifter fra c. 1300 (sald for saldi osv.). Særlig udbredt er den i det danske håndskrift af Flensborg stadsret fra begyndelsen af 14. årh. I de jyske, tidligt-middelalderlige rune-indskrifter er der ingen sikre exempler på apokope. Pjedsted-kisten (Danmarks Runeindskrifter nr. 38) har ganske vist garþ for *gærþæ, men dens indskrift lader sig desværre ikke datere nærmere. Derimod er der i de jyske runeindskrifter eksempler på vokalsvækkelse: -æ for -a, -e eller -æ for oprindeligt -i. Hvis man tør drage slutninger af det spinkle materiale, ser det ud, som om nordjysk står på et ældre trin, nærmere skånsk, end de sydjyske dialekter. I alt fald har de nordjyske indskrifter ingen eksempler på svækkel-se af -a, derimod svækkelse af -i i stedsadverbiet hæræ, der må forudsætte et ældre *hæri.[3]

Apokopen i oprindelige tostavelsesformer anses med rette for et af de mest karakteristiske træk ved de moderne jyske dialekter; den er så væsent-lig, at Skautrup i Det danske sprogs historie under omtalen af infor-tissvækkelsen kan skrive, att denne "når sit højdepunkt i jysk, hvor den resulterer i svind af enhver tryksvag vokal". Som den fremragende kender af de jyske dialekter ved forfatteren naturligvis, at denne påstand er en sandhed med modifikation, i alt fald hvad de østjyske dialekter angår. En undtagelse fra reglen om apokopen er, at infortisvokalen -i er bevaret i østjysk i ikke helt ringe udstrækning. Det mest kendte eksempel er de forholdsvis talrige jyske personnavne, hvis nominativs-i er bevaret til nuti-den; læsere af Blicher vil have stødt på navne som Øvli og Visti.

Aage Hansen gør i 1. bind af sin bog om "Den lydlige udvikling i dansk" med rette opmærksom på, at forudsætningen for det bevarede -i i jyske personnavne er den særlige rolle, som nominativen spiller ved betegnelser for levende væsener i modsætning til andre substantiver. Han henviser bl. a. til, at to af de tre substantiver, der har bevaret deres nom.-r i gamle skånske lovhåndskrifter: þiuvær, nithær og kostær er personbetegnelser. Når nom.–i i de nævnte personnavne har kunnet holde sig til nutiden i jysk, beror det paa det forhold, at en stor del af dem synes at være oprindelige tilnavne. Ikke få af dem har gemineret konsonant, et indicium for, at de (delvis) er hypokoristiske dannelser med kælende eller nedsættende betydning. I-et er blevet betydningsbærende, dels som bærer af den hypokoristiske betydning, dels som angivelse af, at det drejer sig om masculine væsener; -i skulde med andre ord ifl. Aage Hansen være blevet et produktivt suffiks til brug ved dannelsen af hypokoristiske personbetegnelser.

At nogle af disse personnavne på -i virkelig er gamle hypokoristika er der ingen tvivl om, men det gælder også mange andre kortformer af person-

---

[3] Jfr. Glda. Gramm. § 191.

navne, og på adskillige kan forklaringen ikke anvendes. Navne som Amdi og Visti, der stadig bruges i jysk, er således gamle sammensætninger (*Āmundi, Wīsæti). Det vilde vel også være påfaldende, om -i, hvis det var blevet til et særligt hypokoristisk suffiks, kun var bevaret i Jylland.

Det bevarede -i i jyske personnavne må sammenstilles med en række andre eksempler på bevaret -i i østjyske dialekter, både i substantiver, der er oprindelige an-stammer, og andre ordformer. Det østjyske stednavn Agri er et af eksemplerne. Den simple forklaring på navnet er, at det er ordet ager med bevaret dativ-endelse; der synes ganske vist ikke at være andre, sikre eksempler på, at dativ-sing. endelsen er bevaret i jyske stednavne, men det er værd at bemærke, at også dativ-plur. endelsen -um er sjælden i jyske bebyggelsesnavne. Ordet helvede, oprindelige hælwiti, en neutral ia-stamme hedder helledig, hølledig med bevaret -i i store dele af Jylland; Hølledig forekommer også som gårdnavn. Kollektivdannelser til primære trænavne som æspi til asp har bevaret i-et i adskillige jyske stednavne, og på samme måde optræder en kollektivdannelse med et andet suffiks som æmti til alm med bevaret -i (*almiþia>*ælmti>æmti). Trænavnet ene, vn. einir, har i en Djurslands-dialekt formen [*jæni-*] i sammensætningen enebær. En verbalstemme med bevaret i indgår i sammensætningen østjysk [*bræninal*] "brændenælde". Adv. el. adj. ene optræder som [*jæni-*] i sammensætningen [*'jænibow'*] "enebo". Adv. oppe, gammelda. uppi, kan have formen [*åbi*] i Djurslandsmål.

Det bevarede -i i visse jyske personnavne og de andre eksempler fra moderne jyske dialekter kan kun skyldes, at infortisvokalen i i det jyske dialektområde – eller store dele deraf – har været bevaret uden svækkelse fra de ældste tider. At området for bevaret -i tidligere har været større end i nutiden fremgår af, at de sønderjyske skattemandtal fra 16. årh. har talrige eksempler på -i i personnavne, der i moderne sønderjysk ender på [-ð]. Der er altså i nyere tid sket en svækkelse af vokalen, men den har ikke ført til apokope.

De jyske dialekter eller en del af dem står, som man ser, på det her omtalte punkt på et ældre trin end skånsk og afviger således fra hovedreglen om skånskens større oprindelighed. Når bevaret -i trods alt er undtagelsen i jysk – bortset fra personnavne – beror det på analogi fra andre kasusformer af ordet. De masculine an-stammer – stadig med undtagelse af personnavnene samt visse dyrenavne – ender ikke på -i i moderne jyske dialekter, men har vokalsvækkelse og apokope, og det skyldes, at de moderne former ikke udgår fra nom., men fra obl. kasus, hvis -a i jysk svækkes og apokoperes.

Vi skal derefter se på behandlingen af spiranterne og de utstemte klusiler i gammeldansk. For spiranternes vedkommende må vi dog indskrænke os til en enkelt, den palatale eller gutturale spirant, der i håndskriftsproget normalt skrives gh. Udvikligen af den labiodentale eller tidligere bilabiale spirant er af ortografiske grunde yderst vanskelig at følge, og hvad den dentale spirant angår, så tilhører overgangen til halvvokal stort set middelalderens slutning, og bortfald af spiranten eller overgang til t tilsløres i høj grad af traditionel ortografi.

Den spirant, vi beskæftiger os med, går i hovedsagen over til halvvokalerne i og u på et tidligt tidspunkt, sådan at vi først og fremmest får overgang til i efter fortungevokal og overgang til u efter bagtungevokal, regler der dog ikke er uden undtagelser. Det ældste eksempel på overgang af spiranten til i er ifl. Gammeldansk Grammatik og Skautrups sproghistorie navnet Farþein i en møntindskrift fra slutningen af 1000-tallet. Dette eksempel kan man dog formentlig se bort fra. Farþein er som så mange former i møntindskrifterne udtryk for engelsk påvirkning. Møntprægerne har i stor udstrækning været englændere, og det nordiske personnavn Farþein kendes, bl. a. fra engelske mønter netop i formen Farþein. Det ældste sikre eksempel på den nævnte overgang er navneformen Malmøi for oprindeligt Malmhøgh i slutningen af præbendelisten i Necrologium Lundense: denne del af listen må tilhøre tiden omkring eller lidt efter 1170. De ovenfor citerede navne på -høgh i gavebrevet 1085: Flatoige, scialshoge, hildeshoge viser ikke spor af overgangen, idet oi i flatoige betegner ø-lyden. Det må dog bemærkes, at det sidste navn i præbendelisten c. 1123 har formen fletogy (nu Flädie), hvor den omlydte vokal i forleddet sandsynligvis skyldes udviklingen til halvvokal i efterleddet, selv om denne overgang ikke er kommet til udtryk i skriften. Overgangen af spiranten til halvvokal efter ø i skånsk skulde, hvis denne opfattelse holder stik, kunne dateres til tiden mellem 1085 og 1123 eller med et rundt tal c. 1100. I stillingen efter a, hvor spiranten også går over til i i en del af det skånske dialektområde, er det ældste eksempel på overgangen vistnok navneformen Ain bech i Termini Balluncslef 1241. Den ældste grænsebeskrivelse fra tiden lige efter 1200 har endnu Agnbæc.

Saxo har enkelte eksempler på overgangen til halvvokal efter fortungevokal, men ingen i det danske navnestof. Et af eksemplerne er Eidora eller Eydorus ''Ejderen''. Det er et oprindeligt Egidora, som navnet skrives i de frankiske annaler under året 808, og skrivemåden Ei-, Ey- er udtryk for den oldsaksiske udvikling af forbindelsen ægi foran dental konsonant; jfr. de talrige tyske personnavne af typen Reinhart. På overgang til halvvokalen u efter a har Saxo et eksempel i Pariserudgaven 1514, nemlig det norrøne personnavn Suibdauus. Da det middelalderlige Lassenske fragment har -dauus og Jyske Krønike, der bygger på Saxo, har -danus ved en almindelig fejllæsning af u som n, er der ingen tvivl om formens autenticitet. Et lidt yngre eksempel på overgangen findes i navnet øxnechou i et originalt pavebrev fra 1228, fremdraget af Marius Kristensen i en lille afhandling

"Om vokalisering af ældre dansk gh" i Da. Stud. 1929. Sorøbogens afskrift af pavebrevet har desuden en form biaforthon af et navn, der ikke længere kan læses i orginalen. Det er det nuværende Bjæverskov, og biaforthon er formodentlig en fejllæsning af originalens *biafor(s)chou med glemt s og let forståelige fejllæsninger af c som t og u som n; diplomet har således rummet endnu et eksempel på overgang af spirant til halvvokal i ordet skov.

I jysk, specielt i sønderjysk, er spiranten bevaret længere end i de andre hoveddialekter. Et meget tidligt eksempel på overgang af spiranten til halvvokal har vi dog vistnok i et jysk personnavn, der skrives Aucti i en sønderjysk kilde fra 13. årh. Her kan vi ikke direkte iagttage overgangen, men det er klart, at vi ikke i det 13. årh. kan have en diftong, der er bevaret fra olddansk tid. Au synes at måtte forudsætte et ældre *agh, hvor spiranten er gået over til halvvokal. Navnet må antages at være en sammensætning, der i Danmarks gamle Personnavne sammenstilles med formen Augute i Reichenaulisten (fra tidlig middelalder); personnavneordbogen citerer også en form Aughuty i et diplom 1302, der dog kun er kendt fra en afskrift. Det må antages, at der foreligger et oprindeligt *Aghguti, hvor den særlig tidlige overgang af gh til halvvokal er betinget af u-et i efterleddet. M. h. t. k (c) i Aucti beror det på overgang af g til ustemt konsonant foran t, efter at u-et i -guti er synkoperet. At overgangen til halvvokal i dette tilfælde er særdeles gammel turde fremgå af, at der i østjyske kilder fra 1400-tallet optræder et sjældent personnavn, der må være et ældre *Ø̄kti; at det drejer sig om et nordisk navn fremgår af det bevarede nom. -i. Forholdet mellem de to navneformer Aucti og Øyti, ældre *Ø̄kti må forklares på den måde, at overgangen til halvvokal i forleddet Agh- er så gammel, at den nyudviklede au-diftong i nogle dele af det jyske sprogområde, men ikke i andre, er kommet med i den gammeldanske monoftongering. Men udvikligen af Agh-er, som nævnt, er særtilfælde beroende på u-et i efterleddet.[4]

Et vidnesbyrd om at spiranten i sønderjysk – bortset fra det specielle tilfælde Aucti – er bevaret længere end i de andre dialekter, er den lydlukning af foregående vokal (o og ø), der kan konstateres i kilderne. Langt o optræder således som u i adskillige stednavne (el. tilnavne der er oprindelige stednavne). Eksempler er bl. a. Kylnæscugh i Ribe Oldemoder 1291. Østerskugh i Åbenrå latinske stadsret 1335 og Ymdropskugh i et originaldiplom udstedt i Ribe 1343. Mærkeligt er det, at spiranten har været bevaret i det allersydligste danske område i subst. høj. I et kirkeregnskab fra Siseby sogn i Svans fra c. 1603 optræder flere danske højnavne i skriveformen -huch. Ingen af dem er bevaret til nutiden, men endnu i vore dage har nedertyske udtaleformer af andre navne på Høj-, -høj i Svans formen [hyx] med bevaret spirant. At overgang af spiranten til halvvokal overhovedet er

---

[4] Om Aucti se Dialektstudier I (1964–65) p. 215 ff.

sen i jysk fremgår også af, at en stærkt dialektpræget tekst som Flensborg stadsret ingen eksempler har (bortset fra nægtelsen ei). Vi ser altså, at mens den nævnte udvikling – i det mindste i stillingen i udlyd efter ø – har kunnet konstateres i Skåne allerede i det 12. årh., har spiranten været bevaret i det allersydlige danske område så længe dansk sprog overhovedet blev talt i disse egne.[5]

M. h. t. behandlingen af de ustemte klusiler, hvis såkaldte svækkelse er den allermest markante forskel på dansk og svensk sprog i middelalderen, så har både Skautrup og Brøndum-Nielsen i de ovfr. nævnte værker sammenstillet en række eksempler på overgang til media eller videreudvikling til spirant. Ikke alle disse eksempler er dog lige relevante. Adskillige fra Pariserudgaven af Saxo kan skyldes senere afskrivere, og andre er ikke udtryk for normal klusilsvækkelse, men for assimilation med en følgende stemt konsonant, et forhold man også kan finde eksempler på i fornsvensk.

Det ældste, man kunde sige: regulære, eksempel på dansk klusilsvækkelse turde være navnet Westerwigh i Liber Daticus Lundensis fra c. 1225; navnet skrives også -wigh i Valdemars jordebog. Formen citeres i Gammelda. Gramm., hvor Brøndum-Nielsen mener, at den mere eller mindre tryksvage stilling af efterleddet kan være årsag til de tidlige svækkelse. Der findes muligvis i LibDat et endnu ældre eksempel på svækkelse af k, nemlig Blegunc fra sidste tredjedel af 12. årh., men man kan ikke se bort fra, at der her kan være tale om en simpel skrivefejl, ombytning af bogstaverne g og c. Et tredje eksempel Glumstenswig o. 1190, som citeres i Gammelda. Gramm. efter Diplomatarium Svecanum, beror på en misforståelse. Der er i virkeligheden ikke tale om et originaldiplom, som man skulde tro efter Gammelda. Gramm., men om en afskrift i Esrumbogen fra c. 1500, der har formen -wigh. Efterleddet er næppe subst. vig, men gammelda. with, idet den samme hallandske lokalitet i Esrumbogen også kaldes Glumstenskogh. Efterleddet -with i orig. er læst som -wich, og Esrumbogens skriver har da opfattet det som vig og anvendt sin samtids skrivemåde af dette ord. Det eneste eksempel fra det omfattende navnestof i diplomerne fra 12. årh. i Esrumbogen, der eventuelt kunde komme på tale som udtryk for klusilsvækkelse, er Nadebec, der i Danmarks Stednavne II 38 er tolket af et plantenavn identisk med svensk nata "Stellaria media". Tolkningen er imidlertid ikke sikker, idet d også kan stå for dd; der er adskillige eksempler på, at konsonantlængden ikke betegnes i de gamle kilder. Der foreligger da andre etymologiske muligheder; jfr. vn. naddr "pil", i svensk Naddö brugt om en lille odde. Desværre er navnet Nadebec ikke bevaret til nutiden.

Et andet tidligt eksempel på klusilsvækkelse foruden Westerwigh er vistnok tilnavnet Løytenes i et originalt diplom, udstedt af biskoppen i Slesvig

---

[5] Kopenhagener germanistische Studien I 278 ff.

1267. Tilnavnet er identisk med det nordslesvigske stednavn Løjtnæs, en sammensætning med sognenavnet Løjt, der formentlig er et ældre *Løktæ (en afledning med t-suffiks til plantenavnet løg). Formen Løyte- kan sammenlignes med, at adj. tøkær hedder tøycht i neutr. i Flensborg stadsret, der ellers ikke har eksempler på klusilsvækkelse. Lydforbindelsen -kt- indtager, som man kan se af de moderne dialekter, en særstilling, idet den går over til jt eller wt, hvad der forudsætter tidlig overgang af klusilen til spirant med videreudvikling til halvvokal. Løytenes må altså betragtes som et særtilfælde.

Da Saxos navneformer har spillet en stor rolle i diskussionen om klusilsvækkelse, må de omtales særskilt. Hvis vi holder os til Pariserudgaven 1514, er der adskillige eksempler på, at der faktisk skrives b d g for etymologisk p t k. Udgaven har bl. a. personnavnet Sprageleg, af vn. Sprakaleggr, men Jyske Krønike, der går tilbage til Saxo, har formen Spracaleg, der må være den ægte saxoniske form. Et andet eksempel er Herwig (sål. to gange i Pariserudg., Olrik-Ræder p. 199). På det tilsvarende sted har den tyske historiker Krantz, hvis tekst går direkte tilbage til det håndskrift, der var forlæg for udgaven 1514, Heruyck, hvad der tyder på, at hs. har haft en form med c eller k. Rolf Krakes tilnavn skrives Krage, og Saxo oplyser, at det kommer af det danske ord krage = truncus. I de latinske kongerækker, der er trykt i Scriptores minores og som delvis bygger på Saxo, skrives navnet Crake, der er den etymologisk korrekte form og utvivlsomt den, der har stået i Saxos manuskript. På samme måde må bedømmes Saxos form Lothbrog overfor kongerækkernes former Lothbrok, Lothbroki. Et eksempel på svækket klusil, der ikke er grund til at mistænke for at skyldes en senere afskriver, er Suibdagerus = vn. Svipdagr, der forekommer flere gange i Saxos 1. bog. I 5. bog forekommer navnet i den ovfr. omtalte form Suibdauus. Det til Suibdagerus i 1. bog svarende navn skrives med b både i Jyske Krønike og hos Krantz, og b-formen må derfor antages at gå tilbage til Saxo selv. Et andet eksempel fra 1. bog er Gudlandia i Pariserudgaven, som Olrik-Ræder med tvivlsom ret ændrer til Gutlandia (Gotland), den form, der anvendes i de historiske afsnit af værket. Compendiet har her Guthlandia, Krantz Gothlandia. Sammenfattende kan det siges, at de eksempler på klusilsvækkelse, der må antages at være ægte saxoniske, er udtryk for overgang til stemt klusil under indflydelse af en følgende stemt konsonant.

Nogle sjællandske diplomer fra tiden mellem 1272 og 1728 indeholder enkelte eksempler på svækket k: subst. wrag og stednavnene Schienswyt Maglæ, Ølsy Maglæ og Egbyworæ,[6]. Det er måske ikke tilfældigt, at eksemplerne viser svækkelse af oprindeligt k, idet denne konsonant ifl.

---

[6] Ti Afhandlinger p. 158.

Brøndum-Nielsens analyse af litterære tekster er den af klusilerne, der først er udsat for svækkelse. Iøvrigt kan formerne Maglæ og Egby- opfattes på samme måde som de ovfr. nævnte former fra Saxo. Det må også nævnes, at et par tidlige eksempler på klusilsvækkelse næppe, som antaget, er udtryk for dansk sprogudvikling. Det ene er ordet wigbyld "jurisdiktionsområde", det tyske weichbild. Det forekommer i et brev udstedt af Valdemar Sejr i 1216 til borgerne i Lybæk. Da der er tale om Lybæks iustitia "jurisdiktion", som kaldes wigbyld, kan ordet næppe betragtes som et låneord i dansk. Normalt skrives ordet med k i nedertyske kilder, men kan også have en form med g ((Schiller-Lübben har sammensætningen wigbel(d)e recht fra Kiel)). Et andet gammelt eksempel på et sammensætningsled, der ligesom wig- i wigbyld går tilbage til latin vicus, er stednavnet Brunsuig i et diplom fra 1228. Navneformen, det nuværende Braunschweig, turde høre hjemme i den tyske sproghistorie.

Til slut skal omtales et par eksempler på at former, der tilsyneladende er eksempler på klusilsvækkelse, i virkeligheden er udtryk for, at der ikke kan være tale om en almindelig svækkelse af de ustemte klusiler. Et af eksemplerne er stednavnet Egelev på Falster, der i det såkaldte hovedstykke i Valdemars jordebog, den kan dateres til midten af 13. årh., skrives Eklef; det er sammensat med trænavnet eg. I den lidt yngre Falsterliste i jordebogen skrives navnet dels Eglef, dels Ægglef. Disse former er udtryk for assimilation af k til g foran l, men da man ikke før den almindelige klusilsvækkelse kan have stemt, kort klusil i stavelsesudlyd, må den stemte klusil realiseres som lang, og længden betegnes i den ene af Falsterlistens skrivemåder tilligemed forkortelsen og lydåbningen af vokalen foran den forlængede konsonant. En parallel til udviklingen i Egelev har vi vistnok i det nordjyske herredsnavn Skodborg, Valdemars jordebog Skodburgheret, Ribe Oldemoder c. 1325 Skoddburg. Den mest tilfredsstillende forklaring på dette navn får man, om man antager, at det er identisk med et andet Skodborg, navn på et gammelt kongeligt slot ved et vigtigt overgangssted over Kongeåen på grænsen mellem Nørre- og Sønderjylland. Efter slottet havde åen oprindelig navnet Skodborg Å, og dette navn er velkendt i islandske kilder som Skotborgará, der viser, at navnet har gammelt t i l. led. Under forudsætning af navnenes identitet, har vi da i det nordjyske navn det samme forhold som i Egelev. Den ustemte klusil bliver stemt foran den stemte konsonant, og den stemte klusil må ved assimilationen blive lang, således som det fremgår af skrivemåden i Ribe Oldemoder.

Hvis den opfattelse er rigtig, som her er gjort gældende om udviklingen i navnene Egelev og Skodborg, en opfattelse, som i alt fald har den fordel, at den giver en simpel forklaring på navnenes forled, betyder det, at man må være varsom med at betragte løsrevne skrivemåder med henholdsvis g og d som udtryk for normal svækkelse af k og t. De kan tværtimod, som i disse navne, være et indicium for, at en almindelig svækkelse af de ustemte klusiler endnu ikke var indtrådt i det 13. årh.[7]

Selvom der i tekster allerede fra det 13. årh. er nogle få regulære eksempler på svækkelse af klusilerne, tør man ikke tage dem som udtryk for, at klusilsvækkelsen har været gennemført i talesproget, og at det er skriftsprogets konservatisme der gør, at den så sjældent markeres i skriften. Den gennemførte klusilsvækkelse er nok et relativt sent fænomen, og der har, som både de middelalderlige tekster og de moderne dialekter viser, været tale om store geografiske forskelle. Det er også tydeligt, at klusilerne ikke følges ad i udviklingen, men om dette indviklede forhold må jeg her nøjes med at henvise til fremstillingen i Gammeldansk Grammatik.

Betragter man eksemplerne på spirant- og klusilsvækkelse under eet, må man, selv om materialet er spinkelt, komme til det resultat, at spirantsvækkelsen, specielt i skånsk, er det ældste af de to fænomener og ikke afhængig af klusilsvækkelsen. At der ikke behøver at være nogen sammenhæng mellem spirant- og klusiludvikligen, kan man se af forholdet i engelsk. Vi har der en tidlig spirantovergang svarende til den danske: day, law, men ikke klusilsvækkelse: take, gate. Det er derfor vanskeligt at se de nævnte processer under et fælles synspunkt, nemlig som resultatet af en forskydning af stavelsernes accentforhold, et middelalderligt sidestykke til den trykforskydning, der fremkaldte den urnordiske synkope. De ændrede trykforhold, hvorved de stærkest betonede stavelser får yderligere tryk og de svagere betonede stavelser yderligere svækkes, resulterer ifl. Skautrup ikke alene i svækkelsen af infortisvokalerne, men det svagere tryk på endevokalen i ord af typen taka gør det vanskeligt at fastholde en ustemt skarp klusil ved overgangen til den tryksvage stavelse. Den foregående vokals stemthed overføres da på konsonanten og gør den stemt, og de stemte mediæ går som regel videre til spiranter. Vil man derefter undgå et sammenfald mellem de oprindelige ustemte klusiler og de oprindelige spiranter, må spirantrækken forskydes. Denne betragtning forudsætter altså, at klusilsvækkelsen er ældre end spirantovergangene, hvad der, som det fremgår af det foregående, næppe er tilfældet.

Hvad det kronologiske forhold mellem svækkelsen af infortisvokalerne og spirantovergangene angår, synes der, specielt i Jylland, ikke at være nogen sammenhæng, hverken kronologisk eller geografisk, og den ene af infortisvokalerne, nemlig i, må i stor udstrækning have været bevaret langt ned i tiden uden svækkelse og er tildels endnu bevaret i de jyske dialekter. Det resultat, jeg kommer til ved en undersøgelse af de gamle kilder før de gammaeldanske håndskrifters tid og sammenligning med de moderne dialekter er, at de væsentlige sproglige forandringer, jeg har talt om, er meget

---

[7] Om Egelev og Skodborg se Studia Septentrionalia (= Festskr. Ole Widding) p. 249 ff.

komplicerede processer med store geografiske og kronologiske forskelle, som det ikke er muligt at finde en fælles årsag til.

Det er måske lidt utilfredsstillende at komme til dette negative resultat, men det stemmer vel egentlig ganske godt med, at vi heller ikke kan give en dybere psykologisk forklaring på disse sproglige processer. N. M. Petersen mener i sin sproghistorie, at "Sprogets bestandig større og stærkere Overgang til Blødhed", som han siger, kunde være "en Følge af Almuens undertrykte og forkuede Forfatning". Skautrup indvender heroverfor, at vigtige ændringer i det danske sprog finder sted i en storhedstid (Valdemarstiden) med store kulturelle fremskridt, og det kan man i alt fald hævde med fuldt så stor ret.

Jeg tror, at den dybereliggende psykologiske årsag til spontane lydovergange unddrager sig vor erkendelse. Man må, for atter at citere N. M. Petersen, forfatteren af den første nordiske sproghistorie, nøjes med at henvise til "Tiden, som ikke tillader nogen jordisk Form at bestaae i sin oprindelige Tilstand".

Lear: a Tragedy with a Difference; and Shakespeare's Tragicomedies or Romances

By Jeremiah J. Hogan

Professor of English
Formerly President of University College
Dublin, Ireland

I call *Lear* a tragedy with a difference because, unlike Shakespeare's other tragedies, it has something rather close to a happy ending. In *Ham., Oth., Macb.* normality is restored, happiness will again be possible; but it is remote and there is none or very little of it for the chief actors and sufferers. In *Lear* there is more.

I do not know of any critic taking this view. Bradley however approached it. He declared his wish (*Sh. Tr.* 252) that *Lear* had ended happily, adding that the wish was not just the human desire that unhappiness be avoided, but a critical or aesthetic wish; he thought that dramatic logic called here for a happy ending. He added that Shakespeare would probably have ended *Lear* happily a few years later "in the days of *Cymb.* and *W. T.*" But the change to *Cymb.* and *W. T.,* and to *Per.* and *Temp.* which Bradley does not mention, could hardly come without some preparation. As I see it, *Lear* itself contained, or was, a large part of that preparation; so that the romances are not a fully independent group but in a considerable degree repetitions of something already done in *Lear*. *Lear* contains their formula, to complete which it was necessary to limit the tragic beginning, and to increase the final consolation or joy—which *Lear* had already, I believe, presented in a degree far beyond the other tragedies. Having written *Lear*, Shakespeare could later do the tragicomedies with ease and swiftness, almost as holiday work.

Let us examine the places in *Lear* showing *happiness*, of a kind and degree not found in the other great tragedies, which prepares for and leads towards *Lear*'s (as I think) unique conclusion.

First and chief is Act 4 sc. 7, one of the most joyful scenes in Shakespeare.—Cordelia has not seen her father since he disowned her; she has come home to defend him, but he has refused, through shame, to meet her. The Doctor opens the inner-stage curtain, revealing Lear asleep on a chair, and says to Cordelia *Please you draw near*. Cordelia goes up to her father:

Cord. O my dear father!—Restoration, hang
Thy medicine on my lips, and let this kiss
Repair those violent harms that my two sisters
Have in thy reverence made. . . . . .
Had you not been their father, these white flakes
Did challenge pity of them.
. . . .
                           Mine enemy's dog,
Though he had bit me, should have stood that night
Against my fire; and wast thou fain, poor father,
To hovel thee with swine and rogues forlorn
In short and musty straw? Alack, alack,
'Tis wonder that thy life and wits at once
Had not concluded all.—
He wakes, speak to him.
Doctor. Madam, do you, 'tis fittest.
Cord. How does my royal lord? how fares your majesty?
Lear. You do me wrong to take me out o' th' grave:
Thou art a soul in bliss, but I am bound
Upon a wheel of fire, that mine own tears
Do scald like molten lead.
Cord.   Sir, do you know me?
Lear. You are a spirit I know.—Where did you die?
Cord. Still, still far wide.
Doct. He's scarce awake, let him alone a while.
Lear. Where have I been? Where am I?—Fair day light?
I am mightily abus'd; I should e'en die with pity
To see another thus.—I know not what to say;
I will not swear these are my hands; let's see;
I feel this pin prick.—Would I were assur'd
Of my condition.
Cord.   O look upon me sir,
And hold your hands in benediction o'er me.—
No sir, you must not kneel.
Lear.   Pray do not mock me.
I am a very foolish fond old man
Fourscore and upward, not an hour more nor less;
And to deal plainly,
I fear I am not in my perfect mind.
Me thinks I should know you, and know this man,
Yet I am doubtful; for I am mainly ignorant
What place this is, and all the skill I have
Remembers not these garments; nor I know not
Where I did lodge last night.—Do not laugh at me,
For as I am a man, I think this lady
To be my child Cordelia.
Cord.   And so I am.
Lear. Be your tears wet? Yes faith. I pray you weep not.
If you have poison for me I will drink it;
I know you do not love me, for your sisters

Have, as I do remember, done me wrong;
You have some cause, they have not.
Cord.   No cause, no cause.
. . . .
Cord. Will't please your highness walk?
Lear.   You must bear with me;
Pray now forget and forgive, I am old and foolish.

Some say this happiness is utterly destroyed, engulfed by what follows in
Act 5, and even that its destruction deepens the play's unhappiness. I do not
agree. 5.3.197, though far more closely environed with danger than 4.7, is,
for Lear anyhow, not less happy:

Cord. Shall we not see these daughters and these sisters?
Lear. No, no; no, no: come let's away to prison:
We two alone will sing like birds i' the cage;
When thou dost ask me blessing, I'll kneel down
And ask of thee forgiveness: so we'll live,
And pray, and sing, and tell old tales, and laugh
At gilded butterflies, and hear poor rogues
Talk of court news; and we'll talk with them too,
Who loses and who wins, who's in, who's out;
And take upon's the mystery of things
As if we were God's spies; and we'll wear out,
In a wall'd prison, packs and sects of great ones
That ebb and flow by the moon.

Gloster's death is reported, 5.3.179–99, by Edgar. Having learned the truth
and been reconciled to Edgar, Gloster dies happily—*his flaw'd heart
. . . 'Twixt two extremes of passion, joy and grief, Burst smilingly.* This is
capital for the interpretation of Lear's final moments, still to come; Gloster's fortunes have run parallel to Lear's, so that when Gloster dies happily
we may well expect Lear to do so too.

Lear enters, 5.3.254, bearing Cordelia's body—he has killed the hangman
and cut the rope, but too late to save her. At one moment, 256–8, he knows
she is dead, at the next, 258–60, he thinks he was in time and that she lives.
And at 307, having once more concluded her dead, he looks yet again, and
cries:

Do you see this? Look on her! Look her lips,
Look there, look there.

—adding in a moment *Break heart, I prithee break,* and dying.

What is meant by *Look on her! Look her lips?* The second *Look* means
"see", "Look at her, see her lips", so much is undisputed. But what does he
see and ask the others to see? Bradley (291) holds that, though Cordelia is

dead, Lear thinks he sees her lips move, showing that she is alive, and dies from the joy of this error. But to die from the joy of a mistake is surely unsatisfying as the end of such a story. Others hold that he dies of grief, from a true conviction that she is dead, which the pallor of her lips proves to him. That pallor of lips may indicate death is of course true; and Shakespeare alludes to this, *W. T.*, 3.2.206, *R. & J.*, 4.6.99, 5.3.96. But Lear has already indicated that he belives her dead 265–8; further proof of it could hardly be so great a surprise or shock to him. *Do you see this* suggests, not another, needless affirmation that she is dead, but some new idea—and to be new it must contradict the earlier affirmation that she is *dead as earth*. I believe that what he points to is not the colour of the lips, but their expression, a smile which indicates that death is overcome, and that she lives in a better world, where he may in a moment join her. If this is right, Lear dies of joy, seeing on Cordelia's lips the marks of salvation.

One fairly recent critic says Lear cannot die of joy "because there is no joy in this play". This is simply to beg the question—and to ignore 4.7 and the opening of 5.3. There is necessarily this difference between the end of *Lear* and the ends of the soon-following tragicomedies—that as *Lear* is a tragedy, though with differences which enable it to be the spring and source of the tragicomedies, its final happiness must be death—but a death that conquers sorrow.

The tragicomedies or Romances, *Cymb.*, *W. T.*, *Pericles*, *Temp.*, follow the Tragedies in time, and are in considerable measure derived from one of them, *Lear*. Why should *Lear* be followed by, and to some extent *produce* these four plays, when no later plays arose from *Ham.*, *Oth.*, *Macb.?* If *Lear* had been the last of the tragedies in date, as well as containing more of incidental happiness than any of the others, the answer would be fairly simple—the full tragic inspiration was spent when *Lear* was written, but a return to romantic comedy was out of the question, leaving tragicomedy or romance, tentatively begun in *Lear,* as the fresh field. But in fact it seems that four tragedies, *A. & C.*, *Macbeth*, *Timon*, *Coriolanus*, were written after *Lear* and before the tragicomedies. Shakespeare must, when all these were written, have harked back to *Lear,* the one of them differing most from the others, to develop from parts of it his latest plays.

I shall not give any account of the tragicomedies except in their relationship to *Lear*. All are delightful, representing an Indian Summer of the poet, who handled them easily, rapidly, and at times carelessly.

(*i.*) These plays are often called Romances, as they are not closely bound to realistic probability, each being *like an old tale*. The persons are led by beneficent Fortune, or by Providence (*Temp.* 1.2.132), breaking the ordinary logic of cause and effect, from trouble, and the danger of greater trouble, to perfect security and happiness; the price paid for the *miracle* is amends by the old, who have caused or contributed to the unhappiness and danger; the young contribute innocence, good will, capacity for joy.

(ii.) The persons are of two generations, parents and lately grown up children (Lear, we remember, is the only hero of any of Shakespeare's major tragedies who has children). The parents and the children may be separated by quarrel or by mischance. Action covers a long time—in *Per.*, 15 years pass between 3.4 and 4.1, in *W. T.*, 16 years between Acts 3 and 4—allowing the infants or young children of the opening Acts of these plays to grow up. In *Temp.* unity of time is kept, but narration sends us back to earlier, near-tragic action *twelve year since* (1.2.53). *Cymb.* is exceptional in covering a much shorter range of time than the others, but perhaps its variety and range of travel make up for this.

(iii.) Wide stretches of travel correspond to the long range of time; Sicilia, Bohemia, Wales, Naples, Prospero's isle, Rome.

(iv.) The harmony of music accompanies and assists the "miracle" (as in *Lear*, 4.7.25); *W. T.* 5.3.98, *Cymb.* 5.4.30–92. *Temp.* 5.1, *Per.* 5.1.233.

(v.) There is in most of these plays delay in full realisation of the unhoped-for joy, with half-recognition of the dear ones—might they not be *simulacra* only? In some there is painfulness in the progress to full realisation. In all, children then kneel for the blessing of parents from whom they have been sundered.

(vi.) Fresh garments are put on for these scenes of reunion and new life—and Pericles shaves after 14 years (5.3.73).

Abbreviations

Ham. — Hamlet	*Per.* — Pericles
Oth. — Othello	*Temp.* — The Tempest
Macb. — Macbeth	*Cord.* — Cordelia
Sh. Tr. — Shakespearean Tragedy	*Glo.* — Gloster
Cymb. — Cymbeline	*R. & J.* — Romeo and Juliet
W. T. — The Winter's Tale	*A. & C.* — Antony and Cleopatra

Individual Responsibility Within A New Technological Framework

By Margaret Mead

Curator Emeritus
The American Museum of Natural History
New York, USA

(retrospective summary of speech delivered without
a text at Uppsala University, September 1977)

Throughout recorded history and within every known type of human community of every technological level, there has been a close relationship between the character structure that children develop in the course of their socialization and the functioning of the hamlet, tribe, monarchy, empire, or nation state within which they live. Neither the most coercive and tyrannical government nor the most gently persuasive has ever been able to function without depending on an answering resonance in the character of the people, whether this be an abject fear of torture, a willingness to die for a cherished local identity, or a veniality which will accept a materialistic trade-off in return for support of government policy.

However, the relationship between the cultural character of a people and governments has become more complex, as societies have become larger and have divided in the subcultural versions of class and caste, region, religious denomination and occupation and as the extent to which individuals assume any responsibility for the whole has steadily eroded. In the modern nation state, national institutions like the draft army, national taxes, national political parties and national news media have provided a superficial veneer of common purpose and commitment. While early empires had to depend upon very imperfect methods of moulding conquered or absorbed populations into some semblance of consensus, the rapid growth of the new technologies of communication have put at the disposal of national, transnational, multinational and international bodies, increasing means of providing the basis for some kind of consensus. But side by side with these new methods of wielding great populations together, the importance of local ties has remained strong enough to present serious challenges to many previously well consolidated nation states, as well as newly consolidated ones like the large African states or India.

Under existing conditions, the ways in which individuals' loyalties to the groups of various sizes to which they feel allegiance are combined with the wider appeals of globally distributed media messages, is of vital importance. What kind of citizenship can we hope to develop within the present trend towards ever larger economic units as giant corporations, giant trade unions, giant extractive and manufacturing centers develop around the world, as enormous housing complexes obscure all possibility of localized responsibilities, and as decisions made in distant grain markets and chancelleries affect the fate of farmers half a world away? I believe it can be demonstrated that there is a strong relationship between the scale of residence, work, recreational, artistic and religious activities and the capacity of individuals to assume and carry out responsible action. Unless there is such a tie between the way a street or bridge is maintained, crops are planted or land left fallow, or a finished manufactured product is inspected, the conflict between the lack of individual responsibility and the increasingly exacting technological requirements for precision and responsibility will pose greater risks to the entire system. It becomes urgent that new kinds of ties be forged between the primary and local groups, about which we now know how allegience and commitment are forged, and the tremendous gigantic network within which the peoples of the world are now living but are not yet related with responsibility and loyalty.

The earlier types of societies which preceded our current global interdependancy were able to link the experience of the infant in the family, the child in the neighborhood, the resident in the town and region, and the relationship to the most superordinate power in ascending order. The loyalties of the smallest group were congruent, if not isomorphic, with the loyalties to each larger group and could be called on for action when action at high levels was needed in the face of catastrophe and war. Today, the nuclear family has been cut out of its support system of relatives and neighbors so that children grow up with great anxiety about the permanence of their only supports and refuge and with no sense of responsibility for a wider group. This opens the way for a tenuous artificial tie between the remote ideals of the new nation state and the longings and fears of early childhood and provides few exercises in responsibility. Individuals move from a precarious over-dependance on too small a family, to a series of more and more remote and impersonal sets of relationships, to the parts of the system within which almost every detail of their lives are determined: what food they will be able to eat, what dwellings they will live in, what occupations they can follow, and how the largest group to which they owe their allegiance—still often very small and weak—will fare on the world scene.

These current conditions are primarily due to changes which have occurred so rapidly, as with the electronic revolution, that the necessary social infra-structure has not been created either by the usual long term adjustments to change, or by those who have attempted to apply conscious but fragmented planning to the world scene. While the development of simulation by computer has enormously enhanced our capacity to treat the world system as a *world problematique*—a cluster of a cluster of problems—we are still at the beginning of dealing with it as a total system. Any proposed solution to any of the multiple problems that beset humankind today must however, if we are to take another step forward in taking charge of our own evolution, be conceived of as part of a single whole.

The change in scale, of size of units, and numbers of people and items has come about through a technology that has favored large scale enterprises. I believe that we are now entering a new phase in which several important changes in the organization of a global society will make possible, if not necessarily dictate, a new set of relationships between social units of different sizes.

The new technological framework within which new relationships can be formed depends upon the shift, from the ground to the air, of the social arena on which human life has been played out throughout history and partly upon the recognition that energy must be conserved. The preponderant importance of the air for wayfare, communication, and transportation makes obsolete the old geographic boundaries where men stood on frontiers to protect their women, children, and the alters of their gods. There are no defensible boundaries in the air, either against pollution or nuclear, biological, or chemical warfare. Each nation state endangers its own people, as well as its neighbors, whenever it fails to protect them from the consequences of their own air-borne dangers. The defense for any people is to give up the idea of defensible boundaries and turn earnestly inward to protect their own populations from air-borne disasters. This should lead to a softening of the preoccupation with frontiers and a reduction of the importance of a bounded unit in developing loyalty and responsibility for the whole.

In the past, the units of principal loyalty have been those bordered most rigidly between insider and outsider, citizen and alien, predator and prey, human and less than human. The units that were bounded have varied; today the lines around the nuclear family are too strong, identification with neighborhoods and communities is weak, sub-national units of ethnic diversity are becoming too strong, the lines around the nation state which permit any nation to claim allegiance for the purpose of destroying other nation states are too rigid and prevent responsibility for the merging global community. With a recognition of the shared dependance upon and danger from the air, a greater emphasis on neighborhood and community and less on ethnic autarchy and national allegiance, these relationships can be changed so that the trust and dedication learned in childhood can be progressively extended to larger and larger units.

We could not however expect this to occur without a corresponding shift away from the large scale technological basis of economic life. Fortunately the energy crisis can be expected to force, later if not sooner, a decentralization that is congruent with the new sources of energy—solar, wind, and diathermal. With technological development on the side of localization and the new relationships based on vulnerability to and dependance on the air, we should be able to work towards a hierarchical sense of loyalty, allegiance and responsibility adequate to the awesome tasks ahead of us.

Deir el Bahari

By Kazimierz Michałowski

Academician, Professor of
Mediterranean Archaeology,
University of Warsaw, Poland

The term Deir el Bahari for the valley, lying on the west bank of the Nile directly opposite Luxor, is an interchangeable one applied for a long time and up to the present, to designate the Temple of Hatshepsut which stands there. The ruins of this temple, were built into a Coptic monastery near the end of the Antique Period and the name Deir el Bahari, which in Arabic means the Northern Monastery, derives from this. Deir el Bahari had already been the subject of Champollion's and his great successor Lepsius' investigations in the first half of the 19th century. In any case, the name Deir el Bahari appeared for the first time during the thirties of the last century and was employed by Wilkinson in his work "The Topography of Thebes", London 1835. Prior to this, the definitions Assasif Monastery or the Assasif Temple were used, designations which are still to be found in Lepsius' work.

The first work of excavating the temple was performed by Belzoni and later, in the middle of the last century, A. Mariette conducted some investigatory works there. Near the end of the 19th century, the mud-brick walls, the remains of the Coptic monastery, were dismantled and removed from the temple. This operation was performed too hastily and in fact we do not possess any precise documentation of this Coptic monument. The Coptic constructions were removed by E. Naville, who excavated the northern part of the temple in 1894–98 and it was thanks to this that Naville was able to elaborate his 6-volume monumental work "The Temple of Deir el Bahari". He was also the first to investigate the parts of this temple lying to the north of its axis which had earlier been covered with rubble and Christian buildings.

Hatshepsut's temple had been partially rebuilt many times in antiquity and had suffered damage from the huge boulders which were precipitated from the gebel above it during earthquakes. One such disaster during the XX Dynasty times damaged not only the queen's temple, but also that of Mentuhotep and the temple of Tuthmosis III discovered and explored by us in 1962–68. The damage caused must have been extensive, since this sacral-sepulchral complex was abandoned as unsuitable for cult ceremonies.

Only parts of the building were still accessible while among the ruins of the temple from the times of the XXI to the XXVI Dynasties, there spread a necropolis for the priests and priestesses of Amon and the god Mont.

And it was not until the Ptolemaic times that the temple was cleared of ruins and adapted for the new cults of Imhotep, the builder of the stepped pyramid of king Djeser, and Amenhotep, the son of Hapu, the famous architect of the pharaoh Amenhotep III. The shrine of the new gods, cut into the rock behind the old sanctuary of the Hatshepsut Temple, derives from the times of Ptolemy IX Eurgetes II. The latest graffiti of the Greek pilgrims originate from the II century A. D. Then, there must have been another earthquake which caused further destruction and the next epoch was the one during which the ruin was converted into the Coptic monastery referred to above.

At the beginning of the 20th century, American Egyptologists from the Metropolitan Museum, New York, and above all, H. Winlock and A. Lansing conducted extensive investigations within the area of the temple ruins and in front of them. In the thirties of this century, on the other hand, E. Baraize, who was at that time the Director of the Technical Works of the Service des Antiquités, was comissioned to perform some reconstructional works in the temple. These works, however, were not always performed accurately, for although Baraize was an excellent restorer and architect who did much to preserve the antiquities of Upper Egypt, he, himself, was not an Egyptologist, and was not always able to seek the advice of experts, although whenever the opportunity to do so arose, he did approach such outstanding Egyptologists as Lacau, Legrain and Drioton for assistance. These direct contacts, however, did not prevent him from committing several errors, such as for instance, positioning blocks bearing reliefs or inscriptions on them in the wrong places etc.

The entire question of partially reconstructing this architectural jewel of the New Kingdom, has led to an anastylosis of the building from the thousands of decorated blocks and block fragments which had been tentatively put in order in front of the temple and on its terraces by Naville and his successors.

However, the correct classifying of this material, the matching of fragments belonging to one another, is an enormous task which can only be accomplished by Egyptologists working in close co-operation with architects who are qualified for the restoration of antiquities. Some of the block connections can be established correctly only with the help and close co-operation of these two groups of experts. Apart from this there remains another immeasurably complicated, and extremely work-absorbing task, that of comparative investigations and research work.

The re-erection of walls, columns, pillars and architravers is partially carried out in new stone originating from the very same quarry as the original building material of the temple. The new stone is used together with the authentic decorated or inscribed stone blocks which will have to be re-laid in their correct places and height in the walls.

How very difficult and involved this task is, can be evidenced by the fact that a year ago we had to dismantle the south wall of the Upper Court which had been falsely reconstructed by our predecessors so that it could be given a more authentic appearance with the newly discovered original material and in accordance with the block connections.

When I say that we had to do this, I am taking it for granted that it is known that from 1961, the Polish Centre of Mediterranean Archaeology in Cairo on the initiative of the Egyptian Ministery of Culture, has been carrying out revalorization work on this temple for a number of years with the assistance of a group of specialists from the Polish State Ateliers for the Conservation of Historical Monuments. The revalorization of the temple, which has been in course for over 15 years, has produced some visible results, and so for instance after comprehensive investigations, the appearance of the Upper Terrace of the temple, although this is still a ruin, is quite unlike its appearance of twenty years ago.

The first target for reconstruction was the so-called Ptolemaic portico and wall with the niches because it was for this that we had first been successful in selecting and accumulating a considerable quantity of new material from among the blocks lying on the terraces of the temple. This wall had to be completely rebuilt. Far-reaching changes have also been made to the Upper Portico, known as the Osiride Portico, preceding the terrace. Thanks to the reconstruction of the exterior pillars on which the Osiride statues had once stood, and the interior columns of this portico, we were able to consider the possibility of putting a partial roofing on this object, and this changed the entire appearance of the temple auguring a third level of light and shade as an optical effect emphasizing the Lower and Middle Porticoes. The reconstruction of the pillars and columns both in this portico and in the Hypo-style, is, quite obviously, an extremely complicated undertaking.

However, the basic change to this multi-plan façade occurred after we had discovered the rock ledge above the Upper Terrace and had rebuilt the protective wall which covered the cliff face from the wall with the niches up to the level of the ledge. The discovery of this ledge was of basic importance and not only for the recreation of the authentic appearance of this object. We had established that Senmut, the builder of the queen's temple, had already envisaged the threat to the building in the form of stones and fragments of rock falling from the top of the gebel behind it. In his project this ledge cut in the cliff, 9 m wide and about 65 m long, had a low balustrade along its edge towards the back of the temple and this sufficed to contain the smaller pieces of falling rock and to protect the building in normal circumstances. The soundings performed by us on the so-called Mentuhotep Temple (new discoveries have implied that this building may be a treasury, Per—Hedj, and not a temple), permit it to be stated that this building also had a protective ledge of the same type above it. So it seems reasonable to suppose that Senmut, the queen's architect, must have taken this as his model.

During our excavations of the ledge above Mentuhotep's temple, there was one find which was particularly noteworthy. It was a wig-maker's workshop where we discovered the following items: four alabaster vases containing semifinished products for the making of wigs, human hair, bone hairpins adorned with ebony, cornelian bead necklaces, two flint knives, a bronze burin, and substance for glueing, dyeing and perfuming wigs. This is a magnificent find which provides us with fresh information concerning wig-making techniques in ancient Egypt. The most interesting element, apart from the alabaster pitchers, is the wooden model of a human head bearing scratched measures concerning the making of wigs on it.

This is, if I am not mistaken, the only discovery of this kind and one that is unique. This entire workshop must have originated from the end of the Second Intermediate Period or the beginning of the XVIII Dynasty and has remained there, where we found it, from the time it had been concealed during the turbulent days of that period. Among the smaller finds we made within the areas of the temple, worthy of note is the ostrakon bearing the name of Senmut. Furthermore, a statue of him was also discovered in the ruins of the Temple of Tuthmosis III and Mr. Marek Marciniak has devoted a separate study to this, entitled "Une nouvelle statue de Senenmout récemment découverte à Deir el-Bahari", Bulletin de l'Institut Français d'Archéologie Orientale, vol. LXIII 1965. While we are on the subject, it is worth reflecting on the fact that a votive statue of Senmut was discovered in the Temple of Tuthmosis III, which was built after the death of the famous architect.

The real work of reconstruction has to be preceded by prolonged archaeological studies, a few of which now in course should be mentioned. Thus the wall of the Vestibule before the Court with the altar has a highly important text concerning the cult of sun on it, J. Karkowski, Studies on the Decoration of the Eastern Wall of the Vestibule of Re-Horakthty in Hatshepsut's Temple at Deir el-Bahari, Et. et Trav. IX (1976). Studies on the north wall of the Upper Court have led to the correcting of the many erroneous opinions of the scenes represented there. This was achieved thanks to the discovery of many new blocks deriving from this very wall. Furthermore investigations on the Ptolemaic Sanctuary are still in course and investigatory work on the Upper and Lower Porticoes, which had been incorrectly reconstructed by our predecessors, have been going on for many seasons. We have also undertaken investigations on the shrines of Anubis and Hathor and the rate of these investigatory works can be illustrated by the fact that articles dealing with a summing up of some stages of the work of reconstruction (some preliminary reports are appearing mainly in the PKZ Information Bulletin and Etudes et Travaux) are quite often out-of-date before they appear in print because the finding of new block connections and new material brought about a change in the initial reconstructional conceptions.

When I arrived at Deir el Bahari in 1961 to organize our Mission, which was to perform the architectural revalorization of the Temple of Queen Hatshepsut, and was deliberating over the programme of works in this area, I arrived at the following conclusion: Obviously, the reconstructional work for a partial anastylosis of the inscribed and decorated blocks alone would initially entail investigatory-documentary work and, above all, the putting into thematic order of the thousands of whole blocks and block fragments originating from this temple. My attention was attracted by a quite wide mound of rubble and stones lying between the temples of Hatshepsut and Mentuhotep which had fallen from the cliffs of the Gebel. It seemed reasonable to assume that in this mound of rubble there might still be concealed some of the blocks from the Temple of Hatshepsut which had fallen there during an earthquake. I therefore gave instructions to the effect that, apart from the work of classifying and searching for block connections, preparing the masonry for a partial reconstruction of the so called Osiride Portico, we should immediately begin clearing the above-mentioned mound of rubble employing the same procedure as we would when performing routine excavatory work. The real work began in the winter season of 1961–62 and within a short time after this, we discovered a temple of Tuthmosis III, unknown up to this time, which is undoubtedly one of the most important discoveries of Polish archaeologists.

The finding of an unknown royal temple in an area which for tens of years has been the subject of the investigations and excavations of many expeditions, is in itself an unexpected fact which had aroused justifiable astonishment, since the areas of Deir el Bahari and Assasif are so pitted and scarred with holes that they are slightly reminiscent of the battle-field of Verdun after the First World War. What is more, the lower part of the ramp and the monumental road leading to the temple we discovered, had long been found. However, nobody had connected these elements characteristic for Deir el Bahari with the building we had just discovered.

After the completion of the Metropolitan Museum Expedition's excavations in the thirties, Egyptologists basically had all the details concerning the existence of this temple, for not only the parts of the ramp, the road leading up to it, but also the Hathor shrine, fragments of columns, architraves, corniches, and even reliefs from the walls, if they had been thoroughly studied, would have clearly indicated that they originated from a large edifice and not a small pavilion as had been assumed. The crowning evidence of the existence of this building was the group of ostraca which mentioned that a construction of such importance that the supervision of the work was assigned to the Vizier Rekhmire was built within the course of a number of years.

However, in all honesty, it should be said that even we, ourselves, after we had excavated the first elements of the temple in situ, did not realize what all these indications inferred. Mrs. Lipińska, who participated in all the excavatory campaigns and was responsible for one of them, in her book "Deir el Bahari II. The Temple of Tuthmosis III. Architecture", Warsaw 1977, made an attempt at reconstructing the original appearance of this object. Up to then, it had been thought that in the valley of Deir el Bahari, situated on the west bank of the Nile directly opposite the Temple of Amon at Karnak, the principal element was the Temple of Hatshepsut. It now appears that Tuthmosis in erecting his temple at a higher level than Senmut's building, had taken over the central place in the entire architectonic lay-out of the buildings of the valley. The erecting of this temple, which was called Djeser Akhet, meaning "Holy of Horizon" was initiated in the 42nd year of the reign of Tuthmosis III probably simultaneously with the "dishonouring" of Hatshepsut and the erasure of the queen's name at Karnak.

If the reason really was to "dishonour" the queen. We can now have some doubts after the excellent study by a pupil of my friend professor Säve-Söderbergh. I think of the book of Gun Björkman "Kings at Karnak". As it is commonly accepted, Tuthmosis III did not like his aunt and stepmother Hatshepsut, so then, when the proud, clever young ruler came to the throne to rule independently, he began to thoroughly erase every trace of his aunt's name. This above all entailed the hammering out of her names on the buildings she had erected at Karnak and Deir el Bahari. But anyhow the fact is that the ruler decided that his edifice should predominate over Senmut's edifice for the queen. However, there was not much space between the Temple of Hatshepsut and that of Mentuhotpe so the builders of Tuthmosis III levelled the cliff and artificially extended this space by cutting into the rock on the north and the west sides.

As the platform thus made was narrow and irregular in shape, it was extended by the building of strong supporting walls to the east and south, and filling this frame with a mass of taffle, rubble, boulders and rocks. The building of this temple was prolonged and Tuthmosis III died before it was completed. According to what Mrs. Lipińska states in her book, the names of Amon were erased during the "Amarna Period" and then reconstructed. It is not quite certain whether this temple was a mortuary temple, since, as it is known, Tuthmosis III possessed a mortuary temple at Gurna. There were cases of course, when rulers had two funerary temples, but one thing is certain and that is that the god worshipped here was Amon in both his identities as Amon-Re and Amon-Kamutef.

The discovery of the Temple of Tuthmosis III was of importance not only because of the building itself, its location and historical significance, for during our excavations, we discovered a number of sculptures among which, first and foremost, is the magnificent two metre high granite statue of the seated ruler which is excellently preserved and bears traces of polychromy on the *klaft* and beard. There is also another representation of the pharaoh which was discovered in the form of a marble mask. According to Mrs. Lipińska's investigations, the bust to which this belonged, is now in the Metropolitan Museum. The series of reliefs originating from the temple walls are particularly noteworthy for their exceptionally well-preserved polychromy and apart from the royal representations, the processional scenes and the effigies of gods among which those of Amon-Min are of great interest.

Parts of the walls were built of either crystalline limestone or sandstone. The discovery of a great number of hieratic inscriptions written in ink by pious pilgrims most of which were invocations to the goddess Hathor, came as a real surprise to us. These inscriptions all derive from the Ramesside Period and not one of them is later than the end of the XX Dynasty. They have been studied by Mr. Marciniak in his book "Deir el Bahari I. Les inscriptions hiératiques du temple de Tuthmosis III", Warszawa 1974.

The state of preservation of the Temple of Tuthmosis III, leaves much to be desired, for even a partial reconstruction would require a considerable length of time. On the other hand, the archaeological evidence which this object yielded to science just after its discovery, is invaluable for both Archaeologists and Egyptologists.

Alchemy and
Early Chemistry in China

By Joseph Needham

*Director of the East Asian History of
Science Library, F.R.S., F.B.A.,
Cambridge University, England*

I would like first of all to say what a great pleasure it is for me to be with you
in Uppsala on this famous occasion, long to be remembered in history as the
500th anniversary of the foundation of this academy.

First I would like to point out that the kind words said by Lindroth about
me personally are not entirely deserved, because without collaborators it
would not have been possible to do anything. I should like therefore to pay a
tribute to my collaborators, particularly Doctor Wang Ching-Ning, Doctor
Lu Gwei-Djen, who is fortunately with us today, and Doctor Ho Ping-Yü,
among many others, who have contributed to this work. In fact I would say
that it would have been impossible for anybody of either civilization to do it
single-handed, so that it has to be a collaboration from people of two
different civilizations, China and the Western World.

Secondly, before getting in to the matter, I would like to say that I have
scrapped my elegant text because I thought it was more important, more
interesting, to give to you a summary, a resumé, of the contents of our four
volumes in the "Science and Civilization in China" series which deal with
early chemistry and alchemy in Chinese culture.

Chinese alchemy and early chemistry revolve round the concept of *tan*,
which we could translate as elixir, elixir of life or perpetual youth and
immortality; and it also meant the actual elixir itself so that one could divide
it into *wai tan* and *nei tan* according to the substances from which it was
prepared. The *wai tan* conception involved inorganic substances, salts of
metals, heavy metals, and all kinds of inorganic chemicals, some quite
poisonous, while *nei tan* on the other hand (the "inner" as opposed to the
"outer" elixir) meant the formation of a medicine of immortality from actual
juices, secretions and tissues, constituents of the body itself. This last was a
quasi-Yogistic system and I hope to be able to say something about it at the
end of the talk this afternoon. It had certain relations with India though we
do not exactly know what they were so far. And then we have two expres-

sions: *lien tan shu*, the art of transmuting the elixir, and *lien chin shu*, the art of transmuting gold.

These two ideas were intimately intermingled from the very beginning, because in 133 B.C. when Li Shao-Chün spoke to the Chinese emperor, what he said was: "I have a way to make gold artificially from other substances, if you will be so good as to support my researches. When we have made gold artificially from other substances, you'll be able to drink from vessels made of it, and so call up the spirits, the holy immortals *(shêng hsien),* and they will explain to you how to become one of the holy immortals yourself." So already we have this tie-up between the idea of artificial gold and immortality, which spread throughout the Old World cultures right down to the time of Paracelsus of Hohenheim, whom I want to speak of later.

In the course of our work on the alchemy of China, we have been obliged to employ three new words, which link in quite well with the *lien tan shu* and the *lien chin shu;* namely *macrobiotics* on the one hand and *aurifiction* and *aurifaction* on the other. We found we could never get through the maze of materials about medieval alchemy unless we used these conceptions. Macrobiotics, of course, is quite easy, coming from that famous phrase: "The Art is long, but Life is short." Macrobiotics is thus the transmutation of the elixir, the finding of the elixir. But on the other hand, as regards the *lien chin shu,* you have, in the East as well as in the West, two different things, aurifiction and aurifaction. Aurifiction means the imitation of golden or other precious substances, almost invariably with intent to deceive; and aurifaction on the other hand the conviction that you had succeeded in making them from other substances. Now this imitation can be found in the papyri of the Hellenistic world in Egypt in the third century B.C., while the aurifaction idea occurs in the *Corpus Alchemicorum Graecorum* from the first to the tenth centuries A.D. We do not call the people engaged in this alchemists because we regard alchemy as necessarily involving the idea of macrobiotics and immortality elixirs, but we can call them proto-chemists. You have the same differences in China, some people believing that they were able to make gold from other things, and others on the other hand aiming simply to imitate, and most usually to deceive the people who were employing them. These three conceptions are, I think, extremely fundamental in any discussion of the subject.

Aurifiction has another aspect connecting it with the edicts against counterfeit coinage. You get *wei huang chin* (false yellow gold) as early as 144 B.C., before the time of Li Shao-Chün. In Rome you don't really get edicts against coining, making false precious metals, until the time of Diocletian in 296 A.D. That is a point I will come back to, because on the whole the Chinese alchemical tradition was running about a hundred years earlier than the Greek one throughout the centuries. Now the great difference, the fundamental difference, between the Hellenistic tradition (from which all the other traditions in Europe derive) and the Chinese tradition, was that the Greek or Western one had only aurifiction and aurifaction. The macrobiotic idea, the idea of an elixir of life, or youth or perpetual longevity, immortality, arose only in China.

The reason for that can, I think, be traced back to the characteristic Chinese ideas of immortality. In China there was no ethical polarization. We use the term "ethical polarization" to mean the idea that after death there would be a judgment of souls, and that those who were worthy would rise to a kind of other-worldly paradise and continue there for ever, while those who had done evil deeds in their lifetimes would descend into a hell of eternal punishment and remain there indefinitely. But in the Chinese world of the fourth century B.C., Tsou Yen's time, when all this began, there was no such ethical polarization. The general view was that all mankind, all human beings, when they died, went down to a place called Huang Ch'üan, the Yellow Springs, very much like the She'ol of the Hebrews, or the Hades of the Greeks, and everybody stayed there for the rest of eternity, doing nothing much and doing it very well, as one of our poets had it, I think Gilbert O' Sullivan. That was the fate of nearly everybody, but if you knew the right things to do, if you could find the right pills in the right bottle, as it were, the right drug, you would be enabled to avoid the Yellow Springs, and instead to stay here for ever in a state of happiness and bliss, enjoying the change of the seasons and conversing with other members of the elect who had not gone down to the Yellow Springs. In other words you would become a kind of Taoist sage wandering about through the mountains and forests for ever.

Such was the situation of a *ti hsien*, in other words a *hsien*, one of the holy immortals, on the surface of the earth. On the other hand, you might be invited to be a *t'ien hsien,* which did not mean going outside the natural universe, certainly not to a paradise, obviously not to a hell; you might be invited to join the bureaucracy of the universe, which had its seat in the constellations and the clouds. You might be invited, for example, to become Deputy Assistant God of Cattle Plague or something like that, and play a part in the bureaucracy of the heavens, one of the holy immortals but not still existing on the earth. There are some very nice stories of men and women who said: "The earth is quite good enough for us, and we would like to stay here indefinitely; we do not wish to join the bureaucracy in the heavens."

Since in China there was not this ethical polarization, the way forward to the idea of a macrobiotic drug was clearly present. You see, if you have ethical polarization, if people are going to be judged on the basis of their good or evil deeds in this life, then it is not easy to imagine any kind of medicine or chemical substance which would prevent them being sent down to hell if they had done evil or taken up into the heavens if they had done well. But on the other hand, if you do not have that ethical polarization, then it is possible to imagine a chemical substance, as well as many other things, exercises of various kinds in the *nei tan* type of activity, by means of which you could avoid the fate of going down to the Yellow Springs. After all, all medicines keep people in health, or restore them to health, and it was really an extreme case of that pharmaceutical conviction.

I mentioned the word Taoism just now, and I must interject at this point that the whole business of Chinese alchemy and early chemistry was bound up with Taoism. As you know, it was one of the three religions, the *san chiao* of China, quite different from Confucianism and of course from Buddhism, which came in later. Taoism was, one might say, a nature-mysticism. I myself, when in China during the war, heard the eminent philosopher Fêng Yu-Lan say in one of his lectures that Taoism was the only system of nature-mysticism which the world had ever seen which was not profoundly anti-scientific. On the contrary, it was very pro-scientific, and wherever we find the first sprouts of science growing up in Chinese culture, and technology also, we find that the Taoists were there.

The *Tao Chia* was the group of philosophers from the 4th century B.C. onwards who developed Taoist philosophy. But *Tao Chiao* was the Taoist religion, the Taoist church, which arose from the 2nd century A.D. onwards, perhaps as a kind of opposition show to Buddhism based on intrinsic autochthonous ideas but borrowing the forms of ecclesiastical organization. So Taoism became a veritable religion and went down through history in that way. But wherever you find alchemy, wherever you find early chemistry, you find the Taoists. They were always there, and it was in their laboratories that the earliest experiments were done.

I think now that I would like to mention another point, namely what were the metallurgical possibilities in the matter of aurifiction. What did they probably make? A good deal of our work has been consecrated to that, and one of the most probable things was the making of different kinds of brasses, because there are compositions of copper, zinc and tin which do have a very gold-like appearance. And then again there is arsenical copper. As you may know, arsenical copper, when you only have from 2–5 % of arsenic, will give a very silvery appearance, but if you blow off some of the arsenic it will look like gold. Where the Chinese really went to town, as we say in my country, was in their discovery of cupro-nickel. If I was in England now I could show you the coins in my pocket, all those ten new-pence pieces, which have nothing to do with silver, though they are always called silver. They are cupro-nickel, a Chinese discovery which probably goes back to the 2nd or 3rd century A.D. and maybe earlier than that, maybe considerably earlier, because there is evidence that they exported it to Greek Bactria. The earliest cupro-nickel coinage in the world was minted there.

One of the most interesting questions is how it was that the idea of aurifaction could have arisen in the Old-World cultures, which had known the test of cupellation for a thousand years or more before. Cupellation, the "refiners' fire" which tries out gold and silver, as the Bible has it, went back to Babylonian times. There is only one way of explaining how this came about, I think, and that is by the view that in fact the artisans and the philosophers were two different sorts of people. They did not meet very much. The artisans knew about the test of cupellation and defined gold and silver more or less in the way we do now, though knowing nothing of course about atomic theory or about metallic atoms, while the philosophers on the other hand had a very different definition of gold and silver from what we have, depending largely on colour. If they knew about the test of cupellation at all, they probably thought that it would damage their product, which it certainly would have done, and they were not prepared to submit their products to it. I think this may well be the explanation of what we call "recluse environments" as opposed to public ones. The Taoists are always saying that if you want to transmute metals you have to go into the country and do it in remote temples in the depths of the forests; you must not do it where anybody can see you. This was not because they were particularly credulous, but I think they were really trying to get away from the artisans who knew about cupellation. There is a remarkable story dating from 60 B.C. where Liu Hsiang at the Chinese capital got hold of the books of the Prince of Huai-Nan, who had died sixty years earlier, and was actually entrusted with a government program in the Shang Fang, the Imperial Workshops, for making gold and silver artificially, and he failed. He tried extremely hard, tried all the formulae, and it failed because obviously the artisans were there who knew about cupellation, and they could show every time that what Liu Hsiang produced was not the real stuff. Others went away into the mountains and forests and worked alone in remote places, and they were able to produce many things which the artisans did not get a chance to prove false.

If you ask what was probably the greatest accomplishment of Chinese alchemy and early chemistry, I think I should say that it was the discovery of stannic sulphide. The sulphide of tin crystallizes in beautiful golden plates. We believe that *chin i*, potable gold or gold juice, so often referred to by the alchemists, was most of the time suspensions of stannic sulphide. This compares with the most important thing the Hellenistic proto-chemists did, the preparation of calcium polysulphides (usually by the dry distillation of eggs), with all their powerful effects on metal surfaces. These are the two achievements, both concerning sulphur, which were perhaps the most interesting inventions of the early Middle Ages in these particular fields.

In the two civilizations you have a parallel course of development. It is a very remarkable fact, not known to many people, that parallel with the Hellenistic proto-chemists there was a similar succession in China. Bolus the Democratean about 200 B.C. is followed by Pseudo-Democritus, Pseudo-Cleopatra and many others, Mary the Jewess and so on, all round about the first and second centuries A.D. and then by Zosimus of Panopolis in 300 A.D. and Stephanus of Alexandria in 600 A.D. In China things started rather earlier, with Tsou Yen in 350 B.C., Li Shao-Chün in the 2nd century B.C., Liu Hsiang in the 1st century B.C. and Wei Po-Yang in the 2nd century A.D. Wei Po-Yang, by the way, wrote the first book on alchemy in any civilization, the *Ts'an T'ung Ch'i* of 142 A.D. Then comes Ko Hung, about the same dates as Zosimus, and Sun Ssu-Mo corresponding to Stephanus. After that the originality rather died. The golden age, it's true, of Chinese alchemy, was still to come, in the T'ang period, but nothing much more happened in the Hellenistic world down to about 1000 A.D. when Michael Psellos put together the collection now available in the translation of Ruelle as the *Corpus Alchemicorum Graecorum* (or as we should like to call it, *Corpus Proto-chemicorum Graecorum*). Revival came only with the rise of Arabic alchemy from about 750 A.D. onwards, and its transmission into Latin from about 1120 A.D. onwards.

If one asks then about the most important features which we find in this succession in China, which goes on right down to 1500 A.D., I suppose one would be the governmental support which alchemy and early chemistry got in China. You don't hear much about that in the Western world, but in China it was quite marked. I mentioned the case of Liu Hsiang earlier who had the whole facilities of the Shang Fang, the Imperial Workshops, placed at his disposal. Of course it was natural in a bureaucratic society. As you know, China was basically a bureaucratic feudalism, not at all a military aristocratic feudalism, and in such a society it was natural enough that the government might be interested in making gold artificially, or for that matter in acquiring immortal life—for the members of the bureaucracy if not for anyone else. So they were interested, and they did support research, and we find not only Liu Hsiang in the Han, but also in the Northern Wei, in the fifth century A.D., an Imperial Alchemical Laboratory maintained at public expense with large provisions for facilities and funds. There were others in the T'ang period (the seventh to the ninth ceturies) and the Sung (tenth to thirteenth centuries). A laboratory for carrying out alchemical and chemical experiments was attached to the College of All Sages, one of the imperial academies of the T'ang; and another was part of the Han Lin Academy in the Sung. This is one remarkable aspect of the Chinese story.

A second point of great interest, I think, is the fact that women were so often concerned with alchemy in China. This seems to be rather more the case than in Europe, and we have some remarkable examples, like the wife of Ko Hung (ca. 300 A.D.), the wife of Ch'êng Wei (ca. 80 B.C.), and then Teacher Kêng, an account of whose life we translated in one of our volumes, a great favourite with one of the T'ang emperors. Many more examples could be given.

Thirdly, I think it is fair to say that China produced the first printed book on any scientific subject in any civilization. Since printing started in China in the 8th century A.D., earlier than anywhere else, it is fairly natural that this should be the case, and so about 848 A.D. Hokan Chi printed the *Hsüan Chieh Lu* or "Mysterious Antidotarium". It was a description of all kinds of plant drugs by the aid of which alchemists could avoid the dangerous and deleterious effects of taking the metallic elixirs which they had prepared. There were many cases of poisoning in the Middle Ages by elixirs which contained so much mercury and arsenic, to say nothing of bismuth and antimony, and other rather dangerous things, so they had to try to keep themselves going somehow. This book was an attempt to show them how they could avoid the worst effects.

I must pass on now to a few other things. First I think theory: We have in a volume which is going through the press now, a part contributed by our collaborator, Nathan Sivin of Philadelphia, on the theory of Chinese medieval alchemy. For the medicines which they wanted to make he coined the brilliant phrase: "time-controlling substances", because a central idea was the control of time by actual chemical substances. The psycho-tropic drugs that we know about today show that the idea of time-control is in a way very real, but the Chinese idea was rather different. Normally the growth of gold and silver in the earth was, they thought, very slow. It might take a thousand years. But the alchemist should be able to speed it up so that it would only take perhaps a few months. This was a case of acceleration of a process which normally was exceedingly slow. But by the same token there could also be a deceleration, as in the case of human life, normally declining so that three-score years and ten would be the limit and there would be nobody there after that. According to the Chinese alchemical theories, however, it should be possible to bring about *ch'ang shêng,* or very long life, by the elixirs which one could prepare in the laboratory. If you were really successful, you could decelerate mortality so as to become changeless, and ride into the heavens as a *hsien,* a *shêng hsien,* and never die at all.

The concept of time-controlling substances is, I think, a very important one, especially considering that there were in Chinese cosmology and natural philosophy many interlocking cycles of different lengths. For example, the planetary revolutions and many other astronomical cycles, the lunation, the eclipse cycles and so on, all were interlocking. The idea was that if you could attain perfection, the *krasis* of the Greeks, you would no longer be subjected to cyclical change. If you could get an absolutely perfect *Yin-Yang* composition of substances, you would attain extreme longevity or even material immortality. I should have used the word material immortality more often because it is the key to the whole thing. It was not an other-worldly immortality, but a material immortality which would keep a person going on the earth, and nowhere else.

Apart from all this, there were other aspects of theory which are interesting, like the making of cosmic models with circulations of different types, the use of real eggs, and colour symbolism. It was thought that the successful operation of a chemical cosmic model would give the alchemist freedom to escape from mortality.

But now I must come to the question of apparatus, and all I can do is just to tell you that there is a vast amount of hitherto unexpected and interesting information about the chemical apparatus which was developed in China. First I would like to tell you something about the three different types of distillation: the Hellenistic type, the Chinese type and the Gandharan type. In the Greek type the still-head is concave to the still so that the distillate runs down on each side and is taken away by the side-tube from an annular gutter. This is the kind of still that you see depicted in the Greek proto-chemical manuscripts, the sort that Mary the Jewess was concerned with, or Petasius or Pseudo-Democritus, in the early days of Hellenistic proto-chemistry. The annular gutter comes down from Babylonian times, when there were no side-tubes. The Chinese system was exactly opposite because here the still-head surface was convex to the still, so that the distillate ran down to the centre and then dripped into a little cup which caught it and so out by the side-tube. Thus you have two logically opposite methods of distillation, on the one hand the collection annular and on the other hand the collection central. Naturally it is anyone's guess as to what the genetic relation between these two types of still might be. Ideas may have passed in one direction or another, or of course you can say that it must mean they were two independent discoveries. If one asks for the origin of the Chinese still we can say what that is, because in Neolithic times already they had a custom of steaming their food. Anyone who has been to China or lived among Chinese people knows that bread is not baked, it is always steamed. It is very delicious that way because you get the taste of the yeast. But in ancient Chinese times they had a vessel called a *tsêng* with a perforated bottom, and a *li* underneath with legs like a tripod cauldron. So all you had to do therefore was to put a little cup on the grating, and then the cooling bowl on the top, and you will immediately have the Chinese still. Thus the still morphology is a very ancient thing in China and goes back so far that it seems difficult to believe it was a result of an idea coming from anywhere else.

But I have not mentioned anything about the third type of still, which is Indian. You might reproach me for not having said anything about the Indians hitherto, but actually we are very badly informed about their alchemy and early chemistry, partly because of the great difficulty of dating Indian books. However, there is no question that there was in early times a type of still which is more like a retort, and examples have been found at Taxila and other parts of Gandhara. This type did not envisage the collection of any liquid in the still itself at all. Nothing but vapour is going to pass over, and the cooling was applied to the receiver. In that way it was intermediate between the Greek and the Chinese still, in that like the Chinese still it had cooling, but not at the still-head, while like the Hellenistic still it had a concave still roof and not a convex one. All this is only just to give you one example of the fascinating interest in many of the pieces of information we can get about the development of chemical apparatus in Asian history, and a lot more will be found in the volume that is going through the press now.

One of the big problems which arises in this connection is the question of the discovery of strong alcohol. We know that it was first distilled in Europe by the Masters of Salerno in 1155 A.D. or so. And then you get the formula in Marcus Graecus, the *Mappae Clavicula* and other texts. But we also know that the Chinese were distilling *shao chiu*, an exact parallel of *Branntwein*, in the T'ang, that is to say from about 700 A.D. onwards. And the question arises: "Was cooling at the still-head a limiting factor, and was that why the Europeans could not do it?" But on the other hand cooling of the receiver might also be effective and it may be that the Gandharan people in Taxila and other places were doing this on the borders of India a long time before the Chinese started doing it. We just do not know. This is under discussion at the moment.

But there is another item in the picture and that is *tung chiu*, not *shao chiu*. *Shao chiu* is *Branntwein* but *tung chiu* is "frozen-out wine". From about 400 A.D. onwards the city-states in Central Asia, lika Tashkent, Turfan, and so on, were sending presents, gifts, tributes in fact, of frozen-out wine to the Chinese imperial court, and the way it was done was simply to take the wine or the beer and expose it on the top of the T'ien Shan or wherever you could get really cold positions. Then of course the ice freezes and leaves at the centre a small amount of very strong liquor. This was a big discovery in the 17th century in the West. Robert Boyle wrote on it, so did Paracelsus himself in the "Archidoxis", and they were very excited about it in the Europe of the Renaissance. But it had been done much earlier in Central Asia, and the Chinese had been familiar with it for twelve centuries previously. Was this something which stimulated the Chinese, or perhaps the Gandharans, one can't tell, to carry out distillation to subject the wine or the beer to an extremely powerful *Yang* force instead of the extremely powerful *Yin* one which they had been using previously.

Lastly I should like to mention another aspect, and that is the question of what we like to call "comparative macrobiotics". Comparative macrobiotics is a term we use to mean the spread of the elixir conception out from China throughout the Old World. First of all, you don't find anything in the Hellenistic writings about elixirs of life and immortality; anything that looks suspicious is always metaphorical, but the Chinese of course were extremely materialistic; it is not metaphorical there. The Arabs were the first to receive the Chinese influence. Where you get the beginnings of it in Arabic culture is in "Balinas"—which meant Apollonius—and other eighth-century Arabic writings. Then there is a fascinating story about a governor of Basra, Bishr ibn Marwan, who died in 695. He had a person, a Jewish physician who had contact with China, come to him and say: "Would you like me to give you a drink which will permit you to live for ever and not to go to any paradise or descend to any hell?" And he said, yes, he would rather like that. Many of the precepts were very Chinese; he was not to give way to any passions, he was not to have commerce with women, and he was to be extremely calm throughout the six weeks, or whatever it was. But then all of a sudden, the Caliph sent him a letter to tell him that he had been made the governor of Kufa as well. So his joy knew no bounds and he jumped on his horse, and followed by his retinue, rode off to Kufa in great excitement. As they were starting, the man came before him and said: "Bear me witness that you are doing something I told you not to! You will never gain immortality if you get into a state of excitement such as this. Go back to bed at once!" But he would not do it and went on to Kufa. Before they had gone more than a few miles as he was stroking his beard it came off in his hand. This was extremely frightening, so he returned to Basra and lay down, but died a couple of days after. I don't vouch for the historicity of this story, but what is extremely interesting is that just round about 700 A.D. is the first time we begin to hear about elixirs of immortality, longevity and perpetual youth in the Arabic culture-area. After that they come thick and fast. In the Jabirian Corpus from 800 to 950 A.D. you have abundant evidence of this and in other Arabic alchemists also.

Then round about 1070 A.D. you have some very strange Byzantine monks, who offered immortality by the aid of chemical substances to one of the empresses, one of the Theodoras I think. By 1275 A.D. Marco Polo is giving his accounts of the sulphur and mercury elixirs of the "brahmins". Finally the idea comes through to the Latins in 1280 with Roger Bacon, who was, I would say, the very first European to talk like a Taoist. He has a book, for example, *De retardatione accidentium senectutis,* which was only one of his writings on old age, in which he says that there are many ways, if we knew more about chemistry, in which old age could be abolished or retarded.

So at last we come to Philippus Aureolus Theophrastus Bombastus Paracelsus von Hohenheim in the late 15th century who, though admittedly as mad as a hatter, was nevertheless a very great man in his way; perhaps no less a pillar of the scientific revolution than Galileo himself. With his great formula "The business of alchemy is not to prepare gold but to make medicines for human ills" he fully linked up with the first of the Chinese alchemists, Li Shao-Chün and Tsou Yen, though he certainly never himself heard of any of them. He also linked up with everything that has happened since in medical chemistry and chemo-therapy. That really is the main burden of what I wanted to say. I believe that the origins of all medical chemistry lie in China, though practically nobody realises it.

Higher Education: Paradise Lost?

By Clark Kerr

Chairman Carnegie Council on Policy Studies in
Higher Education,
Berkeley, USA

"Paradise lost" is a common theme today among many academics in higher education in many nations. Not alone in Sweden is it being said that: "The university has never undergone so great a change before. It [has been] a free and independent intellectual corporation and has remained so through all the vicissitudes of the centuries. It now faces a future in which its freedom will be drastically cut down ...." (Lindroth, 1976, p. 260). A recent report on German universitites concluded that they have been gravely "weakened" as places of "learning and scholarship". (International Council on the Future of the University, 1977, p. 39).

Joseph Ben-David (1977, p. 180) in surveying developments in Britain, France, Germany and the United States notes "the feeling of crisis and anomie that prevails in many academic circles"; Edward Shils (1975) from his position as editor of *Minerva,* writes about "The Academic Ethos under Strain"; and Torsten Husén (1975, p. 33) states that "universities all over the world .... have during the last few years .... been forced to adapt themselves to what Kenneth Boulding so fittingly refers to as the 'management of decline'." These are among the most knowledgeable, perceptive and respected observers of higher education around the world.

A few years ago I collected the titles of recent essays about higher education in the United States, and the general theme was one of gloom and doom (Kerr, 1975).[1]

In this essay I wish to examine, first, the nature and extent of the current crisis and, second, possible solutions to it. My central theme is that it is mostly elite higher education, not all of higher education, that is in crisis and that this is more the result of specific human choices than of general historical tendencies.

A short-lived golden age. Academic Paradise, in its most recent manifestation and according to many popularly held views, lasted from the end of

---

[1] The titles included *Academia in Anarchy, Bankruptcy of Academic Policy, Chaos in Our Colleges, Down and Out in Academia, Embattled University, Fall of the American University,* and so on through the alphabet.

World War II until the late 1960s or early 1970s. This was a comparatively short-lived Eden or "eternal spring" of about a quarter of a century or a little more. I realize that it might be said that this golden age lasted much longer than a quarter of a century in some countries; that for England it began with the founding of the University of London in 1836 and with the reforms at Oxford and Cambridge beginning in the 1850s; and that for the United States it commenced with the land-grant movement and the rise of the modern university beginning in the 1860s and 1870s. But, for most countries, it began after World War II, and even in the United Kingdom and the United States the renascence after 1945 followed a rather quiescent prior period.

By contrast, Plato's Academy remained productive of new ideas for the first 300 of its 900 years of existence. China had three quite extended periods of about 300 years each of rich scholarly endeavor ("the hundred schools" period beginning with Confucius, and during the Han and Tang dynasties). The golden age of Islamic universities lasted for about two centuries (the 10th and 11th) and in Spain carried on for another century (the 12th). The medieval continental universities reached the peak of their vigor in the 12th and 13th centuries. The English universities were in a particularly active period in the 16th and the first part of the 17th centuries, and the Scottish universities in the 18th century. Uppsala also became renowned in the 18th century (the "Age of Freedom") to be followed by a decline into a period of "romantic idealism" until it evolved for a time into what was once referred to as a "cave of boredom" (Lindroth, 1976, p. 117). The German universities were a model for the world, albeit toward the end a declining one, from 1810 to 1930. Golden ages come and go. Sometimes they are overwhelmed from without—by the Seljuk Turks or by Hitler; sometimes they decay from within when a period of high intellectual vigor, with profound results in terms of the extension of knowledge that gives self-confidence within and public support without, deteriorates into one of learning the classics by rote and of petty criticism. This has often happened in history. Paradise has been lost before, but seldom after so brief a sojourn of about 25 years; and never before for the same set of reasons.

The recent golden age, if it really has ended, was different from others before it not only in its relatively short duration and the reasons for its demise but also in its universality, covering as it did many countries on all continents and representing several intellectual traditions. (I do not include, of course, nations without a system of higher education, nor do I include countries with totally planned economic and social systems where higher education moves along in a highly articulated fashion in keeping with estimated manpower requirements and without intellectual freedom in most areas of learning outside of science and technology, nor a few special cases such as China.) Old universities were re-invigorated. New universities were started. Student numbers soared. Research funds were greatly augmented. Higher education was deeply respected and held many of the hopes of nations for a better future. It had substantial autonomy. It was a time of "great expectations", as Shils (1975) has noted, for "the perfection of society and the individual through the universities".

I have chosen to use the terms "Paradise Lost" and "Paradise Regained" not to make the point, as some do, that the universities yielded to and must now reject temptation whether in the form of affluence or of power and influence or of growth. The greatest temptation of all, according to Milton, was to eat of the forbidden fruit of the tree of knowledge which in his phrase was "able to make gods of men"; and from this weakness came the fall from Grace. Presumably no academic could resist this particular temptation and, under certain circumstances, affluence, influence and growth may follow and indeed have followed. Universities have been established, in large part, in order to respond as eagerly and as effectively as possible to this particular and most seductive form of temptation—to eat the fruit of the tree of knowledge. And may I note with reference to the argument that we all yielded too much to this temptation, that the Japanese universities fell from Grace even though their faculty members were not affluent, and the French even though they did not gain power and influence through scientific research which is largely conducted outside of their universities, and Oxford and Cambridge even though they grew only modestly. Rather, in using these terms, I wish to indicate the tendency at many times and in many places for intellectuals to identify their own times as gravely lacking in merit and as poised between a golden age in the past and a utopian prospect in the future; the tendency to see what is wrong with what is, but what was right about what was and what will be right about what yet may be. Some academics are always mourning the Paradises that have been lost, and moaning that they are the lost angels of some ruined Paradise; and others are burnishing the images of the Paradises that may yet be gained.

How golden was this golden age and to what extent has it been lost? How golden an age is depends, of course, on the "eye of the beholder". There is no precise accepted definition of an academic "golden age". I define it as including these elements: internal and external acceptance of academic freedom, a substantial measure of institutional autonomy, professorial control over essential academic decisions, a wide measure of public respect, rising financial support, opportunities to undertake new endeavours, and significant new intellectual developments in a number of fields. One might add, in terms of service to society, that much of the research is useful in application and that the professional and occupational needs of the labor market are being met. So defined, the quarter century after World War II was, in many nations, clearly a golden age. On a world-wide basis, it was the most triumphant period for universities in history.

But there were many problems.[2] There were arguments whether "more means worse", over the development of the "binary" system in England and similar movements toward mass higher education in almost every industrial society, over the getting and spending of money, over rates and locations of expansion, over the prospective lowering of standards among students and faculty, over the respective roles of the sciences and the humanities—the conflict between the "two cultures", over costs and benefits, over centralization and decentralization, over the merits of alternative plans and the role to be given to market forces, and much else. In the United States, there was the period in the early 1950s of the intimidation of the academic community by Senator McCarthy. There were times when the Paradise now lost seemed more like at least a faint imitation of Hell.[3]

To what extent has the golden age been lost and where? Situations, quite obviously, vary from nation to nation. They also vary within nations. Let me make a generalization that has many exceptions: universal access higher education (or better, universal access post-secondary education) is booming as never before; mass access higher education is in a generally static situation, depending on the specialties involved; and elite higher education overall has experienced some comparative and even absolute decline.

Universal access higher education, as represented in the "technical and further education" institutions in Australia, the community colleges in the United States and Canada and the District Colleges in Norway, continues to expand. It is particularly responsive to the drive for equality of opportunity and to what Torsten Husén (1975, p. 35) has called the demand for "self-fulfillment and cultural enrichment". Mass access higher education, as represented by the polytechnics and the teacher training colleges in the United Kingdom and the comprehensive colleges and universities in the United States, is particularly responsive to the labor market, and the market generally is down in some areas (for primary and secondary teachers, for example) but up in others (such as some types of professional engineers). The situation is mixed.

The only sector that is overall in comparative and sometimes even absolute decline is the historically elite segment of higher education which has

---

[2] For a discussion of the actual situation in the United States, see Henry (1975). Henry notes that in the period after 1945, "The veteran enrollment spurts and the Tidal Wave were so overwhelming in demand for resources that a continuous struggle against inadequacy was normal. Conditions were not 'affluent' or 'golden' or 'easy' in terms of quality maintenance and the effort towards improvement and greater effectiveness; the stresses and strains created apprehension and uncertainty as to the future." (p. 149).

[3] I once wrote of that period in *The Uses of the University* and noted the many problems and tensions (Kerr, 1964).

constituted perhaps 10 to 20 percent of enrollments in Japan, the U.S. and France (and also Russia) and as much as 50 to 60 percent in the United Kingdom; and apparently an even higher percentage in Germany and Sweden; and a still higher percentage in Italy. This is the sector that has concentrated on training for the more advanced professions and on research. The decline has taken place in prestige, in morale of faculty, in rate of growth of enrollments[4] and financing, in reduced independence from external control, and in other ways.

To what extent has the golden age been lost in the elite sector? Here again the answer depends on the individual nation, but also on the aspects of the sector being examined. Rates of enrollment growth have slowed and sometimes become negative (as in Sweden). The elite sector, as a consequence, is a smaller proportion of all of higher education. Research funds are more difficult to obtain and, at least in the United States for a period of several years declined in real terms. The elite sector has been subject to increased internal and external criticism and even attack as compared with earlier times.

Yet, I would suggest that elite higher education in many nations is still in better condition, overall, than at any time in prior history, except for the recent golden age itself. If the point of comparison were any other period except this recent one, it might be said that the elite sector is, in absolute terms, now experiencing a veritable golden age. What we have is the recent golden age in deteriorating condition, and the deterioration in some nations is rather slight. It is, of course, substantial for some aspects of university affairs in some nations as, for example, in the area of internal politicization in Germany and of newly imposed external controls in Sweden; and massive for almost all aspects in Italy where the system has been overwhelmed by numbers. Overall, however, it might be said that elite higher education, viewed historically, is now located on the fifth or sixth of Dante's "seven planetary heavens". The direction of movement, however, has recently been downward from the "seventh heaven" of the great golden age.

The deterioration of the elite sector of higher education. Why has the golden age decayed in the elite sector? To begin with, some rates of growth could not reasonably be sustained whether of student numbers (which in some nations more than doubled in a single decade) or of research funds (which at one point in the United States were increasing at 10 to 15 percent a year). Also, there were excessive expectations which were disappointed. In the developing countries, the costs of higher education turned out to be greater and the visible benefits less than earlier were thought to be the case.

---

[4] "... the only country in which the university sector is continuing to grow more quickly than the non-university is Yugoslavia." (Hecquet *et al.*, 1976).

In the developed countries, university-based science did less to usher in the new world and university training did less to reduce inequality of access to elite positions than had once been hoped. Student unrest and new social priorities in many nations also contributed to the decline, as did labor market surpluses of university graduates.

I think that at least three additional continuing forces or historical tendencies are at work on the elite sector. These tendencies are (1) the transition from elite to mass access to universal access higher education, (2) the internal politicization of higher education which has been largely confined to the elite sector, and (3) the submergence of higher education under more and more external social control. These three forces are to varying extents interdependent, but I should like to concentrate on the first—the massification of higher education. I should only like to note at this point about the second (politicization) that it has come in recent times more from within than from without (Mishan, 1969);[5] and about the third (social control) that higher education is going the way of trade and industry before it in being subject to more and more bureaucratic controls (Schumpeter, 1950.)[6]

I do not believe that there is any inherent reason why mass or universal access higher education *must* be the enemy of elite higher education, although this has often been the case. True, elite higher education which was once the totality of higher education becomes a constantly smaller proportion. But mass and universal access higher education can help identify new talent for transfer into the elite sector; can make it possible for the elite sector to become more elite—both Harvard and the University of California are more elite today than when they, in fact, carried on more of the less selective functions in the absence of a mass sector; and mass and universal access higher education can create a base for social gradations in a democracy that reduce the sharp distinctions (and potential resentments) between the educated classes and the uneducated masses, that help to soften class distinctions and class antagonisms. The continuation of class attitudes is clearly related to the perpetuation of elite access to higher education.

When I was guiding the development of the Master Plan for Higher Education in California in 1959 and 1960, I considered the vast expansion of the community colleges to be the first line of defense for the University of California as an institution of international academic renown. Otherwise the

---

[5] As Mishan has noted: "... owing to increasing student intolerance, the universities have become one of the few places in Britain where free speech and open political debate are no longer assured!"

[6] Schumpeter lays at the feet of the intellectuals themselves partial responsibility for the spread of social controls (see, particularly, "The Sociology of the Intellectuals," pp. 145–155); a process which is now reaching into the universities themselves. Intellectuals create the conditions for some of the loss of their own autonomy.

University was either going to be overwhelmed by large numbers of students with lower academic attainments or attacked as trying to hold on to a monopoly over entry into higher status. That plan, for the first time in history anywhere, guaranteed a place in a community college for every high school graduate or person over 18 otherwise qualified and gave community college graduates preference in transferring into the University of California. The most important reason, by far, for this guarantee was the contribution that the community colleges could make to the development of individual lives. The Master Plan, in all of its essentials, has recently been reaffirmed for another 15 years.

But mass and universal access higher education *may* be the enemy of elite higher education.

(1) They may take money away from elite higher education. But it is hard to know when and if money is taken away from elite higher education because it is not possible to know what money otherwise would have been given. There is no evidence I know of that there is a rigid "wages fund" (or higher education fund) from which all institutions must draw and permitting one institution to get more only by taking away from another. In the United States, however, there is slight evidence that in a few states elite institutions may have suffered at the hands of non-elite (The Carnegie Foundation for the Advancement of Teaching, 1976, p. 71).

(2) They may pave the way for the enmeshing of elite higher education into governmental frameworks that are unduly confining. Non-elite higher education, in the form of teachers' colleges and community colleges, has continuously been under more social and less collegial control than elite higher education, and for good reasons. These types of institutions are more tied in their products to direct and immediate social needs. Autonomy is both less essential and less demanded. If elite and non-elite institutions are placed under the same policies for external governance, then social controls can stifle the elite functions. The very size and cost of the expanded total system, also, invites controls.

(3) They may help to introduce internal forms of governance which are inappropriate or even potentially destructive. (I define "internal" to include the governing boards of the institutions.) The functional authority of the scholar is much more important to the proper performance of elite than of non-elite functions. Participation by non-scholars in detailed governance, which may be neutral or even beneficial in its effects on the performance of non-elite functions, can be destructive to the performance of research activity and of instruction in higher learning.

(4) They may overwhelm the facilities of elite institutions of higher education if the numbers of students they entail are poured into these institutions. Homogenization of students and faculty within institutions of higher educa-

tion can result only, regardless of intentions, in movement in a downward direction academically when working from the historical base of an elite system. Sudden mass attendance at traditional research universities, as in Italy, can inundate both facilities and faculty members. The surest and quickest way to destroy an elite system of higher education is to force enormous numbers of students rapidly into its component institutions. This leads to over-use of facilities, disgruntled faculty members and students, and lowered academic standards. The Italian system, once quite good, is now a shambles. The German system, where 17 new research universities have been opened in the past decade alone to accommodate student enrollments, is in deep trouble; but not for these reasons alone. It is a monumental historical error to try to accommodate mass and universal access enrollments within an "elite" framework. If, on the other hand, elements of the elite sector are placed in mass institutions, then elite standards are also very likely to deteriorate as in the spread of Ph.D. training programs in the United States into institutions with modest standards for admission.

(5) They may over-populate the professions into which the elite institutions have traditionally provided entry, as in Germany (International Council on the Future of the University, 1977, p. 33)[7] with negative economic and political consequences. An explosion of degree holders from traditional universities diminishing the assured inequality of status historically associated with their degrees can overwhelm a profession resulting in unemployment or, more likely, underemployment and intense political resentment.

I have said "may" above, but each of these results has, in fact, happened in one or more actual circumstances. The advent of mass and universal access higher education can and has weakened elite higher education in some situations.

Can Paradise be regained? We cannot go back to the simpler world that once was, to the Athens of Pericles or to the ivory tower of old. When given the chance to participate in the modern age, even the University of Chicago under Robert Maynard Hutchins, who advocated the "Great Books" approach to higher learning and was deeply distrustful of research and science, accepted a major atomic bomb contract during World War II in the Metallurgical Laboratory under the direction of Enrico Fermi and Arthur Compton; and even Columbia University under Jacques Barzun, the humanist, as Provost, who favored an inward looking "House of Intellect", (Barzun, 1959) became one of the great scientific research contractors in the United States. Nor were those earlier ivory towers of fond but imperfect memory

[7] "Thus the 840,000 (20 % of the present youth group) now in institutions of higher education still expect to pass almost automatically into professional positions which only five years ago provided employment for less than 400,000."

so insulated from the surrounding society, so immaculate in their conception, so unsullied by contact with temptation and affluence; they just were an integral part of a different kind of society. Man a long time ago took the first bite of that forbidden fruit of the tree of knowledge. His chosen instrument in many nations for eating away at that fruit, faster and faster, has come to be the university. Not all the longings for a more innocent world, not all the regrets at having yielded to the temptation to become "gods" can take back the current reality that the operation of the world is increasingly dependent upon new knowledge and its application; and that the universities not only are but want to be involved.

I start from the assumption that elite higher education is needed by and useful to society; that it would be so even in a Rawlsian world of more perfect "justice" (Rawls, 1971); that all men can benefit from better knowledge and higher skills properly applied and that generally they recognize this; that the "difference principle" has universal validity; and that under the "difference principle" some individuals, chosen on merit, will be given higher level training and more opportunity to use it than others.

I should now like to change the terminology I have been using. I have been employing the standard terminology of "elite", "mass" and "universal access" higher education. This terminology reflects stages of historical development, with the qualification that elite higher education was not all that "elite"—it was sometimes just smaller in numbers.[8] I should like to suggest that a more operational terminology, now that the stage of universal access higher education has been reached and now that we are moving away from class-oriented to more merit-oriented higher education, and a terminology less loaded with negative implications is:

(1) highly selective higher education,
(2) selective higher education, and
(3) non-selective higher education.

(One might prefer, of course, two, or four, or five or some other number of levels rather than three.)

I think the principle of selectivity is central. Highly selective higher education is that part engaged in admitting and educating persons for those professions that are based on advanced-level high intellectual training and in conducting research that is related to such training and uses persons so trained. Selective higher education is that part engaged in preparing persons for the numerous occupations of modern society that depend on or at least can utilize the advanced knowledge and skill imparted by what, in American terminology, is called undergraduate education. Non-selective postsecond-

---

[8] The average level of mental ability of college students rose in the United States as "mass" replaced "elite" higher education from 1920 to 1960 (Taubman, *et al.*, 1972, p. 19). This may have been reversed with the move from mass to universal access higher education since 1960.

ary education is, by definition, open to all persons of a certain age or background in prior education or employment.

I recognize that there are degrees of selectivity and thus difficulties in drawing lines between and among levels, but such drawing of lines nevertheless has often been done.[9] I think it reasonable to suggest that the highly selective segment might be designed to attract about the top 10 percent in terms of ability of the historical age cohort (which is roughly the practice now in several nations) and be directed toward preparation for professions where some degree of postgraduate training is normally essential; and the selective segment the next 10 to 20 percent, which would cover, between these two segments, preparation for those professions and occupations in society for which some postsecondary education is useful even if not always entirely necessary with some allowance for associated demands;[10] with the non-selective segment open on demand.

I agree in full with Torsten Husén (1976–77) that higher education cannot effectively be organized around a single model.[11] I favor a minimum of three models. One of these (Model X) would center around what Parsons and Platt (1973) have called the "core sector" of graduate training and research, but I would add related pre-graduate training as in the selective liberal arts colleges in the United States. The second (Model Y) would be organized, formally or informally, around the occupational and vocational needs of society for undergraduate training and around the "general education" interests of students. The third (Model Z) would be responsive to social demand based on any reason, subject only to consumer choice. There are, of course, points of overlap. This three model approach, in one form or another and either by official action or informal practice, is now followed in a number of political jurisdictions around the world, including some which look upon themselves as "unitary" or "binary".

[9] Selection sometimes, of course, takes place not at the point of original admission but in the first year or two after admission through a process of elimination of the less able students.

[10] This assumes, as is the situation in the United States, that about 20 percent of the jobs in a highly industrialized nation can make use of postsecondary education to the level of a bachelor's degree or higher, with allowance made for equivalent education of spouses of persons holding such jobs, for some who "drop-out" before or after their degrees and do not use their training, and for some who compete for the degrees and the jobs but do not get them but in the course of competing put some downward pressure on comparative salary levels for the more educated elements of the population and upward pressure on effort and productivity—for an allowance of an additional 5 to 10 percent.

I should like to make clear that these percentages relate to the *total age cohort and not to enrollments* as do other statistics both earlier and later in this paper. For example, about 20 percent of the age cohort attend institutions of higher education in Germany and over 40 percent in the United States. Enrollments in "elite" institutions are about two-thirds of all enrollments in Germany but only about one-fifth in the United States. Thus, more of the age cohort is in "elite" institutions in Germany (about 14 percent) than in the United States (about 10 percent).

[11] See also Husén, 1976.

These three models can be distinguished from each other not only by the levels of their admission qualifications for students but in other ways also: the principles for selection of faculty members, the needed level of financial support per student and per faculty member, the degree of institutional autonomy required for effective performance of the differing functions, the degree of importance of academic freedom to the faculty members, the appropriate forms of governance. Each model needs to be thought through in the light of the particular circumstances of the individual situation, along the lines of these and other dimensions.

The first model operates best at a national and international level of service; the second at the national or regional level; and the third at the regional or local level. The first is tied to the disciplines and their collegial governance (horizontal governance); the second to the schools that train for the occupations and their more hierarchical governance (vertical governance); and the last to consumer choice and a more entrepreneurial form of governance (market choice). The central theme of the first is scholarship; of the second, attention formally or informally to the labor market and the preparation of what economists call "human capital"; of the third, the satisfaction of individual desires for self-development.

The essential principle for a modern system of higher education is differentiation of function from which follows differentiation of financial support and differentiation of governance.[12] There can be no universal "gold standard" for degrees as historically alleged in England; and no eternal and universal connection between teaching and research as historically alleged in Germany.[13] These two cherished doctrines have been in any event more myths than actualities. Some British degrees have always been of higher quality gold than others; and in Germany some teaching and some research have always been more intertwined than other teaching and other research. Degrees will vary in content and quality. Research and teaching need only be combined in the highly selective institutions. The traditional research university, in any event, cannot by itself fully accommodate the new numbers and the new functions, for then it will no longer be the traditional research university. Mass and universal access higher education enrollments cannot just be poured into its "shell"[14] without drastic consequences. An effective modern system of higher education must differentiate its

[12] This view runs counter to what Cerych calls "the trend towards what might be called a diffused system ... with blurred separations". (Hecquet *et al.,* 1976, p. 168). In particular, it runs counter to the idea of a single all-purpose and totally integrated single institution encompassing all aspects of higher education.

[13] Husén (1976) notes that teaching and research have not "always been united in a harmonious marriage".

[14] For use of the word "shell", see Coleman (1973, p. 359 ff.).

component institutions one way or another. Given such differentiation, a highly selective sector can be maintained in a condition of good health; but such differentiation, by itself, is not enough.

Methods of differentiation. Martin Trow (1976) has noted several methods of differentiation. One is to have a highly selective official segment, such as the French *grandes écoles;* another is to have free-standing individual institutions, such as Harvard or Rockefeller University; a third is to have a highly selective level within a less selective institution, such as the graduate level of some "Big Ten" universitites in the United States; a fourth is to have one or more highly selective enclaves at whatever level within a less selective institution, such as a specially protected research center in a mass institution, like the distinguished atmospheric laboratory at one of the otherwise moderately selective American universities, or a selective undergraduate "honors college," as in the University of Alabama, or a "closed" faculty with special (numerus clausus) admission requirements, as in Germany and Sweden. (See Chart I for a schematic outline of these possibilities and variations on them.)

The most generally preferable solution among these possibilities, I believe, is the first—the separate segment; although other solutions can also work effectively under the proper circumstances. This first solution makes more easily possible differentiation in admission requirements, in criteria for selection of faculty members, in financial formulas for support, in forms of governance and much else. The second solution (the free-standing institution) almost requires private sources of support which are not likely in most nations, or public funds treated as though they were private by a special mechanism (the University Grants Committee in the United Kingdom), or by a personal edict of the nation's governing authority (as in Iran). The third solution (the highly selective level) tends to result in clear faculty neglect of the students in and the duties of the less selective level; but, at least in the American context and increasingly the German, has made possible the preservation of high level scholarship within an institution that accepts mass enrollments at a lower level of academic rigor. The fourth solution depends on a degree of tolerance by others of the special enclave, which is not always forthcoming in the face of what have been called, in the field of industrial relations, "orbits of coercive comparisons" (Ross, 1948)—these comparisons are more coercive within than among institutions. Combinations are, of course, possible, and particularly of the first and third which results in separate segments with distinct levels of selectivity for undergraduates and graduate students within the highly selective and perhaps also the selective segment (the fifth solution).

There are problems, of course, with each of these solutions. The first (differentiated segments), for example, raises the difficulty particularly of

CHART I
Alternative Approaches to Differentiation

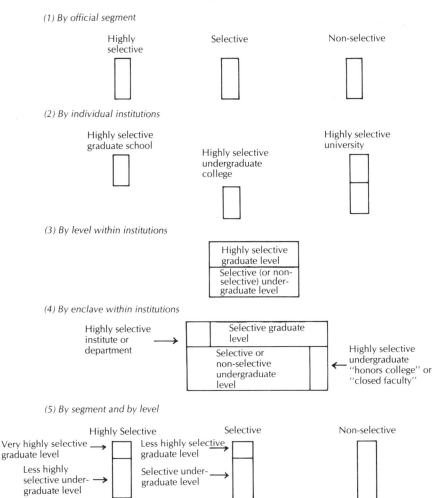

(1) By official segment

Highly selective   Selective   Non-selective

(2) By individual institutions

Highly selective graduate school

Highly selective undergraduate college

Highly selective university

(3) By level within institutions

Highly selective graduate level

Selective (or non-selective) under-graduate level

(4) By enclave within institutions

Highly selective institute or department →

Selective graduate level

Selective or non-selective undergraduate level

← Highly selective undergraduate "honors college" or "closed faculty"

(5) By segment and by level

Highly Selective   Selective   Non-selective

Very highly selective → graduate level

Less highly selective under- → graduate level

Less highly selective graduate level →

Selective under- → graduate level

how to draw and enforce the lines of differentiation and how to care for the status needs of faculty members in the less selective and non-selective segments; but also how to supply "solid legitimization" of the in-between sector with the highly selective sector founded on "competitive excellence" and the non-selective sector on "egalitarianism" and the selective sector floating somewhere in between unattached to so clear a justification unless it be a labor market orientation.[15] There are no problem-free solutions.

[15] See the discussion by Smelser (1974, pp. 9–141).

I see, then, the best generally available solution to the preservation of an effective highly selective segment as being a more-or-less clearcut differentiation of functions among institutions or, if that is not possible, among levels or enclaves within institutions—the highly selective segment organized basically around intellectual concerns; the selective segment around the job market or "general education" or both; and the non-selective segment around consumer preferences whatever they may be.

Preserving the highly selective sector. To preserve selective centers of high excellence in a period of massification of higher education, and realizing that each national situation is different but that some general principles may still be applicable, I should like to suggest the following policies:

(1) Differentiation of functions, as discussed above; with rejection of those remnants of differentiation within higher education based on hereditary class.

(2) All-out support by the highly selective segment of expansion of the less selective segment and particularly of the non-selective segment.[16] I should like to venture a strong statement which points up a strange anomaly: the best way to save a highly selective segment of higher education is to expand and give increased status to the less selective and non-selective segments; is for the highly selective segment to lose its dominant position in terms of total numbers and total financial support for the sake of preserving its highest level intellectual contributions. It is, of course, also easier to differentiate the highly selective segment if it is a small portion of the total than if it is a large portion.

(3) Entrance on merit into the highly selective segment and easy transfer on merit to it from the less selective and nonselective segments.

(4) Concentration of the highly selective functions in a few locations; and distribution of the less selective and particularly the non-selective functions in many locations.

[16] I note that historically elite higher education is in more difficulty in nations where its enrollments are a relatively high proportion of the total (Germany, Italy, Sweden, and the United Kingdom) than where they are a relatively small proportion (France, Japan, and the U.S.A.). Difficulties, in one form or another, rise in intensity almost in direct proportion to the percentage of enrollments in the historically elite research universities:

Italy	90 percent or more
Germany and Sweden	60–70 percent
U.K.	50–60 percent
France, Japan, U.S.A.	10–20 percent

The general rule seems to be that the greater the proportion of the expansion that is absorbed within the once "elite" sector, the greater the problems; the more students forced into the "shell" of the historic research university, the more trouble there ensues.

(5) Acceptance by public authority that, if highly selective functions are to be performed at a level of high excellence, there must be a separate model for them—a separate model of internal and external governance, of financing, of access. A separate model is necessary for each of the three differentiated sets of functions. One cannot fit them all.[17]

(6) Control by members of the permanent faculty in highly selective institutions over appointment of faculty members and over research and curricular policies. These institutions, in particular, should develop what Eric Ashby (1968–69) has called a "Hippocratic Oath for the Academic Profession"[18] as a basis for assertion of their autonomy from detailed public control. Autonomy can be lost as a result of internal conduct as well as it can be denied externally. The faculty in less selective institutions should also control selection of faculty members and curricular content because they involve professional judgments. The curriculum in non-selective institutions is more dependent on consumer choice.

(7) Democratization of governance not in the internal form of "drittelparität"[19] which has sometimes proved so disastrous to academic freedom and academic standards but in the external form of carefully chosen public members of boards of governance. I should like to distinguish as clearly as possible between the two main forms of democratization of governance: (a) the "internal" by sharing power over essential decisions among faculty, students and staff, and (b) the "external" by sharing power over essential decisions with chosen members of the general public. Germany earlier chose the "internal" route, and Sweden more recently the "external". There are, of course, many combinations of these two forms, and each form and its variations may apply more appropriately to the making of some decisions than others. It is a strange commentary on the academic profession that the record of public trustees in protecting institutional autonomy and academic freedom has so frequently been better than that of some internal participants in governance who become so seized with moral purposes that they seek to override standards of scholarly conduct.

---

[17] In Sweden, for example, within the framework of a "unitary" solution, there are "faculty boards" in charge of postgraduate studies and research, but "line boards" with external representatives in charge of the undergraduate curriculum; and there are "closed" and "open" faculties.

[18] For a discussion of these problems, see also Weber (1973).

[19] "Drittelparität" is "not the way to conduct an intellectual institution" which requires "standards of intellectual judgment" (Shils, 1973). Hegel once wrote that "Hell is truth seen too late." The Germans, at least, are now, however, overcoming the worst practices of "drittelparität" through both judicial and legislative action intended to guarantee faculty control over research and curricular policy and over selection of faculty members.

(8) The democratization of occupations, and professions, in the sense of narrowing status and income differentials, so that the prizes awarded for a degree from a highly selective segment of higher education are not disproportionately high—have no monopoly element to them. Democratization of entrance implies the democratization of exit rewards.

(9) Constant efforts by leaders of the highly selective sector to make contact with citizens at large and the mass organizations that represent them to explain the values of the highly selective sector to society at large and to its individual members, as have the land-grant universities in the United States.

I would also agree with Martin Trow (1976) that the highly selective segment is less vulnerable if private as well as public funds are available for its support. Overall, I join Trow in believing that "in most places" highly selective higher education is not an "endangered species" and would add that where it is endangered it is not by historical necessity but by unwise human choices.

Paradise for highly selective higher education has been only partially lost. That was easily done. Paradise when partially lost can be at least partially regained. That will not be easy but is essential, for the further progress of the modern world is ever more dependent on ever higher higher-learning. The preservation and furtherance of higher learning at a level of excellence deserves both high priority and devoted efforts. To conclude with another quotation from Milton: "All is not lost."

REFERENCES

Ashby, Eric (1968–69). "A Hippocratic Oath for the Academic Profession." *Minerva*, VII: 64–66.

Barzun, Jacques (1959). *The House of Intellect*. New York: Harper and Brothers.

Ben-David, Joseph (1977). *Centers of Learning*. New York: McGraw-Hill.

Carnegie Foundation for the Advancement of Teaching, (1976). *The States and Higher Education: A Proud Past and a Vital Future*. San Francisco: Jossey-Bass.

Coleman, James S. (1973). "The University and Society's New Demands Upon It." In: Kaysen, C. (ed.) *Content and Context*. New York: McGraw-Hill.

Hecquet, Ignace, Christiane Verniers and Ladislav Cerych (1976). *Recent Student Flows in Higher Education*. New York: International Council for Educational Development.

Henry, David D. (1975). *Challenges Past, Challenges Present: An Analysis of American Higher Education Since 1930*. San Francisco: Jossey Bass.

Husén, Torsten (1975). "Higher Education's Adaptation to Changing Social Forces." In: Burn, B. (ed.) *Higher Education and the Current Crisis*. New York: International Council for Educational Development.

Husén, Torsten (1976). "Problems of Securing Equal Access to Higher Education: The Dilemma Between Equality and Excellence." *Higher Education*, 5: 407–422.

Husén, Torsten (1976–77). "Swedish University Research at the Crossroads." *Minerva*, XIV: 419–446.

International Council on the Future of the University (1977). *Report on German Universities*. New York: International Council on the Future of the University.

Kerr, Clark (1964). *The Uses of the University*. Cambridge; Harvard University Press.

Kerr, Clark (1975). "The Moods of Academia." In: Hughes, J. F. (ed.) *Education and the State*. Washington, D. C.: American Council on Education.

Lindroth, Sten (1976). *A History of Uppsala University, 1477–1977*. Uppsala: Uppsala University.

Mishan, Edward J. (1969). "Some Heretical Thoughts on University Reform." *Encounter*, 32 (3): 3–15.

Parsons, Talcott and Gerald M. Platt (1973). *The American University*, Chapter 3. Cambridge: Harvard University Press.

Rawls, John (1971). *A Theory of Justice*. Cambridge: Harvard University Press.

Ross, Arthur M. (1948). *Trade Union Wage Policy*, Chapter 3. Berkeley: University of California Press.

Schumpeter, Joseph A. (1950). *Capitalism, Socialism, and Democracy* (3rd. edn.). New York: Harper and Brothers.

Shils, Edward (1973). "The Freedom of Teaching and Research." *Minerva*, XI, 433–441.

Shils, Edward (1975). "The Academic Ethos Under Strain." *Minerva*, XIII: 1–37.

Smelser, Neil (1974). "Growth, Structural Change, and Conflict in California Public Higher Education, 1950–1970." In: Smelser, N. S. and Almond, G. (eds.) *Public Higher Education in California*. Berkeley: University of California Press.

Taubman, Paul and Terence Wales (1972). *Mental Ability and Higher Educational Attainment in the 20th Century*. Berkeley: Carnegie Commission on Higher Education.

Trow, Martin (1976). "'Elite Higher Education': An Endangered Species?" *Minerva*, XIV: 355–376.

Weber, Max (1973). "The Power of the State and the Dignity of the Academic Calling in Imperial Germany, The Writings of Max Weber on University Problems." *Minerva*. XI: 571–632. (Originally published in the years 1908 to 1911.)

The role of universities in the developing countries

By Amadou-Mahtar M'Bow

Director-General of Unesco

I should like to begin by saying how much pride and pleasure it gives me to be taking part with you in celebrating the five hundredth anniversary of the University of Uppsala. This occasion, imbued in itself with such prestige, is especially significant to me in that it marks the outstanding privilege conferred on me by the award of the degree of Doctor *Honoris Causa* by the oldest university in northern Europe. This honour which, through me, is designed for the Organization which I head, bears fresh witness to the commitment of the authorities of this country, both academic and governmental, to the cause of international intellectual co-operation.

I wish, therefore, to pay tribute here to the very active part played by Sweden and the Swedish academic authorities in Unesco's work, more especially as regards co-operation with the developing countries.

Thus, for instance, the Swedish Government, back in 1963, took the praiseworthy step of making available to Unesco, through the Swedish International Development Authority, funds-in-trust which, under a flexible arrangement, make it possible to meet certain urgent needs of the developing countries.

In regard to higher education itself, persons prominent in the academic sphere of Sweden have provided considerable support for the activities of Unesco's European Centre for Higher Education, in Bucharest.

The interest taken by Sweden in the global problems of mankind's survival development and welfare has also been evidenced by its participation in the establishment and the strengthening of the United Nations University, which—as you know—is operating under the joint auspices of the United Nations and of Unesco. I have pleasure in reminding you of the assistance that Mr. Hans Löwbeer, Chancellor of the Swedish Universities, is affording it, as a member of the University Council and as Chairman of its Budget and Finance Committee. I am also very grateful to the Swedish Government for its decision to contribute one million Swedish kronor, in August 1975, to the Endowment Fund of the United Nations University.

So far as the University of Uppsala itself is concerned, I feel that it has special claims to the gratitude of Unesco and of the international community. I am referring here not only to the distinguished part played by the Egyptologist Säve Söderbergh in the saving of the monuments of Philae, an undertaking assisted by Unesco, but also to the persevering efforts of the University to come to the aid of research workers, and to set up research groups in the developing countries while endeavouring to make it easier for specialists to return to their home country and find a suitable place there. With the assistance of the Swedish International Development Agency and the International Atomic Energy Agency, 6,000 research workers have thus been enabled in recent years to follow some forty courses on a very wide variety of subjects.

In saluting the University of Uppsala, on the occasion of this solemn commemoration, as one of the oldest centres of European culture, I am particularly happy to recognize and to stress that it was, without doubt, one of the first universities to plan and direct its activities with an eye to what we now call the new needs of development. Consequently it is on the role of universities in the developing countries that I should like, in accordance with your kind invitation, to offer you today a few reflections. But, for a better understanding of the role, may I first glance over certain aspects of development itself, in the light of the conditions now prevailing in the world.

In this latter part of the twentieth century, it is reasonable to suppose that mankind has indeed reached a turning point in its history. On the one hand, never have the fundamental imbalances in the distribution among nations of the material wealth and the scientific and technological potential of our world, engendered by a long historical process, been so marked. In some respects, these imbalances are even growing and, though it may require a little qualification, the image so often presented to us by the mass media, of a world split into a northern hemisphere possessing immense resources and a southern hemisphere whose inhabitants, although they constitute the majority of the world's population, live in penury, corresponds—alas!—to grim reality.

But never, on the other hand, has there been such a keen awareness of these disparities, of their intolerable affront to the spirit of justice and, above all, of the risks they would entail for the human community if they were perpetuated. We are here witnessing a historical process of paramount importance decisively impelled, since the end of World War II, by decolonization, but also in part rendered possible by the giant strides of modern technology, with the close contacts it permits between peoples and with the serious threats it entails for their future. This historical process leads all nations gradually to perceive the *de facto* solidarity which unites them, going beyond their independence retained or recovered, and to understand that only the establishment of a new world order, desired by all and taken up with full knowledge of the facts, can provide common remedies for the evils affecting not only certain parts of the globe but the contemporary world as a whole.

It is from this dual standpoint, it seems to me, that the notion of development should be considered. If, as stated by Gunnar Myrdal, development is, in respect of the individual country, the upward movement of the whole social system, it should on a world-wide scale be the upward movement of the whole of mankind, in an impulse of fellowship born of the understanding of what unites peoples in a common destiny. In either case, universities, set fast in the national fabric but open to the outside world, have an all-important catalytic part to play, in regard to innovation and liaison. In the developing countries, even more than elsewhere, they can and must be among the chief architects of nationhood while remaining, in accordance with their basic purpose, the essential link with the rest of the intellectual community of the world.

It would no doubt be difficult to draw a precise dividing line, for the purposes of what I have to say, between the groups of so-called "developed" and "developing" countries because, in the latter case, there are increasingly marked differences between the most underprivileged nations and those whose rapid advancement brings them closer—at least from the point of view of global revenue—to the "rich" nations most affected by some of the crises which are unsettling the industrialized world. Moreover, since all countries may be regarded, at their respective levels, as "developing", it will not be surprising that some of the remarks I am about to make on the role of universities in the countries of the Third World apply all round. So, rather than to any particular geographical, historical or economic criterion, it is to the similarity of extremely serious problems currently facing many developing countries that I shall refer here to establish a distinction. As to these problems, you will allow me briefly to name a few, in order to clarify the position of universities in those countries that have to be called "underdeveloped".

Firstly, need it be recalled that for millions of human beings, poverty is still evinced, in this atomic age, by the ravages of hunger, disease and ignorance. The fact that these scourges subsist in many countries which are too poor to set up the basic infrastructures for their development and which are often forced into dire straits by the economic growth of other regions, through a process of accentuation of inequalities characteristic of our times, shows the urgent need for an endeavour to achieve development, social dynamization, for which universities can provide a powerful driving force. We all know that undernourishment and malnutrition, which every year afflict and cause the death of millions of human beings, exist on a scale that is paradoxically amplified by the vast upsurge in the world's population since the beginning of the century. Many diseases, for which there are nevertheless known treatments and cures, also afflict broad sectors of the populations in the Third World, unfitting them for truly productive work, whereas a mere fraction of the 300 thousand million dollars spent annually on weapons of war would suffice to wipe out those diseases and fully revitalize the human potential of those very nations which are most in need of it to provide for their future.

But it is above all on ignorance—which might seem to be a lesser evil than hunger or endemic disease, if it were not directly responsible, through the social paralysis it entails, for their perpetuation—that I should like to place emphasis here.

Ignorance is a key problem in the developing countries, and one which the universities can help to solve.

Just a few facts and figures will give an idea of the extent of the problem. For the developing countries taken together, the absolute number of illiterates went up from 700 million in 1960 to 756 million in 1970, and there is nothing to indicate that this trend may be reversed in the near future since—to take Africa as an example—at the present rate of school-age population growth, the number of children attending school would have to be increased by about 50 per cent merely to keep enrolment rates at their present level over the next fifteen years. In fact, according to Unesco estimates, it seems that, in the Third World, about half of the population aged 15 and over is at present illiterate. In some countries this proportion is much higher. We can visualize the sort of difficulties which may be raised, in such circumstances, for national authorities endeavouring to train key personnel or to organize a university education that shall not be the privilege of an élite which is severed from the people at large and will subsequently be tempted to apply its skills abroad, whereas they are essential to the progress of the nation. We can also gauge—and I shall come back to this presently—the responsibility of universities in respect of a problem which would seem, at first sight, to come essentially within the scope of primary and secondary education but, on account of what is at stake, remains indissociable from the problem of development as a whole.

It is of course not my intention to give here a full survey of the economic and social characteristics of the developing countries, which have in fact been the subject of a great many studies in Sweden, but simply to sketch in the general background of the role of Third World universities in a way which will pinpoint the specific character of that role. In this respect, it is fitting that this brief reminder of a few factual data should also bear on certain crucial problems facing the developing countries in other fields of

Unesco's competence: science and technology, culture and communication.

The introduction of science and technology in the developing countries, and a speeding-up of the growth of this potential, obviously constitute an urgent necessity in a world where—as I have pointed out—the knowledge and expertise involved are concentrated in the developed countries, whereas a considerable proportion of the raw materials essential to industrialization comes from countries devoid of such an infrastructure. Economic growth, which is essential to development even if not identical with it, undoubtedly represents a priority objective for the Third World. But its achievement—as I shall try to show presently by means of a few examples—raises as many issues as it solves material problems. While seeking to acquire gradually the autonomy they lack, a good many developing countries are somewhat uneasy concerning the effects of the scientific and technological models which are suggested to them, since these may detract from other forms of knowledge or, owing to the way in which they are introduced, may bring about a state of dependence on the industrialized countries.

A similar imbalance is observable in the field of communication, and this was discussed at length by the General Conference of Unesco at its nineteenth session in Nairobi in October-November 1976. The distribution of communication media and of the immense power they constitute follows the pattern of the unequal distribution of economic power and of scientific and technological potential among the nations. It is quite clear today that the mass media constitute exceptionally effective instruments of development, particularly in the spheres of education and science, since they enable knowledge to be more readily disseminated in the most underprivileged sectors of the population. From this point of view, the underequipment in communication media of the Third World countries, which simply cannot afford such costly technologies, is a great handicap for them, since the multiplier effect of the communication media is precisely what those countries need. Furthermore, the capacity to issue information enables the nations possessing it to extend their cultural influence—not to say their domination—far and wide in the world. Those devoid of this capacity cannot take part in the dialogue which should be established among all nations and are obliged to be the passive recipients of cultural flows of foreign origin which may, in various ways, run counter to the full development of their identity.

The notion of cultural identity is, as we know, one of the essential aspects of the new conception of development which has arisen as the previously colonial or semi-colonial peoples have, in the second half of this century, attained independence and endeavoured to lay the foundations of a true autonomy despite a host of economic, political and social obstacles. This notion is also increasingly becoming a factor of some consequence in the general problems facing even the highly industrialized countries, where certain groups seek to rediscover or re-establish culture-based communities to break with the limitations of a life that tends to destroy traditional social units. Quite as much as the material requirements to which I have briefly referred in the first part of my remarks, this modern conception of development should profoundly modify the work of universities in the Third World, and I should now like to dwell on this a little.

The notion of development is evidently much more complex than it appeared to be just a few years ago, before being added to and elaborated upon by parallel reflection on the experience of the industrialized countries and on that of the developing countries. Today, development cannot be thought of either as a mere accumulation of material goods or as pure economic growth. The latter is but an aspect—albeit essential—of a multidimensional process, the social and cultural components of which are not the least important. This means that development, far from being an end in itself, derives its value and its significance from its ultimate objectives, which are seen to be both the self-fulfilment of man in the diversity of his aspirations and the conscious progress of the community to which he belongs and for which he works towards goals it has freely chosen. In this dialectical context, man may be regarded as both agent and purpose of development.

Consequently development should, for the whole of mankind, match up to the requirements of individual dignity and individual advancement and to the desire for happiness, which are intimately associated with the human condition. This is one of the facets of the notion of a new international order, which reflects the need for relations based on the interdependence and the common destiny of all mankind. But, at the same time, in so far as man, within a community, is not an abstract being but the product of geography and history, and responsible for an original future which he will have chosen and contrived with his fellow citizens, development, while universal in its fundamental purposes, is clearly multiform in the ways in which it accomplishes itself.

The numerous Third World countries which were unable, in certain periods of their history, to follow original paths to development in keeping with their own circumstances met with failures or with fresh constraints which not only reproduced but aggravated those sometimes sustained by the industrialized countries. These negative experiences led to the evolution of the concept of endogenous development, that is to say development rooted in the specific realities of a country, desired and achieved by the people of that country, probably assisted in various ways by international co-operation, but in accordance with local resources and with the particular spirit of a culture.

Before embarking, in the light of this very brief description of some aspects of the general problem facing the developing countries, on an outline of the traditional or new tasks which may be undertaken by the universities of those countries, I should like to make a preliminary remark.

The expression "universities of the developing countries" in fact covers a complex and many-sided reality. Just as it would be wrong to believe that all developing countries are faced with the same problems in roughly similar circumstances, we should also be mistaken in thinking that the universities of the Third World are all alike and have the same preoccupations. Some of them, such as Cairo's El Azhar University, which dates far back in history have—just like the University of Uppsala—a prestigious past and can pride themselves on having formed very great minds. Others, as a legacy of the period of European colonization, continue to dispense a relatively conventional education or, on the other hand, are undertaking a complete overhaul of their structures, their curricula and their methods so as to adapt themselves radically to the new requirements. Still others, very recently founded (I have in mind various open universities, for instance), have from the outset adopted teaching methods and curricula which put them in the vanguard of innovation, for it is true that one of the privileges of the developing countries is to be able sometimes to take short cuts in the light of the experience gained by other members of the international community.

In the developing countries, universities assume, as elsewhere, their traditional functions of seeking and creating knowledge, transmitting it and providing training; but these functions are often carried out in particular circumstances and in a historical context obliging universities to go beyond the boundaries usually assigned to them.

Basic research in the developing countries thus needs to be conducted vigorously and draw upon increased resources, since it constitutes one of the prerequisites for intellectual autonomy. But whereas, owing to the small extent of industrialization and to the lack of large networks of private institutions such as are to be found elsewhere, the universities of the developing countries often represent the only centres of study and the only research facilities, it would be unthinkable that they should not give the necessary attention to the solution of problems on which the survival of the national community sometimes depends. Basic research and *applied research* may be regarded there, more than elsewhere, as indissociable, since the universities have a duty to seek practical solutions, with a view to contributing to the development of natural resources and to a rational use of the human potential, so as to meet the elementary and vital needs of the population in general, such as improved public health, nutrition, housing, communications, urbanization, education and so forth. Hence the need to place knowledge back in the real social contexts in which it can actually be applied. In other words, it seems essential to associate more closely not only theory and practice but also research, training and production.

Universities are, naturally, in the developing countries as elsewhere, ideal places for thought or for intellectual production, but very few of them are actually associated with the production of material goods. There is of course no question of changing universities into factories or farms but, by associating them with productive work, of enabling them more soundly to test the theories they elaborate and to draw conclusions therefrom for fresh research or experimentation, or simply for new patterns of training likely to help improve productivity. By reducing the time spent on feedback in the basic research-experimentation-application cycle, we make for a faster development process by gauging more surely and more promptly not only its economic but also its human and social impacts. Then, surely, it is normal and even necessary that those who are to be the national leaders of tomorrow—namely the students of today—should be fully aware of the conditions in which the bulk of their people live and work.

In this respect, the universities of the developing countries should also be more fully associated with all the sectoral or global studies on which the processes of national planning and programming, and that of evaluation of impacts and results, are based. A great many developing countries call upon foreign specialists when they possess often unemployed local talent. The false idea, sometimes held by the leaders of some developing countries, of universities as places of pure intellectual speculation severed from national realities, or even as breeding grounds or dissident political ideas, no doubt has something to do with the ostracism from which they occasionally suffer. It is for them, and we shall constantly stress this, to open themselves to the outside world with the rigour, objectivity and humility which mark any worthwhile intellectual approach and any truly disinterested human action.

Since universities have to direct their research towards action, they are naturally led to adopt, in the developing countries, a multidisciplinary approach to ensure that the scientific, technological and cultural talents at their disposal are all concentrated on the purposes of development.

With regard also to *training,* the requirements of development largely determine the work of universities. While, for instance, many industrialized countries have not succeeded, either quantitatively or qualitatively, in the difficult task of gearing training to the demand for manpower, this problem becomes tragic for the young developing nations. For these, higher education represents a very heavy financial burden. Yet, despite their relatively small number of graduates, they see a number of them joining the ranks of the unemployed because they have received a training more in line with foreign models than designed to meet domestic requirements. This is why higher education in the developing countries must, if it is to accomplish its historic purpose, give high priority to the training of the key personnel which the nation needs in all spheres. A number of universities have become aware of this need and are endeavouring to provide courses along original lines, matching precisely defined needs and with subject-matter intended to ensure a high standard of proficiency and to fit students to tackle practical problems, which are usually of a multidisciplinary nature.

Needless to say, such training should, wherever possible, be provided locally, being supplemented, when necessary, by specialized or post-graduate training in other parts of the world. Local training, as compared with that provided abroad, has the advantage of greater relevance in that it represents the result of a determined effort to think out afresh what should be the objectives of training, its subject-matter and its procedures. It enables the student to be set firmly in his environment, promotes the essential two-way contact between the university and the community, and makes it possible to avoid or to check the brain drain, which not only represents a serious waste of financial resources but too often deprives the developing countries of some of their best people.

These essential functions make the universities, in the developing countries, one of the surest safeguards of that *cultural authenticity* without which there can be no true autonomy, and their activities in this respect may take a variety of different forms.

It is, for example, incumbent upon the universities to rediscover, collect, transcribe, conserve and hand down what oral tradition has to teach, together with the rest of the legacy of past generations, their beliefs, their wisdom and their practical skills, their customs pregnant with a meaning that all too often goes unrecognized, their history—marked, in some cases, by an accord with the environment which is now lost—their crafts and their diverse forms of artistic expression. While the process of modernization may be irreversible because it meets the needs of a period in which it is essential to provide for the subsistence and the progress of growing numbers of people, it is by no means incompatible with preservation of the values on which the authenticity of each people is founded. One of the responsibilities falling to the universities in the developing countries is also (as several ministerial conferences have emphasized) to carry out the linguistic research that is needed to restore *local languages* to their rightful place, including, more particularly, the work of transcription, description, codification and unification, and the preparation of glossaries and grammars, that will raise these languages to the status of languages of instruction. In most of the developing countries, instruction is provided in foreign languages inherited from the former colonial powers. This fact contributes to creating an ever-widening gap between a modern élite benefiting from the meagre advantages of development and the bulk of the population.

It is also the task of the universities, in these countries, to see to the *preservation of the whole cultural heritage* and oral traditions. The historians they train must go back to the fountainhead and build, on the foundation of the past a rediscovered cultural identity; with the possibilities this will give them for communion with generations of their ancestors, they will then be able to repair the rifts occasioned by history and to restore that continuity which has been lost by so many countries subjected to colonization. Major responsibility thus lies with the universities as regards the establishment of institutions and research centres, or collaboration with those already existing. What is involved is not, of course, a mere reconstruction of the past, coming under the heads of archaeology, museography, or pure erudition. I just referred to endogenous development: such development rules out the perpetuation of anything in the past which hampers liberty and progress; and presupposes instead that a new significance will be attributed to the values and practices of societies, one of whose basic features is that they ensure for all the necessary conditions for the achievement of their full potential.

While the universities in the developing countries have a responsibility for strengthening the cultural identity of their peoples through the preservation of their intellectual and artistic heritage, they can also be of considerable assistance in safeguarding that identity in various areas where outside influences may threaten it.

This is the case, in particular, in the sphere of science. While it may be said that science knows no frontiers, in that it uses a language through which all may communicate, it is none the less true that the applied sciences and technology are not culturally neutral, for they very largely reflect the ways of life and the values of a society as well as influencing them. Endogenous development thus necessitates the application of specific formulas and the devising of appropriate technologies which, having regard to the conditions peculiar to the socio-cultural environment, will succeed in reconciling a heritage consciously assumed with the requirements of modern science. In the working out of such distinctive combinations, the universities in the developing countries have a vital part to play: they alone, in fact, can rediscover and study in depth the heritage of the past and, more particularly, take critical stock of the intellectual resources to which their role as links with the international community of scientists and researchers gives them access.

Similarly, the growing importance of the major *communication* media in the dissemination of knowledge and the shaping of attitudes, and the role of communication as a factor in national cohesion and as a means of access to international information, make it necessary for the universities in the developing countries to extend and rethink their activities in this sphere.

The information of all sorts (recordings, films, etc.) conveyed by the media tends in fact to bulk still larger, alongside the school and the university, in the developing than in the industrialized countries, and imposes on the public in those countries models imported from other parts of the world, which have consequently been designed in and for alien social and cultural contexts. Universities in the developing countries are morally bound to strive by every means in their power to correct this situation, to train specialists and to assist in the formulation of communication policies that are truly linked with endogenous development.

In order to be able to blaze the trail to really endogenous development in this way, the universities need, in the Third World countries, to strike deep roots in the community, which is, in truth, their very *raison d'être*. It is no longer sufficient—although it is still indispensable—for the universities to organize extramural activities as they have been doing in many countries for several years past. They should open their doors wide, through new structures, new admission procedures and the use of new methods, such as distance teaching, to new categories of students, many of whom, by force of circumstances, will not have had the opportunity of following a normal scholastic or academic career; they should organize meetings or seminars to provide information or further training for various social groups and broad strata of the population; and they should try, too, to play an active part in literacy campaigns, working shoulder to shoulder, in the national development effort, with the population at large—which in most cases is a rural population. In other words, the community of teachers and researchers formed by the university should henceforth in each country be more directly associated with, if not actually take charge of, the organization and conduct of systematic campaigns to eradicate illiteracy and to educate the masses, in particular the rural masses.

Participation in these joint tasks, drawing knowledge from the population as much as from academic studies should, then, constitute one of the new functions of the universities in the developing countries. But to do this, the university must relinquish the position to which it has sometimes clung, as the citadel in which, like a garrison taking refuge behind high walls, a small band of custodians of knowledge live in isolation, refusing to share the learning on which their power is based.

It is interesting, in this connection, to find that several developing countries are beginning to work out systems that combine study with community service or, according to circumstances, voluntary work by young people, so as to associate them with rural development and to meet the immediate needs of the people at large. Students, hitherto subjected to a passive learning process and theoretical teaching in higher education establishments, thus have the opportunity to take part in active life and in the working world. Such programmes promote an understanding of rural problems among students and the teachers in charge of them, and develop a sense of responsibility and initiative. Education may then cease to be the status-conferring process that paves the way to urban societies, neglectful of poverty, the realities of manual work, and village life.

Attempts of this type, which can, and no doubt should, be extended to underprivileged urban environments, obviously offer manifold advantages: they enlist the efforts of those who have had the privilege of access to learning for the purposes of development, they contribute to the education of the mass of the people, which is the essential condition for any progress, they strengthen the sense of fellowship and national unity and they tend to bring about genuine democratization; but, in addition, and perhaps most important of all, they have an outstanding educational value inasmuch as they bring the student into contact with working life and the realities of society and production. Moreover, political and administrative leaders, whether in the public or the private sphere, would be liable to fall short in the discharge of their national responsibilities—to an even greater extent than those in the developed countries—if they were not acquainted by practical experience, with the realities of their people's day-to-day life.

This means that the university must necessarily become an integral part of the developing society around it and must cease to hold aloof from the rest of the educational system, from which it has too often been isolated. It can, by setting its own house in order, provide the educational system with a foundation on which to build in overhauling its arrangements, and encourage it to adapt institutions and curricula, too often carried over from the colonial past or designed on the lines of foreign models, to the facts and new requirements of national development, fostering among other things the merging of formal and non-formal education and the linking of education with work. The university can also play a vital part in research in the education sciences. No one can help being struck by the very small place that this has so far held in university research in the developing countries, whereas it should cover a very broad range of disciplines. I have in mind not simply pedagogics and educational technology, but psychology, sociology, social psychology, and the language sciences, the importance of which needs no further emphasis. It seems to me that institutes dealing with educational research and the sciences of education could, without thereby sacrificing their intellectual independence, set themselves the task of studying the problems facing ministries and the various authorities responsible for educational policies, and guiding them by this means in their policy decisions. The university would, by so doing, assume a task of vital historic importance in the development of national education systems.

In order to carry out these new functions and to adopt an approach differing so markedly from the traditional attitude in many industrialized countries, the universities in the Third World countries are being increasingly induced to change their institutional structures and the content of their teaching, together with their methods, their relations with society and with everyday life, and the rules governing their own functioning and their management techniques. Every lecturer then becomes at once a researcher and an instructor, an expert and an organizer, and, at times, an adult education worker and a community leader; his responsibility *vis-à-vis* the students and society in general is thereby considerably increased. He is often called upon, too, to co-operate with specialists who, although not trained for teaching, can revitalize conventional education by bringing to it their professional experience. The university is, in this way, led to embark on a reconversion process which will enable it to take on the dual function of initial and recurrent education in order to meet the needs and to observe the spirit of lifelong education. It is, moreover, impossible to lay too much stress on the university's responsibility with regard to continuous training in countries where, to a greater extent than elsewhere, intellectuals and specialists are liable, for lack of the necessary infrastructures and means of professional contact, to find themselves so unfortunately isolated that only frequent refresher courses can remedy the serious disadvantages due to the rapid obsolescence of knowledge which is a feature of the present time, especially in the scientific field.

To round off my thoughts on the university's new roles in the developing countries, I should like to say a few words about two requirements which seem to me to be complementary.

First of all, there is the need for *co-operation among universities in the same region* so that, through the distribution of personnel training or research tasks among institutions in countries whose needs are very similar, development problems may find a solution within a wider context. By avoiding duplication among neighbouring countries, the necessary resources can be released for concentrating efforts on the institutions of highest international standing so that national capacity is thereby strengthened.

But collaboration is also possible and desirable between countries which, although not in the same region, have much to gain from pooling their experience because of the similarity of their social structures, their natural conditions, their level of development or their policies.

I would add, lastly, that close *co-operation* is increasingly necessary *between universities in developing countries and in industrialized nations:* the collaboration among scholars and research workers which was always consistent with the university's responsibilities and its long-standing practices, is seen today to be the essential condition for the working out of that more equitable international order to which all people everywhere aspire, and which cannot be conceived otherwise than as a new humanism born of the hopes and thinking of the university community as a whole. The theme that you have prompted me to develop on this solemn occasion is sufficient indication that you share this conviction with me, and I do not think that any other setting could have been more appropriate for it, in the circumstances, than the University of Uppsala.

A Confrontation between the Theory of Democracy and the Theory of Social Choice

By William H. Riker

Professor of Political Science
University of Rochester, USA

The theory of social choice is a theory about the way that the tastes, preferences, or values of individual persons are amalgamated and summarized into the choice of a collective group or society. As such, this theory must include, among other elements, a theory of voting because voting is one method of aggregating values. Voting itself is in turn an indispensable feature of democracy because, whatever outcome of justice is attributed to democracy, it does involve as its method some kind of popular participation in government. Necessarily, therefore, the theory of social choice is highly relevant to the theory of democracy.

It is only recently, however, that the relevance has been recognized. One reason recognition has come slowly is that students of democracy have, typically, not been interested in the mechanism of voting, which they have tended to regard as a trivial subject. Political philosophers, engaged in the pursuit of justice, have in fact treated the theory of voting as something best left to the attentions of municipal employees.

About thirty years ago, however, Duncan Black rediscovered the paradox of voting and showed that voting is not such a simple thing after all. This paradox occurs thus: Suppose every individual voter is able to order his or her preferences. This means that for three objects, a, b, c, say candidates or motions, voters can say that they prefer them in the order abc, with a best and c worst. Still, it may happen that, when these ordered preferences on individuals are voted on, society may not have an order: a beats b, b beats c, and c beats a. When this happens, no one knows what the social arrangement is because everything is in a cycle: abca or bcab or cabc.

A few years after this rediscovery, Kenneth Arrow showed that, in effect, no reasonably fair system of voting could avoid this paradox. And recently Allen Gibbard and Mark Sattertwhaite have shown that, among other things, Arrow's theorem means that *any* system of voting can be manipulated.

All these are disconcerting results. They raise doubts about whether or not voting can in fact do what, in democratic theory, it is supposed to do. So my question for today is: Can democratic means achieve democratic ends?

First, let me say a few words about democracy, which is a quite complex set of ideas about freedom and equality and participation. These can be regarded as both means and ends and in democratic theory they are in fact both. As a means, participation is a way to control one's social environment. Freedom in turn is necessary for participation because, as Madison said, "Liberty is to faction what air is to fire." One can't have political parties to organize participation and debate and voting without civil, religious, and economic liberty. Similarly, equality is necessary for participation because participation is without meaning unless the participants do in fact have some opportunity to influence outcomes, which requires roughly equal chances.

These democratic means are also the democratic ends in themselves. Liberty and equality are traditional human ideals and the notion that participation or self-control is the essence of human dignity goes back at least to Aristotle.

So whether we think of participation as a means or as a goal, it is the essence of democracy and the purpose of liberty. Furthermore, voting is the essence of participation, because in the end all of political debate and party organization comes down to voting, which is one subject in the theory of social choice.

In the democratic tradition there are at least two interpretations of voting, really two traditions about what participation means. One is the Liberal, or Madisonian view; the other is the Populist, or Rousseauean view.

The Liberal view is that the function of voting is to control officials and nothing more. Madison, for example, defined a republic (which was his word for what we now call democracy) entirely in terms of regular popular elections. They were, he thought, both necessary and sufficient to prevent tyranny and to ensure both liberty and popular control of government. In short, he saw elections as a check on power and he assumed that, if power were effectively checked, liberty and participation would flourish naturally. This remains the Liberal view, with added emphasis that what the voters decide is neither right nor wrong, but merely the choice they have made.

The Populist view, on the other hand, interprets voting as a way to determine the content of liberty. Rousseau, for example, asserted: "Liberty is obedience to a law we have prescribed for ourselves." This is not quite the medieval blasphemy that "the voice of the people is the voice of God", but recently a contemporary American populist actually asserted that "righteousness .... can only become wholly visible in .... the life of a people" and went on to assert that the works of the participating people were not only their liberty but *absolute* righteousness as well. Even without such excesses of enthusiasm, the Populist view is:

(1) Participation in making law is necessary for liberty.

(2) The laws thus made *must* be respected as right and proper because they thus embody popular liberty. Since law is a fair and true amalgamation of the values of the people, if it is not respected and obeyed, liberty itself would vanish.

This is in sharp contrast to the Liberal view in which the outcome of voting has no special moral character.

The question I want to put today is: Can either of these interpretations of voting stand up in the face of the recent discoveries in the theory of social choice. There are three kinds of discoveries I want to talk about.

One is that different methods of voting give different results even though voters' preferences are the same.

Another is that no method of voting can guarantee logical consistency.

A third is that every method of voting can be manipulated. Let me discuss these discoveries in turn.

First I will discuss the proposition that different methods of voting give different results. Most people are not aware of this fact simply because our voting methods are fairly crude. They give us a choice; but they do not give us enough information to know what the choice might have been with a different method of voting. It is often the case—and I have in fact found a number of real world examples—that a motion will pass in a legislature that could have been defeated by an amendment which was in turn rejected early in the amendment process. But most of us never realize this because usually there is not enough data provided by the voting method to check out possible alternative results. That is, we don't know voters' full preference orders. Usually we only learn their first choices, or in voting on motions and amendments, some of the possible comparisons, but not all of them.

There is one instance, however, in which a researcher collected full preference orders from all voters and then applied different methods of voting to those orders. In 1972, when beginning to plan for the recently launched Voyager probes of Jupiter and Saturn, Ralph Miles, an engineer at the Jet Propulsion Laboratory in Pasadena, conducted a vote on the trajectories. While the Laboratory was of course responsible for selecting the trajectories and the experiments, it had ten teams of scientific advisers, composed mostly of university professors, on such subjects as magnetic fields, infrared radiation, etc. These teams were responsible for suggesting experiments in their specialties and, ultimately, for interpreting the data that would be gathered. While the rockets had to be launched in August and September of this year, there was considerable leeway in possible trajectories, and the Jet Propulsion Laboratory picked out over 100 pairs. These were winnowed down to 32 pairs. Mr. Miles then had the ten teams rank order these 32 pairs and, furthermore, he had them use the so-called Von Neumann-Morgenstern experiment to generate cardinal utility numbers in the range from zero for lowest to one for highest for each of the 32 pairs. So, as a result, he had just about complete data on the team's preferences. Furthermore, in most cases it was good data. Most of the teams took the task of voting very seriously. They spent several months discussing it by mail and phone, and each team gathered for one weekend to discuss their preferences. Certainly the choice of a trajectory meant a lot to them. For many of the team members these probes would be a significant part of their lives' work as scientists. Furthermore, the trajectories made a difference to them. For example, one trajectory was ranked first by one team, third by another, and 32nd by three others. So for the most part these preferences were important to the voters and were carefully thought out by intelligent people. Finally, Mr. Miles attempted not to let the teams manipulate the outcome by voting contrary to their true taste or by forming coalitions, as would certainly have happened had they been allowed to behave politically. Instead, he simply had them report their cardinal utilities in (apparently) total ignorance of what other teams were doing. Presumably, therefore, he learned their true preferences. Then he used his data to count their votes by four methods.

There are three main categories of voting methods, which vary mainly in the way that data on preferences is used to determine the winners. The first category I call *majoritarian,* which with exactly two alternatives, is just simple majority voting; but, with more than two alternatives is defined thus: The winner is that alternative which can beat all others by a simple majority vote. Such a winner is called a Condorcet winner after the eighteenth century philosopher who coined this definition. Since it can often happen that no alternative is a Condorcet winner, there are a number of ways to define further a weaker kind of winning. But in this case it was not necessary because trajectory pair no. 26 was preferred by a majority to each other pair. It was the Condorcet winner.

A second category of voting methods I will call *positional* because they are based on data about where alternatives stand in all voters' preference orders. Plurality voting is one such method. Another is the Borda count which operates them: For each person's preference order and, say, 32 alternatives, give the person's highest alternative 31 points, the next highest 30 points, on down to the lowest, which gets zero points. Then sum the points for each alternative in all preference orders and the alternative with the most points wins. By this method trajectory pair no. 31 was the winner.

The third category of voting methods I call *utilitarian* or Benthamite, after the English utilitarian, Jeremy Bentham. One such method is to define as the winner that alternative which has the largest sum of individual cardinal utilities. By this method, trajectory no. 26 won. Another such method is to multiply each person's cardinal utility for an alternative by each other person's cardinal utility for that same alternative. The winner is then that alternative with the largest product of utilities. By that method, trajectory pair no. 31 was the winner.

Thus, by two methods no. 26 won; by two other methods no. 31 won. Which was the *true* winner? Which method best amalgamated individual values into a social choice? I do not believe this question can be answered. There is something good and something bad about each of the categories of methods.

Majoritarian methods do obtain a majority choice, if one exists, and that is desirable, I believe, because it assures a minimal consensus. On the other hand, majoritarian methods can violate a fundamental logical rule of *Consistency*, when two groups of voters, like two legislative houses, vote on the same alternatives.

Positional methods are, on the other hand, always *consistent* but, even when a Condorcet or majority winner exists, positional methods may select something else.

Utilitarian methods are also *consistent,* but they have two serious defects: One is that they may choose something that a huge majority opposes. Another is that they involve adding up my utility numbers and your utility numbers, which is about like adding beautiful ladies' heads and lionesses' bodies, and birds' wings to get sphinxes, whose meaning, if any, is an unsolvable riddle.

So there is no method of voting that is wholly defensible, either logically or morally. Consequently, with the same set of individual judgments, different outcomes result using different voting methods, and no outcome is clearly superior to any other. It follows, therefore, that the social outcome depends just as much on the accident of which voting method is used as it does on the true tastes and values of the voters.

This seems to me to raise deep questions about Populism. If laws supposedly embody the values of voters, yet if it may happen that each particular law is adopted as much because of the method of voting as because of the beliefs and values of the voters, the populist justice depends in good part on which imperfect method of voting happens to be used. I do not believe even the most extreme Populist would want to assert that. Liberalism, on the other hand, is somewhat less affected by this discovery of the influence of methods on outcomes. Liberalism does not anticipate that voting will truly and fairly amalgamate the values of voters. In the liberal view, all that voting does is get rid of unpopular officials and keep officials who aren't unpopular. No other meaning is or can be attributed to electoral decisions.

This is, however, just the first question raised by the theory of social choice. A much deeper question is raised by Kenneth Arrow's general possibility theorem. To prepare for this theorem, Arrow placed certain minimal conditions of fairness and efficiency on the method of amalgamating individual judgments and a condition of logicality on the outcome of the amalgamation. He then proved—and this is the striking theorem—that no method of amalgamating individual values over three or more alternatives into a social choice could simultaneously satisfy the fairness condition and the logicality condition. From this one infers that an always fair voting system must sometimes produce illogical results or that logical results can always be obtained only from a voting system that is sometimes unfair.

Let me list the conditions of fairness and efficiency:

(1) Everyone should be free to choose whatever preference order he or she wants. Many writers have tried to evade the force of Arrow's theorem by tinkering with this condition; but it seems obvious to me that elementary fairness requires that individuals be allowed to make their own judgments on an alternative.

(2) A second fairness condition is that the voting system be such that, if an individual raises the valuation of an alternative, then its chance of winning does not decline. Since voting systems are supposed to reflect voters' values, it would be the utmost in perversity if the fact that a voter came to like an alternative better meant that it had less chance to win.

(3) A third fairness condition is that the social choice not be imposed from outside the system. The desirability of this condition from the point of view of democracy seems obvious.

(4) A fourth fairness condition is that the method of voting always give the same result every time it is applied to the same set of ordinally ordered individual preferences. This is simply the requirement that the method of voting not itself be capricious and seems an obvious condition of fairness. Yet it does rule out utilitarian voting methods.

(5) A final fairness condition, the most obvious of all, is that there must not be a dictator.

These are all reasonable conditions and, it seems to me that nearly everyone would agree with them, especially the last one, that there not be a dictator.

The condition of logicality, often called a condition of rationality, is that the social outcome be transitive. This is simply the requirement that, if x is chosen over or ties with y and if y is chosen over or ties with z, then x is chosen over or ties with z.

Arrow's theorem is that the five fairness conditions are incompatible with the rationality condition. This means that it is always possible for a fair method of social decision to produce an illogical result. In practice, since most decision methods satisfy all fairness conditions except non-dictatorship, this theorem boils down to the assertion that voting systems that always produce a logical result must have a dictator.

This is a pretty gloomy conclusion and naturally there has been a continuing effort in the last decade to find some way around it. But there just doesn't seem to be any good way to do so. For example, one can weaken transitivity, while still retaining some kind of ordering principle; yet the best one can do is to change from needing a dictator to needing an oligarchy. So that method of evading Arrow's result doesn't get one very far.

Another way to evade the theorem is to say that society need not be rational or logical. After all, one might argue, rationality is a property of human beings and a *group* of humans is not itself human. So there is no reason why the group as a whole should behave like a human. Just as it is an anthropomorphic fallacy to attribute human emotions to an animal, so it is an anthropomorphic fallacy to attribute human logicality to the Leviathan. One ought to expect, on these grounds, that social decisions will often be illogical.

Since I am, myself, not willing to give up on any of the fairness conditions and since I believe most democrats are also unwilling to do so, we are forced to accept the possibility of social illogicality. This fact has never particularly bothered me because I have never really expected society to be rational in the same sense people are rational.

What has surprised me—and I believe also most other political scientists—is that in accepting social illogicality, I am also forced to accept the possibility that social choice can be manipulated. Gibbard has shown that any non-dictatorial ordinal voting system is subject to manipulation in the sense that some voter can, by voting contrary to his true preference order, bring about a result that is more attractive to him than if he voted "sincerely". Of course, this is precisely what is involved in logrolling, agenda-fixing, and introducing new alternatives—all the usual techniques of manipulation. Satterthwaite has further shown that, for a voting system to be immune to strategic voting is exactly equivalent to being socially rational. Hence, the only way to avoid strategic manipulation is to violate one of the fairness conditions, such as non-dictatorship.

Again, one can weaken this result by weakening the requirement of transitivity. The weakest such requirement—which does not really avoid manipulation—is the condition that, if choosing is broken up into several steps, the ultimate social choice be something that is, at least, chosen at one of the steps. This does avoid the necessity of a dictator, but it does not avoid all manipulation and it does involve the possibility of choosing an alternative that *everyone* would prefer not to have.

From all this I conclude that any expectation of social logicality necessitates something quite undesirable morally, some kind of unfairness such as a dictator or choosing something no one wants. So it seems to me that we might as well face up to the fact that all our social choice procedure are going to be manipulatable in some way or another.

Many social choice theorists have feared that Arrow's theorem meant that we would have to have some kind of concentrated power in society in order to guarantee a logical ordering of outcomes. This seems to me to get things backward. What Arrow's theorem and Gibbard's theorem tell us is something quite different. Democratic societies are, for certain, not going to allow concentrated power. Consequently, they are going to have to put up with social illogicality and the manipulation of decision procedures. This is the political interpretation of Arrow's theorem: that manipulation is always possible in democracies.

In this way we political scientists have been led by the force of the mathematical argument to see what parliamentary and democratic political leaders have always known but what idealistic philosophers have tried to hide: namely, that it is usually possible to manipulate political outcomes. Indeed, once I began to look at politics through the spectacles of social choice, I realized that the main content of political life and the true art of democratic and parliamentary politics is planning and executing maneuvers of manipulation. What began as a mathematical exercise has, for me, at least, become a descriptive explanation of political life.

There are, I believe, two main kinds of manipulation, corresponding to the two main situations of political life, namely winning or losing or being in or out of power.

The manipulation by those in power is carried out through control of the agenda. Political leaders have always known that is possible by controlling the agenda to produce social decisions that are not fair amalgamations of individual values. Farquharson opens his study of strategic voting with an example from the Roman Senate, surely one of the earliest parliamentary bodies. Pliny the Younger was presiding and he realized that his preferred outcome would lose if he put the question in the usual way. So he put the question in a novel way and his side won. Presiding officers have been doing this ever since. Indeed, Charles Plott has shown that is perfectly easy in laboratory experiments on the control of the agenda to defeat a motion that is preferred to *all* others. I have repeated this experiment in my own laboratory with identical results. Give a group of, say, 21 subjects preferences over several alternative motions by guaranteeing to pay to each one differently various amounts of money for the victory of the various motions. This gives each subject a preference order over the motions, a different order for each person. Plan to pass motion x; present the group with an appropriate agenda and it passes motion x. Plan to pass motion y; give exactly the same preferences to another group but with a different but appropriate agenda and it passes motion y. But if the true preferences of the subjects were followed motion z would pass! Control of the agenda is an immense power and this is what winners always have.

But losers have something also. They can introduce new motions and create new platforms. Winners like the old issues because they won on them. Losers naturally don't like the old issues because they lost on them. So losers have a continual motive to introduce new issues and these always have the potential of rearranging politics so that old losers become new winners and old winners become new losers.

The simplest way to introduce a new issue is to bring into consideration an otherwise irrelevant alternative through a vote trade. A minority about to lose on a motion buys enough votes to win from some members of the erstwhile majority with the promise of support on some other issue.

This maneuver is so well known that I don't want to waste time describing it. Let me instead explain some other related techniques, one of the cleverest of which is the cycle-generating amendment. To give an example, let me tell about the election of U.S. senators. In the Constitution of 1787 it was provided that they be elected by state legislatures. But by 1900 it was widely believed that they should be chosen in popular elections; a number of states had adopted procedures that in effect provided for it; and there probably were enough senators, mostly Southern Democrats and Western Republicans, to pass a Constitutional Amendment. Eastern Republicans, a fairly small minority, were mostly opposed; but they had a brilliant parliamentary strategist, one Chauncey DePew. When the proposed Constitutional Amendment came up, he proposed to add to it the requirement that the national government supervise the senatorial elections. This was in effect a proposal to go back to the era of Reconstruction, twenty-five years previously, when the Army supervised polling places in the South to be sure that blacks voted. All Republicans, regardless of their attitude on senatorial elections, were agreed on the desirability of this arrangement. So DePew's proposal passed. But now the Constitutional Amendment was unpalatable to every Southern Democrat for at that time most blacks lived in the South and only whites could vote. All the white Southern Democrats who had previously favored the Constitutional Amendment, now despised it because of DePew's addition. So the Constitutional Amendment failed. Altogether this amendment was delayed for seven or eight years by this elegant maneuver by losers. Ultimately they lost; but they managed to stave off losing for quite a while.

Another technique of introducing new issues is the majority-splitting platform. The best example I know of this concerns the development of that great and persisting issue of American politics, namely the role of blacks in society. That issue underlay the Civil War and never since has been far from the surface of American politics. To describe its development, let me point out that in the 1820s American politics consisted on the whole of trivial bickering. Alexis DeTocqueville visited the United States in 1830 and wrote that the great national parties of the 1790s had broken up into confused factions. But at the very time DeTocqueville wrote, President Andrew Jackson was re-creating the great national parties, largely along economic lines. Jacksonian Democrats were mildly radical, agrarian, and anti-mercantile, while the opposing Whigs were mildly conservative and mercantile in orientation. In the 1830s Democrats were big winners and had they been able to keep the economic issues of the 1830s going, they could have won forever. But there was no reason why the Whigs should allow this. And they didn't.

I first came across the explanation in the diary of President Polk, a Jacksonian Democrat who held office from 1845–1849. He was a successful President, but a very strange and obsessive man who kept a private diary that was never intended for publication. In this diary he frequently complains that the Whigs had made slavery an issue simply to split the Democratic Party. When I first read this, written only twelve to fourteen years before the Civil War, I wondered how Polk could be so blindly partisan that he could not see what was plainly in front of him, namely that slavery was a profound moral issue. Then I realized he was probably right. The Whigs promoted slavery as an issue exactly because it would split the Democratic party. It did. It also destroyed the Whigs; but President Lincoln, an old Whig, created the Republican party as a descendant of the Whigs; and it won elections pretty steadily for about seventy years thereafter.

What made it possible for the Whigs to split the Democrats on slavery, which up to that time had been a relatively minor issue in American politics? The answer is that by 1840 the Democrats were a national party with strength divided about equally between the North and the South, while the Whigs were almost entirely Northern, the non-slavery area. If Whigs could make slavery an issue, they would split their opponents without hurting themselves much, precisely what Polk feared. And the Whigs did. The best evidence of their success is that they terrified Northern Democrats into becoming anti-slavery themselves. Martin Van Buren, a conventional Jacksonian Northern Democrat, was President from 1837–41 and, so far as I can discover, did nothing to attack slavery. He simply played out the drama of Jacksonian economic issues. In 1848, however, and with great moral fervor, he ran for President as a third party anti-slavery Democrat. Of course, all he accomplished was the election of the Whig. Within the next ten years the Democratic party was hopelessly split and many Northern Democrats joined with Whigs to form the Republican party, which established itself under the ex-Whig, Abraham Lincoln, one of those Whig Congressmen in 1847–48 who Polk believed were trying to split the Democratic party by trying to exclude slavery from the lands conquered from Mexico.

This is the power that losers have. They can create new issues that old winners lose on. From mere vote trading to complete reorientation of politics losers can manipulate outcomes by introducing what appear to be irrelevancies.

I return now to the question with which I started this discourse: How does democratic theory fare in light of the discoveries of social choice theory?

We have two main discoveries: One is that the same set of individual values may be added up by different, but equally defensible voting systems, to get different results. The other is that, given the inevitable inconsistency of voting results, every method of voting can be manipulated, either by the winners' method of controlling the agenda or the losers' method of introducing new issues.

How does the Populist interpretation stand up against these discoveries? Since the discoveries imply that the method of voting and the agenda setting of leadership have as much to do with the outcome as popular values, it is no longer possible to claim that the results of any particular election reveal the wants and wishes of the people. To save the Populist position at all, it is necessary, I believe, to reduce the Populist claim to the proposition that popular values are expressed in a series of elections (in which presumably the effects of voting methods and agenda manipulation cancel out). But in a series of elections there is always the prospect that the repeated revelation of any particular set of values will be thrown off track by the creation of new issues. Thus, the Jacksonian economic issues were put on the back burner by the introduction of the slavery issue. I believe that the Populist cannot claim these new issues that tap a new dimension of popular belief are false. To claim they are false is to claim, as Marxists do, that they know more about popular values than the people themselves. So the Populist position is undercut two ways: It is impossible to claim that the popular will has been truly revealed in a single election, nor is it possible to claim that the disruption—by new issues—of new revelation of popular will in a series of elections is unfair or false. Thus, social choice theory has made it extraordinarily difficult to sustain the Populist interpretation of voting.

It is not that the Populist interpretation is indefensible. One can emend it to say that true popular will is revealed over time in what becomes substantial agreement. What is indefensible is the Populist political tactic of claiming to have discovered popular values in a single election and thereby justifying radical changes in society on the basis of one election alone. So it seems to me that Populism as a theory can survive in a highly damaged form the discoveries of social choice theory, but Populism as a practical political tactic cannot be intellectually justified.

What about Liberalism? While Liberalism makes no claim that the outcome of elections embodies the popular will, it does claim that the people can exercise control over disliked rulers by getting rid of them. And the inference from any particular election is that an ejected ruler is disliked. But, of course, given the doubts I have raised about the system of counting and about the possibilities of manipulation, one cannot take that claim very seriously either. All that can be said of a particular election, even in the Liberal view, is that it had a particular outcome which may or may not have truly and fairly expressed popular belief.

Where does all this leave us? It should, I think, make us highly sceptical of interpretations of particular elections. Liberalism is much less hurt by this scepticism than Populism because liberals have never placed great emphasis on particular elections anyway. But nevertheless all interpretations, whether Liberal or Populist, that attribute meaning to particular elections are somewhat damaged.

It seems to me that we are by social choice theory forced to say that in any particular election there is very little meaning. It is only in series of elections that all seem to go the same way that we can discount the effects of the method of vote counting and of manipulation.

What then does this mean as a practical matter? I believe it warns us that we ought not tolerate radical action on the basis of single elections. Indeed, taking radical action on the basis of single elections seems to me to be a major occasion for at least class hatreds and at worst civil wars. My hope is that one of the effects of social choice theory, as an understanding of it spreads, will be increased scepticism about the interpretation of particular election results, increased scepticism about Populist claims of revelations of popular will in particular elections, and increased reluctance to make significant changes in the status quo on the basis of particular elections. It will doubtless take a long time for this kind of scepticism and reluctance to permeate popular consciousness. In the meantime, it seems to me that social choice theory provides a powerful justification for institutions that make it difficult to take radical actions on the basis of particular elections. Here are some of the institutions that are justified: multiparty systems, where clear majorities seldom exist or even two-party systems which are fragmented into many factions; multiple legislative bodies each with a veto over the others, even judicial review of legislative action. On the other hand, here are some institutions that are not justified and about which one ought to have doubts: responsible, clear-cut two-party systems of and single sovereign legislative bodies. The basis for the justification and condemnation is, of course, whether or not the institutions allow winners of single elections to enforce a claim for a popular mandate for major changes in political life.

Nothing in social choice theory is in conflict with the fundamental methods or ideals of democracy. But there is, I believe, an irreconcilable conflict between the moral and mathematical revelations of social choice theory and Populist enthusiasm. My conclusion is, therefore, that in planning political institutions from a democratic point of view we ought to try to be liberal; we ought to render institutions responsive to popular control but at the same time we ought to insist these institutions prevent precipitous action based on one election.

"Where Are We Growing?"

By Maurice F. Strong
Chairman, Petro-Canada
Canada

It is a very special privilege indeed to have this opportunity of participating in the programme celebrating the 500th Anniversary of the establishment of Uppsala University. The life of the University has spanned the most rapid and dramatic period of transition that the human community has ever experienced. Few of the institutions which existed at the beginning of this period exist today; few have contributed more significantly or positively to the changes in the human condition which have been effected during this period; and even fewer have retained the intellectual vitality and social relevance required to deal with the unprecedented challenges which confront our societies in the period ahead.

It is to these challenges that I would like to direct my remarks today. I would remind you that I am neither scientist, economist nor politician. My views are those of a layman who has had the privilege of working for some years at the interface of science, economics and public affairs where so many of the conflicting pressures and issues which are shaping our future converge. Here it is necessary to try to see the multitude of forces which bear on the future course of our societies within a holistic framework. It is clearly not easy to do this; for the methods by which we can perceive, let alone evaluate, the complex system of cause and effect relationships by which our future is being shaped are as yet poorly developed—one must still rely primarily on one's individual observations and intuition for the attempt to understand this system and how our own actions within it can affect our future course.

The environment issue has, more than any other, made us aware that the planet Earth is a single system in the physical sense, that the future survival and well-being of the whole human family depends upon the continued health of this physical system and that technological man now has the capacity to make changes in this system which could be decisive for the human future. The United Nations Conference on the Human Environment held in Stockholm in June 1972 was the first major step by the nations of the world in recognizing that these realities require a response at the political level which is beyond the capacity of any individual nation state or group of states and requires in fact co-operation on a global scale amongst all nations. It pointed up the fact that we cannot expect to be able to manage effectively a physical and technological system which is intrinsically global without creating an effective political system that is also global in scale.

But, what has happened since Stockholm can give us little cause for confidence that these new perceptions of the need for a global approach to the human future are influencing to any significant degree the attitudes and policies of the leaders of nation states.

It is true that the establishment of the United Nations Environment Programme, the expansion of environmental activities by other international agencies and scientific organizations together with the establishment of environmental organizations and policies by most national governments have provided the institutional basis for a significant increase in national action and international co-operation in respect of specific environmental issues.

It has also been demonstrated that many specific environmental problems—for example, various kinds of air and water pollution—will respond to technological solutions if we are prepared to spend the money required to do this. And most industrialized societies have shown a good deal of willingness to accept these additional economic costs.

This is encouraging. But it is not nearly enough. Indeed, there is a danger that because of this proliferation of activity in the name of environment people will be lulled into feeling that protection and improvement of the environment are now well in hand. Nothing could be further from the truth.

But, while we have shown the capacity to deal with some of the simpler manifestations of environment problems which Stockholm pointed up, there has been little or no progress in tackling the underlying source of our problems, the fundamentally unsound and unhealthy process of growth on which our modern economic system is based. Indeed, the economic difficulties which most governments have faced during the past several years, coupled with the manifest difficulties of reaching agreement on complex issues at the international level, have resulted in an almost universal regression by our national governments to more inward-looking, narrowly nationalistic attitudes and policies. Thus, as the need for global co-operation has continued to grow, the political will required to achieve it has receded to a degree which I feel is extremely dangerous.

Although the political force of the environmental movement has remained encouragingly strong as evidenced by the successful efforts in many countries to slow down the development of nuclear energy, environmental considerations are still viewed largely as an added cost to the economy and an irritation to governments rather than a central element in their national objectives. The truth is that the environment issue cannot be dealt with as an issue separate and distinct from others any more than we can deal in isolation with such issues as inflation, unemployment, energy and rich/poor disparities.

At a high level of generality we all accept the premise that these issues must be dealt with as inter-related aspects of the larger task of maintaining the security and well-being of our societies. But the structure of our institutions, our governments, our financial organizations, our universities and our professional lives continues to be based largely on a narrow, sectorial or disciplinary approach to these issues. Both our educational system and our career patterns tend to re-enforce the attitudes and the incentives which continue to impel us along the narrower paths. Inertia is a powerful force in the political and social arena as it is in the physical world. While we talk about the need for a new and more integrative approach to society's problems, we are caught up in a set of attitudes and processes which are inexorably moving us in the same direction we have moved since the inception of the Industrial Revolution.

I am convinced that at the heart of our dilemma is the growth process itself. It is through the growth process that we create the economic means for meeting so many of our social needs, that we impact on the environment, that we use energy and natural resources, that we create employment and make possible leisure. The inflation, unemployment, environmental degradation, social conflicts and economic disparities which now bear in upon us with increasing intensity are not isolated phenomena. They are manifestations of fundamental deficiencies within the growth process which is central to our present economic, social and political systems. It is based on the premise that growth in the purely material sense, in the production and availability of material goods and services, will bring about a corresponding increase in human satisfaction and well-being. The concept of "gross national product" was invented as a means of measuring growth and soon the level of "gross national product" came to be equated with standard of living. The increase in "gross national product" became the central objective of national governments. In practical terms, this has tended to be the case whatever the underlying political ideologies of the governments.

Of course, it has been true up to a point. The explosion of our capacity to produce a multitude of material goods and services which accompanied the Industrial Revolution has brought unprecedented benefits to the peoples of the industrialized world. It has also made it technically possible to make vastly improved conditions of life available to the entire human population. Despite this, economic and political barriers continue to prevent the two-thirds of the world's people who live in the developing countries from realizing these benefits. The modern industrial system, based on mass production and mass-marketing, has proven to be an amazingly efficient means of meeting the needs of people for a wide variety of basic goods and services. But today, the mass market in the industrialized world for whom the mass production was designed has been largely satisfied, if not over-saturated. Most of the unsatisfied needs in industrialized societies today are of a non-material nature which industry rarely searches out as they do not accord with its traditional industrial logic. The remaining unsatisfied markets for material goods and services are largely in the third world where people cannot afford them. But the response of our industrial machine is to expand its markets by creating new wants and new appetites amongst the people who can afford them. We are thus caught in a paradox in which we have created an industrial system capable of meeting the basic needs of all the world's people but are in fact using it largely to foster further growth in the demand by the wealthy minority for goods and services well beyond what we need or is good for us.

Perhaps worse, this forced new growth is increasingly illusory. Illusory because the industrial-economic system we have inherited aims at the largest possible production of the most simplified goods. Thus competition, which has been vaunted as the essential condition driving our systems to offer greater and greater choice on the market place, has gradually lost that function. In fact, it has been reversed.

The financial need for large production makes innovation into a dangerously expensive risk. To avoid that risk, competition increasingly pits almost identical products against each other in sectors where basic markets have already been established.

The principal differences within that competition are in presentation and publicity. In other words, this forced growth is not real; it simply offers greater and greater quantities of increasingly similar products—which is to say, of fewer and fewer real products.

This system, like the bicycle, can only maintain its equilibrium when it is moving forward at a sufficient speed. Now that growth has slowed down in most industrial countries we must deal with some of the basic weaknesses which have always been inherent in the system. One of the most important of these is the parallel increase in the amount of capital and decrease in the amount of labour required to achieve a given unit of production. This in turn means that a disproportionate share of the rewards, and perhaps more importantly, of the power, go to those who control the capital. At the same time there is a reduction in the amount of employment available for a given level of production. And, although those who are employed can be well paid, many of the jobs available to them provide limited opportunities for personal satisfaction. And, for those growing numbers who are not employed, there are limited opportunities outside of the mainstream of the industrial system either for maintaining their income or employing their time in a satisfying way.

The great backlog of unfulfilled basic needs in the industrialized countries together with the massive reconstruction required following the two world wars of this century gave our industrial system a dynamic momentum which has now receded. There is nothing in prospect that is likely to see this momentum renewed in the foreseeable future. We are now in a transitional period which is almost bound to be more turbulent and difficult than what we have experienced in the past several decades. The pressures on our present economic, social and political systems are bound to escalate. It could well be a period of degeneration for western industrial civilization. But it could also be a period of renewal.

Social degeneracy has always been marked in history by overkill through concentration on quantity rather than quality. This was true in ancient Greece where concentration on quality was a sign of the civilization's innate rigor; its subsequent degeneracy being marked by encrusting that quality with a plaster-like over-emphasis which eventually dragged the society down.

In 17th and 18th century France, the decline of the monarchy and its society was first marked by apparent obsession of quality under Louis XIV. However, this was a false and superficial obsession which was merely the decoration or facade which surrounded the court and everything it stood for. There was a very real decline in the actual quality of life during that period as exemplified by the disappearance of adequate sanitation and water supply systems, even in the palaces.

Interestingly enough, the decline of efficient sanitation and water systems has symbolized the decline of societies since before the Greeks. One of the effects of our society's concentration on linear production has been the abandonment of water systems in the third world, the pollution of our own water systems, the decline in the quality of water available for consumption, especially in urban areas and a massive growth in the sale of bottled waters which bypass the system.

During a long siege, Athens eventually fell to Sparta because of an epidemic caused by the polluted water running through the city.

Medieval Europe's inability or unwillingness to deal with the waste produced by a growing urban population led to an increase in rats which carried the plague which in turn proved so destructive to that society. Degradation of water systems in China in several periods led to disastrous floods, rivers changing routes, agricultural disasters, followed by revolts and the collapse of the empire. Similar circumstances affected the histories of Rome and of Egypt.

The question is not whether pollution, especially water pollution, was caused or produced by degenerate societies. Pollution simply is and always has been one of the signs of societal decline. Following all of the historical precedents, our present pollution problems could point out the degenerative influences now operating in our societies.

We must face the fact that the long period of rapid growth experienced primarily in the industrialized world since the advent of the Industrial Revolution is both unprecedented in history and unsustainable. Nor can the industrial system which has developed during this period be patched up to meet the needs for a secure and promising future. Fundamental changes are needed both in this system and in the growth process of which it is the engine. If this period of turbulence is to be one of renewal for our societies, this renewal must be based on a new conception of growth, new attitudes towards the purposes of growth, and a re-structuring of the system of incentives and penalties which motivate the growth process.

Let us examine briefly the consequences of continuing along the growth path that has been followed by the industrialized countries since the Industrial Revolution. The first assumption we must make is that the developing countries will also choose to continue along a similar path. In order for all of the present population of the world to reach a standard of living equivalent to that of the United States in 1970, it would require extraction of some seventy-five times as much iron as is now extracted annually, 100 times as much copper, 200 times as much lead, 75 times as much zinc and 250 times as much tin, and increases of similar orders of magnitude in the production of many other basic resources. (1)

As for energy, such a standard of living would require the equivalent of 7 times as much oil, 8 times as much gas and 9 times as much coal as is now produced annually. All of that at a time when, as a recent international report by the Workshop on Alternative Energy Strategies pointed out, just keeping up with the growing demands of the more developed world may bring us to a supply gap of 20 million barrels a day equivalent of energy by 1990 and that gap may begin as early as 1982. (2)

But long before we confront the absolute physical limits of the Earth's supplies of petroleum and other key non-renewable resources, our use of these resources will be limited—in some cases drastically—by the economic, environmental and social costs of extracting and processing them as well as problems of distribution.

While large supplies of some of these materials might theoretically be made available through extraction of the minute quantities which exist in much of the earth's surface and the oceans, as well as a total commitment to recycling of metals, it is unlikely that the environmental impacts of such a vast increase in industrial activity could be kept within tolerable limits. And it is inconceivable that such levels of industrial activity could be achieved without a degree of political, economic and social mobilization and regimentation which would be incompatible with the maintenance of free societies and the rights of the individual.

And if the industrialized societies should attempt to continue on their present growth paths with little regard for the growth requirements of the developing countries, there is bound to be escalating conflict between the appetites of the rich and the needs of the poor. It is impossible to envisage a secure and prosperous world for either rich or poor under these circumstances. However, our pursuit of present growth patterns would, as I have said, be limited by organizational, institutional and social constraints long before it reached the limits of physical resources. The social costs and economic disparities which we now see as byproducts of this kind of growth and the increasing alienation of large sections of the population of industrialized societies make a change in the system inevitable long before these theoretical physical limits have been reached.

In short, I believe that the present approach to growth is simply not viable, that basic changes are necessary. I also believe they are possible.

"No growth" does not commend itself to any national government today as a viable policy. But no growth will nevertheless be the probable outcome of the policies most governments continue to pursue. The conditioned response to the problems which the present slavish adherence to material growth has produced is to provide more of the same. This is understandable. The prime function of politicians is to manage the issues which are of most immediate importance to their constituents. And today, most political leaders are so overwhelmed by the number and complexity of issues confronting them that they are less and less able to deal with immediate problems effectively, let alone consider seriously the fundamental changes that are necessary to secure the future of their constituents. Industrial societies are on the verge of becoming virtually ungovernable under the present system.

And there is no new body of economic and political theory on which they can construct new political platforms. Both Marxist and Keynesian theories have now been shown to be largely obsolete and no new body of ideas has yet emerged. We desperately need such a new body of ideas. And they must centre on the need for a new attitude towards growth.

First, I would suggest the objective of growth must be clearly seen as to make possible the greatest number of alternatives for individual choice and self-fulfillment which is compatible with the rights and well-being of society as a whole. This, of course, is easier to conceptualize than measure. I share the skepticism of Gunnar Myrdal as to the value of the social indicators that many have suggested as a substitute for gross national product. However, I do not believe that the difficulty in measuring the non-quantitive elements of growth should be a serious deterrent to adopting this objective.

We should also accept as the basic parameters for a "new growth" approach the needs:

1. To assure that every person on the planet has access to the means of providing the basic needs required to assure a life compatible with human dignity and wellbeing; and

2. To assure that our collective activities do not transgress the "outer limits" of the capacity of the biosphere to sustain human life at acceptable levels.

Within these two parameters, the growth process should be designed to facilitate equal opportunity for all people to pursue an infinite variety of interests, aspirations and life styles.

Conservation must become a prime element in the new growth system. Waste must be reduced to a minimum by redesigning industrial processes and careful planning of plant location to assure that the residues of one process become the raw materials of another. Technologies for recycling and reuse of materials and abatement of pollution must be integrated into production systems and not merely added on to them. A prime measure of the health of the system will be the degree to which it incorporates effective measures for the preservation of the resource and environmental capital base on which continued development depends.

This is already a practical goal in many areas. For example, steel can be produced from steel scrap with a 75 % energy saving over production from iron ore. And aluminum produced from discarded cans conserves 95 % of the energy used to produce it from bauxite. (3)

The logical way to measure progress is by the length of time the stock of processed materials is in active use; not by the speed of product turnover. Governments can encourage this in many ways. For example, by offering incentives for recycling facilities and removing or reducing depletion allowances for mining industries.

In many cases, new conservation oriented systems are on the verge of cost breakthroughs. They require major government support. A prime example is the solar industry. The land areas of the world receive some 690 Q (Q = a thousand million kilowatt hours of electric energy) of solar radiation per year after filtering by clouds. In comparison, the world energy production in 1970 was in the area of 0.24 Q or 2,800 time less.

At the present time, ERDA estimates are that one kilowatt of photo-electric power at a sunny location costs about $15,800. But, by 1986, they expect the cost to drop to $1400. At the same time, they expect the cost of electric power generated through nuclear fission to rise in real terms due to more sophisticated safety features and the rising cost of both uranium and waste disposal. By 1986, nuclear power could cost more than solar photo-electric power. (4)

The new growth concept must be rooted in the need to create an effective and functioning world economic system which recognizes that the policies and actions of each nation affect and are affected by the whole system. The growing interdependence of nations requires an increasingly effective international system of institutions and measures for the effective management of the system. This should in no way preclude the development by each nation of the maximum degree of self-reliance. Indeed an interdependent world system is likely to function most effectively when its national components have a significant degree of self-reliance, particularly in their ability to meet the basic needs of their people. This kind of self-reliance should be encouraged and strengthened, particularly in the weakest members of the international community. But self-reliance is not autarchy and no nation, however self-reliant, will be able to assure its people the maximum security and well-being outside of the world system.

It is industrialized societies for whom the "new growth" concept will require the most radical changes. It will require a major transition to a less physical kind of growth, relatively less demanding of energy and raw materials. It will be one which is based to an increasing degree on the satisfaction of peoples' intellectual, moral and spiritual needs and aspirations in such fields as culture, music, art, literature and other forms of individual self-development and fulfillment. These, after all, are the areas in which man achieves his highest levels of growth in human terms.

The industrialized countries must also be prepared to facilitate and support the establishment of most new industrial capacity, particularly that which is resource or labour intensive, in the less developed parts of the world. This, of course, must be done under conditions which enable developing countries to avoid many of the environmental and social costs we have paid for our industrial development.

The marriage of ecology and economics which I call "ecodevelopment" would be designed to assure that the precious natural resources of soil, forests, water, plant and animal life of the developing world are exploited in ways which make best use of their own skills and labour and harmonize with their own culture and value systems to produce maximum benefits for their people without destroying the resource base on which sustained development depends. It means, too, assuring that they have full access to the latest technologies and support for the development of their own scientific and technological capabilities so that technology will serve rather than determine their own growth patterns.

"New growth" will thus require new dimensions of co-operation between industrialized and developing nations. Interdependence, which is now a

physical and environmental reality, must become a working reality in economic, social and political terms. There must be a revamping of the present
international system of arrangements and institutions to enable them to
better support and serve the interests and aspirations of the developing
world. The healthy functioning of our interdependent technological society
requires the full participation and active co-operation of the two-thirds of
the people who live in the developing world and this dictates that we meet
their demands for a more just and equitable share of the benefits which this
technological civilization makes possible.

The transition to a new growth society has, perhaps, its best analogy in
the human body. From the birth of a child to the time it achieves physical
maturity, the principal emphasis is on physical growth. Indeed, healthy
physical growth and continued physical health are essential pre-conditions
to the growth of human personality in its social, cultural, intellectual, moral
and spiritual dimensions. Yet growth in these non-physical aspects of human development has only nicely begun at the time that physical maturity is
reached. Real growth is still to come. Our industrialized societies are very
much like the physically mature human being. For us to continue to pursue
purely physical kinds of growth would be as unhealthy and self-destructive
to our societies as it would be for an adult person to indulge himself so as
simply to add to his physical dimensions. And it would be just as wrong to
say that societies must stop growing when they reach the stage of physical
maturity as it would be to say that people stop growing when they stop
growing physically.

The real growth of our societies in human terms can still be ahead of us.
But it demands that we change our ways and adapt to a more mature kind of
growth that is less physically oriented and less demanding of resources and
the environment. On the other hand, developing countries are at a much
earlier stage of growth in which they must continue to grow in physical
terms if they are to meet the needs and aspirations of their people. But, they
too, must emphasize the kinds of physical growth which are healthy and
sustainable and provide expanding opportunities for self-expression and
fulfillment in human terms for their people.

Technology can be an ally in reducing the physical content of growth. The
most advanced technologies today, particularly in the fields of information
processing and communication, are moving dramatically in the direction of
less material and less energy intensiveness. For example, the same computer capacity which in the 1950's cost several hundred dollars and required a
machine that would fill a moderate-sized room is now available for a few
hundred dollars on a hand calculator. Similarly, it is technologically feasible
to reduce energy consumption by some 50 % without significantly impairing
present standards of living. And technologies are available to make even

further significant reductions in the energy requirements of many production processes. Thus technology can be enlisted to support the drive for achievement of the new growth society.

Similarly, I believe that the public policy levers which governments can today deploy are capable of altering the system of incentives and penalties to which our economic life responds so as to make it profitable to carry out those activities which are environmentally sound and socially desirable and unprofitable to do those things which impair environmental quality, destroy resources and detract from social goals. We have clearly demonstrated this in fighting or preparing to fight wars. For it is not the operation of the free-market economy which produces the massive market for war materials. That market is created by an act of public policy by governments, responding to the belief of their people that their security is at stake.

In fact, the arms industry is the industrial sector to have shown the greatest growth over the last years. In the arms industry, our physical growth oriented society has found its most dependable crutch.

In 1974, the GNP per head in the Middle East was $845. Of that $135 or 16 % was spent on arms. (5) Almost 30 % of all manufacturing industry in California is tied to arms; which makes that sector the largest employer in the state—one and a half million people. (6)

American military aerospace exports went from $840 million in 1972 to $2.5 billion in 1975. (7) Between 1973 and 1974, the United States almost doubled its arms exports from $3.9 billion to $8.3 billion. (8) Among the clients was Iran which spent almost $10.5 billion on arms in 1975–76. That is nearly one-third of its GNP. (9)

What is more, each piece of this equipment is incredibly expensive; as if the most creative edge of the industrial system has been devoted to creating these complex weapons. A single Chieftain tank costs $400,000—more than 20 tractors—while a Tomcat fighter costs $20 million or enough to buy a thousand tractors. (10)

In 1975, the world spent almost $300 billion a year on arms and the developing countries spent more on arms than on health and education together. (11)

What is the meaning of this extraordinary growth in one sector while most others were stagnating or advancing with difficulty? Part of the explanation lies in the fulfillment of the principal material needs in the developed countries. There is less room for growth and yet our economic system drives industry on.

Gradually the industries have turned to one of the rare growth areas left. In other words, it is easier for an industry to grow by selling arms than by selling tractors. That growth is not hindered by the fact that both the need and the market are artificial. In fact, a warped form of competition is encouraged as nations build up their arsenals. It is a fertile growth market because there are no real limits to demand and that demand is not limited by traditional market factors.

Today the threat to our security through the physical and social imbalances generated by present growth patterns is as great as the threat of nuclear warfare. Indeed, it is even more difficult to deal with because it seems less immediate and less traumatic. The threat of a nuclear war may be averted right up until the moment the button is pushed. But the threat of ecodisaster or economic and social collapse can only be averted by foreseeing it far in advance and acting to prevent it. By the time it is upon us it will be too late.

New growth does not mean a retreat to a more primitive or less desirable standard of life or to a static economy. Indeed, it should be seen as an advance towards a more qualitative, humanly satisfying lifestyle.

Far from being negative to the economy, a commitment to "new growth" would unleash new and dynamic economic forces and stimulate creativity, innovation and economic activity across a broad front.

If governments can create markets for arms they can surely create markets for other things which society needs but cannot translate into economic demand through the operation of the free market alone.

Also, if expenditures on war materials, which are inherently wasteful whether they are used or not used, can be a major stimulus to the economy, surely expenditures on building better and more liveable cities, improved cultural, educational facilities, recreational areas and opportunities for meaningful leisure, can be just as stimulating to the economy while at the same time adding positively to the real capital stock of our societies.

So I believe it is feasible to make the transition to the new growth society. But that does not mean it will be easy. For it requires basic changes in the attitudes, values and expectations of people—in effect a cultural revolution. Governmental action will not be possible unless it is undergird by this cultural change. It must be a culture that places highest value on quality rather than quantity, on conservation rather than waste, on co-operation above competition. It requires that we learn to applaud and look up to those who adopt lifestyles that are modest in terms of the amount of space they monopolize or the amount of materials and energy they consume; that ostentatious, wasteful and indulgent living become socially reprehensible. The person who drives alone into the city in an over-sized automobile will be scorned, even spat upon, rather than envied. There must be an acute sensitivity to all activities which create risks of damage to our natural heritage or impair the quality of life for others. People of industrialized societies in particular must again nourish their communal values and downgrade their competitive drives.

The transition to the "new growth" society implies some profound changes in our traditional notions of the distinctions between private and public rights and responsibilities. Here, we must re-think our conceptions of the public and private domains. In a technological society, private acts increasingly affect public interests, and actions taken in the public interest intrude on private interests and rights.

The conditions which determine the optimum balance between individual freedom and collective constraint will be complex and decision-making will not be easy. It will call for a vastly improved method of evaluating the interactions between private and public interests in particular situations, of presenting and disseminating information and of assuring a maximum degree of citizen participation in decisions which affect them.

There is little evidence at present that we can realistically expect this kind of cultural transition to take place wilfully. The status quo continues to have a powerful grip even on those who concede that such a transition is necessary. We owe a great deal to those people in our societies who are already demonstrating that more qualitative, less materialistic lifestyles can be not only feasible but highly desirable and rewarding. But it is not easy to pursue such lifestyles today even for those who wish to do so. We should encourage and support more experimentation by people in new lifestyles, both within existing communities and by the creation of new communities. If more of the leaders of thought and opinion in our society could themselves adopt such lifestyles, it would have a powerful exemplary effect on the changes in our value system that are needed to make the new growth society possible.

Up to now the human species has changed its ways significantly only after having been chastised by bitter experience. Man's history has been based on repeated cycles of advance, tragedy inflicted by nature or by war, collapse and rebuilding, often for many centuries on a lower level than that which was destroyed, and often without rediscovering its most advanced aspects, such as the architecture and democracy of Greece or the porcelain of China.

A sobering thought for those of us in the industrialized world is that the rebuilding rarely takes place on the site of the destroyed societies. The centre and benefits of civilization rarely prosper a second time in the same place. Now that, for the first time in our history, we possess the means of total self-destruction, can we risk repeating these cycles? Even if we could, it is surely doubtful that the wholly unprecedented scale and nature of risk we now face would enable us to have another chance if we were to wait until eco-disaster or economic and social collapse is imminent.

Our present growth process which is based on greed and conflict is a cancer which is now eating away at the body and soul of society. It will destroy the very fabric of our society if we do not bring it under control. We must know where we are growing. We must become masters of the growth process and not its slaves. We must use it to expand our unlimited potential for human growth and not subordinate our humanity to its requirements. It is not only our survival as a race which is at stake, but the survival of those very qualities which distinguish us as human.

BIBLIOGRAPHY

1. Ehrlich, P. R. & Ehrlich, A. H., 1972, *Population, Resources, Environment,* W. H. Freeman and Co., page 62.
2. Report of the Workshop on Alternative Energy Strategies, *Energy: Global Prospects, 1985–2000,* McGraw-Hill, N. Y., 1977.
3. Laszlo, Irving, et al, Report to the Club of Rome on the New Horizon of Global Community, *Goals for Mankind,* 1977, page 296.
4. Laszlo, Irving, et al, Report to the Club of Rome on the New Horizon of Global Community, *Goals for Mankind,* 1977, pages 289 and 291.
5. Stockholm International Peace Research Institute, Yearbook, 1976, pages 62–63.
6. Los Angeles Times Supplement, Business and Finance, Part VIII, May 16, 1976.
7. Aerospace Industries Association of America, *Aerospace Facts and Figures,* 1975–76.
8. Sampson, Anthony, *The Arms Bazaar,* 1977.
9. International Institute for Strategic Studies, London, *The Military Balance 1975–76.*
10. WMSE Publications, *World Military and Social Expenditures, 1976,* Leesburg, Virginia, 1976, pages 5–6.
11. WMSE Publications, *World Military and Social Expenditures, 1976,* Leesburg, Virginia, 1976, pages 5–6.

Structure of molecular physics and its relations with other sciences

By Raymond Daudel

Professor of Quantum Chemistry
Sorbonne, Paris, France

Introduction

It is sometimes admitted that philosophy establishes a bridge between science and ideology:

$$\text{science} \rightleftharpoons \text{philosophy} \rightleftharpoons \text{ideologies}$$

Such a scheme leads to the conclusion that there is a kind of dialectical relation between science and philosophy. With such a theory the philosophical implications of science become a necessity and furthermore scientific implications of philosophy must be expected.

This kind of interaction can be examplified by a statement of a famous scientist, professor Wheeler, who said that:

"The Universe has given rise to an observer and the observer gives a meaning to the Universe."

I should like to mention here some epistemological implications of new physics. More precisely I want to show how wave-mechanics gives a particular structure to a large region of the scientific knowledge.

I shall take as an example molecular physics because I am working in this field. But I shall try also to precise relations of molecular physics with other sciences.

For such a purpose it is useful to use a good classification of sciences.

Perhaps because I live in Paris, at the corner of the avenue of the Observatory and of the August Comte street I have always been interested in the classification of sciences.

The classical classification suggested by Auguste Comte during the nineteenth century does not seem to be convenient nowadays.

It is possible to present another classification in which the various sciences do not appear isolated but appear as a whole. Such is the tetrahedral classification I suggested sometime ago.[1]

---

[1] R. Daudel, La Chimie Quantique, Presses Universitaires de France, Paris (1973). R. Daudel, Nouveau Journal de Chimie, 1, 91, (1977).

To each summit of a tetrahedron is placed a large group of sciences (Fig. 1):

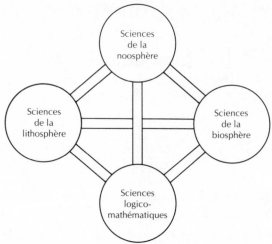

Fig. 1.

1) The methodological sciences: linguistic, logic, mathematics.
2) The lithospheric sciences related to the lifeless, the inanimate.
3) The biospheric or biological sciences related to the living beings.
4) The noospheric or psychosocial sciences concerning the thinking.

To each edge of the tetrahedron appear naturally the science which establishes a bridge between two groups. For example along the edge joining summit one and summit two lie the various mechanics (classical, statistical, relativistic, and wave mechanics) which permit to set up a mathematical government among molecular populations. See Fig. 2.

Fig. 2.

Syntaxic Polarity

Science mainly produces discourses and laboratory instruments. The very well known statement:

"To publish or to perish"

underlines the importance of written discourse in the production of science. It is why the analysis of a scientific discourse is a good procedure of obtaining information on the nature of scientific knowledge, and therefore on its structure.

A large amount of constraints characterizes such type of science discourses. The statement being in some language must be in accord with the syntax of this language. These syntaxic constraints are explicited by the corresponding element grammar and transformational grammar.

Formal systems can be used to formalise the syntaxic rules. Le us give a simple example. Consider the following formal system. Its alphabet Σ is made of three kinds of symbols:

(1) symbols $a_1, a_2, a_3 \ldots$.
(2) symbols $n_1, n_2, n_3 \ldots$.
(3) symbols $v_1, v_2, v_3 \ldots$.

The ensemble Φ of sentences of type P is built by using the following rules
(1) $a_1 \, n_1 \, v_1 \, a_1 \, n_1$ is a sentence of type P.
(2) another sentence of type P is obtained by substitution in that sentence of any symbol of a given type by another of the same type.
(3) no other sentence of type P can be written.

If now we give to this formal system the following interpretation:

(1) symbols a represent articles
(2) symbols n represent substantives
(3) symbols v represent verbs

the formal system can be used to formalise the syntax of many sentences of the English language.

For example,

"the current creates a field"

is a sentence of type P.

In the framework of lithospheric sciences the discourses must be in agreement with the usual logic.

The new constrains which follow can be formalised by the very classical proposition calculus.

We know that this formal system alphabet contains symbols like:

$$\neg, \wedge, \vee, \longrightarrow, \longleftrightarrow$$

which are respectively interpreted as: no, and, or, implicate, is equivalent to. We also know from Gödel's theorem that unhappily this formalisation is not completely satisfactory.

In the field of molecular physics the mathematical problematic must encompass the architecture of such a scientific discourse.

This new kind of constraint introduces at the syntaxic level a new formal system: the predicate calculus.

PHYSICO-MATHEMATICAL DOCTRINES AND OPERATIONALIST NATURE OF MOLECULAR PHYSICS

But the more specific kind of constraints which arise is related to the physico-mathematical doctrines. In the field of molecular physics two main doctrines have to be considered: quantum mechanics which describe molecular properties and statistical mechanics which describe the behaviour of molecular populations.

The discourses of molecular physics must be consistent with the principle of those doctrines which have been created to establish a connection between the mathematical structures and the laboratory operations.

Let us analyze first the consequence of the first principle of wave mechanics.

Following this principle "to each observable A (i.e. a measurable property) we associate, following certain rules, a certain mathematical operator A_{op}. Each measurement of this magnitude is an eigen-value of the operator."

Therefore to obtain the possible values of a certain magnitude (for example the energies of a hydrogen atom) two independent procedures are possible:
1) we measure the magnitude in a laboratory.
2) we calculate the eigen-value of the corresponding operator with the only help of paper and pencil.

Theoretically the two procedures must lead to the same numbers. In fact, that identity is observed very often.

Thus, the first principle of wave mechanics associates to an ensemble G of observables an ensemble Ω of operators.

Let us analyze, a little more, the nature of the ensembles G and Ω.

Following Bridgmann[2] an observable is a set of operations.

"In order to find the length of an object, for example, we have to execute certain physical operations. The concept of length is therefore established when the operations measuring length have been found, i.e. the concept of length is not more and not less than the set of operations measuring the

[2] P. W. Bridgmann, The logic of modern physics, Mc Millan ed. (1928).

length. In general an observable is synonymous with its corresponding operations."

Very often these operations are both experimental and theoretical. For example to measure a wave length we have to use the usual theory of light. As a conclusion we can say that an observable is a set of theoretical-experimental operations.

Therefore ensemble G is an ensemble of sets of theoretical-experimental operations.

An operator is defined by of set a mathematical operations. The ensemble Ω is an ensemble of sets of mathematical operations. Such are the ensembles associated through the first principle.

But this principle goes a little farther. "With the sum of two observables is associated the sum of the corresponding operators. With the product of two observables is associated the product of the operators." Therefore the

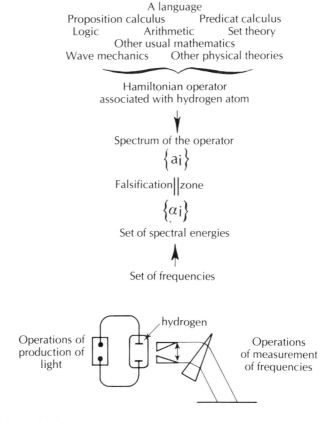

Fig. 3. Analysis operations of Balmer spectrum.

ensemble G and the ensemble Ω are both provided by two internal composition laws.

The correspondance between ensemble G and ensemble Ω is therefore an isomorphism. Such is the structure of the correspondance which is established through the first principle of wave mechanics between theoretical-experimental operations and mathematical operations.

Figure 3 summarizes all we have said until now. We can add that the foregoing isomorphism corresponds here to the Popper falsification zone, because if a discrepancy appears between the numbers calculated and measurements there is something to improve in the purely theoretical discourse, in the theoretical-experimental operations or in both.

To end this section we can recall that Hempel has remarked that the Brigdmann statement is simplification of the reality and that in fact an observable is something more than a simple set of measurement operations. We have no time to discuss this problem here.

We must also underline the fact that Fig. 3 shows how the physico-mathematical doctrines establish a bridge between the operations of the logic which are mainly substitution of symbols and the laboratory operations which are much more complicated.

But for doing both kind of operations a special training is needed which requires practical work.

For example to do symbolic substitutions correctly you have to recognize the same symbol when it is written in different ways.

If I speak of a wave-length of 7 500 Å you see red only if you have a certain training in spectroscopy.

Stochastic nature of molecular physics

Let us consider now the second principle of wave mechanics.

Following that principle:

"The probability of obtaining a certain value during the measurement of an observable is related to the projection of the vector representing the particle system on to the eigen-vector associated with the corresponding eigen-value."

Therefore, the only information which is given by the wave-mechanics is a probability of obtaining a certain value. As very often this probability is far from being unity it is far from a certainty. The famous Heisenberg uncertainties are consequences of that principle.

It is interesting to underline the consequences of the probabilistic nature of atomic and molecular physics.

In various cases the amount of information contained in a probability is very small.

The knowledge of the life-time of a radioactive type of nuclei gives very little information about the behaviour of one such nucleus. It can desintegrate immediately or at the end of time.

Recently I suggested a way to reduce this kind of uncertainty.[3]

Let us consider an example: the helium atom, in its first excited state. In the old Bohr theory it would be considered as made of two electrons rotating around the nuclei, the first one on the K circle, the second one on the L circle.

In the framework of the wave mechanics the picture of the atom is very different. It is not possible to describe the trajectories of electrons. We can only calculate the probability of finding one of them in a given small volume. Furthermore, as a consequence of the indistinguishability principle the two electrons must play the same role in the atom. It is not possible to distinguish a K electron and a L electron. But we can produce a certain geometrical description of the atom. Let us consider a sphere of radius R, the value of R being completely arbitrary.

Three different possible electronic events are possible:

(a) the two electrons are found in the sphere
(b) they are found outside the sphere
(c) one is found in the sphere, the other outside.

The wave function associated with the electrons permit to calculate the respective probability P_1, P_2 and P_3 of those three events.

To such a set of probabilities information theory associates a certain amount of information. More precisely this theory introduces the missing information function:

$$I = \Sigma_i \ P_i \ \log_2 \ P_i^{-1}$$

As the various probabilities P_i depend on the radius R the missing information function is a function of R.

If we like to obtain the maximum amount of information we must look for the value of R which corresponds to a minimum of the missing information function. Calculations lead to the value

$$R = 1.7 \ a_o$$

For this value of R the probability of finding one electron into the sphere and the other outside reaches the value:

$$P = 0.93$$

Therefore the probabilities of the other events are small. The foregoing events is said to be the leading event. The sphere corresponding to this value of

[3] For a review see: Localization and Delocalization in Quantum Chemistry, O. Chalvet, R. Daudel, S. Diner and J. P. Malrieu, Wiley ed. Vol. I (1975) Vol. II (1976).

R can be called the K loge, the remaining part of the space being the L loge and we can say that when a helium atom is in its first excited state there is a probability of 93 per cent of finding one electron in the K loge and the other in the L loge.

Finally we found a procedure giving a certain geometrical description of the atom. The description is such that the probability of one of the events is very large (near one). We have replaced the uncertainty by a quasi certainty.

Such a method which amounts to describe a phenomenon in such a way that high probabilities appear is called a method of quasi-certainties.

Let us consider now the molecule BH in the approximation of Born and Oppenheimer (the nuclei replaced by charges fixed at the equilibrium positions). It is a six electron problem. Let us select the best way of partitioning in three "loges", one being a sphere of radius R centered on the boron nucleus, the other two separated by a cone of angle θ with BH direction as the axis (Fig. 4). The missing information function is minimised for R = 0.7 a_0 and θ = 73°. The dominating event corresponds to two electrons in each loge. The sphere will be called the core loge of boron atom. The interior of the cone constitutes the BH loge and the exterior the lone pair loge.

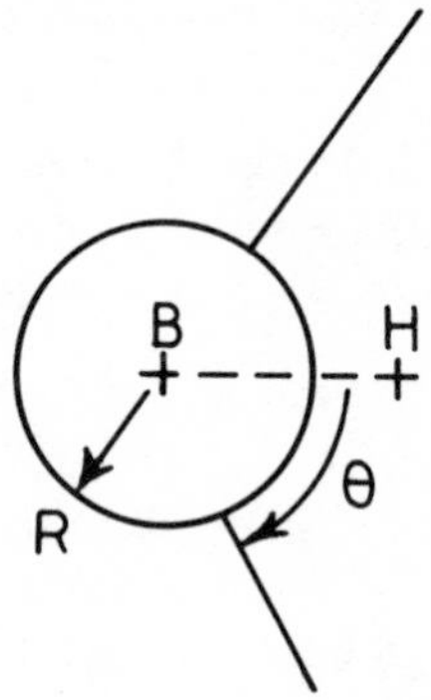

Fig. 4.

Figure 5 shows that the fluctuation $\wedge$ of the number of electrons in the loges of the BH molecule if minimised at the same time as the missing information. A chemical bond thus becomes a region of the molecular space whose number of electrons fluctuates very little. Moreover, it is found that the *virial theorem* can be often applied locally in such zones and that in a loge the correlation between the positions of electrons is strong but it is weak between the electrons moving in distinct loges. Finally, chemical bonds appear to be regions possessing a certain autonomy and it is proved that their organisation effectively resists strong perturbations. Thus the bond loge of BeH remains almost unchanged in HBeH. The addition of a new atom has not perturbed the BeH loge in a significant manner.

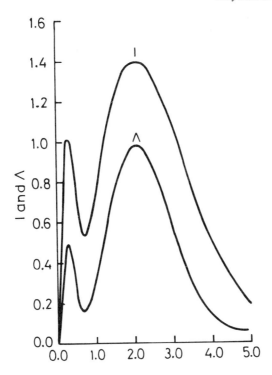

Fig. 5

Molecular physics and its relations with other sciences

Molecular physics is one of the sciences of the lithosphere. Its position among them can be pointed out by considering the following classification:

elementary particles and fields,

nuclear, atomic and molecular sciences,

gases, liquids and solids,

mineralogy, geology,

astronomy,

cosmology.

It is seen that it is no longer necessary to distinguish between physics and chemistry: that distinction becomes archaic.

Molecular physics and chemistry are molecular sciences, the frontier between them is nowadays very vague. The relations between them are therefore obvious. For example the theory of chemical reactions is mainly the study of collisions between molecules and molecular beam experiments is chemistry for physicists. Wave mechanics also plays a very important role in this field.[4]

---

[4] See for example: R. Daudel, R. Lefebvre and C. Moser, Introductions to Quantum Chemistry, Interscience (1959).

There are various bridges between nuclear physics and molecular physics. I established one by predicting the dependance of the life time of some radioactive nuclei on the nature of the molecules in which they are introduced.[5] This phenomenon is nowadays very well known and is particularly important in the case of electron captures and isomeric nuclear transitions. It is related to the fact that the life time of such radioactive nuclei depends on the electronic density near the nuclei which itself depends on molecular structure. This phenomenon generates one of the most precise procedure of measuring the electronic density near the nuclei.

The bridge between molecular sciences and life sciences is mainly established by molecular biology.[6]

An example of contribution of quantum molecular sciences to biology will be given by studying an aspect of the theory of mutations produced by radiations.

Figure 6 shows the coupling between cytosine and guanine, two of the four molecules which produce the genetic message contained in nucleic acids. The duplication of nucleic acids during the cell division is based on the fact that a cytosine is normally always coupled with a guanine and a thymine with an adenine.

Quantum molecular calculations show that if cells are irradiated with U. V. light and a cytosine excited to its first excited state the nitrogen of the NH_2 group becomes positive and therefore repulsive for a proton and the

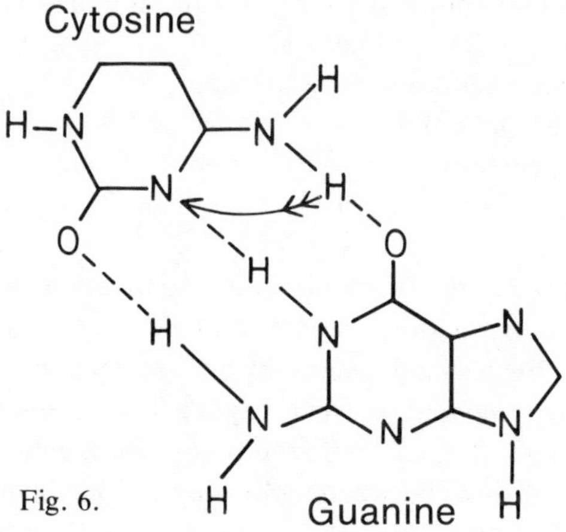

Fig. 6.   Guanine

[5] R. Daudel, La Revue Scientifique, *85,* 162 (1974); J. de Physique *13,* 557 (1962).
[6] See for example A. and B. Pullman, Quantum Biochemistry, Wiley (1963).

neighbouring nitrogen on the contrary becomes more negative and therefore more attractive for a proton.

As a consequence, a proton transfer occurs, a proton of the NH_2 group going on to the neighbouring nitrogen (this transfer is indicated by an arrow on the Fig. 6).

If during that time duplication occurs, there is no longer room for a guanine before that tautomeric form of cytosine but it is easy to see that the new organisation of the atoms is convenient for a coupling with an adenine. This miscoupling will produce a mutation. It is believed that simple ideas, simple perceptions could be associated with circulations of nervous influence in certain circuits of neurons of the brain called engrams. Let us assume that the perception of the colour blue is associated with a certain engram A. Let us assume now that the word blue is associated with the engram B. If when a young child sees a colour blue we tell him the word blue the two electric circuits A and B will work very often simultaneously.

Little by little some molecular reorganisation will produce connexions between the two circuits in such a way that when the circuit A is excited the circuit B is also excited. The word blue becomes associated with the impression of blue.

Such would be the molecular basis of memory.

This kind of theory is also helpful to produce new pharmaceutical drugs. I was asked to establish relations between the electronic structure of a set of morpholine derivatives and their analgesic power by a group of pharmacologists. The pharmacologists were able to observe a fixation of the morpholine derivatives on trytaminergic receptors. By calculating the map of the electric potential contours created by the molecules I was led to predict an interaction between the drugs and noradrenergic receptors.[7] The pharmacologists effectively observed such an interaction and concluded that some of the morpholine derivative could be used as antidepressors. Clinical tests have shown that it is so.

[7] R. Daudel, L. Esnault, C. Labrid, N. Busch, T. Moleyre and J. Lambert (Eur. J. Med. Chem.)

The present Formulation of the Undation Theory

By R. W. van Bemmelen

Professor of Geology,
University of Utrecht, The Netherlands

It is my intention to give a concise review of the present formulation and the future research possibilities of the Undation Theory. This comprehensive synthetic model of the diverse aspects of the terrestrial evolution has been developed by me in the course of half a century of professional activities, by

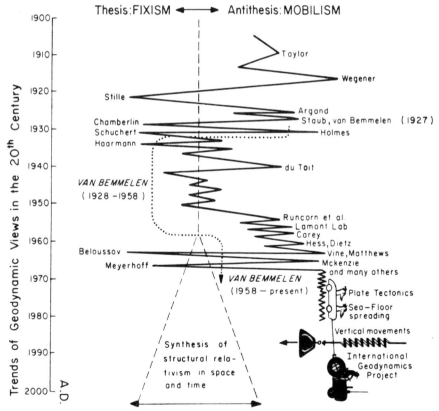

Fig. 1. Trends of geodynamic views in the twentieth century (from van Bemmelen 1974).

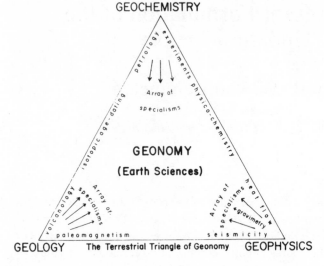

Fig. 2. The triangle of the Earth-Sciences (Geonomy) (from van Bemmelen 1975 a).

progressively adapting it to the growing fund of basic facts. It represents a persistent search for synthesis, especially between two major concepts in geodynamics, fixism and mobilism.

Since the last world war the enormous advances in geophysical and geochemical researches caused a rapid increase of exact data of observation ('diagnostic facts'), so that the Earth Sciences can now be called *"Geonomy"*, having acquired the same level of scientific exactitude as the Star Sciences, called "Astronomy". Pre-isotopic geology was largely an art of intelligent guessing, whereas present day geonomy became in many respects a more exact science by measuring the magnitude of the relevant parameters.

Geonomy occupies a central position in *the Sciences of Nature,* extending from the dimension of colloids (about 10^{-6} cm) to the distance of the Moon (about 10^{+11} cm).

It is embedded between the basic sciences on the micro-realm, (nuclear physics, physics, chemistry) which reach down to the critical Planck length of observation, and the macro-realm which reaches out into cosmic space to the farthest objects of observation (quasars, at a distance of about 10^{+28} cm).

The *driving forces of the endogenic evolution* of our planet belong to two different categories; Category I belongs to the micro-realm, obeying the laws of thermodynamics, and Category II belongs to the macro-realm being governed by relativistic inertia (gravitative, rotative), obeying the mechanical laws of moving masses. In the field of geodynamics this means that the fundamental principles of geo-rheodynamic have to be applied. All terrestrial processes of evolution result from the forces derived from potential (free)

TABLE I. *Central place of the Earth-Sciences (Geonomy) in the field of observation covered by the Sciences of Nature (from van Bemmelen 1976).*

Fluctua-tions of the elec-tric field become all important	10^{-13} cm critical Planck length	man: ca. 1.7 x 10^{2} cm PHYSICAL SCIENCES — of the observable interval —	ca. 10^{+28} cm farthest observable objects	Various other probability waves in "super-space" (Wheeler, 1968)
← infra-observable	(1) BASIC SCIENCES or Physico-Chemistry ← lower interval of → observations	(2) EARTH SCIENCES or Geonomy ← central interval → of observations ca. 10^{-6} cm ca. 10^{+11} cm	(3) STAR SCIENCES or Astronomy ← upper interval of → observations	→ ultra-observable
	nuclear physics + *physics + chemistry*	*geology + geophysics +* *geochemistry + selenology*	*cosmology +* *astrophysics*	
	particle-interactions by physico-chemical forces (electro-magnetic field) ↓ (time)	interactions between geonomic units caused by forces of electro-magnetism and inertia ↓ (time) *geonomic evolution by* *entwining equilibrio-petal* *chains of reactions* geothermodynamics ↓↑ georheodynamics	internal and external interactions of cosmic units by forces of inertia ↓ (time)	

energy in the micro- and macro-realm of matter and their mutual interactions.

This gives rise to a wide variety of successive geological situations with cumulative effects. The temporary situations never recur in complete similarity, though the causative forces are immutable.

Nevertheless, *periodicities* of certain features can be distinguished in the successive situations. These periodicities are the result of accumulations of potential energy which are intermittently released ('relaxation oscillations').

Periodic circuits of masses in the solid earth (homogeneous and heterogeneous convections systems) can cause differential vertical movements at the surface, which are called *'undations'*.

For practical purposes of descriptions and interpretations these undations are subdivided into five classes of extent; they range from mega-undations (which measure several thousands of kilometers across and have a life-cycle of more than 100 m. y.) to local undations (which have a diameter of some hundreds of meters and a life-cycle of some hundreds of years). (Fig. 3.)

The mass-circuits in the solid earth are reaching progressively deeper according to the diameter of the undations which they cause at the surface.

The radial movements of the causative mass circuits build up mechanical potential, which is released by countercurrents. Thus internally coherent energy-systems of convection come into being which strive for a net drop in their mechanical potential (Ramberg, 1967). Convective systems of diverse

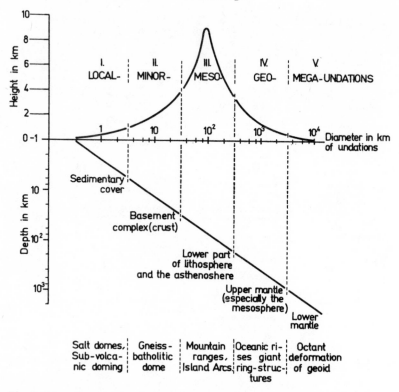

Fig. 3. Five classes of undations (from van Bemmelen 1976).

magnitudes and velocities can be mutually super-imposed, being either cumulative or compensatory in their effects.

We will now give an outline of the geo-dynamic effects of undations, starting with the largest (mega-undations), then the successively smaller ones.

In the case of *mega-undations* the great diameter points to causative mass-circuits in the lower mantle (at more than 1 000 km depth), which are probably the ''motor'' for the geo-dynamic processes in the upper mantle. The lower mantle encloses (as a cooling envelope) the terrestrial dynamo, which is active in the outer core; it absorbs the heat produced by the magneto-hydrodynamic turbulence in the geo-dynamo. Thermal expansions at the base of the mantle will result into buoyancy, so that convective systems are created. The ascending columns in the largely oxydic lower mantle, however, cannot pierce the more or less gradual (and therefore seismically vague) transition zone with the outer mantle. The latter has lower mean densities because of the decrease of the P and T conditions, which determine a physico-chemically different composition (silicates).

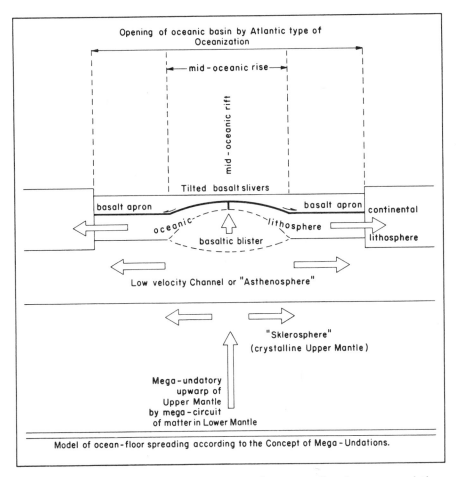

Fig. 4. Model of continental drift and sea-floor spreading by mega-undations (from van Bemmelen 1976).

Consequently, the upper mantle is passively deformed into a broad upwarp, a mega-undation.

Three structural levels can be distinguished in the upper mantle: (1) the presumably crystalline "meso-" or "sklero-sphere", (2) the seismic low-velocity channel, called "asthenosphere", and (3) the "lithosphere" which might be again preponderantly in a crystalline state.

These passive upper-mantle spheres will react almost immediately to the mega-undatory upwarp by spreading under gravity, like a pile of slightly tilted books. The lithosphere will move sidewards with a higher velocity and over a greater distance than the underlying, lubricating asthenosphere. This is a mechanism of continental drift or plate movements by *inherent* mechanical potential, resulting from disturbed gravitational inertia of all mass particles concerned. This mechanism of driving forces is the reverse of that proposed by the model of plate tectonics. The latter suggests that the lithospheric plates are dragged by *external* forces, transmitted from convective systems in the deeper parts of the mantle. In that case the convective mantle circuits should have much higher velocities than the lithospheric plates which they carry on their backs.

'Dragging' is an anthropomorphistic concept, which does not take into account the difference between the magnitude of the parameters in the human workshop and those of the terrestrial reality (v. B. 1975c, see also right upper corner of table II on p. 130 in "Geodynamic Models", 1972a.)

The mechanism for the sidewards drift of huge lithospheric units by means of their inherent mechanical potential leads to the opening of *deep oceanic basins of the Atlantic type*. The floor of these basins is formed by aprons of basalt outflows of the "trap-type" (Deccan Trap, f. i.), issuing from more or less diffusely distributed centres of eruption at the surface of the upper mantle that is deeply exposed over the crest of the mega-undation.

Geo-undations

In a later phase of evolution, with a time-lag of some dozens of million years, a buoyant blister of anomalous upper mantle matter (containing pockets of eutectically segregated basaltic magma) will have been formed at the top of the mega-upwarp. Such an "oceanic asthenolith" is a geo-chemical 'after-effect' of the megaundation. It produces a mid-oceanic rise, which measures some 1000–1500 km across. The eruptive activity of basaltic magma is then concentrated along a longitudinal rift on the crest of the rise. This newly formed oceanic crust glides from the shoulders of the rise, becoming characterized by a symmetrically striped pattern of paleomagnetic reversals.

Geo- to meso-undations

Another type of upper-mantle upwellings, which causes sequences of geo-dynamic and geo-chemical processes in the lithosphere, has recently become known; giant circular centres of igneous activity and diastrophism appear in sialic crustal shields from the early pre-Cambrian onward (Van Bemmelen 1973, 1976; Kloosterman 1975; Körner, 1977 a and b).

These centres of igneous activity are reworking the sialic crust, and they measure many hundreds of kilometers across (up to about 1000 km).

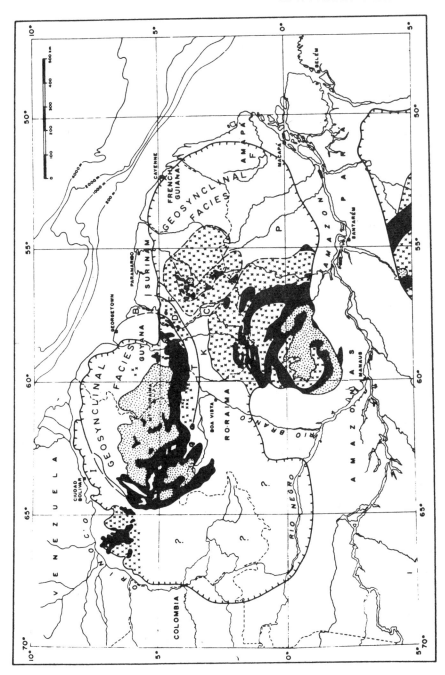

Fig. 5. Giant-ring-structures of the Guiana Shield of South America (from Klooster-man 1975).

Meso-undations

Such centres of mantle activity are surrounded by annular belts of mountain- and island-arcs with compressive structural features, meso-undations some 100–200 km wide. In the Caribbean and Mediterranean areas as well as in the western part of the Pacific, these orogenic belts have the tendency to migrate radially away from their centres of diastrophism (V. B. 1972a, 1973; Stride et al. 1976).

An orogenic evolution by means of sideward displacements of crustal waves differs from the picture given by the model of plate tectonics, which envisages a fixed position of orogenic belts along the destructive margins between colliding plates. Moreover, the subduction of drifting plates is not the cause of alpine-type orogeny; on the contrary, it is a passive process. It is the combined result of being overrun by step-wise advancing orogenic crustal waves in the first place, and the "aging" of the oceanic plate (which increases its mean density by cooling) as an additional factor. The further subduction of the plate along seismic Benioffzone's is promoted by the formation of high-density minerals according to the increasing pressure (V. B. 1974).

Meanwhile, in the centres of diastrophism themselves, irreversible geochemical processes are going on. Diapiric off-shoots of the asthenosphere into the lithosphere invade and corrode the overlying sialic crust.

The Pannonian Basin, surrounded by the Carpathian mountain belt, is a type example. Its evolution began already in Mid-Mesozoic time, when the

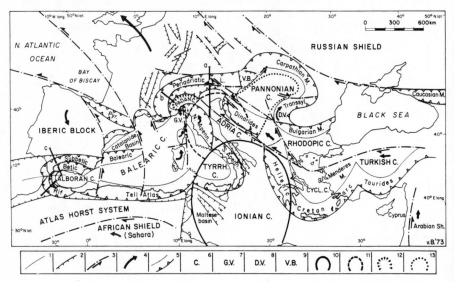

Fig. 6. Ring-structures of the Mediterranean area, forming centres of the Alpine-type of diasthrophism (from van Bemmelen 1974).

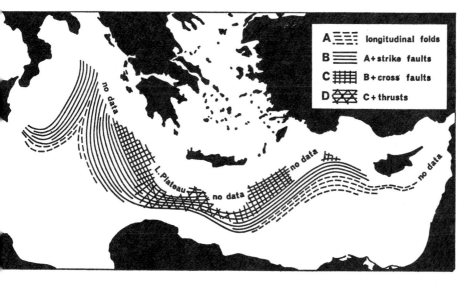

Fig. 7. Evolving mio-geanticlines of the East Mediterranean (from Stride *et al.* 1976).

centre emerged as a tumescence of the European continental shield; this bulging up was volumetrically compensated by a ring-syncline, into which products of erosion from the centre were deposited as flyschoid sediments. In later stages of its evolution the central bulge was intruded and pierced by magma's, and then collapsed in young Cenozoic time, forming the present

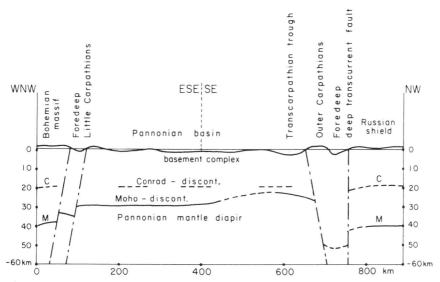

Fig. 8. Schematic section across the Pannonian Basin in Europe (from van Bemmelen 1974).

basin. This basin is underlain by a sialic crust of reduced thickness, being 10 km thinner than that of the surrounding continental shield. The seismic Moho-discontinuity between the sialic crust and the mantle forms a closed cupola. An analysis of possibilities of this *in situ* removal of the sialic crust shows that it occurred largely in a geochemical way; namely by means of a process of overhead stoping, which accompanied the diapiric activity of an off-shoot from the asthenosphere into the continental lithosphere (V. B. 1973; 1974, p. 104–105).

In the terminal phases of this geochemical process the cooling roof of such asthenopsheric diapirs crystallizes into high-density matter of mafic to ultra-mafic composition, mixed with katametamorphic matter of the sialic crust. Huge blocks are detached from this roof by their sheer weight and plunge down through the hotter deeper parts of the diapir. This downward movement of huge blocks, up to the size of more than 10 km in diameter, will be accompanied by intermittant relaxations of their mechanical potential causing earthquakes with hypocentres at intermediate depths. The initial movements of the focal mechanism of such earthquakes will be a subvertical pull. This expectation (prognosis) of the model is confirmed by diagnostic facts of observation. Analyses of earthquakes in Rumania show, that they are caused by sub-vertical movements, such as the one of 10 November 1941 (Ritsema, 1969, p. 4, 7) and the recent one of 4 March 1977 in the Vrancea district at a depth of about 95 km.

This *Mediterranean type of oceanization* is a geo-chemical process, that stands in contrast to the fore-mentioned Atlantic type of oceanization. It leads to a reduction of the volume of the sialic crust, which is progressively incorporated (consumed and digested) by the mantle (V. B. 1958, 1969, 1972, 1975, 1976, 1977b). This aspect of the Undation Theory is another major difference from the model of Plate Tectonics, which adheres to the classic ideas of onion-skin growth of the sialic crust by juvenile granitic excretions from the mantle.

The crustal waves (meso-undations), which emigrate step-wise from the centres of diastrophism, are also accompanied by seismic activity, though of a different character (shallow foci with compressive initial movements).

Ando (1975) studied the geodetical results of historical earthquakes in Japan (see also V. B. 1976, p. 172/3). The seismic catastrophe in the Friuli district of NE-Italy in 1976 has been the subject of a special conference at Udine at the end of that year (V. B. 1977).

This Friuli seismicity is a good example of geophysical events which accompany the arching up of a crustal wave of meso-undatory dimensions, cp. the Eastern Alps. The Alps are about 150 km wide in this sector and they are in the final state of Alpine-type orogenic evolution, the Molasse-phase (V. B. 1973).

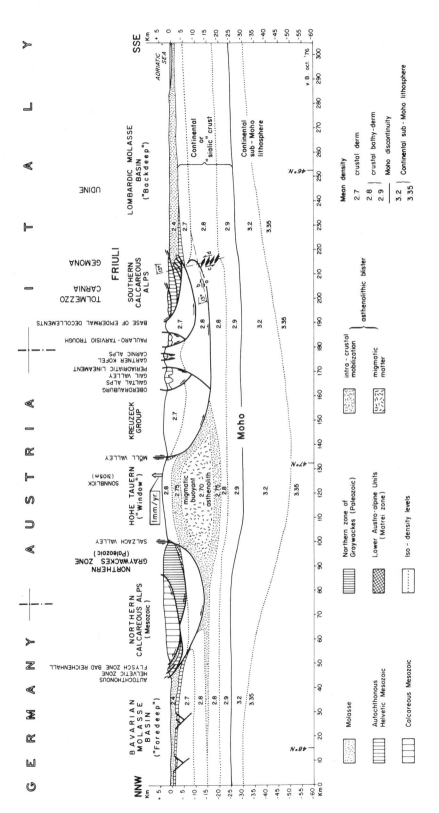

Fig. 9. Schematic section across the Eastern Alps (from van Bemmelen 1977).

The crest of the East-Alpine vault is formed by the tectonic Hohe-Tauern window, about 40 km wide, which is rising at a rate of 1 mm/yr. This is the result of the presence of a geophysically determined low-density blister inside the sialic crust, called an 'orogenic asthenolith'. The north- and south-flanks of the vault are spreading under gravity over the adjacent molassic basins, the fore- and backdeeps, which are volumetric compensations of the meso-undatory arching up. The present author advanced stringent arguments (V. B. 1977a) for his opinion that the seismic line Verona-Vienne, on which Friuli is situated, results neither directly from the differential vertical movements of the alpine uplift, nor from the NW-directed thrust of the Adriatic microplate. These are both very slow geo-dynamic movements which are mainly released by slow isostatic creep adjustments underneath the Moho. The direct cause of the frequently recurring Friuli-seismicity at depths of 10–20 km has to be sought in the fact, that the foot of the southern limb of the alpine vault breaks intermittantly through the supporting floor, formed by the lower part of the continental crust. Since the main shock of 6 May 1977, 395 aftershocks occurred, the latest two mid-September 1977.

Examples of Minor- and local undations are so well studied geologically, that they need not be discussed in this short review.

Thus the following sequence of geodynamic processes of diminishing magnitude can be distinguished:

V. *Mega-Undations,* which are accompanied by continental drift, with newly formed deep oceans (Atlantic type of oceanization) in their rear, and passive subduction of the ocean floor at the frontal side of the sialic shields.

IVa. *Oceanic Geo-Undations.* The mid-oceanic rises which result from geochemical after-effects in the rear of the drifting continent.

IVb. *Continental Geo-Undations.* Centres of diatrophism formed by geochemical processes in the lithosphere, underneath the sialic crust. In the cases of the Tethys belt and the East-Asiatic island arcs these disturbances of the physico-chemical equilibrium occur at the frontal side of the drifting continental shields (V. B. 1973, 1974).

III. *Meso-Undations* are crustal waves which migrate radially outward from the centres of diatrophism. They are related to intra-lithospheric mantle diapirism.

II. *Minor-Undations* are culminations of regionally restricted extent, resulting from intra-crustal geochemical processes, gneissic domes such as exposed in the Hohe-Tauern window of the Eastern Alps, and in the Bergell-culmination of the Western Alps. The Caledonian belt of Norway shows good examples of early Paleozoic age, and the domes in Southern Rhodesia are early Precambrian.

I. *Local-Undations* are the smallest class of undations, resulting from still shallower sediment-tectonic and magma-tectonic processes inside the non-metamorphic sedimentary veneer, such as halokinesis and laccolithic uptrusions.

This is a genetically coherent sequence of geodynamic events of diminishing magnitude, resulting from the interaction of driving forces in the micro- and macro-realms of planetary matter. Alternatively mechanical potential is built up by disturbances of either the physico-chemical equilibrium or of the gravitational and rotational inertia, and this free energy is then periodically released by convective circuits of masses in the solid earth (V. B. 1975, table 1, 'causes of geodynamic processes in the lithosphere', on pages 16–17).

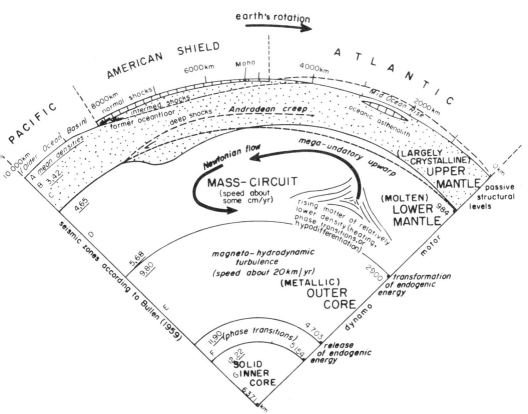

Fig. 10. Step-wise flow of endogenic energy from the inner core to the global surface. Heat production in the zone of transition between the inner- and outer-core might be the result of turbulent frictional movements resulting from the different rates of rotation of the inner core (the initial centre of accretion of the proto-Earth during the cosmogenesis) and the remaining part of the solid Earth both in response to the tidal forces of the Earth-Moon system (from van Bemmelen 1972a).

The foregoing review of the present formulation of the Undation Theory might be terminated by some words about the most recent checking of the functional correctness of this model, by means of an analysis of the relationships between the major gravitational gravity anomalies of our globe on the one side and its megatectonic features on the other.

The gravity anomalies of the geoid are represented numerically in meters of deviation from the spheroidal form of rotative flattening. Of course this does not mean that real bulges and depressions occur at the surface. It only points to inner instabilities formed by the presence of masses with relatively too low and too high mean density in relation with the place they occupy in the mantle. Only the most important deviations from gravitational equilibrium can be detected in anomalies of the earth's gravity field, namely those related to the mega-circuits of matter in the mantle, which produce mega-undations at the surface. Negative gravity anomalies coincide with ascending matter in the mantle and positive ones indicate matter possessing a mechanical potential for descent. The geoidal bulge at the north pole coincides with the arctic ocean basin, the floor of which is descending; whereas the negative dent at the south pole coincides with the Antarctic shield, which is emerging.

The correlation between the major gravity anomalies and the global tectonic features have been analysed in my papers 1975a fig. 2 and p.p. 14–15, and 1976 fig. 10 and p.p. 165–178 (a correction of fig. 10 has been published by Hédervári in Tectonophysics 40 (3/4), July 1977, p. 369 and in Geologie an Mijnbouw, Vol. 56, (3), September 1977).

Here only some salient aspects will be pointed out:

The greatest field of negative gravity anomalies is centred over Ceylon (Sri Lanka:—113 m). This active mega-undatory upwarp gives mechanical potential to the Indian sub-continental shield on its north flank which is drifting northward (as a huge gliding mass) towards central Asia, pushing up the Himalayan orogenic system and the Tibetan platform.

Central Asia itself coincides with another negative field, which coincides with the Tibetan-Mongolian mega-undation. The crest of the latter presumably coincided originally with the N-trending Dalai Nur depression, but thereafter it has shifted north-westward to the Baikal rift-zone in Siberia. Russian submerging vessels are presently exploring this deepest lake of the earth (−1620 m). Geodetical investigations indicate that the Baikal rift widens at a rate of 2 cm/yr. This rift is comparable to the Red Sea rift on the crest of the Afro-Arabian mega-undation, and it might become a new deep ocean basin in the distant geological future.[1]

In my paper on the mega-tectonics of the Tethys belt (1969b) I pointed out

[1] See also special issue of Tectonophysics 45 (1), Jan. 17, 1978: "Geodynamics of the Baikal Rift Zone". (Note added to proof).

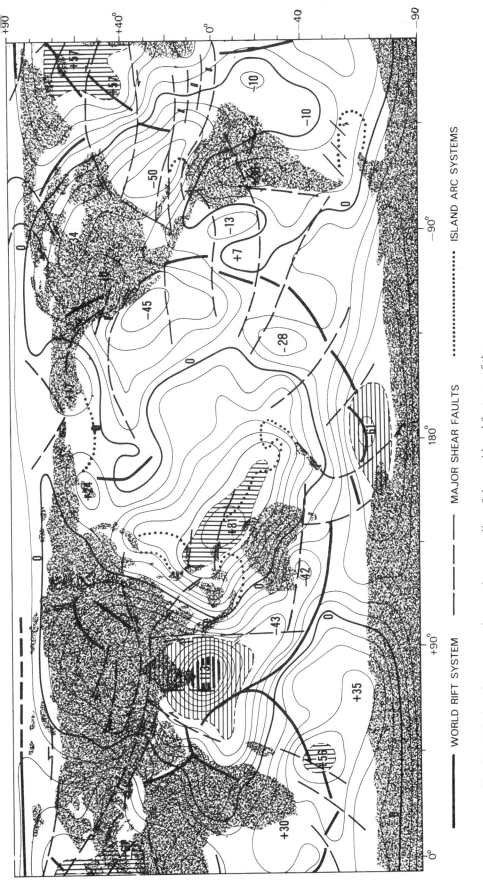

Fig. 11. Relations between major gravity anomalies of the geoid and features of the lithosphere (from van Bemmelen 1976).

WORLD RIFT SYSTEM ———   MAJOR SHEAR FAULTS — — —   ISLAND ARC SYSTEMS ·········

that the Himalayan sector has been displaced northward by the northward drift of the Indian shield in Cretaceous—Cenozoic time. The older sialic crustal units in front of it have meanwhile been displaced by sideward flow of micro-plates, which drifted along more or less E.–W. trending shear-fault systems towards areas of positive gravity anomalies, where descending currents close the mega-circuits in the mantle. These shear-faults are dextral between Tibet and the field of positive gravity anomalies in Europe (+ 57 m), and sinistral in S.E. Asia (to the East of Tibet), where the sialic crustal units move towards the positive anomaly field of the western Pacific.

The geodynamic evolution in Mesozoic to Cenozoic time in the border area between the Indian Ocean and Southern Asia is a gigantic example of the relativistic interplay of mass-circuits in the mantle and drift movements in the lithosphere. It is a struggle for place of incompressible and unsinkable sialic crustal units, which move like floes of ice over the earth's surface in response to megaconvection systems in depth. According to the rheological principles of gravity tectonics *sensu lato,* these floes ('plates' and 'micro-plates') have obtained mechanical potential for their lateral displacement by forming the horizontal connective link between ascending and descending currents in the mantle (=mega-undatory circuits). The active geodynamic developments in Central Asia are clearly correlated with the major gravity anomalies of that part of the globe.

Another example of the correlation of geodynamic flow movements in the lithosphere and the major gravity anomalies can be found in the southern part of the Pacific, where an extensive field of positive gravity anomalies occurs in the Melanesian area, with a maximum value of + 81 m.

Menard (1964) gave the name of 'Darwin Rise' to this slowly subsiding part of the Pacific floor. It has been interpreted by the present author (1976, p. 168–169) as the final stage of evolution of a mega-undation, which originated in the Central part of the South Pacific (Polynesia), and then its crest migrated westward to Melanesia in the course of some 100 m y. It left in its wake straight chains of islands such as the Tuamoto, Society, and Tubua Islands. These chains can be interpreted as 'nemataths'. They are comparable to the Ninetyeast Ridge and the Maladive—Laccadive Chain which are nemataths formed in the wake of the northward shifting crest of the Indian Ocean—mega-undation with the Gondwana fragment of India drifting as its north-flank. The mean velocity for the westdrift of the Darwin mega-undation is comparable to that of the westdrift of the Atlantic mega-undation which migrated from its original site in the mid-Mesozoic (the Atlantic rise-rift system) to the present belt of negative gravity anomalies in the western part of the Atlantic (V. B. 1976 pp. 173–176). The Atlantic mega-undation is still in a somewhat younger phase of evolution, so that it possesses a buoyant crest (the Bermuda rise, for instance), whereas the

Darwin Rise represents an extinct mega-undation, which has been active in younger Mesozoic time, but its crest has been subsiding already in the course of the Cenozoic.

Nevertheless, the 'Darwin Rise' still is an obstacle for the island arc systems which are advancing towards the inner Pacific. The East-Asiatic arcs flow around its north-western corner, showing dextral shear-faults between the Mariana, Yap, and Palau ridges. The Philippine and Indonesian Archipelagoes drift along the western margin of the Darwin Rise, showing sinistral shear faults (V. B. 1976, p.p. 169–170).

The Banda Arcs of Indonesia eventually veered entirely eastward, by-passing the south-western corner (c.q. the Sula Spur) by means of the sinistral, E–W trending Sorong Fault. They now form an eastward facing orocline with eastward extension, which is manifest, for instance, in the more than 7000 m deep Weber trough. The nematathic character of the island ridges in the southern Moluccas, the discordant course of the volcanic and non-volcanic arcs, as well as the tightly curved contours of the seismic Benioff zone are also evidence for this active eastward flow (see f.i. Fig. 5 in *S. Tokrosapoetro,* 1977).

Paleomagnetic researches in the Southern Moluccas might confirm this interpretation which leads, among other geodynamic events, to the prognosis of strong rotations in the islands Ceram and Buru during young Cenozoic Time.

Island arc systems which migrate towards Australia and New Guinea (instead of moving towards the inner Pacific, like the East-Asiatic island arcs), are found along the southern margin of the Darwin Rise (New-Britain, Solomon Islands, New Caledonia, New Hebrides). This mega-tectonic contrast to the East-Asiatic island arc systems is not easily explained by the model of plate tectonics. On the other hand, it is quite conform to the expectations of the Undation Theory. When the Darwin Rise represents the final stage of a mega-undation, it will have acted earlier as a centre of diastrophism, from which island arc systems migrated outward, like the East-Asiatic arcs move away from the still active Tibet-Mongolian (Chinese) mega-undation (see Van Bemmelen, test case III, 1974).

At a distance of some 5000 km east from the Banda "whirl" of eastern Indonesia, another spiralic structure can be distinguished which rounds the SE corner of the Darwin Rise. The Fiji islands form the "eye" of it, from which arms evolve in opposite directions. One arm begins at the western side of Viti Levu with the tightly curved row of the Yasaway islets; it unfolds eastward over the Horn islet, and then southward, linking on to almost straight nematathic ridge of Tonga-Kermadec-Raoul-Macauley-Curtis, which reaches on to the major islands of New Zealand, and beyond to the Macquari Ridge, extending over some 45° latitude.

Another arm starts from Vanua Levu, pointing first eastward, then curving southward into the Lau Ridge.

The counterpart of these eastern arms of the whirling Fiji structure is a spiralic ridge which evolves westward. It starts from the SE corner of Viti Levu with the southwest trending arc of Kandavu-Conway-Hunter-Matthew. This NE–SW arc has also a nematathic character, and it shows sinistral shear faults. It then links on to the SSE–NNW ridge of the New Hebrides. The latter is a young Cenozoic, westward migrating system, consisting of a volcanic inner arc, a non-volcanic outer arc a foredeep in front of it, and an eastward dipping seismic Benioff zone at its rear. The New Caledonian arc system to the west of the New Hebrides shows also a westward migration, though being an older orogenic wave, emigrating from the Darwin mega-undation, during Late Cretaceous to Early Miocene (see Van Bemmelen, 1974, pp. 97–98 and Fig. 7 on p. 99).

This spiralic Fiji structure at the SE corner of the great field of positive anomalies in the SW Pacific is remarkably analogous to the whirl of the Indonesian archipelago at its SW corner. The Macquari-Tonga-Fiji arm is equalled in length by the Sunda arc (Andaman-Buru), both being some 6000 km long. The South- and North-Islands of New Zealand (which show a longitudinal dextral sheat-fault system, the ''Alpine Fault'') are the counterpart of the islands of Sumatra (with the longitudinal dextral Semangko shear-fault) and Java. The nematathic ridge extending from New Zealand to Fiji is comparable with the eastern part of the Sunda arc (Lesser Sunda Islands and the South Moluccan arcs). Moreover, the westward evolving arm of the Fiji whirl is represented in Indonesia by the westward curving island of Halmahera in the northern Moluccas and the anomalous arc structure of Sulawesi (Celebes), which are situated respectively to the North and West of the Sula Spur.

There is apparently a far-reaching similarity between the geotectonic features of the Indonesian and Fiji Archipelagoes. Both present a spiralic, whirl structure which clearly indicates that their geo-dynamic evolution has to be interpreted by means of rheological principles, and not by ideas of collisions between 'rigid' lithospheric plates, and their spreading from more or less straight rifts.[1]

[1] *Note added december 1977.* A good example of the differences between the way of geodynamic analysis by means of the model of the Undation Theory and the model of Plate-Tectonics can be obtained by comparing the foregoing picture of the evolution of the Central Pacific with that recently given by A. *Nur* and Z. *Ben-Avraham* (''Lost Pacifica continent'', Nature, Vol. 270, 3 November 1977, pp. 41–43).

Conclusion

In the preceding pages an outline of the present formulation of the Undation Theory has been given. This geodynamic model shows a clear conformity with the modern results of geonomic researches, accepting also the continental drift and the sea-floor spreading, which are the main-stay of the Plate Tectonics.

But the Undation Theory differs from Plate Tectonics in its mechanical concepts (inherent instead of external driving forces), and in its geochemical views (reduction of the sialic crust by mantle corrosion instead of the principle of its onion-skin growth by mantle secretion).

The resulting rheological view of geodynamics is checked in some detail by analysing the correlations between the major gravity anomalies of the geoid and the mega-tectonic features of eastern hemisphere (Asia and the central Pacific).

LITERATURE REFERENCES

Ando, M.: 1975: "Source mechanisms and tectonic significance of historical earthquakes along the Nankai Through, Japan". Tectonophysics, *27:* 119–140.

Embleton B.J.J. and L.A. Valencio: 1977: "Paleomagnetism and the reconstruction of Gondwana-land". Tectonophysics *40* (1/2): 1–12.

Hédervári, P.: 1977: "Plate Tectonics and the Undation Model—a rectification". Tectonophysics *40* (3/4): 372–374.

Kloosterman, J. B.: 1975: "Roraima, Tafelberg and Nutuma formations of the Guiana Shield; a correlation". Geologie en Mijnbouw, *54* (1/2):55–60.

Kröner, A.: 1977 a: "The precambrian geotectonic evolution of Africa: plate accretion versus plate destruction". Precambrian Research, *4* (1977), 163–213.

— 1977 b: "Precambrian mobile belts of southern and eastern Africa—ancient sutures or sites of ensialic mobility? A case for crustal evolution towards Plate Tectonics". Tectonophysics, *40* (1/2): 101–136.

Ramberg, H.: 1967: "Gravity, deformation and the earth's crust". Academic press, London, New York, 1967, 214 pp.

Ritsema, A. R.: 1969: "Seismo-tectonic implications of a review of European Earthquake Mechanisms". Geol. Rundschau *59* (1): 36–56.

— 1975: "The Contribution of the Study of seismicity and earthquake mechanisms to the knowledge of Mediterranean geodynamics". Progress in Geodynamics. Proc. Dutch Symposium, Amsterdam 1975, pp. 142–153. Geodyn. Project Sci. Rep. nr. 13.

Tjokrosapoetro, S.: 1977: "Holocene Tectonics on Timor island, Indonesia, Paper submitted to the international symposium on recent crustal movements, Palo Alto, California, July, 1977" (in press).

Stride, A. H., R. H. Belderson, and N. H. Kenyon: 1976: "Evolving miogeanticlines of the East Mediterranean (Hellenic, Calabrian, and Cyprus outer ridges)." Philosophical Trans. The Royal Society London. Series A : Mathematical and physical sci. Vol. 284, no. 1322, 255–285.

van Bemmelen, R. W.: 1931: "The Bicausality of diastrophism (Undation and Gliding)". (Dutch with English Summary). Natuurkundig Tijdschrift Nederlands Indië, *91:* 363–413.

— 1932: "The Undation Theory, and its application to the western part of the Sunda Arc". (Dutch with English Summary). Ibidem, *92:* 85–242 and 373–402.

— 1949: "The Geology of Indonesia". State Printing Office, The Hague. Reprinted with updated literature references by M. Nijhoff, The Hague, 1970.

— 1954: "Mountain Building". M. Nijhoff, The Hague, 177 pp.

— 1958: "Flow systems in the silicate mantle". (Dutch with English Summary). Geol. Mijnb. *20* (1): 1–17.

— 1969 a: "On the origin of the western Mediterranean: an example of oceanizations". Trans. Roy. Geol. Mining Soc., the Netherlands, *26:* 13–52.

— 1969 b: "The Alpine loop of the Tethys Zone". Tectonophysics, *8* (2): 167–113.

— 1972 a: "Geodynamic Models, an evaluation and a synthesis". Elsevier, Amsterdam, 267 p.

— 1972 b: "Driving forces of Mediterranean orogeny (Test-case I: The Tyrrhenian area)". Geologie an Mijnbouw, *51,* 548–573.

— 1973: "Geodynamic models of the Alpine type of orogeny (Test-case II: The Alps in Central Europe)". Tectonophysics, *18,* 33–79.

— 1974: "Driving forces of orogeny, with emphasis on the blue-schist facies of metamorphism (Test-case III: The Japan Arc)". Tectonophysics, *22,* 83–125.

— 1975 a: "Berlage's accretion model of lunar origin and its geochemical consequences". Proc. Roy. Acad. Sci. Amsterdam, Series B, *78,* 169–187.

— 1975 b: "Some basic problems in geonomy". Progress in Geodynamics, Proc. Geodynamics symposium Amsterdam; 9–22. Geodynamics Project Sci. Report, nr. *13.*

— 1975 c: "Kritik der Plattentektonik". Geologie en Mijnbouw, *54,* 71–81.

— 1976: "Plate Tectonics and the Undation Model: a comparison". Tectonophysics, *32,* 145–182.

— 1977: "Note on the seismicity of NE-Italy (Friuli area)". Tectonophysics, *39,* T 13—T 19.

— 1978: "The Undation Theory". Chapter in Vol. X of the Encyclopedia of Earth Sciences (in press). Preprints in the Geosurvey Newsletter of Indonesia (Berita Direktorat Geologi), *9* (II), March 1977, 117–128, and in "Geologie en Mijnbouw", Vol. *56,* nr. 3. 263–269, Sept. 1977).

Pollination Ecology: Trends and Problems

By Knut Fægri

Professor of Botany,
Bergen's Museum, University of Bergen,
Norway

The transfer of pollen grains to receptive stigmas is a necessary condition for the production of seeds in higher plants—apart from apomictic species. Pollination ecology is the study of the external factors influencing this transfer.

The nature and manifestation of sexual differences in animals, as in man, has undoubtedly been realized by early and primitive societies. Both hunters and cattle-raisers depended on—and knew that they depended on—the fertility of animals for their own livelihood.

Not so with plants. Even in cases when we to-day know that existing agricultural practices aim at securing pollination of crops, the ancient peoples hardly had any clear conception about the real significance of their practices. The question of sex in plants remained an enigma during the Classical Ages, the Middle Ages and well into the modern era. Not that the problem was not discussed, but scholastic argumentation was hardly the most expedient pathway towards a solution. The philosophic criteria for maleness and femaleness were constructed ex analogia with animals and, especially, humans, leading to somewhat incongruous results. Of the two most common European fern genera the one was coarser, the other more graceful, so the former was considered the male, the second the female. The specific epithets still in use for the two main species *(Dryopteris) filix-mas* and *(Athyrium) filix-femina,* meaning respectively, male and female fern, even to-day reflect this long ago forgotten misunderstanding.

The history of pollination ecology closely follows and reflects the history of biology. The first step was the recognition of the sexual apparatus and the external part of the sexual process in plants. What the church-dominated and inhibited earlier periods had not realized was clearly brought out during the more liberal periods to follow around 1700 when the pollination process was discovered and described independently by various botanists. Half a century later, the great Linnaeus constructed his *sexual* system of plant taxonomy: evidence of the understanding of what constituted the sexual process in plants.

We know to-day that, strictly speaking, what we observe is not the real sexual process: the plant is an asexual diploid, and only the haploids, the pollen grain and ovule are sexual, i.e. able to produce sex cells. However important this is theoretically, it has no significance for the early conception of the sexual relation of plants or for the study of pollination ecology. In practice, pollination can be equated with the sexual process.

The work of the first pollination ecologists, Camerarius (1694) and Koelreuter (1760), can be considered the last arguments in the long debate about the sexuality of plants; the title of the work of Camerarius being quite simply *De sexu plantarum:* on the sex of plants. But at the same time as these and other papers represent the end of a long quest for the truth, they also opened up a new line of investigation. Their observation of the sexual manifestation in plants had shown a certainly unexpected variation, and, above all, had shown that the sexual process in the immobile plants presumed a mobile *vector,* an external helper who could transfer pollen from anther to stigma: pollination ecology was born out of the discussions about the sex of plants.

Whereas the latter discussion had come to an end, the former had just started, and the first major contribution in pollination ecology for its own sake is a hundred years younger than the pioneer contribution of Camerarius: Sprengel's famous: *Das entdeckte Geheimnis.* Even if the secret was a hundred years old, it had been an esoteric part of biology, and also Sprengel's observations of and understanding of the pollination process far superceded those of his predecessors. He was the first real pollination ecologist, and his book is a marvel of acute observations and deductions, many of which, after having been neglected and ridiculed, have only been confirmed by modern experimental research.

Both Camerarius and Koelreuter were to a great extent preoccupied by the utilitarian aspects of pollination ecology: the effects in agriculture and plant breeding. Sprengel was the pure scientist. Only rarely has a science been born more brilliantly than Sprengel's pollination ecology. Why did nothing more happen? The main reason was that unlike the work of Camerarius, that of Sprengel was unrelated to any major trend in contemporary biology or contemporary thinking. To the pious Sprengel the description and praise of the manifestations of the Lord's wisdom was a goal in itself. Praiseworthy as this sentiment might be it did not carry pollination ecology through, and it slept for another fifty years.

Then another explosion shook science: Darwin's evolution theory, the first evolution theory to become a major scientific, philosophical and political issue. In the discussion of evolution the problem of adaptation and, even more, of coadaptation was of primary interest, and where could finer adaptations be found than in pollination ecology? Pollination ecology is nothing but the study of adaptation, and the Darwinians, with Darwin himself leading, with extreme eager took up pollination studies. The period of discussion of the evolution theory was the golden age of pollination ecology.

Fifty years later the evolution concept had been accepted by biologists. The argumentation from pollination ecology had been important in the fight, but had become redundant now that the fight was over, and pollination ecology again relapsed into a second-rate preoccupation, far removed from the mainstream of the advancing experimental biology.

This time, the interval was shorter, but again the impulse came from the outside, not from within pollination ecology itself: insect ethologists needed an experimental field, and, again the adaptation to flower visits represented a very effective and simple field. Thus Knoll during the 1920's again established pollination ecology as a respectable science, this time on an experimental basis in contrast to the former, purely observational aspect.

In the knowledge of pollination ecology there are two trends which have developed a little independently of the study of the basic problems. One is the study of pollination of cultivated plants. Once the importance of pollination and pollinators for the production of seed was realized, agriculturists took a natural and lively interest in studying it. This actually goes back to the agricultural practices coming down to us from the Classical Age in visual and verbal descriptions. One of the early triumphs of this trend was the unravelling of the basic principles of the terribly intricate pollination of the edible fig by Solms-Laubach in the 1880's.

As many cultivated plants are wind-pollinated, the study of wind pollination came up as a separate trend, in contrast to the animal—mostly insect— pollination that had formerly been the central part of pollination ecology. Especially in forestry wind pollination is of paramount importance, and the study of wind dispersal of pollen grains of trees received increased impetus from two other sources: dispersal of spores of plant parasites followed the same rules as do pollen grains, and the young science of (geological) pollen analysis, born in 1916, soon demanded a better knowledge of the fate and origin of the pollen grains studied.

The last trend has been the basis for investigations with sophisticated equipment for the study of the quantity of pollen grains in the air under different conditions: airplane reconnaissances, collecting apparatus etc. It is only during the latest decennium we have gained a deeper insight in the phenomena and can form a picture of how pollen grains of trees are dispersed with the wind. Most grains simply fall down to earth, through the canopy, and are found within a radius of some 50 m from the stem. A majority of the grains do not fall directly, but adhere to leaves and twigs from which they are again dislocated, above all by rain but then the receptivity period of the stigmas is usually past, and the grains may be dead.

Another part of the pollen grains released from the crown of trees are subject to horizontal transport: they are picked up by wind and transported horizontally a certain distance, depending on the velocity of wind and the rate of fall of the grains. Now, wind is a turbulent current, and the rate of fall of most pollen grains is rather small in relation to the velocity of air particles in a turbulent wind. Consequently, pollen grains behave more or less as parts of the air current with one important exception: grains are sieved out of the air by obstacles on the ground, especially vegetation. Experience shows that the majority of the horizontally transported grains do not reach beyond 300–500 m from the mother tree. There is very little horizontal transport within the forest itself. The distance of horizontal transport is obviously very much dependent on the level of release of pollen grains in relation to the surroundings. On a horizontal level the horizontal transport will necessarily be limited, as the grains will be filtered out very fast.

However, there is a third component: the vertical turbulence. During periods of clear sky and rising temperature—conditions during which most wind dispersed pollen is released—air near ground level is heated by sun energy and rises turbulently, carrying pollen grains with it. The rate of rise of turbulent air currents may in extreme cases be of the order of ten times the rate of fall of pollen grains, which will therefore again behave more or less like air particles, and in this case there is no sieving out effect. The warm air rises like bubbles or air cells of limited dimension (some hundred metres) and life-time (less than half an hour). However, on collapse they don't drop their pollen load immediately: new bubbles form, and form a larger cell of longer duration which continues to rise until it is in thermal equilibrium with the surrounding air, being cooled off adiabatically. This means that the upper limit for this transport is the thermal inversion layer in the air, the layer which on a fair day manifests itself as the basis of the cumulus clouds. In the end a pollen cloud can hang underneath the inversion layer. During this process a lateral transport takes place, and the pollen cloud can in the end be dropped into a vegetation completely different from that of its origin. In the afternoon and evening the process is reversed: the general cooling off of the bottom layer causes a downward air movement which, together with the natural fall of the pollen grains clears the night air of pollen. A good average of this type of transport will be some 5 km, with 50 km as a maximum.

In very dry air no inversion layer forms, and the pollen grains may be raised into the higher atmosphere. The dispersal distances of this group of pollen grains is virtually unlimited, and they are found thousand of kilometres away from their place of origin. On the other hand, even a very short rain-shower will clear the air of all pollen grains.

The heavy incidence of pollen grains due to direct fall and horizontal transport is the major agent in pollination, and the further the distance, the more sparse the pollen grains and the less the chance of pollination. Even if such long-distance pollinations are rare, they are very important, not only for trees growing in isolated positions, but also for the transfer of genetic material from one population to the other, whether this is in the individual instances desirable or non-desirable, the latter in specialized cultures of obligate out-breeders.

Characteristic of wind-pollinated plants are: small, inconspicuous, well exposed flowers, often before the leaves are out; small, dry buoyant pollen grains that are dispersed singly; large, well exposed stigmas; frequently dioecious, preventing self-pollination. As the vector, wind, is non-discriminating, there is the danger of indiscriminate pollination between species; this, less important in trees, is counteracted in grasses by extremely short flowering time, all pollen being released in a few minutes and cleared out of the air before the pollen of the next species comes out, as shown by Soviet botanists for grasses in the Arctic. Since the chance that two pollen grains shall hit the same stigma is almost infinitesimally small, the ovary is usually one-seeded.

The animal-induced pollination is a much more complicated process, often leading to very sophisticated adaptations. The orchids are well known for this, but other adaptations, perhaps not as spectacular, are often equally intricate. In a short paper it is not possible to go into details, so we shall have to look at some questions of principle, taking as a starting point that some animal vector carries the pollen from the anthers to the stigma of a compatible flower. What constitutes a compatible flower is highly variable. There are all transitions from complete self-compatibility to equally strong self-incompatibility. The concept of compatibility should not be confused with sterility. A sterile plant produces no seed in any combination, an incompatible plant can produce excellent seed, but not in this special combination, e.g. with pollen from the same plant: self-incompatibility. Self-incompatibility is a logical consequence of the sexual process. The effect, one might say the desired effect, of the sexual process is to mix genetic material from two parents, and if both gametes in a fertilization process come from the same plant, there is no real mixing. On the other hand strict self-incompatibility may be dangerous if external circumstances are unfavourable to the pollination process. It is therefore often seen that the degree of incompatibility varies during the anthesis, usually breaking down towards the end so that the own pollen may then function if no foreign pollen has been brought to the stigma. Similarly there may exist a certain self-compatibility all the time, only the pollen tubes from foreign pollen grow much faster, so the own pollen will come too late if foreign pollen has been deposited on the stigma. The effect again is one of self-incompatibility.

The basis for compatibility reactions has been studied by geneticists who have been able to define a set of genes regulating the process. More recently, it has also been studied biochemically, and it appears that it is at any rate in many cases a function of the existence of certain "recognition substances", presumable of protein nature, located on the outside of the pollen grain. It has proved possible to kill a pollen grain without destroying the recognition substances; afterwards this recognition substance has been used to open the road into the stigmatic papillas for pollen tubes from own pollen. Self-incompatibility in those cases seem to be a negative process: lack of recognition substance. Other observations indicate that there may also be positive factors, the own pollen carrying substances that prevent germination or even kill the stigmatic papillas.—The lack of recognition substances also explains the lack of success in crosses between species too remotely related.

An animal vector is usually able to carry a great number of pollen grains, and transfer many of them to the stigma during a visit. Also, the flower may experience several visits. Consequently, the ovaries of plants with biotic pollination are usually many-seeded with orchids as the extreme, corresponding to the very great number of pollen grains contained in the pollinium and being transferred as one packet. On the other hand, these sophisticated pollination syndromes depend on so many variables that they are rather unreliable, and many orchid flowers are never visited at all, since conditions were not right. As one visit is enough to ensure fertilization of all ovules, subsequent visits would be futile in relation to this flower, but might deprive other, not yet pollinated flowers from receiving a visit, and one therefore sees that many flowers, and those of orchids especially, wither a very short time after being pollinated. A pollinating insect in a commercial orchid greenhouse is a catastrophy!

However, other plants may be even more refined in this respect than orchids. The flower of the horse-chestnut *(Aesculus hippocastanum)* has a yellow nectar guide, which changes to red after a few days. The red-marked flowers are dry, and are not visited, so why are they there? A flower that, by the red mark, warns prospective pollinators from visiting is a paradox. Because of the very complicated morphology of the *Aesculus* inflorescence flowers in all stages of anthesis are mixed, and withering of pollinated flowers like in orchids would leave a rather messy-looking thyrse. By keeping the old flowers "on pension" the inflorescence achieves a very fine distance attraction and at the same time the red dot prevents useless visits to flowers already visited (*Aesculus* ovaries are one- or few-seeded).

Visits by pollinators to flowers are induced by attractants, the best known being, of course, nectar and pollen, of which nectar, through its carbohydrate content, chiefly functions as an energy food whereas pollen, with high percentages of protein and fat, is the predominant food for development, e.g. for growing insect larvae. Even though nectar contains some amino acids, and pollen does of course give a great output in energy, the usual pattern is that pollen is collected by females of brood-rearing insects, whereas nectar is consumed by males and by non-brood-rearing species. However, this is a rule with important exceptions even among insects. The pollen-collecting females also need some energy food.

Neither pollen nor nectar is particularly showy, and the existence of a specific odour, which has been suggested for pollen, is doubtful. Consequently a flower cannot attract pollinators simply by presenting these *primary* attractants. They must be supplemented by *secondary* attractants which are in themselves of no use to the pollinators, but serve as visual or olfactoric cues to the existence of the primary attractant. The pollinator will start by reacting to one of these secondary attractants and gradually be lead by them to the place where the primary attractant can be found.

Secondary and primary attractants are therefore interdependent: without the latter, the former become meaningless; without the former, the latter cannot be utilized. The relative importance of visual and olfactoric attraction varies with the pollinator species: some animals are more olfactoric, others more visual, even if few are as exclusively visual as man. It also varies with the pollination syndrome: for pollination at night odour is a more important attractant than sight, and night-pollinated flowers can fill the air with fragrance even in temperate areas, immensely much more so in the tropics. Many features seem to indicate that olfactoric attraction is the more primitive—showy flowers being a later development whereas olfactoric attractants, not always agreeable, are found also in gymnosperms, e.g. in *Cycas*. Also, most of the known deceit syndromes (cf. below) are based on olfactoric attraction.

Pollen as an attractant is easy to understand. Pollen (microspores) were there long before higher anthophytes came into existence, and certainly were utilized by spore-eating small animals. After the establishment of oospory with consequent need for the transfer of spores, both the vectors and mechanisms were already there. There is therefore every reason to consider biotic pollination as a primitive condition. In phanerogams, wind pollination is derived.

In contrast to pollen, nectar is an enigmatic substance. Did it exist before pollination and what was its function? Nectar does exist independently of the pollination syndrome. Extra floral nectaries and extra floral nectars are well known and whereas some of them have a function in a pollination syndrome, others e.g. those on young *Pteridium* fronds, definitely have not.

Nor have the efflorescences of sugar that can be seen in the areoles of cactus plants indoors. In nature such things are rarely seen both because sugar is washed off by rain and dew, and also because sugars are so attractive as to be immediately consumed by any animal that happens to be near. It seems that this apparently senseless waste of good assimilation material is a more or less regularly occurring phenomen in rapidly developing plant organs—possibly because the ascending sap has a surplus of carbohydrates in relation to other substances used by the developing organ. Therefore, we must surmise that also nectar existed before the advent of flowers, and that the use of nectar as an attractant in pollination also represents utilization of an already existing mechanism, which is supported by the immense morphological variety of nectaries: nectary is a function, not a definite type of organ. On the other hand, the utilization of nectar in pollination syndromes certainly puts nectar and nectaries to a new use, and to-day floral nectar production is much more important than extra floral.

Nectar-carbohydrate and pollen-protein are the two sources of nourishment taken by almost 100 % of those pollinators who visit flowers to feed. Recently, Vogel has discovered a small class of flowers that present fat oil as a food. Again, this is larval food—apparently the digestion of protein and fat is a too slow process to suffice for imagines. The oil attraction syndrome, which was originally described from South America, especially in *Calceolaria,* has later also been found elsewhere. In Europe, some species of *Lysimachia* apparently belong to this group. This discovery increases the number of known primary attractants, but in principle it is not different from the other two food-seeking syndromes.

The possibility of other primary attractants has been discussed, e.g. for nest material etc. However, the matter is rather unsettled and doubtful.

Secondary attractants are advertisement, advertising the existence of food. Not all advertisements are quite truthful, and so it is also in the flower world: flowers cheat and advertise a non-existing product.

The classical deceit is represented by flowers that smell of decaying proteins—carcasses or dung—and thus attract animals that live on or oviposit in such material. The olfactoric attraction is usually—but not always—accompanied by a visual one: the flower or inflorescences having a characteristic greenish-brownish-purple colour reminiscent of putrid meat and similar substances. The smell can be overpowering and attract great numbers of the animal(s) in question, which are attracted to the area of maximum odour concentration, during which process they are also led past anthers and stigma. Whereas trap flowers are far from unknown in other syndromes, they are very common in connexion with this attraction. The animals, once having "found out" that they have been cheated, have no inducement to remain in the blossom—usually an inflorescence. However, if there is a case of stigmas being receptive before anthers open—which prevents self-pollination—it is important that the pollinators stay for some time, and such blossoms are therefore temporarily impossible to get out of. Later, after anthers have opened, they wither and the insects can crawl out.

In this syndrome, visitors usually do not profit themselves. To keep them alive, the blossom may furnish them with a little sugar during the imprisonment, but that is all. Especially for those individuals who have entered in the hope of being able to oviposit, the visit is a total failure, which may be lethal if the oviposition is induced, as the larvae find no food. However, there is no rule without an exception: blossoms have been described in which there is a special tissue in which the larvae may develop. These cases represent transition cases towards the brood-rearing syndrome (cf. below).

Interesting variations on this theme have been described; blossoms that form death-traps in which the pollinating insects regularly die; attraction of blood-sucking insects by smell imitating that of vertebrate skin; attraction of mycetophilous insects by fungus-like organs in the blossom etc. All of this is in reality parasitic behaviour of the plant in relation to the pollinator.

Whereas the food deceit attraction has been known and understood very long, the sexual deceit was not discovered until the beginning of this century. By odour and shape the flower—chiefly of the genus *Ophrys,* but also in other genera—"imitates" the female of certain insects to such a perfection as to induce males to settle on the same and attempt copulation, during which process pollination takes place. "Imitate" is a much too anthropomorphic word; a more exact description would be that the flowers release and maintain a chain of reactions that under normal circumstances would lead to copulation. In reality it is the same phenomenon in both these deceit cases: a chain of reactions is started and maintained that normally leads to an important event in the life cycle of the insect, but in this case goes wrong because it has been started by a blossom and not by the right agent.

The pollination of the genus *Orchis* has been much discussed. The flower has no primary attractant—reports to the contrary are based on misinterpretations. After hundred years of search pollination ecologists are now seriously discussing if this is a case of visual deceit: can the flower be so like other, nectar-containing flowers that they are visited by mistake?

Some other examples of possible visual deceit have recently been brought up for discussion. *Begonia* is monoecious and has no nectar; pollen is the attractant in the male flower. In the female flower the exceptionally massive, anther-like stigmas may imitate anthers and induce visits from pollen collectors. In *Saintpaulia,* another flower with pollen attraction, the very conspicuous anthers remain apparently unchanged during the later, female phase of the anthesis and may serve to attract pollinators, even if they are by that time empty.

Odour has till now been considered only in its function as a secondary attractant. However, Vogel has shown that odour, or rather perfume, may also be a primary attractant. Whereas some male bumblebees possess organs (Nasonoff glands) that produce a perfume which is certainly of importance in the sexual syndrome, other bees have not got this possibility. Some male bees extract perfume from various flowers. They are equipped with special sponge-like oil-collecting organs on the hind legs, and transfer to those organs the ethereal oil they scrape up, sometimes under such excitement as to render them apparently momentarily unconscious. After having filled their perfume containers, the bees take up a position from which the odour may spread. The most interesting feature of this syndrome is that these males have an exceptionally long span of life for an insect male, about six months, whereas most male hymenopters live six days or less. These males therefore represent a pollination ecological vacuum, as their feeding instinct is very low.

The concept of rendez-vous attraction is still rather vague. The well-known tendency of insects to establish a rendez-vous territory seems to be utilized by flowers in some cases (*Orchis* species may come in here), but the matter needs much closer investigation to find out if this is of any importance in pollination.

However, we have learned that flowers do not only attract by appealing to the feeding or sexual instincts of animals, but also, as we shall see, to their brood-rearing instinct. Within this sphere we find some of the most complex mutual adaptations in pollination ecology. These adaptations are both instinctive—as always—and structural, the latter to a higher degree than in other syndromes.

The general pattern can be defined thus: female insects oviposit in the ovary, and, during this process, also transfer pollen to the stigmas. The larvae eat some of the developing ovules, whereas others escape this predation and develop into seed. This is an extremely delicate balance between the predator and the plant: too high predation would kill the fruit and thereby, indirectly, also the next generation of the predator.

In some ways this may be seen as a host-parasite relation, but in contrast to other host-parasite relations in pollination (deceit attraction), as elsewhere, this one is not dependent on being in the minority. In its classical expression it is a regular part of the life-cycle of both insect and flower, but there are other, less balanced cases in which the predation aspect is more prominent and can lead to destruction of the plant population.

A comparatively simple case is that of *Trollius europaeus*. The flower is closed and rarely visited by larger insects. A small fly, *Chiastochaeta trollii*, enters between the imbricate tepals, partakes of the nectar present in the flower, and oviposits at the bases of some of the ovaries of the apocarpous gynoecium. During this process it becomes dusted with pollen, which is carried on to the next flower. The developing larva will eat the ovules of "its" ovary, after which it tunnels out and pupates, presumably in the ground.The non-infected ovaries develop seeds. Seed production is high enough to tolerate this loss. The fly has no morphological adaptation to the mode of life to which it is ecologically programmed.

The extremely complicated pollination syndromes of the genus *Ficus* is in reality the same pattern with the added refinement that the pollinators—fertilized females of chalchidoid wasps—are also equipped with morphological adaptations, veritable pockets into which pollen is stored and from which it is also brought out by a regular series of movements on oviposition/pollination. Other differences from the *Trollius* syndrome are the morphology of the blossom, in this case an inflorescence—a syconium—and the fact that the larvae both develop and pupate inside the blossom, that the fertilized female once having entered, cannot escape after oviposition, with the result that pollen release does not take place until the next generation of wasps leaves the syconium to enter another generation of syconia in the receptive phase. Seed-set is here safeguarded by varying lengths of styles: oviposition can only take place in short-styled flowers.

The genus *Ficus* has ca. 1000 species and, so far, only a few, rather highly developed ones have been investigated. Probably, there are more primitive syndromes in less highly developed species. On the other hand, the usual edible fig of world trade *(F. carica)* is a complicated, functionally dioecious plant, the staminate part of which is the so-called caprificus, the fruits of which are full of insects and totally inedible. However, both the caprificus and the parasitic wasps are necessary if the edible fig shall develop its fruits to perfection. The principles of fig pollination was elucidated about 100 years ago, but only during the last 10–20 years have the finer, decisive details become known, and they are still very much under investigation.

The classical case of brood-place pollination is that of the genus *Yucca*, the drooping, waxy flowers of which are pollinated by a moth, *Tegeticula yuccasella*. The fertilized female actively scrapes up the waxy pollen from the anthers, places it in a special organ under her head, transports it to another flower and actively pushes it into the stigma before oviposition. The larvae eat some of the ovules of the very large capsule, whereas the rest give ripe seed. Both *Ficus* and *Yucca* are examples of strong mutual adaptation, of active pollination and, above all, of complete interdependence. There is no reason to presume that the largely unknown pollination syndromes in tropical countries do not exhibit more examples as wonderful as these.

Scientific pollination ecology was born in Europe, a continent characterised by extreme poverty both in flowers and pollinators. No wonder that pollination became synonymous with insect activity in flowers and even the classes of insects recognised were few. Especially, the enormous importance of beetles in pollination, perhaps the original pollinators at the first development of phanerogams, was overlooked until discovered outside Europe. Although the role both of birds and bats as pollinators was seen and correctly interpreted before the year 1900 their importance has not been realized until rather recently, after pollination had been studied in the tropics. Even so, there is no doubt that insects are the most important pollinating animals, followed by birds and bats, but there are subordinate groups gradually being discovered. Both pollen and nectar are easily obtainable, easily digestible foods, and there is no reason why an animal that can utilize these sources of food should not do so if they are satisfactory and nothing much better is available. In spring, the sparrows can demolish the crocuses in search of nectar; later in the year they find other food more satisfactory. Inside many groups of small animals this utilization of flower food has become so important that the subsequent adaptations have taken place. Small marsupials are dependent on nectar and pollen, their mouths being developed accordingly. Whereas the rat pollinating *Feycinetia arborea* in Hawaii is not known to be especially adapted for flower visits, another rat in Western Australia has definitely lost its feral characteristics and structurally developed towards flower dependence. With all the small primates living in the tree-tops of tropical forests it was not unexpected to find a pollinator among them. Probably, there are more, but their habitat is difficult of access, and their nocturnal habits do not make observations easier to make.

One of the features that restricts vertebrate pollinators to the tropic is their energy demands. Most insects are short-lived. So-called monolectic insects (insects taking food from one flower species only) usually have an active lifetime more or less coincident with the period of flowering of their host plants. After that, they hibernate (sometimes during the summer months!) until next time the plant flowers. Other insects are polylectic and live longer—at any rate as a species even if the individuals are short-lived. But again, insect life and flower season are coincident. Some insects do not feed at all, like the *Yucca* moth, but are for other reasons geared to flowering time.

In contrast vertebrates are long-lived, at least a year, they have an active metabolism during all that period, and they must have a constant source of food during the whole of the year. Some birds can and do migrate northward with the developments of flowers in spring: hummingbirds even reach Alaska, and return again in the autumn; but most vertebrate pollinators are fairly stationary and must find their food there and then. The high temperatures of the tropics are not in themselves so important: the operating factor is the absence of seasonality. Pollinating, flower dependent birds are found in the high alpine zone of tropical mountains "where there is winter every night and summer every day", and where the mean temperature is very low. The ability of some so-called homoiothermic vertebrates to go into a semi-dormancy with depressed metabolism certainly is a factor of importance in this respect.

However, energy output is also important for insect/flower relationships. To extract nectar or pollen from a flower and bring it back to nest or hive does require energy, and unless more energy is gained than spent, the undertaking goes on an energetic deficit which will very soon make it impossible. Energy relations have chiefly been studied in bumblebees, which usually maintain a body temperature close to the ambient one. However, a cold bee cannot fly: before starting flight in cold weather it must heat up, which it does by a shivering motion. Of the three segments of the bee's body, only the thorax, where the wings sit, needs heating, which saves a lot of energy: head and abdomen remain cool.

These considerations of energy relations give some conclusions.

1. An insect can only use nectar sources of a certain size; if the blossom contains too little nectar, the energy expense for a heavy insect is too great: it does not pay to collect the small quantities. It is like using a big truck to hawl a small can of fuel: it burns up more fuel than it transports.
2. A visit at low temperature involves a higher energy expenditure to keep up the thoracic temperature than at high ambient temperature. Consequently, at low temperatures only such flowers can be visited which yield much nectar. Many flowers secernate much nectar during the night, and are well filled in the morning. In spite of high energy losses due to heat loss a matinal visit will give more energy from this flower than a mid-day visit which involves much smaller energy loss, but also gives very small amounts of nectar (=energy) from the already emptied blossom.
3. Crawling is a cheaper mode of locomotion than flying. Large blossoms (inflorescences) which can be visited by crawling from one flower to another, letting the thoracic temperature drop, can therefore attract large insects even if the individual flowers deliver tiny amounts of nectar.

At any rate to higher hymenoptera, pollen is no source of energy. Apparently they do not possess enzyme systems capable of dealing as effectively with protein and fat as would have been necessary to use pollen for energy. A pollen-collecting flight (not to speak of perfume-collecting etc.) therefore goes on an energetic deficit. Before leaving for pollen-collecting insects therefore "fuel up", bringing some nectar with them from the stores in nests or hive. This nectar is not, as was sometimes surmised, for moistening the pollen and make it adhere to the hindleg corbicular, but it is energy food for the collecting trip. Other pollen collectors, which do not bring nectar with them, will interrupt pollen visits by a visit to a nectar sourse, e.g. from oak to buttercup and back again. The nectar flowers are the roadside petrol stations.

Energy relations also govern the behaviour of vertebrate pollinators. Hummingbirds which maintain and have to defend a personal territory, spend so much energy for that purpose that they are confined to the neighbourhood of a large source of nectar, that is a clump of flowers. Non-territorial species carry out extended flights, usually following the same route from day to day, visiting the same scattered, hopefully un-tapped sources of nectar each day ("trap-lining"). Obviously, from a polli-nation point of view, the latter are much more effective.

If there is another new trend in pollination ecology coming up recently to take over after the ethological trend of the last 50 years, it may be this study of energy relations. Is it fortuitous that this comes up at a time when world considerations of future energy consumptions have become one of the major political themes both nationally and internationally?

Some Remarks on the Behaviour of the parasitic Hymenoptera

By Karl-Johan Hedqvist

Research assistant
Swedish Museum of Natural History
Stockholm, Sweden

Parasitica (Hymenoptera parasitica) are the group which contains the most species within the order of Hymenoptera. It has been estimated that there are over 150,000 species in all parts of the world. In Sweden, we have a good 6000 species. It goes without saying that, on account of this large number of species, our knowledge of the parasitica way of life is very deficient. If, to the abundance of species, we also add the fact that the determination of the species has been and still is difficult, the deficiencies in our knowledge of the biology of these flies will probably be understandable. However, apart from the difficulty of determining their species, the glimpses that we have obtained of their often quite complex behaviour should stimulate us to more intensive studies.

How do the sexes find each other out? This is perhaps the first question that is put with regard to these flies. The answer is that we know almost nothing about this, especially as regards the species that are parasitic on free-living hosts. Probably the sex pheromones play an important part. On the other hand, we are better informed about species which live on bark beetles and other insects which live under the bark or in the wood of trees. Thus, in my studies of these parasites on the bark beetles, I was able to observe that the males are hatched before the females. The males then remain on the hatching site, where they roam about, waiting for the females to hatch out. If a roaming male comes across a female which is gnawing her way out of the bark, he stays on the spot. He then drives away all other males which approach. Now and then, he checks on how far the female has got in gnawing her way out. When the female begins to force her way out, the watching male hurries to the spot, but so do all other males of the species in the vicinity. Then there is often a savage struggle for the female's favour and the watching male does not always come off victorious. This is the common behaviour of the chalcid wasps (Chalcidoidea) belonging to the Pteromalidae family. There are different patterns of behaviour in other groups of parasitica, for example, the Braconidae family. If we take as examples species of the *Ecphylus* Först. genus (belonging to the Doryctinae sub-family within the Braconidae family), which are very common parasites on two- and four-toothed bark beetles (*Pityogenes bidentatus* Hbst. and *P. quadridens* Hart.), often 4–6 males gather round the spot (Fig. 1) where a female is gnawing her way out. With their heads pressed together, they wait for her to crawl out.

After mating, the females need protein-rich food for their egg production. In order to satisfy this need, many of them seek out the flowers of especially umbelliferous plants (Apiaceae) and eat the pollen, which contains protein, among other things. Other females obtain protein by puncturing their host with their ovipositors and then licking up the body fluid that trickles out. Some species belonging to the *Habrocytus* Thoms., *Spintherus* Thoms. and other genera use more complicated methods. *Habrocytus cerealellae* (Ashm.) is a parasite on the caterpillars of the butterfly *Sitotroga cerealella* (Oliv.). When the female has paralysed the caterpillar in its cell within a grain of corn (Fig. 2A), she withdraws her ovipositor slowly until only the tip remains in the cell or cavity. In this phase, a fluid is secreted from the tip of the ovipositor. This fluid congeals and forms a thin film around the ovipositor, which is slightly twisted. At the same time, the female inserts it slowly until the tip reaches the spot where the caterpillar was previously punctured when it was paralysed. The fluid congeals and after a few minutes the female withdraws the ovipositor. In the tube which has now been formed by the congealing fluid, the caterpillar's body fluid rises upwards by capillary force. The female then turns round and is able to lick up the body fluid (Fig. 2B). This may be likened to someone using a straw to drink squash from a glass.

After feeding, the females are ready to seek out their hosts. They seem to make, first of all, for the plant on which the host lives. The search is then continued by the sense of touch, among other things. If the host is a

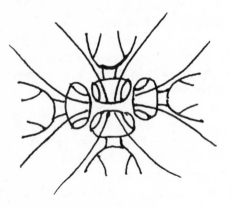

Fig. 1. Four males of the *Ecphylus* sp. with their heads pressed together, waiting for a female who is engaged in gnawing her way out. (Hedqvist del.)

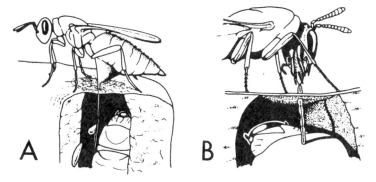

Fig. 2. A. A *Habrocytus cerealellae* (Ashm.) female withdrawing her ovipositor after having punctured the caterpillar. B. The female has made a tube and is licking up the fluid which forces its way up the tube by capillary force. (After Fulton.)

free-living insect, scents would seem to play a certain part. In some groups of parasitica, there are species which do not seek out the host insects but lay their eggs on the leaves of the plants, after which the newly hatched larvae, which are very mobile, actively find their way to their hosts. There are such species in the Eucharitidae and Perilampidae families.

If the host insects live inside plants, for example, as miners in leaves, or gnaw out passages under bark or in wood, the difficulties are much greater. It is now a matter of the female not only tracking down the host insect but also of boring her way into its refuge with her ovipositor. Her most important tools in the search for such hosts are her antennae, which are used in different ways. Chalcid wasps have two predominant positions for their antennae. In the first position, the antenna flagellum is kept hanging straight down from the upwards-directed scape (Fig. 3A), in which case only the club tip touches the surface of the bark. In the second position, the antenna club is bent at an angle to the flagellum (Fig. 3B). In both cases, the females roam in zigzag fashion over the surface. In this way, the surface of the bark can be carefully investigated. In the Braconidae family, the antennae are

Fig. 3. A. The antenna is allowed to hang straight down from the upwards-directed shaft. B. The antenna club bent at an angle to the lash. (Hedqvist del.)

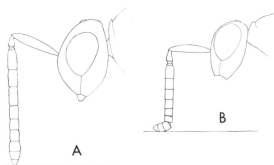

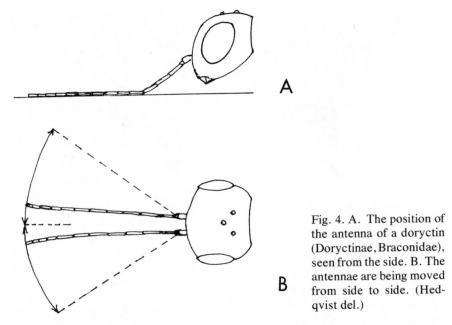

Fig. 4. A. The position of the antenna of a doryctin (Doryctinae, Braconidae), seen from the side. B. The antennae are being moved from side to side. (Hedqvist del.)

used in a different way. They are held parallel to the surface of the bark (Fig. 4A), after which they are moved from side to side (Fig. 4B) with sweeping movements.

The parasitica which attack hosts which live in wood or under bark are often equipped with long ovipositors. However, these ovipositor are not always strong enough to bore holes in wood. The following case is an illustration of this. Amongst other insects, saw-flies of the *Xiphydria* Latr. genus live in dead alder trees. On the most common species, *Xiphydria camelus* (L.), live three different parasites, namely, two ichneumons and a chalcid wasp. The two ichneumon species have ovipositors which are approximately the same length. One species, *Rhysella approximator* (F.) can bore its way into the Xiphydria larva, while the other, *Pseudorhyssa alpestris* (Holmgr.) cannot do this. Instead *Pseudorhyssa alpestris* seeks out the boreholes made by *Rhysella approximator,* inserts its ovipositor in them and is thus able to lay its eggs in the Xiphydria larvae. The larvae of the two species hatch out at approximately the same time. However, the *Pseudorhyssa alpestris* larva has a more powerful head with larger jaws and is always victorious in the subsequent struggle. The third parasite is *Xiphydriophagus meyrincki* (Ratzb.), whose ovipositor is too short to enable it to reach the Xiphydria larva. In order to get at the larva, the chalcid wasp has to make use of old bore-holes and, once inside the trunk, it gnaws its way to the larva.

Appearances may be deceptive, as regards the use of a long ovipositor.

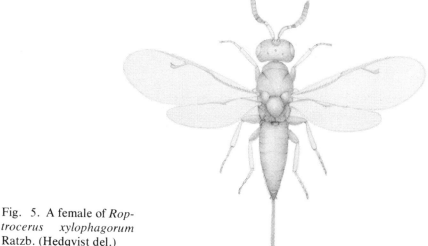

Fig. 5. A female of *Rop-trocerus xylophagorum* Ratzb. (Hedqvist del.)

Thus, among the chalcid wasps, one may be easily deceived by the *Roptro-cerus* species. Judging from their appearance (Fig. 5), these wasps should easily be able to reach the bark-beetle larvae under the bark. But, instead of boring their way in through the bark, the females seek out the holes by which the bark beetles entered and creep in there. The egg-laying may seem to be difficult but it appears to work satisfactorily, considering that the species are common.

Among the great number of parasitica which attack bark beetles, there are also those which specialize in attacking the fully grown beetles. They include species of the *Cosmophorus* Ratzb. genus, which are easily recognizable by their large heads and enormous jaws (Fig. 6A, B). In my

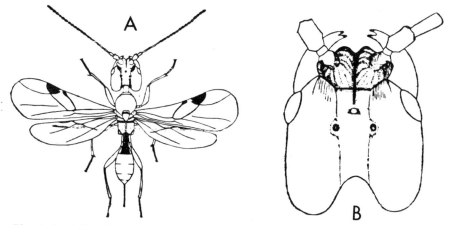

Fig. 6. A. A female of *Cosmophorus regius* Niez. B. The head enlarged. (Hedqvist del.)

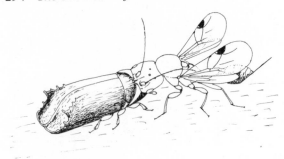

Fig. 7. A *Cosmophorus regius* Niez. keeping firm hold on a spruce-bark beetle. (Hedqvist del.)

studies of bark-beetle parasites, I observed on several occasions how the females of these species behaved in laying their eggs. When a female roaming about on pine logs, for example, meets a bark beetle, she always tries to get into a head-to-head position, after which she takes hold of the bark beetle with her great jaws just behind the neck shield (Fig. 7). She then holds the beetle firmly while she lays her eggs.

The *Cosmophorus* Ratzb. genus belongs to a group of ichneumon flies (the Euphorinae sub-family within the Braconidae family) which attacks exclusively fully grown insects. Thus, *Syntretus splendidus* (Marsh.) attacks bumblebees and *Syntretus lyctaea* Cole attacks ichneumons of the *Phaeogenes* Wesm. genus. On one occasion, I witnessed an attack by another imaginal parasite, *Dinocampus coccinellae* (Schrank.), on a seven-spotted ladybird (*Coccinella septempunctata* L.). The ladybird was sitting on a leaf when an ichneumon fly of this species alighted on the same leaf. The fly at once noticed the ladybird, hurried up to it and directed its vibrating antennae under it. The ladybird then lowered its body to the leaf. The fly tried another place and the ladybird lowered its body there instead. The fly walked around the ladybird, which parried its attacks by lowering its body at the places where the fly touched it with its antennae. After a while, the fly grew tired and stood still at a little distance from the ladybird and began to clean its antennae. When the ladybird moved the fly hurried up to it and the same procedure was repeated. It was not until the fourth time that the fly succeeded in laying its egg in the ladybird.

Even among the chalcid flies, there are species which parasitize fully developed insects. The *Tomicobia* Ashm. genus comprises species which live on bark beetles. In the U.S.A., extensive experiments have shown that *T. tibialis* Ashm. is attracted by what are called aggregation pheromones, which are emitted by certain bark beetles (among others, those in the *Ips* DeG. genus). This is certainly the case also with species in Sweden, such as *Tomicobia seitneri* (Ruschk.) (Fig. 8), which attacks the spruce-bark beetle (*Ips typographus* L.), and *Tomicobia acuminati* Hedqv., a parasite on the sharp-toothed bark beetle (*Ips acuminatus* Gyll.). If one of these chalcid

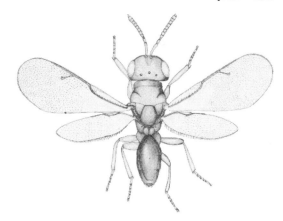

Fig. 8. A female of *Tomicobia seitneri* (Ruschk.). (Hedqvist del.)

flies encounters a bark beetle, it leaps on its back (Fig. 9) and rides on it until it has laid an egg.

Some species of parasitica have developed peculiar methods of laying eggs, for example, the species in the *Laciochalcidia* Masi and *Hybothorax* Ratzb. genera, which are parasites on the larvae of the ant-lion. The females of these species simply go down into the holes occupied by the ant-lion larvae and when the larvae get hold of them (Fig. 10), the females take the opportunity to paralyse the larvae by stinging them. The females can then lay their eggs in peace and quiet.

It happens quite frequently that two or more eggs are laid. The parasitica larva that hatches out first then kills all its rivals, which is seemingly a great waste. However, certain species have developed behaviours which prevent the laying of more than one egg. Such species are to be found especially in the *Scelionidae* (Proctotrupoidea) family, which comprises mainly egg parasites. Species of the *Trissolcus* Ashm. genus specialize in laying their eggs in the eggs of the bugs in the Pentatomidae family of the Hemiptera order. When a Trissolcus female has found a collection of the eggs of these bugs, she first examines all the eggs, a behaviour whose significance will be made clear below. She then lays her egg in the egg of a bug. Before she leaves the

Fig. 9. *A Tomicobia seitneri* (Ruschk.) busy laying eggs in a spruce-bark beetle. (Hedqvist del.)

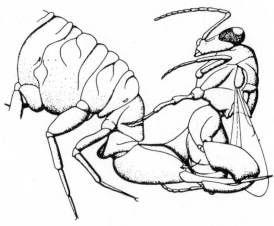

Fig. 10. A *Lasiochalcidia igilensis* Masi attacking a larva of an ant lion. (After Steffan.)

egg, she takes the opportunity of scratching a mark on it (Fig. 11) with her ovipositor. She later recognizes these marked eggs and avoids them, as do other females of this species.

Another family of exclusive egg parasites is the *Mymaridae* (Chalcidoidea), which are, without exception, small to very small parasitica. The female of one species, *Caraphractus cinctus* Walk., is capable of estimating the sizes of the different eggs of diving-beetles (Dytiscidae) which she comes across and thus of regulating the number of eggs that she should lay. If she comes across the small eggs of *Agabus* species, she lays only one egg in each Agabus egg. If she comes across the somewhat larger eggs of *Ilybius* species, she lays 2–3 eggs. If, on the other hand, she finds the relatively large eggs of *Dytiscus* species, she lays many eggs.

In conclusion, I shall mention yet another specialization. The species in the *Platygasteridae* (Proctotrupoidea) family are well known to be parasites on gall midges. Detailed investigations have shown that the platygasterid females lay their eggs in the gall-midge eggs. The platygasterid eggs are not hatched until the gall-midge eggs have been hatched and the larvae have passed through the first and second stages. The plastygasterid larvae then grow very rapidly.

Fig. 11. A female of the *Trissolcus* sp. marking the egg of a bug in which she has laid her egg. (After Askew.)

Water under Tension, its Fundamental Role in Capillarity, Osmosis and Colligative Properties

By P. F. Scholander

Professor of Zoophysiology,
Scripps Oceanographic Institute,
Santiago, USA

Honorable chairman, distinguished audience: Let me introduce my presentation with some elementary facts: when a little sugar or salt is dissolved in water the vapor tension is lowered, and osmotic pressure develops, the freezing point goes down, the boiling point up: it is indeed an astounding fact that there is no accepted kinetic explanation for this, nor for the startling fact that all these so called colligative properties display exactly the same relative changes. Furthermore, when an osmotic difference is produced across a semipermeable membrane the flux is caused as a hydraulic, not a diffusive effect. Sure enough, most of this has with admirable success been correlated numerically with a variety of coefficients introduced by thermodynamicists but none of it is understood on a kinetic basis. It is my task to demonstrate that a simple kinetic explanation is applicable to all of this and was in essence proposed already in 1903. Independently it has been proposed by several later authors, including colleague Ted Hammel and myself.

So, let us go back a hundred years to the celebrated physicist Sir William Thomson (1871), alias Lord Kelvin, at Cambridge University. In 1870 he made the following proposition: A capillary containing a drop of water in its closed end is placed into an isothermal evacuated enclosure, which contains a layer of water (Fig. 1 a). Vapor will obviously distill down into the capillary until the height of the meniscus reaches an equilibrium and this level will be the same as if the capillary were open at the bottom. At this height the vapor pressure of the meniscus matches that which rises to the same height from the flat surface. Otherwise distillation would take place and the Second Law would be violated. Lord Kelvin considered that the vapor pressure was lowered by the curvature of the meniscus, and expressed this in a simple equation.

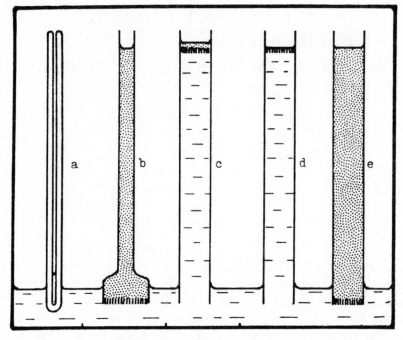

Fig. 1. (a) Kelvin's capillary, (b) Arrhenius' osmometer, (c) Noyes' osmometer, (d, e) Hulett's water and osmotic columns. All of these are standing in water within an isothermal, evacuated chamber.

Eleven years later, in 1881, John H. Poynting, who worked in Lord Kelvin's laboratory, suggested that the reason for the lowered vapor pressure is not the curvature, but the fact that the hydrostatic pressure at the meniscus is lowered, in other words, that the curvature is *correlated* with the lowering of the vapor pressure but is not the *cause* of it. This conclusion was based on the theorem of equipartition of energy and would pertain also for flat surfaces, for which he wrote a simple thermodynamic relation bearing his name.

In 1884 Svante Arrhenius at the age of 24 submitted his doctoral thesis on the dissociation theory of electrolytes to the University of Uppsala. It was based on comparisons between freezing points and electrical conductivites in a series of solutions. Two years later Jacobus van't Hoff (1886a,b) published his first papers on his astounding gas-solute analogue, facing grave difficulties regarding electrolytes, however. On this matter Arrhenius came to his aid, so that van't Hoff in his major paper of 1887 could gratefully include most electrolytes also. And the question naturally arose: what is the nature of osmotic pressure, which so closely simulates the behavior of a perfect gas?

Van't Hoff based his gas analogue on data obtained by others, mainly Pfeffer and Raoult. He suggested two possibilities for the mechanism of osmosis, one a solute bombardment and the other a solute-solvent interaction, but declared his lack of interest in speculating on this subject inasmuch as the thermodynamic aspects were perfectly clear anyhow. This *laissez faire* attitude towards the osmotic mechanism is still prevalent.

In 1889 Arrhenius saw in the elegant deductions of Kelvin and Poynting an important application to an osmotic column. Instead of Kelvin's capillary Arrhenius considered an osmometer with the semipermeable membrane dipping into the water of the isothermal evacuated chamber (Fig. 1b). He let the solution rise to equilibrium height *h*, and stated that the vapor pressure over the solution surface must be the same as that rising to *h* from the water surface in the enclosed chamber; otherwise, distillation would take place. This would apply to any osmotic pressure he thought, provided the density of the solution were near 1.

Eleven years went by, and Arthur Noyes at M.I.T. introduced an important change in Arrhenius' model inasmuch as he moved the semipermeable membrane to the top of the osmometer and covered it with an infinitely thin layer of solution (Fig. 1c). He could then readily say that, in this situation at least, an equilibrium osmotic pressure would be equal to the weight of the water beneath the free surface; in other words, the osmotic pressure produced a *negative* pressure in the solvent.

Let us eleborate a bit on Noyes' beautiful deduction. Instead of the solution, let us place a thin layer of wet sand on the membrane with enough capillarity to support the water column. The sand would interrupt the water and propagate the hydrostatic pressure according to the principle of Pascal. If we now were to grind the sand down to colloidal dimensions, thermal motion would add to the *lift,* even more so if it were ground to solute dimensions. We may ask: at what stage would the water be "diluted" rather than *interrupted* by the particles? When would "molfraction of water" acquire a physical meaning?

Finally, in 1901 George Hulett conceived the complete picture of what we have called the *solvent tension theory* of osmotic pressure. Hulett earned his doctoral degree under Wilhelm Ostwald in Leipzig and returning to the United States at the age of 35, he wrote a paper ('03) in which he stated:

"When a solute is being dissolved in a solvent, it diffuses under influence of the osmotic pressure in all directions to the boundaries of the solvent. There, and only there, is the solute stopped from further progress. When equilibrium is reached and the concentration is uniform, there remains an outward pressure by the solute on all points of the fluid boundaries. This pressure tends to enlarge the fluid volume, but it is checked by the cohesiveness of the fluid. One may therefore consider osmotic pressure as a negative pressure on the solvent. From these deliberations one may see why the vapor pressure of the solvent decreases when the solute is added, namely, because the osmotic pressure renders the solvent pressure negative."

He clarified this point by referring to two Kelvin columns (Figs. 1d, e). To the right, figure 1e, is an osmometer with a semipermeable membrane at the bottom, and an equilibrium height at the top. To the left, figure 1 d, is a water column of equal height, *hanging* by capillarity from a porous membrane. Each of the columns must have the same vapor pressure as that rising from the free water surface. Therefore, within the solution the water would simply be lifted under tension by the solute impact on the free surface. He considered a solute-solvent interaction *within* the solution[1] as unlikely and unnecessary, and explained why the vapor pressure over a solution is lowered, namely by Poynting's relation.

Hulett also clearly saw that all colligative properties must be referred back to one single property of water, namely its state of pressure or tension. Consider for example his two columns (Figs. 1d,e), and let us lower the temperature until the vapor pressure at the upper surfaces just becomes that of ice. In this situation ice will be in equilibrium with the water in either surface, whether a solution or a matrix, and the common denominator is the *water tension* (Hammel and Scholander, '73). A similar deduction is easily made for the boiling point.

In this whole sequence there remained the crucial question of solute solvent affinity *within the solution*. Clarification of this problem is one of the great landmarks in the atomic theory and it came about in 1909 by the great French physicist, Jean Perrin. Perrin was already famous for having demonstrated the corpuscular nature of cathode rays. He became fascinated by the Brownian motion as potential evidence to support atomic theory. Already Robert Brown had suggested that the motion he observed was induced by the thermal motion of the water molecules. Perrin reasoned that, if there was a complete *independence* in the random motions of the dancing particles, they would settle in a logarithmic fashion, in the same way as the atmosphere on our globe. From this Boltzmann's distribution he could then calculate Avogadro's number, provided all other constants were known. So he set out to study emulsions of uniform rosin spheres barely visible in a microscope. For the sedimentations he used a 100 micron deep blood-counting chamber and lowered the objective 30 microns at a time. By ingenious techniques he made thousands of counts, and, indeed from them he derived Avogadro's number, within 10 % of the modern value. He also found his number by observing the lateral displacements of the particles and

---

[1] A solute molecule includes its water of hydration.

even by observing the rotation of 20 micron spheres, corresponding to a "molecular weight of 200,000 tons"! All of these approaches gave the same result; equipartition of energy and random motion held from water molecules to giant spheres and he could now infer the existence of atoms and molecules! Needless to say, his elegant experiments had a profound impact on the world. As a modest spin-off, they also overcame the last hurdle in Hulett's tension hypothesis of osmosis. But alas, all of this was forgotten in the development of modern osmotic *theory* not to mention its *mechanism!*

In 1935 the tension theory of osmosis surfaced again, and independently, through the renowned physicist Karl Herzfeld. He gave a full kinetic account of the pressure effect on the free surface when solute molecules of different kinds are reflected from it, leaving behind their double momentum and how this phenomenon induces tension of the solvent, which is the cause of the lowering of the vapor pressure via Poynting's relation.

More recently Karol Mysels in his textbook on colloidal chemistry ('59) also invoked the tension theory independently with an excellent picture of an equilibrium situation between vapor pressure and solvent tension within and outside the solution. And in 1965, J. Duclaux, likewise, saw osmosis as an expression of negative solvent pressure, and rightly drew a parallel between the "swelling" of a solution within a semipermeable bag and the swelling of a gel.

In the middle sixties we, also independently, had followed another lead, namely osmotic equilibria in mangroves (Scholander, '66; Scholander et al., '65). These are trees or bushes growing in sea water, and it turned out that most of them transport essentially fresh water through their stems and up into the leaves where one finds an intracellular salt concentration which is considerably higher than that in the sea water. We also devised a technique for accurate measurement of negative pressure in the xylem, and we pronounced that in a wilted twig where there is no turgor, the intracellular freezing point depression corresponded closely to the negative pressure in the salt-free xylem sap, in other words, we measured in the *xylem sap* the thermal pressure generated in the *parenchyma cells* by the solute molecules. This very strongly suggested to us the solvent tension theory.

Some recent experiments

Because of the general use of the thermodynamic term *interaction*, in connection with solute-solvent or matrix-solvent relations, let us temper its frivolous interpretation by a simple experiment (Scholander, '72) (Fig. 2). To the left is a column of sedimented starch in a test tube. Two capillaries furnished with a wick separate the water from the starch so one can measure the hydrostatic pressure gradient through the column. The upper wick is

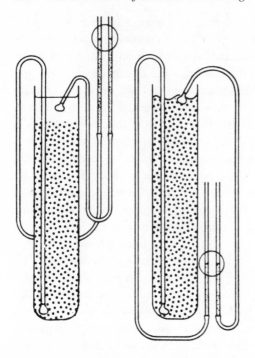

Fig. 2. Sedimented starch columns at equilibrium. Pure
water gradients are measured
with wick-capillaries (Scholander, '72).

placed in the clear supernatant fluid and the read-out capillary shows the
meniscus above the free surface according to the capillary blank. The lower
wick is placed at the bottom of the column and has its identical read-out
capillary parallel with the other.

Sedimented starch has a very strong gradient in it, which is evident when
one tries to stir it, thus a quick stroke by a rod will easily fracture the bottom
layer by its starch-starch interaction. In spite of this, the water is readily
mobile through this column so we can measure the hydrostatic gradient.
After some time, when the sedimentation has come to rest, one finds, of
course, a normal gradient from the surface to the bottom of the sediment,
i.e., the menisci in the capillaries will stand exactly level; otherwise we
could connect them and create a perpetual flow.

On the right side more starch has been added so that it *presses against the
surface,* lifting it up by capillarity. The consistency turns pasty, and right
away we get negative (subambient) pressure in the water. Again, the menisci in the capillaries from top and bottom must stand level; otherwise the
Second Law is violated. *This holds for all dispersed systems through which
water can be transported by an infinitesimal force.* There is no interaction
with the motile water within the column: it cannot be. A crucial point added
to the kinetic reasoning of the role of free surface as a reflecting boundary in
a pure solvent as well as in a solution was contributed by Hammel 1976.

Or in Hammels words[1]:

"When the molal volumes of solute and solvent in a solution are equal, then the number of molecules per unit volume may be the same in pure solvent and solution. The number of molecules (solute and solvent) reflected per unit time from a unit area of solution surface is the same as the number of solvent molecules reflecting from a unit area of pure solvent surface. The thermal force due to the rate of momentum change at a unit of surface is the same for this solution as for its pure solvent. This thermal lift on the surface at 20°C for water at 55.5 mols per liter is some 1300 atm and would be the same as in an aqueous solution as described above. However, in this solution, the area of the water per unit area of solution surface is less than one, i.e.

$$\frac{\text{(vol. of water in solution)}}{\text{vol. of solution}}$$

so the hydraulic tension in the intermolecular forces between the water molecules will be the force per unit area of solution surface divided by the area of the water in that unit area of the solution surface. Thus the water tension in the solution is enhanced, such as a measure of the osmotic pressure will show. This enhanced solvent tension is the kinetic basis of all colligative properties plus the hydraulic flux."

Now, if we were to accept that the dispersal pressure of solute molecules (like the starch) produces increased solvent tension through impact with the free surface, then any force which could modify this *lift* should have a read-out in the osmotic pressure. There are several ways we can test this notion. One of the most striking techniques is by the use of magnetic force. There are commercially available stable colloidal magnetic solutions made from an iron oxide. We have used one of these which has an osmotic pressure of some 17–18 cm of water. It gives ample accuracy when acted upon by a weak magnetic field, and near equilibrium conditions are rapidly achieved when only a shallow (3–5 mm) layer of solution is used in the osmometer.

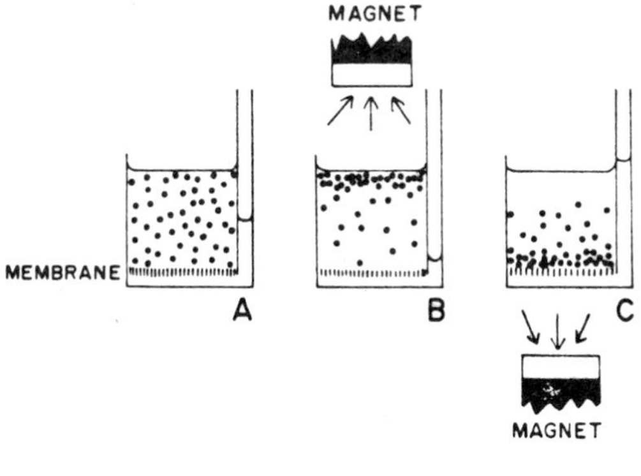

Fig. 3. Theoretical osmotic effect by colloidal ferro solution at equilibrium. (A) no magnet, (B) magnet above, (C) magnet below. Normally convection adds some pressure in the capillary.

[1] Personal communication.

In Figure 3, we present an idealized case of the results. To the left is an osmometer with the colloidal solution resting on a semipermeable membrane, showing the pure osmotic pressure as a depressed meniscus in the capillary. When a magnet is applied from above, the colloidal particles are forced against the surface and we get an increase in the osmotic pressure, note well, in spite of the fact that the "concentration gradient" of the water across the membrane is diminished. Conversely, if we put the magnet underneath the osmometer and increase this "molfraction gradient" of the water across the membrane the osmotic pressure initially turns negative by drag, but gradually approaches zero as the particles settle in a Boltzmann distribution supported by the membrane.

Figure 4 shows a schematic drawing of how this experiment was done. The osmometer is mounted on an aluminum spring which can be loaded with weights which correspond to a known hydrostatic pressure in the osmometer. The magnet can be moved up or down and a constant level of the osmometer is maintained by a null point indicator. If one weight is removed the osmometer rises and if the magnet below is now elevated we can pull the osmometer back to the null position and can thereby maintain a known vertical component of the magnetic field. The effect on the osmotic pressure is measured simply by elevating the capillary until there is a balance.

With the magnet *below* we find a close correlation between the magnetic force and a *decrease* in the osmotic pressure. In contrast, when the magnet is *above,* there is an *increase* in the osmotic pressure, again matching the magnetic vector. If we change the magnetic force stepwise from above and from below we can draw a magnetic-osmotic diagram where the empirical data are compared to a theoretical diagonal of equivalence where the site of force coupling is the free surface (fig. 5). We see how the experimental data

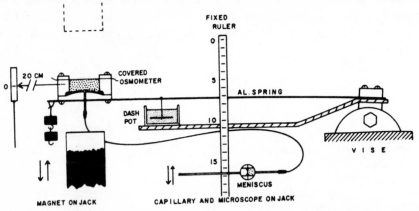

Fig. 4. Known vertical vector of magnetic force imposed on a colloidal ferro fluid in an osmometer. Negative pressure of the solvent is measured by the level of a movable capillary below its capillary blank value at 0 on the fixed ruler.

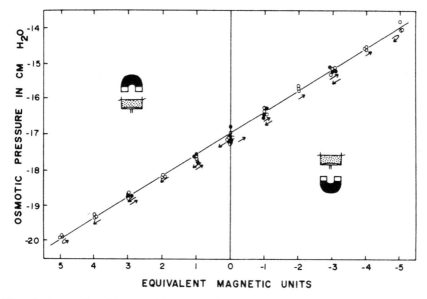

Fig. 5. Composite of 3 runs with magnet above and 3 with magnet below osmometer. Arrows indicate sequence in change of magnetic force. Diagonal is the theoretical equivalence line between osmotic and magnetic force, with interaction (coupling) at the free surface.

run close to this line, supporting the point that osmotic pressure *at equilibrium* is caused by interaction at the free surface and nowhere else.

We can also do the same in a more gentle way by using the buoyant force of the solute molecules in a tall reversing osmometer (Fig. 6). When filled with pure water it can be inverted without change in meniscus E (Scholander and Perez, '71).

Fig. 6. Pivoting osmometer. Right: upright position. Left: inverted position, drawn displaced to the left. (A) location of membrane; (B) pivot arrangement; (C– – –C) axis of rotations; (D) Saran film clamped loosely on the surface; (E) meniscus read with traveling microscope: (C) left, connection to manometer.

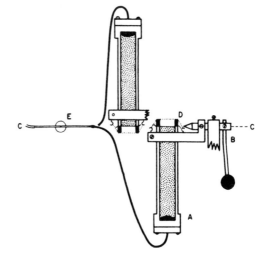

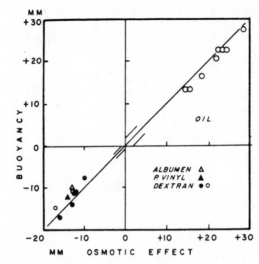

Fig. 7. Experiments with reversing osmometer. Changes in colloidal osmotic pressure by buoyant drag, in mm H₂O. Diagonal is theoretical line. (Scholander '72.)

With the free surface facing up (Fig. 6, right) the light oil suspensions *add* their positive buoyancy (through drag) to the osmotic lift of the surface; whereas the heavy suspensions subtract their negative buoyance. In either case the resulting osmotic change correlates with the surface (Fig. 7).

We shall now take a critical view of current ideas. First, let us point out that they offer no physical explanation why the vapor pressure is lowered over a solution, and the general idea is that it does not matter, for thermodynamic nomenclature can easily handle the situation anyhow. However, this is not quite true as we can see in figure 8. Let us consider a cylinder submerged in water and closed at either end by a rigid semipermeable membrane. It is filled with a 1 mole solution which at 20°C registers +24 atm gauge pressure at equilibrium. It is generally postulated (Ray, '60; Slatyer, '67) that the solvent within this column is under +24 atm pressure. Clearly, however, this cannot be so; for, if the water in the solution were under any pressure greater than on the outside, it would be heavier and would continuously sink through the solution, in violation of the Second Law.

This fictitious elevation of the solvent pressure calls for a thermodynamic ghost to stem a solvent leak out through the pores. It is postulated that a "molfraction effect" lowers the water concentration and thereby the "chemical potential," and that this effect is somehow linked to impact of solute molecules on the pore openings. However, at least in a dilute solution, it would seem clear that only a small fraction of all openings would be hit at any time, while the majority of the pores would allow back leak; once more we have a violation of the Second Law.

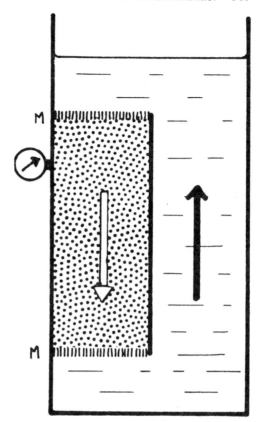

Fig. 8. Cylinder closed by semi-permeable membranes M. M. submerged in isothermal water. Solution is 1 mol with 24 atm osmotic pressure. If the solvent were compressed by 24 atm its increased density would make it sink perpetually through the cylinder (white arrow). Obviously, the solvent throughout matches the hydrostatic gradient on the outside.

According to the solvent tension theory, the ambient *water pressure* transmits through the membrane and in between the solute molecules and there is no local gradient anywhere. The elevated *solution pressure* is caused by the dispersal pressure of the solute molecules alone, hemmed in as they are by the solution boundaries.

The solvent tension theory explains the vapor pressure lowering over a solution, the equivalence of osmotic and hydraulic flux, and osmotic flux against a water potential. It unifies osmosis and imbibition, and it explains the colligative properties; most important: starting with the brilliant work of Perrin, it is backed by incontrovertible experimental evidence.

Acknowledgments

This work was made possible through Grant HL 13893 from the National Institutes of Health and Grant GB 29363 from the National Science Foundation.

LITERATURE CITED

Arrhenius, S. 1884. La conductibilité galvanique électrolytes. Bih. K. Vet. Akad. Handl., 8 (#13 and 14).

— 1889. Einfache Ableitung der Beziehung zwischen osmotischem Druck und Erniedrigung der Dampfspannung. Z. Phys. Chem., 3: 115–119.

Duclaux, J. 1965. Théorie de gas. J. Chim. Phys., 65: 435–438.

Hammel, H. T. 1976 Colligative properties of a solution. Science 192.

Hammel, H. T., & P. F. Scholander 1973. Thermal motion and forced migration of colloidal particles generate hydrostatic pressure in solvent. Proc. Nat. Acad. Sci. U.S.A., 70: 124–128.

— 1976. Osmosis and Tensile Solvent. Springer Verlag, 133 pp.

Herzfeld, K. F. 1937. Thermodynamics und Kinetische Betrachtungen über das Zustandekommen der Dampfdruckerniedrigung von Lösungen. Phys. Z., 38: 58–64.

Hulètt, G. A. 1903. Beziehung zwischen negativem Druck und osmotischem Druck. Z. Phys. Chem. 42: 353–368.

Mysels, K. 1959. Introduction to Colloid Chemistry. Interscience Publishers, Inc., New York, 475 pp.

Noyes, A. 1900. Die genaue Beziehung zwischen osmotichem Druck und Dampfdruck. Z. Phys. Chem. 35: 707–721.

Perez, M., and P. F. Scholander 1972. Molecular buoyancy and osmotic equilibrium. Proc. Nat. Acad. Sci. U.S.A., 69: 301–302.

Perrin, J. 1909. Mouvement brownien et realité moléculaire. Ann. Chim. et Phys., Ser. 8, Transl. F. Soddy in Taylor and Francis, Red Lion Court, Fleet Street, London, 1910.

Poynting, J. H. 1881. Change of state: solid-liquid. Phil. Mag. 5th series, 12: 32–48.

Ray, P. M. 1960. On the theory of osmotic water movement. Plant. Physiol., 35: 783–795.

Scholander, P. F. 1966. The role of solvent pressure in osmotic systems. Proc. Nat. Acad. Sci. U.S.A., 55: 1407–1414.

— 1972. Tensile water. Amer. Sci., 60: 585–590.

— 1975. Water states and water gates in osmotic processes and the inoperative concept of molfraction of water. J. Exp. Zool. 194.[1]

Scholander, P. F., H. T. Hammel, E. D. Bradstreet & E. A. Hemmingsen. 1965. Sap pressure in vascular plants. Science, 148: 339–346.

Scholander, P. F., & M. Perez. 1971. Effect of gravity on osmotic equilibria. Proc. Nat. Acad. Sci. U.S.A., 68: 1569–1571.

Slatyer, R. O. 1967. Plant-Water Relationships. Academic Press, Inc., London.

Thomson, W. 1871. On the equilibrium of vapour at a curved surface of liquid. Phil. Mag., fourth series: 42: 448–452.

van't Hoff, J. H. 1886a. Une propriété générale de la matière diluée. Svenska Vet. Akad. Handl., 21: (# 17, 43).

— 1886b. Lois de l'équilibre chimique dans l'état dilus gazeux ou dissous. Svenska Vet. Akad. Handl. 21: (# 17, 217).

— 1887. Die rolle des osmotischen Druckes in der Analogie zwischen Lösungen und Gasen. Z. Phys. Chem., 1: 481–508.

---

[1] Much of this talk is based on this paper.